CAMBRIDGE LATIN AMERICAN STUDIES

GENERAL EDITOR
SIMON COLLIER

ADVISORY COMMITTEE
MARVIN BERNSTEIN, MALCOLM DEAS
CLARK W. REYNOLDS, ARTURO VALENZUELA

50

HOUSING, THE STATE AND THE POOR

For a list of other books in the
Cambridge Latin American Studies series
please see page 320

HOUSING, THE STATE AND THE POOR

POLICY AND PRACTICE IN THREE LATIN AMERICAN CITIES

ALAN GILBERT

*University College and Institute of
Latin American Studies, London*

and

PETER M. WARD

University College, London

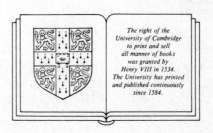

The right of the
University of Cambridge
to print and sell
all manner of books
was granted by
Henry VIII in 1534.
The University has printed
and published continuously
since 1584.

CAMBRIDGE UNIVERSITY PRESS

Cambridge
London   New York   New Rochelle
Melbourne   Sydney

Published by the Press Syndicate of the University of Cambridge
The Pitt Building, Trumpington Street, Cambridge CB2 1RP
32 East 57th Street, New York, NY 10022, USA
296 Beaconsfield Parade, Middle Park, Melbourne 3206, Australia

First published 1985

Typeset and printed in Great Britain at The Pitman Press, Bath

Library of Congress catalogue card number: 84-9521

British Library Cataloguing in Publication Data
Gilbert, Alan, *1944 Oct. 1–*
Housing, the state and the poor. – (Cambridge
Latin American studies; 50)
1. Housing policy – Latin America   2. Poor
– Government policy – Latin America
3. Urban policy – Latin America
I. Title   II. Ward, Peter M.
363.5′9   HD7287.96.L29

ISBN 0 521 26299 2

Contents

Figures

Tables

Acknowledgements

We should like to thank the Overseas Development Administration for funding the research from 1978 to 1981 and the Department of Geography of University College for providing additional financial assistance during 1981 and 1982. We are also grateful to the Institute of Latin American Studies, London, and the Instituto de Geografía of the Universidad Nacional Autónoma de México for providing office space and institutional support. The research was carried out by several people who contributed enormously to the final outcome even if their names do not appear as authors. Dr James Murray and Ms Ann Raymond worked with us from May 1978 until September 1980. They helped us in the design of the project, in the collection of data and in the ordering and processing of that data on our return to London. Dr Carlos Zorro Sánchez provided two base papers on urban housing and law in Bogotá which helped us extend our knowledge of those phenomena in that city. Bill Bell worked with us from 1980 to 1981 helping to process the statistical material and to refine our understanding of the theory of the state. Needless to say, none of these people or institutions is responsible for the contents or views expressed in this book.

We should also like to thank Joanne Stone, Colin Titcombe and Patrick Nunn for their patience with our early efforts at word processing and computing, and Alec Newman, Richard Davidson and Sarah Skinner for preparing the figures. Claudette John, Debbie Ryan, and Gwenneth Vardy helped continuously with their prodigious efforts on the word processor. Croom Helm, Pergamon Press, and Sage Publications are also to be acknowledged for allowing us to reproduce sections from previously published material.

Finally, we should like to thank all those Latin Americans who spent time answering our questionnaires and responding to our enquiries. Their friendliness and cooperation not only made the data collection relatively painless but also turned the whole research effort into a real pleasure.

Abbreviations

AD	Acción Democrática
Adeco	Supporter of Acción Democrática
ANAPO	Alianza Nacional Popular
APRA	Alianza Popular Revolucionaria Americana (Peru)
AURIS	Acción Urbana y de Integración Social
BANOBRAS	Banco Nacional de Obras
BCV	Banco Central de Venezuela
BNHUOPSA	Banco Nacional Hipotecaria Urbano de Obras Públicas
CADAFE	Companía Anónima de Administración y Fomento Eléctrico
CANTV	Companía Anónima Nacional Teléfonos de Venezuela
CAR	Corporación Autónoma Regional de la Sabana de Bogotá y de los Valles de Ubaté y Chiquinquirá
CAVM	Comisión del Agua del Valle de México
CEAS	Comisión Estatal de Aguas y Saneamiento
CFE	Comisión de Fuerza y Electricidad
CMA	Corporación de Mercadeo Agrícola
CNC	Confederación Nacional de Campesinos
CNOP	Confederación Nacional de Organizaciones Populares
CODEUR	Comisión de Desarrollo Urbano
CONASUPO	Companía Nacional de Subsistencias Populares
COPEI	Comité de Organización Política Electoral Independiente
COPEVI	Centro Operacional de Poblamiento y de Vivienda

Copeyano	Supporter of COPEI
CORDIPLAN	Oficina Central de Coordinación y Planificación de la Presidencia de la República
CoRett	Comision para la Regularización de la tenencia de la tierra
COVITUR	Comisión Técnica de la Vialidad y Transporte
CTM	Confederación de Trabajadores Mexicanos
CVP	Caja de Vivienda Popular
DAAC(M)	Departamento de Asuntos Agrarios y Colonización (Mexico)
DAAC(B)	Departamento Administrativo de Acción Comunal (Bogotá)
DANE	Departamento Administrativo Nacional de Estadística
DAPD	Departamento Administrativo de Planeación Departamental
DDF	Departamento del Distrito Federal
DF	Distrito Federal
DGAyS	Dirección General de Aguas y Saneamiento (DDF)
DGAyT	Dirección General Aguas y Tierras (SRA)
DGCP	Dirección General de Centros de Población (SAHOP)
DGCOH	Dirección General de Construcción y Operación Hidráulica (DDF)
DGHP	Dirección General de Habitación Popular (DDF)
DGOH	Dirección General de Operación Hidráulica
DUEB	Departamento de Urbanización y Servicio de los Barrios (Department within the old Banco Obrero)
EAAB	Empresa de Acueducto y Alcantarillado de Bogotá
EDIS	Empresa Distrital de Servicios Públicos
EDTU	Empresa Distrital de Transportes Urbanos
EEEB	Empresa de Energía Eléctrica de Bogotá
FIDEURBE	Fideicomiso de Interés Social para el Desarrollo Urbano de la Ciudad de México
FINEZA	Fideicomiso de Netzahualcóyotl

FUNDACOMUN	Fundación para el Desarrollo de la Comunidad y Fomento Municipal
FUNVAL	Fundación para el Mejoramiento Industrial y Sanitario de la Ciudad de Valencia
IBRD	International Bank for Reconstruction and Development
ICSS	Instituto Colombiano de Seguro Social
ICT	Instituto de Crédito Territorial
IDEMA	Instituto de Mercadeo Agropecuario
IMF	International Monetary Fund
IMSS	Instituto Mexicano de Seguro Social
INAVI	Instituto Nacional de la Vivienda
INCORA	Instituto Colombiano de Reforma Agraria
IND	Instituto Nacional de Deportes
INDECO	Instituto Nacional de Desarrollo de la Comunidad
INFONAVIT	Instituto Nacional del Fondo de Vivienda para los Trabajadores
INOS	Instituto Nacional de Obras Sanitarios
INPI	Instituto Nacional de la Protección a la Infancia
INVI	Instituto Nacional de Vivienda (Mexico)
ISS	Instituto de Seguros Sociales
ISSSTE	Instituto de Seguridad y Servicios Sociales de los Trabajadores al Servicio del Estado
IVAC	Instituto Venezolano de Acción Comunal
MARNR	Ministerio del Ambiente y los Recursos Naturales Renovables
MAS	Movimiento al Socialismo
MINDUR	Ministerio de Desarrollo Urbano
MRC	Movimiento Restaurador de Colonos
OMPU	Oficina Municipal de Planeación Urbana
ONDEPJOV	Oficina Nacional para el Desarrollo de los Pueblos Jóvenes
OPEC	Organization of Petroleum-Exporting Countries
ORDEC	Oficina Regional de Desarrollo de la Comunidad
PAN	Partido de Acción Nacional

PARM	Partido Auténtico de la Revolución Mexicana
PCM	Partido Comunista Mexicana
PCP	Procuradaría de Colonias Populares
PDM	Partido Democrático Mexicano
PEMEX	Petróleos Mexicanos
PFV	Programa Financiero de Vivienda
PHIZSU	Programa de Habilitación Integral de Zonas Subnormales
PIDUZOB	Plan de desarrollo urbano para la zona oriental de Bogotá
PNR	Partido Nacional Revolucionario
PPS	Partido Popular Socialista
PRI	Partido Revolucionario Institucional
PRM	Partido de la Revolución Mexicana
PST	Partido Socialista de Trabajadores
SAHOP	Secretaría de Asentamientos Humanos y Obras Públicas
SARH	Secretaría de Agricultura y Recursos Hidráulicos
SENA	Servicio Nacional de Aprendizaje (Colombia)
SERFHA	Serviço Especial de Recuperação de Favelas e Habitaçãos anti-higiénicas
SIB	Superintendencia Bancaria
SINAMOS	Sistema Nacional para el Apoyo de Mobilización Social
SPP	Secretaría de Programación y Presupuesto
SRA	Secretaría de Reforma Agraria
SRH	Secretaría de Recursos Hidráulicos
SSA	Secretaría de Salubridad y Asistencia
UAM	Universidad Autónoma Metropolitana
UDO	Unidad de Ordenamiento
UNAM	Universidad Nacional Autónoma de México
UNICEF	United Nations Children's Fund
URD	Unión Republicana Democrática
WHO	World Health Organization

1

Introduction: the research issues and strategy

State intervention and the urban poor: major issues concerning housing, planning and servicing in Latin American cities

The main objective of this study is to improve understanding of the social conditions and the role of the poor within urban society in Latin America. More specifically, the aim is to understand how the needs of the urban poor with respect to housing and servicing are articulated and satisfied. The study examines the aims, development and implementation of government policies towards low-income housing dwellers, tries to relate those policies to the wider interests of the state and the constraints within which it acts, and examines governmental success in meeting the needs of the poor. We examine the needs of the poor, their understanding of the main constraints on *barrio* servicing and improvement, their involvement in community organizations and the role that the community and its leaders play in influencing state action. Since housing and servicing directly impinge on the interests of politicians, bureaucrats, landowners, and real-estate developers, as well as those of the poor, they represent critical elements in the relationship between the poor and the wider urban society. Essentially, therefore, the research is interested in how resources are allocated within urban society and how political and administrative power operates at the municipal level.

The research was conducted in three Latin American cities, Bogotá, Mexico City and Valencia, as a reaction to the dominant trend in urban studies to concentrate on a single centre. Most previous work has either sought to generalize across much of the globe or has focused on individual cities or even individual settlements. Our study seeks to combine many of the virtues of both approaches in order to make generalizations across cities about the nature of urban development, government practice and local politics. While the analysis has been confined to countries with non-military governments, Colombia,

Mexico and Venezuela, there are sufficient differences between the chosen countries and cities to make interesting comparisons about the nature of poverty and urban growth. We construct a series of statements about urban development since 1965, specificially concerned with the prospects for self-help housing development.

We are primarily concerned with housing and the poor, but we try to place our discussion within its broad social setting. That housing is not merely a matter for architects and planners has been a recurrent theme in recent literature. Decisions about housing, land and services are part and parcel of the wider economic and political scene. For this reason we dedicate more time than previous studies of housing to the economic, political and social context. We seek to emphasize that the housing of the poor is an outcome of the overt and covert policies of the state and that the form and role of the state must be understood if those policies are to be correctly explained. Whom the state seeks to help through its policies, where its priorities lie, and how it responds to the poor as a social class are vital factors in an understanding of housing.

In the following sections of this introduction we raise the principal issues to be discussed in the study. These issues include some which have received unsatisfactory answers in previous work and others on which little work has been carried out. We have no wish to examine the huge literature in the field with which we are concerned since there already exist several excellent reviews. On housing in Third World countries we would recommend Drakakis-Smith (1981), Dwyer (1975), Grimes (1976), Lloyd (1979), Payne (1977) and Ward (1982a); on the urbanization process in poor countries Abu Lughod and Hay (1977), Friedmann and Wulff (1976), Gilbert and Gugler (1982) and Roberts (1978); on the nature of the state Saunders (1979), Roxborough (1979), Miliband (1977), Castells (1977) and Poulantzas (1973); and on community participation and self-help Nelson (1979). More specific works will be noted in our detailed discussions below. Here there is only room to identify current issues. We are not concerned with describing the current state of knowledge nor do we wish to describe the current housing situation in poor countries. Our aim is simply to explain our principal hypotheses and to show why they are important.

The nature of the state

Recent work in the social sciences has profoundly changed academic perspectives on the state (Castells, 1979; Saunders, 1979; Poulantzas,

1973). Previously, the state was often viewed as a liberal entity that was interested in developing a form of welfare society, engaging in rational planning, and spreading the benefits of economic growth to most groups in society. Such a conception underlay much of the writing on housing, urban planning and economic development; the state was seen to be acting in the best interests of society. Recent work has taken a different stance: the role and nature of the state is an outcome of the class structure of society and of the role that the society performs in the international division of labour. The form of insertion of a given society in the world system broadly conditions the structure of classes, the level of economic development and the nature of the state. To understand specific state responses, therefore, a more holistic, class-based, political-economy approach is required. Since most nation states contain highly unequal societies, few governments will represent all social groups fairly. As a result, most analyses of state policy have ceased to examine the neutral decisions of a technical and objective state; they have begun to examine the policies of a state which responds to class conflict and the constraints posed by the international situation. The state is no longer seen to choose freely between alternatives on the basis of rational judgement; it chooses policies in the light of the major constraints on its action. The state is once again regarded as a political entity not as a futuristic, benign and fair-minded arbiter of change.

Two broad sets of issues are of interest to this study. The first concerns the debate about the nature of the link between the form of the state and the level of economic development. Clearly, the relationship between economic and political development is bound to be complex but its nature has long exercised the minds of academics. Until recently, it was argued that rising levels of economic development would encourage the growth of political democracy. Writers such as Lipset (1959) and Johnson (1958) argued that economic growth would create numerous interest groups which would enter the political arena. This pluralism would encourage the emergence of political democracy with the state responding to and representing the different interest groups. The rise of a series of military dictatorships in Latin America during the sixties and seventies led to a reformulation of this model. Authors such as Cardoso (1978; 1979) and O'Donnell (1973; 1977; 1978) argued that, rather than leading to democracy, the special situation of Latin America would lead to a gradual change in the dominant form of state. The state dominated by an export-oriented oligarchy would give way first to a populist form of state, and thence to more complex bureaucratic and authoritarian kinds of government. This debate is clearly vital to any analysis of state efforts in the fields of housing and service provision. There is little point in recommending community participation, for example, if the dominant form of the state relies on technocratic bureaucracies backed by authoritarian rule.

Linked to this issue is the question: who does the state represent? If it represents only the rich and powerful why should it adopt housing policies to help the poor? If on occasion the state does attempt to remedy the problems associated with low incomes, poor housing conditions and lack of services, what determines the form and timing of its actions? Alternative models of the state exist which we have discussed in detail elsewhere (Gilbert and Ward, 1982b). These models may be broadly characterized as the liberal state, the instrumentalist state and the structuralist state. We have already crudely summarized the liberal state. The instrumentalist perspective differs insofar as it argues that the state is the tool of the dominant class in society, and the state ensures that the interests of that class are maintained and extended. The state is manned by representatives of the dominant groups and fosters an ideology that is compatible with the interests of those groups. By contrast, structuralist perspectives show that the state frequently acts against the clearly defined interests of the dominant groups. Structuralism seeks to avoid this difficulty by arguing that the state responds to class conflict in ways that sustain and reproduce the conditions which favour the maintenance of the dominant groups. At times the state is required to act autonomously in order to maintain the structure of domination. It is no longer necessary for the capitalist class to dominate the state apparatus because it controls the structure to which the state responds.

Numerous difficult questions can be raised in connection with these three perspectives. First, is there a necessary conflict between the different perspectives at least in terms of our search for models with which we can understand the functioning of the state? Is it necessary to select one perspective or is it possible to combine the insights provided by each in turn? This question in turn raises another: what flexibility does the state have in choosing between different kinds of housing and servicing policies? Do urban administrators make the key decisions with respect to land allocation and service distribution, or are those decisions effectively resolved at higher levels by the budgets that are made available for housing or servicing (Pahl, 1975; Harloe, 1977; Saunders, 1979)? This is a critical issue in planning as it questions the autonomy and scope for action of rational decision-making processes such as planning. It tends to argue that the real decisions are made by those with power over the state apparatus or control over the economy. However we resolve these questions one point is clear. Without a broadly accurate view of the state's relationship with the political, social and economic structure of society, little of use can be said about housing, servicing and community action. Integral to any interpretation of poverty and low-income settlement is an implicit or explicit view of the state.

The nature of the housing and land markets

Housing and land markets are often discussed in terms of a dichotomy consisting of the 'formal' and 'informal' sectors. Here we use the terms 'formal' and 'informal' not in the sense of ILO-type studies which imply that there is no link between the two (Hart, 1973; ILO, 1972; Sethuraman, 1976), but in the way of studies which object to the dichotomy argument on the grounds that the 'petty commodity' sector is linked to the dominant capitalist sector (Nun, 1969; Moser, 1978; Bromley and Gerry, 1979; Quijano, 1974; Bromley, 1978). Formal systems provide private housing and land for those who can afford to pay the market price on the legal market; such systems also supply a certain amount of public housing. Higher income groups either buy or rent completed houses and apartments or they purchase land and hire their own battery of architects, lawyers and builders to provide custom-built homes. Financing is usually arranged privately through the banks or mortgage companies and the state frequently gives tax relief on interest repayments. The size of the private formal market depends upon the distribution of income and the affluence of the city; in certain Latin American cities it may account for as much as half of all housing. The formal sector also provides public housing for limited numbers of the lower-middle income groups. Such housing is limited in quantity, usually constituting around 10 per cent of the housing stock. Public housing is limited because it costs more than most poor people can afford. As a result governments are often forced into a difficult position. They either subsidize such housing at great cost to provide benefits for a small group in society or the houses remain unsubsidized and few poor people can afford to buy or rent them. Characteristically, public housing is not allocated to the very poor and seems to serve three functions in society. It serves the ideological purpose of showing that the state is attempting to build housing for the poor. It helps to create jobs and more importantly helps to sustain the private construction industry. Finally, it provides homes for government supporters, for members of working-class groups in strategic industries (e.g. transport, armaments, etc.) and for government officials (Laun, 1976; Malloy, 1979). It serves, in short, both growth and legitimacy objectives.

Those groups which are excluded from formal private or public solutions find accommodation mainly in the informal sector. Those members of the poor who want their own property are obliged to enter land markets of dubious legality and to participate in the construction of their own dwellings. The forms of this 'illegality' vary greatly from city to city but all informal housing suffers initially from a lack of services, because it lies beyond the main service grids, and from certain doubts about security of tenure.

While the distinction between formal and informal housing markets has a certain validity, recent work has clearly demonstrated the following problems with such a dichotomy. First, in reality the two markets are integrally linked. Second, housing and land often change categories through time; land that is occupied illegally may later be legalized and serviced, thereby turning informal housing into formal housing; former elite housing may be converted into rental slums that fail to abide by government regulations on rent rises and contracts. Third, the dichotomy omits the important distinction between those who own and those who rent or share accommodation. Renters and sharers are found in both sectors, although the proportions vary greatly from city to city; poorer renters were traditionally located in the city centre but are increasingly found also in most low-income settlements; in addition, many people – usually the old and recent arrivals to the city – share accommodation with kin.

Critical, therefore, is the relationship between the formal (public and private) and informal markets. The major issue relates to how land is allocated to different land uses and to different residential groups. To some extent historical factors affect the availability of land for the poor. In many African and Asian cities, land is owned by tribal communities whose land has been absorbed by the growth of the city (World Bank, 1978). In Latin America, communal land sometimes remains from the time of the Spanish Conquest or has been re-established by post-independence reforms. Most typically, however, land is allocated by the market with the passive and active intervention of the state. In chapter 3 we argue that market forces are the primary determinant of land allocation with the state exerting a critical influence over prices by determining which areas will be serviced and which will be neglected. The outcome of these forces in Latin America is to divide cities socially: housing areas have become segregated according to income. The rich occupy the best-located and serviced areas, the poor the most-polluted, least-serviced and worst-located land.

Within this context it is interesting to consider how the poor acquire land, for the mechanisms whereby land is allocated differ markedly between countries (Gilbert and Gugler, 1982). In some countries the poor invade land (Collier, 1976; Leeds, 1969), elsewhere they purchase land from property developers (Doebele, 1975), in some places they rent it from private landlords (Payne, 1982), and where community land is widespread they may acquire temporary rights informally (Peil, 1976). Variations of this nature are not only observed between nations but also within each country between cities. There have been numerous detailed studies of particular forms of land acquisition by the poor but there is a remarkable lack of research analysing why these differences occur. For example, why are invasions of land permitted in some cities and not in others? How do the different forms of land acquisition relate to the political economy of individual cities and to the form and role of the state? It is only recently that research has sought to address the relationships between the various forms of land and housing development and the wider socio-political system. We still lack information and theories on this issue and this is a principal theme of this book.

Clearly, the reactions of the state are critical. In some countries illegal squatting on government land has won tacit approval, elsewhere invasions of land are strongly resisted. It is commonly assumed that public land has in the past offered major opportunities for low-income housing development and that attempts to increase public ownership of land are likely to benefit the poor. And yet, since many public agencies commercialize their land in similar ways to private land-owners, such an outcome is uncertain; clearly the responses of the state are highly contingent on local circumstances.

Where governments have adopted a benign attitude to incursions upon their land, the poor are likely to benefit from cheap land. But, where this form of occupation is not permitted, what formal and informal initiatives have emerged to make land available? How has the private sector responded and what has been the state's response to the often illegal processes that have emerged? How have government decisions such as those concerning regularization and servicing affected the value and demand for land from different groups? Answers to such questions provide important insights into state–private sector relations, the workings of the land market and the housing situation of the poor.

How land is allocated and alienated in different cities helps shape the housing market. The form of land acquisition will affect land costs; where squatting is resisted and land is scarce, prices will be high. The likely outcome is either to restrict home ownership or to reduce lot size. Clearly, there are important implications for the poor. We believe that the proportions of the urban population owning, renting, and sharing accommodation is largely explicable in these terms. Where land is difficult or expensive to obtain, alternatives such as renting or sharing with kin are likely to become essential and the proportion of owner-occupiers will decline. So far these propositions have not been tested for one city, let alone on a comparative or cross-cultural basis, and this represents one of the major aims of this study (see chapter 3).

Changes in the housing and land markets

Recent work has tended to view the production of housing and social systems as integral components of the process of peripheral capitalism (Roberts, 1978; Castells, 1977; Portes and Walton, 1976; Peattie, 1974; Perlman, 1976). Within this approach, 'formal' and 'informal' housing processes are seen to form different but related parts of the same production system: a marked contrast to the 'dualistic' view of society in which the formal and informal sectors are viewed as being separate and unrelated. The relationship between the 'formal' and 'informal' sectors is seen to be unequal. Economic groups linked to international and national capital dominate the economy and dictate the forms of employment and housing in the informal, petty commodity and even the pre-capitalist economies. Poverty is a direct outcome of this pattern of social relations. It is, moreover, an inevitable outcome of peripheral capitalism. Without the different kinds of subsidy produced by the cheap labour of the poor, the formal sector would be unable to expand given the nature of the national economy's insertion into the world economic system. More specifically, different studies of employment have demonstrated how various informal sector activities 'serve' the formal sector, directly, through providing the formal sector with inputs and, indirectly, through the provision of cheap services which lower production costs and cheapen the reproduction of labour (Bromley and Gerry, 1979; Roberts, 1978).

Similarly, recent studies of housing have shown how different forms of housing production are linked to the capitalist economy. Pradilla (1976) and Burgess (1978) identify two forms of housing production, the first dominant and expanding, the second subordinate and increasingly penetrated by the first. 'Industrialized' production, which is dominant, is characterized by large enterprises which use high-level technology to produce housing that is sold through exchange. The intervention of numerous actors (such as financiers, commercial developers, real-estate agents) in the production and sales process turns housing into an expensive product. The subordinate 'petty commodity' production of housing assumes two sub-forms: the 'manufactured' form, which is organized into small-scale enterprises with few paid workers, using labour-intensive methods of production and employing local, non-standardized raw materials; and the 'self-help' form in which the producer and consumer are the same and raw materials are purchased from the 'manufactured' sector or take the form of recycled throw-aways. This recent work argues that the capitalist economy is only viable if there is constant expansion in the production of commodities for exchange in the market. Hence, the 'industrialized' form of production will expand at the expense of the 'petty commodity' forms. Although some authors accept this proposition as a matter of faith, it is as yet unsubstantiated in many respects. Nevertheless, the proposition is important because it underlines the need for a better understanding of the relationship between the formal 'industrialized' and informal 'petty-commodity' sectors. The major issue here is to establish whether the relationship is 'benign', 'complementary' or highly 'competitive'. Is the classic Marxist explanation correct in suggesting that the industrialized housing form and the related building-supplies industry will eventually displace petty-commodity production? Alternatively, will the latter form survive in the conditions of peripheral capitalism? Or, finally, might the expansion of the capitalist economy increase the ability of the 'self-help' and 'manufactured' forms to produce housing by raising income levels for the poor or by producing better construction materials? If more profitable opportunities are available to large-scale capital, might it leave housing construction to petty-commodity forms? Should real incomes rise among the poor, might the ability of 'self-help' builders not improve? At the present time, theory has not been matched by empirical investigation; how and to what extent do contemporary practices and policies threaten to undermine the viability of informal housing processes?

In order to answer this kind of question we need to examine how dependent the informal sector is upon the formal sector for the supply of construction materials, and how international monopoly pricing systems have affected the consolidation process. What arrangements has the formal sector made to develop its distributive systems to facilitate the penetration of informal housing markets? To what extent are industrialized building materials and components used in the construction of low-income housing compared with petty-commodity forms? Are the industrialized forms more expensive or cheaper than the petty-commodity forms?

The answers to these questions will allow us to discover more about the impact that penetration has upon the consolidation process. Is self-help consolidation today more expensive relative to incomes than it was ten or twenty years previously? In the event that housing costs are higher, it is probable that rates of home improvement will have fallen.

There is certainly evidence to suggest both that urban land prices are rising and that the land market is being dominated increasingly by large, integrated and powerful organizations (Baross, 1983; Durand Lasserve, 1983; Geisse, 1982). Similarly, it is possible that growing state intervention in planning, regularization and servicing has had a negative effect on the supposed beneficiaries of more rational and liberal planning policies. Has regularization of land tenure and the servicing of low-income settlements had a beneficial or negative impact on the poor? One of the points we seek to examine is the extent to which self-help housing solutions have become less or more accessible to the poor. What impact has the growth in formal bureaucratic procedures regulating informal housing development had upon the ease with which the poor gain access to a plot? In some instances greater bureaucratic complexity may have encouraged informal processes; elsewhere it may have reduced them. In short, where does state intervention fall along our 'benign' – 'complementary' – 'competitive' continuum?

Finally, what effects are changing patterns of employment and income distribution having upon low-income housing consolidation? A common theme in many earlier studies was to describe how labour and housing markets were mutually supportive. Informal patterns of home-ownership involved minimal land payments, utilized spare time through self-help and were supportive of families engaged in low-paid and irregular employment (Leeds, 1971; Mangin, 1967). They allowed the poor to choose accommodation in line with an individual's position in the employment structure (Turner, 1967; 1968). Yet little research has adequately demonstrated the impact of changing trends in the employment structure of a city's economy upon the forms and dynamism of its housing (Peattie, 1979). Industrialization and the expansion of job opportunities fuelled urban expansion and the demand for housing, yet we know relatively little about how, for example, rising levels of un- and under-employment or trends in real wages affect the housing fabric. How have changing employment structures and the possibly growing difficulties of gaining a secure job in the manufacturing sector affected the demand for different forms of low-income settlement? If there is increasing economic hardship, how has this affected residential improvement? Do fewer households become home owners and does dwelling consolidation suffer as a consequence of lower investment potential? Are the poor obliged to rent or share with kin for longer periods until they have generated sufficient resources to contemplate becoming home owners? Or do the poor adopt alternative strategies to survive and thereby sustain the process of home improvement? The relationship between the two markets is clearly a profound one, yet it is inadequately understood. The outcome of these different changes in employment, in the form of state intervention and in relations between the formal and informal sectors, determines the degree to which the poor are able to exercise a choice over their housing situations.

The nature of choice and the way in which migrants adapt their housing preferences to their needs at any specific moment of time are issues that have long fascinated English-speaking scholars (Turner, 1967; Mangin, 1967). This approach, however, perhaps exaggerates the role of residential preferences and underplays the constraints on residents' ability to obtain housing. In short, it neglects the question whether housing preference is determined exogenously or whether it is a response to the urban environment. Settlers are not the only actors in the urban process. The interests and priorities of the commercial and public sectors frequently conflict with low-income groups and 'what is more important . . . tend to exert, usually jointly, a dominating

influence over the total context in which housing choices are made'
(Brett, 1974: 189). In order to understand residential movement, both
residential preferences and constraints need to be considered (Gilbert
and Ward, 1982a). The latter can only be included through an analysis
of wider structural factors such as government policy towards land and
servicing, the changing price of land, the impact of increased densities
on land use in low-income settlement and the effects of increasing
urban diseconomies.

We need to question whether residential movement is best explained
as an outcome of the constraints imposed by the dynamic of the land
and housing markets or whether it reflects a real choice on the part of
the low-income families? To what extent do market forces condition
the opportunities for low-income residents whatever their housing
preferences?

Changing forms of state action with respect to housing, planning and
servicing

State responses to housing, planning and servicing vary markedly both
geographically and temporally. Clearly this variation reflects the
changing role of the state in each country. Specifically, policy formulation, implementation and the rules that govern public administration
will differ between 'bureaucratic authoritarian' and 'populist' governments. Yet it is worthwhile asking whether there are any general trends
in state policy towards housing and servicing. At the risk of overgener-
alization, past approaches can be depicted as having fallen into two
broad phases. The first, which persisted until the middle of the 1960s,
consisted of a neglect of housing investment combined with a lack of
support for informal housing solutions. Few governments regarded
housing as a productive sector, following the ruling bias among
economists on this issue (Gilbert and Gugler, 1982), and therefore
directed little investment in this direction. In addition, governments
assessed housing and servicing conditions according to Western European and North American planning standards. These standards were
inappropriate to the environmental, social and economic conditions of
Latin American societies, but settlements that fell below these official
norms were sometimes subjected to demolition and removal. Demolition, artificially high standards and lack of investment led to rising
housing 'deficits'. Only during the Alliance for Progress was sufficient
capital invested to create large numbers of 'social interest' housing

units. Even then, rising demand and relatively high building costs meant that 'social interest' housing often missed most of the very poor. During this early period most governments neglected the low-income settlements which developed without official authorization, were inadequately serviced and were built through informal processes by the poor themselves.

Major policy shifts appear to have taken place from the late 1960s onwards. While most governments have continued to invest in conventional housing projects, there has been a perceptible shift towards support for unauthorized settlements (United Nations, 1981; World Bank, 1980a; Habitat, 1982). Existing settlements have been provided with basic services and, where necessary, land tenure has been regularized. In addition, new settlements have been developed in which house construction has been left largely to the residents themselves while the state has provided a basic range of services (Angel, 1983).

Several factors appear to have informed this change. Research into low-income groups and settlements revealed the ability and potential for self-build urban development (Abrams, 1964; Mangin, 1967; Turner and Fichter, 1972; Turner, 1976). Self-help advocacy rapidly became the conventional wisdom and won influential support from international funding agencies. Another factor was the realization that traditional policies and approaches had failed to deal with the housing 'problem' either quantitatively or qualitatively (Turner, 1976). Since low-income settlements had become so widespread, governments could no longer afford to ignore the demands from residents for services and land titles. Indeed, the opposite was often true; politicians recognized the opportunities that low-income communities offered for social control, political manipulation and vote catching (Collier, 1976; Cornelius, 1975; Nelson, 1979).

If we are correct in our description of the change in the form of state intervention, then a critical issue is to evaluate the impact of this change on low-income housing conditions. A first step is to examine the quantitative effect of new policies upon service conditions in low-income settlements. Put simply: have servicing levels improved as a result of government interventions (Gilbert and Ward, 1978)? And, insofar as governments have sought to stimulate low-income settlements, how many 'solutions' have been provided in the form of serviced lots, core houses, etc.? It is also important to consider the possibly negative effects of growing state intervention (Peattie, 1979).

As we suggested earlier, it is conceivable that legalization of land tenure may encourage investment by higher-income groups, thereby raising land values and putting self-help housing beyond the pockets of the poor (Angel *et al.*, 1983; Ward, 1982b). One consequence of such a trend might well be higher proportions of renters and sharers in the housing market. In this case a growing polarization might be apparent between those low-income owner occupiers and those groups which are excluded from this housing option (Edwards, 1982a; Gilbert, 1983). In many cities, renters form the majority of households, and non-owners often make up a significant proportion of households in low-income unauthorized settlements. Growing government assistance for owner-occupiers may actually help to exclude the majority of families from ownership. And, insofar as government actions have largely ignored non-owners, has this led to greater political, social and economic differentiation between tenure groups? Have *barrio* improvements led to increased rents forcing poorer renters out of the settlement?

Increased government intervention is also likely to have other repercussions. It will affect the form of community organization by modifying community and state relations. These changes may increase 'social control' or may sharpen political conflict by encouraging class solidarity over the provision of infrastructure and collective services. One determinant of these outcomes is the manner in which the state handles service provision. Different political and community consequences will arise from different kinds of state-agency operation. State agencies that operate according to clearly laid-down procedures will have a different social impact from those that follow more opportunistic policies and where rules are consistently bent. Agencies differ in their responses to partisan political pressures and in their bureaucratic structures. In some institutions personnel are appointed almost entirely on the basis of personal patronage, regardless of merit; elsewhere technical knowledge, proven skills and ability are important. Most institutions are located somewhere in between the two extremes, but where precisely they fall has important implications for the covert and overt aims of an agency and its performance.

Several important issues require clarification. Why, for example, do the rules and patterns of behaviour that govern bureaucracy performance differ so markedly between land, housing and servicing agencies in different cities? Why are certain sectors of public administration more efficient at carrying through their tasks than others? What factors govern their efficiency? We examine these issues in chapter 4.

Forms of social organization and the housing process

One of the primary motives for increasing state intervention in low-income settlement in the 1960s was the fear that such areas constituted a major risk to social stability. Events in Cuba added further to these fears. Writers such as Fanon (1967) envisaged the shantytowns as crucibles of revolutionary activity. The 'lumpen proletariat', denied access to basic services, employment and adequate shelter, yet surrounded by the symbols of wealth in urban centres, would rise up and overthrow existing regimes. Research soon showed that this image bore little relation to Latin American reality (Goldrich *et al.*, 1967; Ray, 1969; Cornelius, 1975). Although irregular settlement populations were poor, they often had secure employment. And for a large number, particularly those who were originally migrants from rural areas, life in the city represented a major improvement in living standards. Once they had gained a foothold in the land market their outlook was essentially conservative: why mobilize to overthrow the regime that had allowed them a certain degree of 'progress'? Material benefits were supplemented by more subtle forms of social and political control: patron–client networks in which residents offer their support to high-ranking government officials or to politicians in exchange for assistance to the *barrio* (Leeds, 1969; Ray, 1969; Cornelius, 1975); cooptation or the buying-off of local leaders to ensure that they moderate their demands (Eckstein, 1977); repression where communities resist cooptation and incorporation.

For the authorities these mechanisms usually worked well; for the poor, radical demands were curtailed in return for limited material improvements. Few associations developed a radical position *vis-à-vis* the state; only the Movement of the Revolutionary Left (MIR) in Chile (Handelman, 1975; Castells, 1977) and isolated cases elsewhere (Montaño, 1976).

Castells' work (1977, 1977a, 1981) argues that hope for radical political activity remains. The declining rate of profit in the capitalist economy obliges the state to increase its responsibility for the provision of such collective goods as housing, water supply, schools and roads. This responsibility is clearly defined and the class struggle can be encouraged by mobilizing residents' political activities around servicing issues. As we shall observe in chapter 5, there are several problems with this line of argument, not least that within any single settlement there are conflicting interests directing servicing needs and priorities (Saunders, 1979; Pickvance, 1976; Harloe, 1977). Nevertheless, the possibilities for the formation of 'urban social movements' remain a key issue in Latin American urban analysis (Castells, 1981; Janssen, 1978).

For the authorities, community organization has become an object of concern not simply as a means of social control but also as a means of improving local housing conditions. Recent housing policies require the active collaboration of the community. Resident associations are encouraged to install services through community labour, reducing the overall costs of service provision for the state.

Past research either emphasized the means whereby the demands of communities are controlled by the state or focused attention upon the characteristics of local leaders and examined the role that these figures play in community affairs. Consequently, there are few comparative analyses which identify the reasons for spatial and temporal variations in state–community relations. As a result, there are few general statements about the factors that have shaped state–community relations, the covert and overt motives for state involvement, and the relationship between party politics and neighbourhood organizations.

There is also limited knowledge about the nature of community leadership. In most cities many somewhat cynically regard community leaders as being corrupt, exploitative and opportunist. While some do fit this picture, as do some government officials, it is less than certain that this is an accurate characterization of most leaders. It is important to clarify the nature of leaders' career patterns, the nature of their involvement, the basis of their legitimacy, their aspirations, and indeed whether the quality of leadership is a critical ingredient in successful demand making.

The corollary of community leadership is the level and form of community participation. Previous studies have suggested that the intensity of participation in community organizations is high in the immediate post-formation phase of a settlement, or when it is threatened by a significant crisis (Ray, 1969; Mangin, 1967). At these times there is an ethos of mutual cooperation, with most households participating in community meetings and public works. Once success is achieved or the crisis passes, active collaboration tends to decline.

Yet few studies have investigated the degree to which most residents participate. Is everyone involved or is it a small minority that is almost entirely responsible for petitioning and public works? This is a key issue if the effectiveness of state projects using community participation is to be assessed. Do men and women participate equally or is there an effective division of labour? What are the implications of different tenure interests for community participation? Do non-owners participate less actively than owners in settlement improvements? Are certain sorts of projects (schools for example) more likely to gain effective support than, say, land regularization that is of interest only to owners?

It is also important to determine how mechanisms of social control through community mobilization actually operate. If leaders are corrupt or linked to official organizations that provide few benefits for the settlements, why do residents continue to support them? Finally, how effective is community petitioning in obtaining services and help from the state? Do different forms of popular participation differ in their effectiveness? Are independent associations, say, more successful than state-directed schemes? Does the adoption of different tactics and strategies of demand making make any significant difference? These questions are also important to the state in its efforts to increase social control. For community experiences will clearly have an important effect upon how settlers perceive the governmental system and will respond to it in future. Does their experience induce cynicism and alienation or goodwill and hope? We investigate many aspects of this complicated range of issues in chapter 5.

The welfare of the poor

All the issues raised above are directed towards the critical matter of establishing how to analyse and improve the living conditions of the poor. Despite so many studies, we know remarkably little about some aspects of how the poor live and the reasons for their poverty. We certainly know very little about whether housing, employment and general welfare conditions are improving or deteriorating (Da Camargo, 1976; Gilbert and Ward, 1978). In chapters 3, 4 and 5 we address this issue. If we know too little about the conditions of the poor and the precise causes of that poverty, to judge by the results of government policies we know even less about how to remedy those conditions. It would be satisfying to pretend to provide solutions, but in all honesty we believe the problems and issues to be too great to do so.

In this book we can only raise those issues which we believe to be critical. Among these issues are those relating to the nature of the state. In short, do certain political systems favour the poor in the allocation of resources more than others? Is democracy or populism preferable in this respect to authoritarianism? What role should bureaucracies play in political systems? Should current trends towards more technical and commercial public utilities be commended or are these agencies simply providing better infrastructure for those who can pay?

It is perfectly clear that certain improvements could be made and indeed must be made if the welfare of the poor is to be improved. The redistribution of land is essential both in the urban and in rural areas. Better servicing and provision for the needs of the poor is vital. More credit and assistance to poor households in their housing situation is necessary. Of course, this is part of the political debate and herein lies a major paradox. Academic enquiry is increasingly moving away from the formulation of objective laws to a realization that the important matters are resolved not by logic but by those who hold power. In the final analysis this book is about political and economic realities; conditions cannot be changed without changing those realities. It would be academically satisfying to propose a new model for urban development that would resolve the problems of the poor. Unfortunately, subsequent chapters show why such a model would be inappropriate.

The research strategy

An important feature of this study is its comparative nature. It aims to compare and contrast the processes of housing and service provision in several Latin American cities. The comparative nature of the research added both interest and difficulty to the work. It required a methodology that would enable us to make meaningful comparisons across countries. Most readers will not be interested in the details, which we describe in appendix 1, but it is important that we sketch the general strategy. Here we provide a broad outline of how we went about the study.

The choice of cities

Our first task was to choose a number of cities sufficiently similar to permit comparison, but sufficiently different to pose provocative questions as to why essentially similar economic, social and political environments could generate distinct local responses.

In 1977, when the broad outlines of the study were being formulated, the Latin American political scene was dominated by authoritarian, military regimes. In fact, meaningful elections were held during the middle seventies in only four countries. A basic question was posed, therefore, whether we should study public intervention and housing in military or democratic regimes or in both. The last alternative seemed unworkable, since decision-making processes are very different in military and non-military countries. While most countries in Latin America are authoritarian, there is much greater possibility for political participation and mobilization in the non-military than in the military countries. Although social control and direct repression are not unknown in the countries which have elections – indeed repression had been increasing in intensity in several – channels do exist whereby community organizations and representatives can communicate with the authorities. Since one of our principal interests was the process of communication between the authorities and low-income populations, and such communication is likely to be much more limited in the military regimes, this swayed our choice. To include both sets of regimes would have complicated the study and made meaningful comparison between countries too difficult.

In a sense the limited number of non-military regimes in Latin America eased the task of selecting the countries for study. Effectively we chose to study the region's three largest non-military regimes: Colombia, Mexico and Venezuela. This choice was strongly influenced by the fact that the project directors had previously worked in Colombia and Mexico and both had limited experience of Venezuela.[1] It was assumed, rightly as it turned out, that this local knowledge and acquaintance with local people would ease the research task and accelerate the collection of data. The decision meant that we would study three countries each with non-military regimes but which were very different in terms of their political and economic structures. Mexico continued to be dominated by the Institutional Revolutionary Party (PRI) which had emerged during the 1930s; Venezuela had been governed by different political parties in a highly competitive democracy since the last military government fell in 1958; and Colombia had been ruled for the greater part of the period since 1958 by a unique power-sharing arrangement between the two major parties. In economic terms, Venezuela was by far the richest nation with a *per capita*

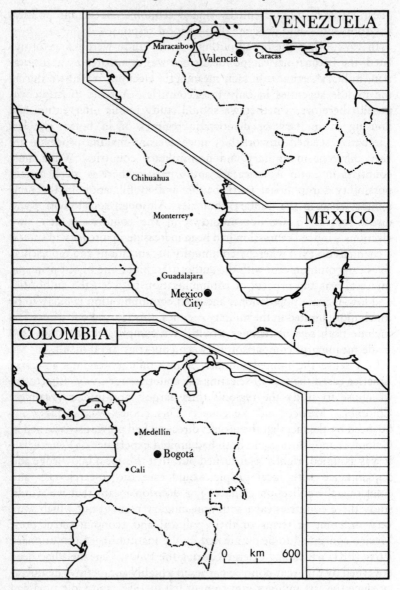

Fig. 1 Locations of the study cities

gross national product of 1,960 US dollars in 1974, Mexico followed with 1,090 dollars and Colombia was much the poorest with a mere 500 dollars (World Bank Atlas, 1977).

The choice of cities was to a considerable extent motivated by similar kinds of argument: the need for a range of urban types and the need for some familiarity with the local situation. One author had previously worked in Bogotá, one in Mexico City. The Venezuelan city, Valencia, was chosen without the benefit of prior acquaintance. Caracas, the obvious candidate for selection as national capital, was rejected because the short period which we could spend in Venezuela would not have been sufficient for a detailed study of such a complicated city. Among the smaller Venezuelan cities, Valencia was chosen because several previous studies were available which would serve as the basis for the research. While they had different foci, they covered important complementary areas of our work, either in terms of the time span covered (Cannon *et al.*, 1973) or in terms of their systematic focus (CEU, 1977; Healey, 1974). This choice gave us a considerable range of city types. In terms of population, they ranged from Mexico City's 10 million inhabitants, through Bogotá's 3 million or so, to Valencia's 600,000 (figure 1). They also varied in terms of levels of service provision, methods of land acquisition and housing tenure (see chapters 3 and 4).

Methods of data collection

The study was conducted by two teams each consisting of a project director and one research assistant. One team worked in Mexico for the full period, the other spent some time in Bogotá and the rest in Valencia. As a first step we sought to identify the broad context of housing and land-use patterns in each city. How important were low-income settlements in each city? What impact had previous housing policies had upon the poor? How was the servicing bureaucracy organized? In order to begin to answer these questions we relied heavily upon secondary sources such as newspapers, census data, agency reports and research theses.

The rationale underlying the field work was to collect information from all levels of urban decision making in order to distinguish between policy and practice, between rhetoric and action. We sought to combine interviews with those making decisions and those affected by them. With the aid of contextual analysis, this approach was designed to give us clear insight into variations in government policy and the reasons underlying those changes. But, before proceeding, an important decision had to be made with respect to the time period under study. It seemed sensible to limit the study to a relatively brief period. If too early a date were chosen it would be difficult to find interviewees who were involved in the important decisions, and in addition their memories might be less than reliable. Eventually, we decided to concentrate on the 1970s, with only brief incursions into the events of the sixties. We proposed, also, to pay more attention to past policies than to those of current administrations on the grounds that the past is generally less controversial than the present. We believed that those who had been responsible for making decisions, and who were no longer directly accountable for the consequences, were more likely to speak frankly. In addition, many of the results of past decisions would already have worked themselves through – a fact which would assist detailed study. In retrospect, we probably under-estimated the willingness of contemporary decision makers to collaborate quite openly. The information that might have been lost by interviewing active decision makers, who necessarily had to be careful about what they said, was amply compensated for by greater access to a wider range of personnel and higher recall of minor, but sometimes important, detail that was often omitted in analyses of past administrations.

We found that an unstructured interview format most suited our discussions with top decision makers whom we interviewed about policy and practice in the housing, planning and servicing fields. We talked with directors of land regularization and servicing agencies, government ministers, councillors, mayors, and party politicians. Our concern was to determine the overt and covert rationale underpinning decision making. We sought their views about how specific decisions or policies had been reached, the adequacy of resources allocated to tackle particular problems, and the relative success of actions undertaken. Before conducting these interviews we studied the local and national press to identify particular crises and problems that had emerged since 1965 and which had directly affected the land, housing and servicing situations. In addition, less senior government personnel were consulted to obtain detailed insights into agency performance and relationships with low-income populations. Unfortunately, it is not possible within the confines of this book to develop many of the insights gained from our discussions with top decision makers and other agency personnel. Suffice it to say that this information added enormously to our understanding about bureaucracy functioning, performance and change, and it informs much of the subsequent analysis.

Parallel to these interviews we visited numerous low-income settlements in order to obtain the *barrio* view of government policy and intervention. Settlement leaders, both past and present, were interviewed about the formation, regularization and consolidation of the settlements, with particular emphasis being placed on the links between the settlement and individual politicians, planners and administrators and how those links had changed over time. Also, by getting to know some of the leaders personally, by attending community meetings, by accompanying delegations to politicians and agency directors, we were able to judge the skills of the leaders themselves. Through initial meetings with leaders and by taking care to explain our interest openly and honestly, we were invariably provided with a wealth of information about and insight into community organizations.

The earlier settlement visits produced an inventory of suitable settlements where we might carry out household surveys. The rationale of how we selected the settlements is explained in greater detail in appendix 1. Clearly it was necessary to select a large number of *barrios* for detailed study in those cities where the urban structure was particularly complex. Hence our decision to interview in six settlements in Mexico, five in Bogotá and two in Valencia. We chose settlements that were between four and fifteen years of age, most of which had been provided with some infrastructure and services. The settlements were chosen to incorporate several methods of land acquisition: invasions, illegal subdivisions and *ejidal* land alienation.[2] They were chosen from different areas of the respective cities (see figure 2) and none had less than four hundred households. A description of each settlement and its history is included in appendix 2. Broad differences in settlement size, housing tenure and average densities were observed both within each city and between cities (table 1).

Our household survey was designed to provide information about the origins, socio-economic characteristics, political attitudes and housing responses of low-income populations in each city. The aim was to provide the context within which we could evaluate the response of the poor to urban decision processes. How were the poor affected by decisions about land allocation, servicing and planning, to

Table 1 *Comparative data for the 'barrios' sampled in each city*

MEXICO CITY	Isidro Fabela	Santo Domingo	El Sol	Liberales	Chalma	Jardines
Number of house lots	1,324[1]	7,500[2]	7,000[3]	640[4]	2,300[5]	1,780[6]
Number of households[2]	3,494	12,200	11,270	755	4,270	4,330
Average household size[8]	5.8	6.0	5.7	5.9	5.9	5.8
Approx. total population	20,000	73,500	64,000	4,500	25,200	25,000
Consolidation score[9]	25.4	21.2	23.3	17.9	20.7	23.8
Density: average lot space per person (m²)[10]	29	25	33	25	34	52
% owner households[10]	63	81	70	82	74	66
% renter households[10]	15	4	13	13	10	19
% sharer households[10]	18	14	12	5	15	11
Number of households interviewed	144	120	120	60	73	114

BOGOTA	Juan Pablo I	Casablanca	Atenas	Britalia	S. Antonio
Number of house lots	NA	NA	NA	2,846[11]	NA
Number of households	131[11]	604[12]	1,042[11]	1,664[11]	415[11]
Average household size[8]	6.6	5.2	5.5	5.8	5.6
Approx. total population	730	3,150	5,730	9,650	2,320
Consolidation score[9]	14.9	23.2	21.5	18.4	23.9
Density: average lot space per person (m²)[10]	25	23	21	23	22
% owner households[10]	89	57	56	71	55
% renter households[10]	11	42	43	28	43
% sharer households[10]	0	1	0	0	2
Number of households					

VALENCIA	Nueva Valencia	La Castrera
Number of house lots	—	—
Number of households	1,200	850
Average household size[8]	6.2	6.1
Approx. total population	7,440	5,180
Consolidation score[9]	19.2	24.2
Density: average lot space per person (m^2)[10]	99	52
% owner households[10]	97	93
% renter households[10]	2	7
% sharer households[10]	0	0
Number of households interviewed	94	84

Notes:

1. Estimate based upon total plot count.
2. FIDEURBE (1976:57). Based upon a total census for regularization.
3. Cisneros (n.d.).
4. Registration of lots and *socios*: Leaders' archive.
5. Estimate based upon our pre-survey listing of 14 (of 120) blocks.
6. Estimates provided by the leader. The figure relates to the original subdivision. Most plots of 400 m^2 have been further subdivided.
7. Estimates based upon survey data of average number of households per plot multiplied by the total number of plots.
8. Calculation derived from *barrio* survey data.
9. An unweighted points score incorporating data about physical structure of the dwelling, services enjoyed, number of rooms and material possessions.
10. Calculations derived from *barrio* survey data.
11. House count or household listing in whole *barrio*. Note that in Britalia there are 2,846 house plots, of which only 1,450 are occupied.
12. 210 houses with *placas* with 328 families.

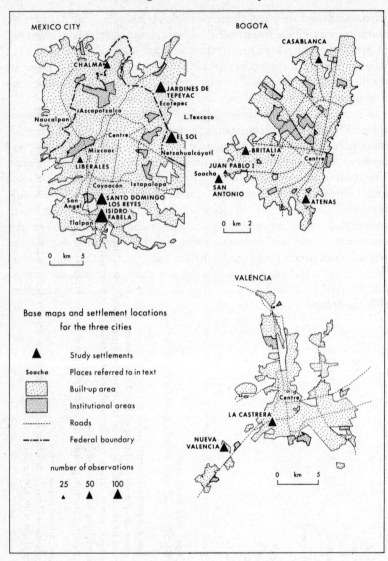

MEXICO CITY

BOGOTA

CASABLANCA

CHALMA

JARDINES DE
TEPEYAC
Ecatepec
Azcapotzalco
Naucalpan
L. Texcoco
Centre
EL SOL
Mixcoac
Netzahualcóyotl
BRITALIA
LIBERALES
JUAN PABLO I
Centre
Coyoacán
Ixtapalapa
Soacha
SAN
ANTONIO
San
Angel
SANTO DOMINGO
LOS REYES
ISIDRO
FABELA
Tlalpan
ATENAS

0 km 2

0 km 5

VALENCIA

Base maps and settlement locations
for the three cities

▲   Study settlements

Soacha   Places referred to in text

          Built-up area

          Institutional areas

-------- Roads

—··—··—   Federal boundary

Centre

LA CASTRERA

number of observations

25   50   100

▲   ▲   ▲

NUEVA
VALENCIA

0 km 5

Fig. 2 Locations of the study settlements

what extent did they feel themselves disadvantaged, how did they go about remedying the situation? To what extent are there consistent sets of problems which are characteristic of all low-income settlements; to what extent are there major variations between settlements? How far do the problems perceived by planners, politicians and administrators find an echo in the complaints and needs of the poor?

We carried out interviews on most Sundays and holidays and on some Saturdays. Representative households were chosen through random sampling from previously derived household counts, and between 60 and 150 households were interviewed in each settlement. The study team carried out many of the interviews but also employed local university students. The questionnaire was long but could normally be completed in about half an hour. Most households cooperated in an amazingly open and friendly fashion. Very few questions caused any embarrassment or concern and our problems related more to our interviewers than to our interviewees; one assistant thought he was better at answering the questions than the sample households! Our faith in Latin American census results was undeniably weakened.

2

Bogotá, Mexico City and Valencia: the social, economic and political backcloth

The different responses to housing and servicing in the three cities cannot be adequately understood without examining the nature and policies of the state both at the national and the local level. For land, housing and servicing are only elements in the total relationship between the state and the poor. Without some understanding of recent trends in economic and social change and of state participation in that process, our explanation of policy towards the urban poor is bound to be superficial. For this reason the chapter examines first the broad patterns of economic growth in each country, second, the nature of each country's political and social development and, finally, the economic, social and political characteristics of each city. This resumé is included in the hope that individual state responses to the specific issues of land, housing and servicing for the poor can be related in the later chapters to the wider issue of how the state conceives the whole dynamic and objective of development and change.

The national economies

There are numerous similarities between the Colombian, Mexican and Venezuelan economies. All showed quite high rates of growth during the late sixties and early seventies (table 2). All have a common dependence on the export of primary products, though the nature of the commodity and its role in the national development process differs. Coffee has long been paramount in Colombia even if marijuana sales became a major, if illicit, source of income from the middle seventies. Venezuela's economy has depended on oil exports since the 1920s whereas Mexico has only recently become a major oil producer. While Venezuela exports little but oil, Mexico also produces sugar and coffee in quantity. As well as all three countries being exporters of primary products, there are also similarities in the industrialization policies

28

Table 2 *Growth of real gross national product and population, 1965–80*
(per cent)

	Colombia[1]		Mexico[2]		Venezuela[3]	
	PIB	Population	GDP	Population	GNP	Population
1965-6		2.7		3.5	2.3	3.4
1966-7	4.2	2.7	6.9	3.5	4.0	3.4
1967-8	6.1	2.7	6.3	3.4	5.2	3.4
1968-9	6.4	2.7	8.1	3.4	3.7	3.4
1969-70	6.7	2.7	6.3	3.3	7.1	3.4
1970-1	5.8	2.7	7.0	3.3	3.3	3.4
1971-2	7.8	2.7	3.5	3.4	3.0	3.4
1972-3	7.1	2.7	7.3	3.4	6.7	3.1
1973-4	6.0	2.7	7.6	3.8	5.8	3.1
1974-5	3.8	2.7	5.9	3.6	5.2	3.1
1975-6	4.6	2.7	4.1	3.3	8.4	3.1
1976-7	4.9	2.7	2.1	3.2	7.0	3.0
1977-8	8.9	2.7	3.3	NA	3.0	3.0
1978-9	5.1	2.1	7.1	NA	0.9	3.0
1979-80	4.0	2.1	7.8	NA	-1.2	2.9

Notes:

1. PIB 1966–70 Colombia, Ministry of Finance, Prospectus for external finance 1973.
   1970–80 *Revista del Banco de la República*, April 1981, p. 118.
   Population 1964–78 DANE (1981) *Colombia Estadística*, 1981, p. 39.
   1978–80 *Colombia Today*, Vols. 15 and 16.

2. GDP 1966–1979 IMF (1980) International Financial Statistics, Mexico.
   Population 1965–76 Nacional Financiera (1978), *La economía mexicana en cifras*, p. 7.
   1977 Consejo Nacional de Población (Mexico) (1978), *México demográfico*, p. 10.

3. PTB 1965–75 BCV *La economía Venezolana en los últimos 35 años*, p. 36.
   1976–7 BCV *Informe Económico*, 1979, p. A-208.
   1977–80 BCV *Informe Económico*, 1980, p. A-198.
   Population BCV *La Economía Venezolana en los últimos 35 años*, p. 11.

29

adopted in each. From the 1940s, import-substituting industrialization was encouraged by the state through fiscal and tax incentives, the provision of infrastructure and facilities for finance. The common aim was to create employment and to increase self-sufficiency through the development of manufacturing industry. Each country has progressed through the stage of producing consumer goods for the home market to the establishment of heavy industry. The state has been a major actor in this process and its power and responsibilities have increased enormously. Government revenues and personnel have increased dramatically and the areas of state intervention have expanded greatly. All three countries are very much 'mixed' economies.

Economic development has brought concomitant demographic changes. Improvements in health and environmental conditions have led to rapid population growth, especially since the 1950s. Industrialization and socio-economic change in the countryside have led to major movements of people to the cities and a decline in the relative size of the agricultural labour force (table 3). Rapid urbanization occurred from the 1940s and today most people live and work in urban centres, many of them in cities with more than half-a-million people (table 3). Unfortunately, the benefits of economic development were less widely distributed than the changes induced by rapid economic and social change. Major inequalities have emerged; most of the population earn a relatively small proportion of the national wealth while a small minority receive a disproportionately large share.

However, the similarities between the three countries should only be taken so far. Among the important differences is the level of national prosperity. Venezuela is in the big league of oil exporters, Mexico has just joined it, whereas Colombia now needs to import oil. Largely as a result, Venezuela's *per capita* income is almost double that of Mexico which, in turn, is substantially higher than that of Colombia. The countries differ, also, in the size of their populations and national territories (table 3).

The national states

The nature and role of the state[1]

Early work on the state in Latin America was heavily influenced by the 'democratization' approach which formed an important part of the much wider body of modernization theory. Such an approach predicted that political democracy was positively correlated with the level

Table 3　*Colombia, Mexico, Venezuela: key economic and social indicators*

	Colombia	Mexico	Venezuela
Population			
Population 1979 (millions)	26.1	65.5	14.5
Annual Growth: 1970–9	2.3	2.9	3.3
Annual Growth: 1960–70	3.0	3.2	3.4
National income and product			
GNP *per capita* 1979 (dollars)	1,010	1,640	3,120
Annual growth 1960–79	3.0	2.7	2.7
GDP annual growth 1970–9	6.0	5.1	5.5
GDP annual growth 1960–70	5.1	7.2	6.0
Structure of production and employment			
Agriculture in GDP 1979	29	10	6
Manufacturing in GDP 1979	21	29	16
Other industry in GDP 1979	7	9	31
Services in GDP 1979	43	52	47
Labour force in agriculture (%) 1979	27	37	19
Labour force in industry (%) 1979	21	26	27
Labour force in services (%) 1979	52	37	54
Social indicators			
Adult literacy (%) 1976	NA	82	82
Life expectancy at birth 1979 (years)	63	66	67
Infant mortality rate 1978 (per thousand)	65	60	40
Population per doctor 1977	1,970	1,820	930
Urban population			
Urban population (%) 1980	70	67	83
Population in cities with more than 500,000 inhabitants (%) 1980	51	48	44
Average annual urban growth rate 1970–80	3.9	4.2	4.2

Source: The World Bank (1981), World Development Report 1981.

of economic development. The dominant hypothesis of writers such as Lipset (1959) was that stable democracy was the product of economic development and industrialization, and that Latin America as a semi-developed region was in transition towards democracy. The assumptions underlying this theory were that economic growth would create new interest groups in the political arena which would lead to political pluralism and hence democracy. The emergence of the middle class would be an important force leading to the replacement of authoritarian by democratic political systems (Johnson, 1958).

This work was roundly rejected as a result of methodological critique and the resurgence of authoritarian rule in numerous Latin American countries in the middle and late sixties. As such, the breakdown of democratic government in Latin America came to be seen as a more pertinent topic for analysis than the identification of the prerequisites for the development of democratic government (Linz and Stepan, 1978).[2] One branch of this work is associated with the emergence of authoritarian and 'technical' forms of government in the 'southern cone'. Authors such as O'Donnell (1973, 1977) have explored the relationship between the emergence of dependent industrialization, social structure and political system. His model of political development in Latin America envisaged a stage dominated first by an agro-export oligarchy, thence by a populist alliance between industrialists and working classes favouring import-substitution policies, and, ultimately, by 'bureaucratic authoritarianism'. The shift from the populist alliance was brought about by the failure of import-substituting industrialization with its uncompetitive industrial structure, high rates of inflation, foreign indebtedness, limited export potential and slowing rate of economic growth. The introduction of stabilization policies designed to cope with these problems contributed to the crisis of the populist state. Since the populist state depended on economic growth to finance benefits to the unionized labour force, it was placed in something of a dilemma by economic recession. This dilemma was made worse by the introduction of 'orthodox' economic policies such as fiscal austerity, currency devaluation, restrictions of welfare expenditure and wage restraint. The popular sector responded forcibly to these policies, thereby creating a political crisis. Combined economic and political crisis created a consensus among the dominant groups in society that popular participation must be limited in order to achieve economic and political progress. The response was either to introduce an authoritarian state or to limit political pluralism in some way. In Colombia and Venezuela, and in Peru between 1964 and 1968, limited pluralism took the form of a coalition or co-associational democracy; most of the rest of Latin America established some kind of bureaucratic–authoritarian state often headed by a military junta.

The concept of the authoritarian state is derived from Linz' classic definition:

> . . . a political system with limited, not responsible, political pluralism, without elaborate and guiding ideology . . . without intensive or extensive political mobilization (except at some points in their development), and in

which a leader (or occasionally a small group) exercises power within formally ill-defined limits but actually quite predictable ones (Linz, 1964).

These systems are 'excluding' and emphatically non-democratic. Central actors in the dominant coalition include high-level technocrats – military and civilian, inside and outside the state – working in close association with foreign capital. This new elite eliminates electoral competition and severely controls the political participation of the popular sector. Public policy is principally associated with promoting advanced industrialization (Collier, 1979: 24).

Later work has embraced this definition and has attempted to refine it for use in the countries of the southern cone of South America. Such work has principally attempted to describe the nature of government decision making in these countries, essentially by considering the nature of bureaucracy. The best-known such definition is that of O'Donnell (1978: 6):

The defining characteristics of the bureaucratic authoritarian state are: (a) higher governmental positions usually are occupied by persons who come to them after successful careers in complex and highly bureaucratized organization – the armed forces, the public bureaucracy, and large private firms; (b) political exclusion, in that it aims at closing channels of political access to the popular sector and its allies so as to deactivate them politically, not only by means of repression but also through the imposition of vertical (corporatist) controls by the state on such organizations as labor unions; (c) economic exclusion, in that it reduces or postpones indefinitely the aspiration to economic participation of the popular sector; (d) depoliticiza-tion, in the sense that it pretends to reduce social and political issues to 'technical' problems to be resolved by means of interactions among the higher echelons of the above-mentioned organizations; and (e) it corresponds to a stage of important transformations in the mechanisms of capital accumulation of its society, changes that are, in turn, a part of the 'deepening' process of a peripheral and dependent capitalism characterized by extensive industrializa-tion.

O'Donnell clearly sees the political developments that have occurred in Argentina, Brazil and Chile as being closest to his model. Neverthe-less, there are important elements of the bureaucratic-authoritarian state model apparent in most Latin American countries, including the three selected in this study. Indeed, we might depict the states of Colombia, Mexico and Venezuela as falling in different parts of O'Donnell's (1973) classification. Colombia and Mexico might well be classified as inclusionary authoritarian states and Venezuela as exhibit-ing limited pluralism associated with developmental populism.

The importance of the concept of bureaucratic authoritarianism, however, lies not merely in the classification of our states as much as providing a scenario by which we can understand the processes occurring in each country and city. It poses the question whether similar tendencies are occurring in each Latin American country which are leading to similar kinds of bureaucratic authoritarianism. The elements of the model which are of most interest to us concern the nature of political participation and exclusion in each state, the degree to which socio-economic policy making and administration is being 'depoliticized' by delegation to 'technical' agencies, and the extent to which the nature of the development model requires the state to hold down the welfare levels of the poor. We examine these issues with respect to Colombian, Mexican, and Venezuelan experience in greater depth in later chapters. Below, our concern is to provide an overview of the nature of the political structure in each country without which the detailed material about the three cities will not be understood.

The Colombian state

Colombian politics is unusual in Latin America insofar as it has long possessed two elitist parties which have dominated the political system. And yet, long as the Liberal and Conservative parties have coexisted, they have failed, until perhaps recently, to institutionalize a *modus vivendi* by which they could adjust to the loss of an election to the other party. As a result of this failure, and the traditional socialization process which ingrained party identification at all levels of society, severe and often violent competition between the parties has frequently broken out: the Thousand Days War at the beginning of the century, the violent 1922 election, the inter-party struggles of the late thirties and forties, and the *Violencia* which culminated in the military coup of 1953 which brought Rojas Pinilla to power. The essential source of conflict between the parties was the weakness of the state. In Solaún's (1980: 14–15) view, the state and the formal organizations of government lacked sufficient autonomy to stand as a national focus outside the realm of party loyalties and politics and consequently to withstand the destabilizing tendencies of party competition. The consequence was to politicize the state and subsume it within the partisan dictates of party. The two parties sought to limit conflict by allowing cabinet representation to the minority party.

The essence of the deal was four-yearly presidential alternation by the two parties and the equal division of all legislative and important appointed offices in the bureaucracy (Kline, 1980: 72; Dix, 1967).

Legislation had to be passed by a two-thirds majority in Congress and 10 per cent of the national budget had to go to education. The two-thirds rule was breached in the 1968 constitutional reform which extended the parity principle for cabinet ministers, governorships, mayorships and administrative positions until 1978. Despite considerable intra-party factionalism, and the possibly fraudulent fixing of the 1970 election to prevent General Gustavo Rojas Pinilla's ANAPO party obtaining power, the arrangement survived until 1974, when greater party competition was restored.

Bagley (1979: 126) characterizes the Colombian state under the National Front as falling into O'Donnell's (1973) category of 'inclusionary authoritarianism'.

The system was authoritarian rather than democratic because it limited political participation to the oligarchically-structured traditional political parties and the dominant class interests they represented. Pluralism was limited. Yet the *Frente* was an 'inclusionary' rather than an 'exclusionary' regime because it did allow for periodic elections, independent voluntary associations, the formation of anti-*Frente* political factions, and the initiation of reform legislation. Moreover, the *Frente* leadership ruled primarily through consensus and co-optation rather than repression, although repression was used selectively against radical opposition groups.

Under the Front there was a strong shift of power away from the legislative to the executive branch of government. The aim was to reduce political conflict and to accelerate the pace of social and economic change. The president's already considerable powers were augmented during the Front especially by the 1968 Constitutional Reforms. These reforms cut Congressional control over the national budget and gave the president power to introduce emergency economic measures over and above his powers under the provisions for a state of siege.[3] '. . . The *Frente* arrangement functioned to preserve and protect the interests of the capitalist class as a whole while simultaneously permitting continuing conflict among the different class factions making up the bloc-in-power' (Bagley, 1979: 82). To a considerable extent, therefore, the arrangement excluded low-income groups from participating in decision making. In this respect, the National Front was merely a continuation of a traditional pattern.

During the National Front, and indeed through the administrations of Alfonso López Michelsen and Julio César Turbay, the surface forms of state–poor relations were highly variable. Rapid economic growth was creating a more complicated and less well-trodden pattern of growth; the traditional method of legitimation and control through partisan political activity was now partially restricted and newly designed bi-partisan institutions developed. In addition, great reliance was placed on economic growth to produce additional resources which would benefit all groups in society. However, since there was never any intention by the dominant elites to give up any of their power, they were faced by something of a dilemma: 'how to preserve the power and status of the ruling class while at the same time accommodating the demands from peasant-, working- and middle-class groups as a result of capitalist development' (Bagley and Edel, 1980: 257–8). Their response has been ambivalent: 'on the one hand, the *Frente* leaders have striven to establish institutional links between elites and masses by promoting local organizations. On the other hand, they have taken care to insure that the power and influence of such groups remained channeled and circumscribed' (*ibid.*, 259).

ANAPO posed the main exception to this pattern. Rojas Pinilla managed to organize a 'mass-based, hierarchically-structured organization' which created a moment of acute discomfort to the National Front (Dix, 1980). The 1970 vote for Rojas received massive support from the poor (and also the lower-middle class) in Bogotá and the two other major cities. If there was little suggestion of socialism in ANAPO's programme, its populist leadership, supported by dissident Liberals and Conservatives, managed to generate 'a massive expression of protest against the policies of the National Front' (Dix, 1980: 143).

The National Front attempted to limit the degree of day-to-day political partisanship in public administration (see chapter 4). It sought to improve the pace of economic growth, the technical basis of government and to spread some of the benefits of development to the poor. But during the administration of Lleras Restrepo it seemed to many to be a highly undesirable process. Economic growth had slowed, inflation had accelerated and the attempts to introduce more technically based government seemed only to have produced corruption in the government. In addition, Lleras' total commitment to modernization had alienated the 'political class'. His constitutional reform of 1968 had taken power away from Congress, departmental assemblies and local councils and given it to the national executive. Public policy came increasingly to lie in the hands of government technicians who had control over the national budget and increasingly had the support of the multilateral lending institutions, such as the World Bank, which controlled important sources of investment funding. A major consequence of this process was that 'popular political initiative and response became less and less relevant to the making of public policy' (Cepeda and Mitchell, 1980: 245).

Much of the reaction to this process was channelled through ANAPO, an organization which offered the complete opposite to technocratic management by an elite executive and which had spent a great deal of effort organizing the *barrio* population. Indeed, during the late sixties, it had organized mass rallies, offered patronage to the low-income population and recruited a large number of members. The result was that it was much more highly regarded in the low-income settlements than the aloof Liberal/Conservative Front. 'In a survey of *barrio*, district, and national party leaders carried out in Bogotá in 1969, *Anapista* leaders reported significantly more attention to *barrio*-level organization, more involvement in 'social work', and more frequent visits by national leaders to the *barrios* than did Liberal or Conservative leaders' (Dix, 1980: 153).

The threat of ANAPO was contained by dubious means in 1970, had weakened by 1972 and virtually disappeared in the presidential elections of 1974 (Dix, 1980: 162–3). The National Front continued its attempts to improve bureaucratic efficiency and to reduce partisan political patronage. But, after Lleras, the approach was laced with a liberal sprinkling of politically inspired policies and attempts to enlist the support of the poor. In Bogotá, the Liberals were trying successfully to 'reconquer the city' and the National Front's Conservative leadership was trying to enlist popular support for its motorway project in the east of the city. The latter badly backfired and eventually brought more credit to the Liberals than the Conservatives (Revéiz *et al.*, 1977; Gilbert, 1978), but it was typical of the efforts underway to accelerate economic growth and legitimate the development model in the eyes of the poor. Major projects were introduced to benefit the city and its population; a few such as the plan to provide water to the peripheral settlements actually helped the poor. In addition, community-action committees were being mobilized by the major parties at this time to enlist electoral support (Gauhan, 1975; Bagley and Edel, 1980: 270) and the distribution of jobs in the bureaucracy continued to be an important cooptive instrument. This combination of major projects, stronger presence in the *barrios* and continued patronage through jobs proved successful in containing the situation. Until 1978 repression was limited in extent; it occurred when land was invaded, and it was used irregularly against trade unions (notably in 1977).

After 1978, however, it became an integral element in the state's response, the Security Statute was employed all too regularly against loosely defined 'terrorist sympathizers'.

But the Front continued to rely heavily on economic growth and modernization to legitimate the system. Hence, the technical agencies sought their own direct contacts with the *barrios* and tended to bypass the more partisan agencies. Our own interviews with *barrio* leaders showed clearly that they now petitioned the agencies directly rather than through the politicians or even through the Department of Community Action (chapters 4 and 5). The planning authorities eased the regulations controlling low-income settlement, which helped communities to deal directly with the service agencies. But all initiatives have come from above. Mobilization from below has been strongly curtailed. The National Front and later administrations have continued to prescribe the terms on which they are prepared to negotiate with the poor. The channels they have developed to accommodate the petitions of the poor have been carefully modulated and controlled. They have offered much in terms of rhetoric but little in terms of real resources.

The Mexican state

Although it is nominally a democracy, the Mexican State is widely perceived as being 'authoritarian'. If the nature of its authoritarianism is less marked than that characteristic of Argentina, Brazil and Chile in the seventies, those states most closely associated with O'Donnell's model, it nevertheless shares certain similarities with those military regimes. Mexico's form of democracy has two principal features. First, it is dominated by a single official party, the PRI, which consistently wins 85 per cent of the total vote (Smith, 1979: 55). Second, competitive parties are narrowly circumscribed and, until 1979, only those parties which never questioned the dominance of the PRI were permitted to compete in elections. These included, on the right, the National Action Party (PAN) and the Authentic Party of the Mexican Revolution (PARM) and, on the centre left, the Popular Socialist Party (PPS). Of these, only the PAN ever figured as an electoral force, winning 15 per cent of the vote in 1976. To ensure that there is always an 'opposition', one-quarter of the seats in Congress are allocated to the opposition parties, divided on the basis of proportional representation. Political reforms in 1973 and 1978 allowed additional parties to contest elections; as a result, the Mexican Communist Party (PCM), the Workers' Socialist Party (PST) and the Democratic Party of Mexico (PDM) were granted representation in 1979. The reforms were designed to revitalize the political system and to provide an electoral outlet for opposition without necessarily detracting from the pre-eminence of the PRI. In essence, they constitute an attempt to restore the somewhat tarnished legitimacy of the government. As a consequence of this make-up, the legislature is compliant to government proposals which it 'rubber-stamps'. The three-quarter dominance by PRI members in Congress and the reliance upon party patronage means that few oppose government proposals. In addition, the real functions of the PRI have little to do with representing the 'aggregate interest' of affiliates or with influencing government policy. The role of the PRI is to legitimize the government by mobilizing the vote at elections, by reducing the demands that local groups place upon the system, and by increasing social control through its powers of patronage, cooptation, and manipulation (Padgett, 1966; Eckstein, 1977; Reyna, 1974; Hansen, 1974; Smith, 1979).

The PRI has a pyramidal structure built around the organization of the farmworkers (CNC), labour (CTM), and the 'popular' sector (CNOP). These huge federations incorporate a myriad of organized groups which encompasses a large proportion of the work force. The CNOP, the most heterogeneous social group, tends to dominate other federations in the legislature (Smith, 1979: 227–9). While the government acts to organize the working classes through the three sectors of the PRI, it is careful to ensure that effective and autonomous power is not devolved to these groups (Eckstein, 1977: 25). Where social organizations critical to the regime threaten to emerge, swift action is likely to divert and demobilize them.

Thus, the *prima facie* impression that the PRI is representative of low-income groups is erroneous and the overall level of working-class participation in politics is low. While abstentionism in Mexico is lower than in Colombia (voting is compulsory in Venezuela) this is largely the result of the PRI's massive efforts to mobilize the vote in support of the state and of individual fears of penalties that might arise from a failure to vote.[4] There is little genuine belief in electoral politics in Mexico.

The Mexican state is commonly described as being led by a 'Revolutionary' or 'Ruling' coalition (Hansen, 1974; Purcell and Purcell, 1980). The political system can best be envisaged as a delicate balancing act involving all elite interests incorporated into a 'political bargain' which is constantly renewed in day-to-day action (Purcell and Purcell, 1980: 194–5). It is 'inclusionary' insofar as all groups or interests are represented, though inevitably certain groups are more assertive or influential at different times. The feature that characterizes the Mexican system is the adherence displayed towards the 'bargain' which is built around a common understanding of the modes of political action (Purcell and Purcell, 1980).[5] Critical is the notion of political discipline: specifically, agreement to defer to the authoritarian leadership and not to seek to criticize nor undermine it. Failure to stick to these rules (as happened during the Echeverría presidency) may result in severe reprisals being taken against the offending bodies. Political negotiation is conducted between personalized leader–follower alliances, usually called *camarillas* (cliques) (Grindle, 1977: 5, 56). These groups are often identified with different ideological positions but are shaped by an implicitly understood set of rules governing individual behaviour (Fagen and Tuohy, 1972: 27; Smith, 1979: chapter 9). The relative influence exerted by any clique waxes and wanes as its leaders move in and out of office or are given particularly prestigious portfolios. While the political 'bargain' demands that all interests be accommodated, any sharp change of policy will, inevitably, advance certain interests at the expense of others. The effects of such action are usually minimized, and a tacitly agreed aim is to avoid the existence of outright 'winners' and 'losers'. However, every administration will, inevitably, create certain imbalances. The expectancy is that imbalances will be redressed in the following administration, which helps explain the tendency to shift back and forth between 'activist' and 'consolidatory' presidents (Purcell and Purcell, 1980: 222). The critical task of the president is to achieve and maintain an appropriate balance within his administration (Smith, 1979: 303–4).

Working-class interests are articulated via formal and informal channels. Pressure exerted through the leadership of CNC, CTM or CNOP is likely to be accorded significance but not predominance. The coalition can ill afford to alienate the *ejido* sector or organized labour (Purcell and Purcell, 1980: 202), but the degree to which the executive is prepared actively to support the interests of these groups depends upon the balance of forces within the coalition at any point in time. Working-class groups pursue their interests informally through clientelistic links with 'patrons' in government but the results are likely to be both partial and discretionary.

Several factors explain the stability of the Mexican state over the years. First, many of the possible destabilizing forces have long since been removed from Mexican politics. Regionalism has declined: the original 'official party' was designed as a coalition to unite and reconcile regional strongmen into a national party (PNR). Later, Cárdenas replaced the PNR with the party of the Mexican Revolution (PRM), built around the labour, agrarian, military and popular sectors, and thereby further eroded any tendency towards regionalism (Hansen, 1974: 93–4). The influence of the military has also waned; it no longer forms one of the main sectors of the PRI, and it has a significant presence within the cabinet. Expenditure on the military has declined from 53 per cent of the public purse in 1923 to 1.5 per cent in the 1970s (Smith, 1979: 38; Eckstein, 1977: 34). Similarly, the Constitution curtails the influence of the church thereby removing it from politics.

Second, the *sexenio* structure and the prohibition on re-election have contributed to stability by allowing the regular turnover of most government jobs. The regular and predictable change in government policy that occurs every six years also allows for a realignment of interest groups and renewal of the political 'bargain' referred to earlier.

Third, as elsewhere, patronage of jobs and resources has enhanced political and social control. Appointees know that they must toe the line if they are to receive adequate budgets. Similarly, concessions can be made to low-income groups that threaten to embarrass the government. Economic growth is important insofar as it enhances the opportunities for patronage; economic decline strains the distributive system (Purcell and Purcell, 1980: 201). One danger associated with Mexico's future oil revenues is the enormous potential for patronage that they offer.

Fourth, the structure of the political system itself adds to stability. The illusion of democratic processes provides an outlet for dissent, the political 'bargain' embodies the coexistence of conflicting ideologies within the state. In addition, the success of the PRI in fulfilling its role as legitimator, mobilizer of the vote, and appeaser or manipulator of potential troublemakers has maintained stability.

Finally, when all else fails, the state has resorted to repression to ensure the continuance of the system. Social dissent unappeased by any of the less drastic measures mentioned earlier, is vulnerable to political pressure, intimidation and force.

Whether or not the Mexican state will continue to be as adept at maintaining stability is uncertain (Whitehead, 1981). Some argue that the Mexican political system is in crisis and believe that the PRI will be unable to cope with rising pressures, so that 'antidemocratic' regimes are likely to arise (Johnson, 1971; Cosío Villegas, 1972). Others believe that the PRI can respond to changing needs so long as incremental reforms are made to alleviate Mexico's socio-economic problems. In Hansen's opinion, the major threat comes from the conservative demands of business groups; if successful, their short-sighted stand against change might precipitate a crisis (Hansen, 1974: xxviii).

The Venezuelan state

Venezuela, like Colombia, is dominated by two political parties: Democratic Action (AD) and the Christian Democrats (COPEI). Unlike its neighbour, however, two-party domination is a recent phenomenon. Before 1958 the typical Venezuelan ruler was a military *caudillo*, who traditionally obtained power through rallying armed supporters under a mock revolutionary cause (Bigler, 1977: 113–14). It is estimated that there were 354 major instances of political violence and bloodshed between 1830 and 1935: a long period of turmoil based little on principle and much on personal ambition for power. The nineteenth-century condition of coup and countercoup terminated at the turn of the century with the initiation of the *Táchira* hegemony of first Castro (1899–1908) and then Gómez (1908–35): regimes maintained through superior arms and close reliance on political allies from the home region. The Gómez years witnessed the origins of a professional military which constituted the main foundation of a state that like the Colombian lacked intrinsic and formal legitimacy. Gómez' successors, who both came from Táchira, initiated liberalizing trends that were in part a response to the expansion of the middle class and growing socio-economic differentiation, which accompanied the creation of the oil economy, and the emergence of serious party activity. The 1945 coup that initiated the *Trienio*, the brief interlude of AD-directed civilian rule, resulted from collaboration between the party and these young military officers, who were discontented at the lack of mobility available within an organization still dominated in its upper reaches by the older Andean generation. AD's success in politicizing the army against the consistent wish of the army command to professionalize its rank was a significant reason for the coup of 1948 and the severity of the military repression of the party's leadership and organization. Martz (1977: 94) also argues that AD's wish to introduce major reforms brought strong opposition from the church, land-owners, and business groups.

Military rule was initially directed by a three-man *junta* advised by senior officers. In 1952, however, an unsuccessful attempt to legitimize military rule by a popular election for Marcos Pérez Jiménez was unsuccessful and required annulling the victory of the Revolutionary Democratic Union (URD) candidate and the introduction of a fully-fledged dictatorship led by the losing candidate. The ensuing dictatorship lasted until 1958 and dedicated itself to achieving national prosperity through investments in major public works in housing and roads.

In 1957, opposition from within the military combined with civil riots and strikes in Caracas brought the Pérez Jiménez regime to an end. It was replaced by an experiment in party rule and open elections. The three major national parties, AD, COPEI, and URD, pledged support for a coalition government and, in the subsequent election, AD's Betancourt became president with 49 per cent of the vote. Although URD later withdrew from the coalition, continuing AD–COPEI collaboration led to the institutionalization of civilian rule. Since 1963, when AD won again, the presidency has alternated between the AD and COPEI parties. This swing of the electoral pendulum has been accompanied by increasing dominance of the two main parties in the national vote. In 1978, COPEI and AD together commanded 90 per cent of the national votes compared to only 64 per cent in 1958 (Martz, 1977: 99; Penniman, 1980: 276). What had emerged by 1978 is what Myers (1980: 247) has called a two-and-a-quarter party system. Power lies essentially in the hands of the AD and COPEI parties but with the left increasingly likely to make a substantial dent in the main party dominance.

There is little difference between the voters of AD and COPEI. Middle-class and working-class groups are about equally split between COPEI and AD, but both the upper classes and the poor tend to favour AD. Interestingly, the growing vote on the left comes less from the poor than from secondary-school and especially university-edu-cated people. To date there has been no direct threat from the poor to the main parties.

The power of the two main parties rests in their control over the public administration and the posts within the bureaucracy. They possess almost unlimited powers of job patronage and sources of funds through which to coopt enemies and reward allies. Their power comes from both the lack of restraining forces and the size of the Venezuelan-government budget. As Gil Yepes (1981: 21–2) says: 'In a state with enormous economic resources – generated either by foreigners or directly by the public sector – this means a quasi-monopoly of power in the hands of political parties, because they do not depend upon any other national sector, except for the government which they control.'

Venezuelan party politics is highly organized. The two major parties and, more recently, the parties of the left, have created permanent organizations which extend from the grassroots through provincial and regional assemblies to the national leadership. It is the last that makes the vital decisions with respect to party strategy and in the selection of presidential candidates. And yet, despite this centralism, Venezuelan parties are rent by factionalism and intra-party contests. Potential leaders compete by mobilizing new members and building up supporting groups within the rank and file. In Venezuela, leaders do not emerge from the bureaucracy to the same extent as in Mexico, nor are they drawn from a socially exclusive caste of natural rulers as in Colombia. The system means that executives at municipal, state and national level must regard the party as a major constituency to be satisfied rather than ignored. In this lies the vital importance of party affiliation and conflict in Venezuela. Indeed, it is this factionalism that acts as the principal constraint on presidential action. Most difficulties facing the president can be attributed to leadership conflicts and the intra-party conflicts so created.

Clearly, democracy has been institutionalized since 1958 in the sense of allowing power to change from one party to another as the result of an election. What appears to have developed only in a limited way is a mechanism through which the majority of the population may partici-pate in decision making. If it would be inaccurate to call the Venezuelan regime authoritarian, neither is it open or democratic. Gil Yepes (1981: 21) has suggested that it is pluralist, but this is arguable in the sense that only certain groups have genuine access to power. 'The present regime seems to be searching for balance by establishing communication channels among elites. To achieve this, it allows political parties, the military sector, entrepreneurs, and the church – in that order – a certain degree of interest articulation.' These groups are all relatively autonomous in the sense that they have their own sources of power and direct access to government. By contrast, other groups, such as the bureaucracy, professional groups, and especially peasant and labour unions, have access only through the parties. This poses certain paradoxes for the political system because, as the economy and political rhetoric have developed, certain expectations have been created among these latter groups. Urbanization, increasing literacy, regular elections and growing social awareness are creating major pressures for improvements in health, education, housing and employment. This pressure and growing representation through the parties creates a major dilemma for the political parties about allocating resources between investment and consumption expenditures (Gil Yepes, 1981: 22–3). 'Pressure to participate has paradoxical effects on the political system. While it shows identification with its values and goals, it also tends to erode the means available to achieve such goals, tearing down the organization on which the system works' (Gil Yepes, 1981: 25). The Pérez government (1974–8) made an attempt to balance these contradictions as, arguably, most regimes since 1958 have done. As Myers (1980: 221) puts it, 'Pérez and his supporters argued that some mixture of developmentalism and populism would be the most effective intellectual brew for maintaining effective linkages between *Acción Democrática* and the Venezuelan people.'

But, if there are paradoxes facing governing parties and intra-party constraints on the incumbent president, there is no doubt that the national executive holds great power. This power is based both on Venezuelan oil wealth and upon the centralization that is endemic to the system. As we have said, the major parties resolve major issues at the national level. The same is true of Venezuelan government, and few students of Venezuela fail to comment on this characteristic feature. Gil Yepes (1981: 79), for example, states that 'The main characteristics of government organization are centralism, presidentialism, and politicization of bureaucracy.' Stewart (1977) has noted how most decisions are made in Caracas by a limited number of key personnel within the government administration. This centralism of decision making is a source of inefficiency and buck-passing. It also leads to major difficulties for provincial and municipal administration; effectively they are excluded from direct access to resources and are reliant on central government for any but the smallest investments. The result is that only individuals with favoured access to the central decision makers in Caracas can obtain swift and effective action.

In sum, the state in Venezuela is not undemocratic, but is highly centralized, highly politicized, affluent and populist. It does not listen much to popular demands, however, and is not accustomed to spending large sums of money on the poor. When it does spend money on the poor that money is often allocated in a politicized way. Insofar as the state responds to demands from Venezuelans independent of the party apparatus, these demands are most likely to emanate from the military, from business or from the church. The consequences on the social and economic situation of the poor will become apparent later.

The three cities

Bogotá

Since 1938, Bogotá's population has grown from 350,000 to over 4 million people. In 1973, over 70 per cent of the city's inhabitants had been born in other parts of the country; in that year it contained 13.6 per cent of Colombia's population compared to only 4.1 per cent in 1938. Bogotá's rate of economic growth has tended to exceed that of most other large cities. Its national share of industrial employment grew from 26.5 per cent in 1958 to 28 per cent in 1979, while its share of building construction in the largest seven cities increased from 36 per cent in 1954 to 54.4 per cent in 1978 (Colombia, DANE, various *Boletines Mensuales de Estadística*). While Colombia is blessed with a number of dynamic industrial and urban centres, those cities are highly dependent on decision makers in Bogotá (Gilbert, 1975). Regional decisions are heavily influenced by national policies and regional political elites have tended to become national elites and to operate from the national capital. Bogotá has increasingly become the centre of Colombian political and economic life.

Between 1960 and 1975, Bogotá's *per capita* income increased 30 per cent in real terms (Svenson, 1977). The main sources of this growth has been the expansion of commercial and financial activities. In 1973 the labour market was dominated by three broad sectors: commerce and finance which employed 26 per cent of workers in specified employment, services which employed 33 per cent and manufacturing 25 per cent (table 4). The booming economy has meant that the city's *per capita* income is higher than that of most provincial cities (Lubell and McCallum, 1978), and unemployment is lower; figures from 1963 show that unemployment has varied from a low of 6.1 per cent to a high of 16.1 per cent (in June, 1967). There is no tendency for the unemployment rate to deteriorate, the low of 6.1 per cent was recorded for June, 1979. The employment problem in Bogotá consists less of a shortage of jobs than the low productivity and remuneration of so many economic activities. Large numbers of workers are employed for long hours in unremunerative activities such as construction, handicraft production, street vending and domestic service. There were 82,000 domestic servants in 1973 among a total labour force of 831,000 (Colombia, DANE, 1978b); 20 per cent of poor male workers still work over 60 hours per week (Mohan and Hartline, 1979). According to the 1973 census, 62 per cent of all income earners were earning, in 1978 dollar equivalents, less than 70 dollars per month.

The social consequences of this poverty are obvious, one-fifth of all seven- to nine-year-olds do not go to school, malnutrition among the young is rife, the incidence of infectious diseases is high and one-third of the population make no use of the health services (Bogotá, *Servicio Seccional de Salud*, 1977). In terms of housing, poverty has an inevitable consequence: in 1973, there was an average of 1.6 persons per room, 27.6 per cent of houses had more than two persons per room, half the population were renting accommodation and among the families who rented only one-third occupied more than 110 square metres (table 5; Colombia, DANE, 1977).

However, by Third World standards, and even by the standards of rural Colombia, these statistics are quite respectable. What is worrying is that there are few consistent signs that welfare levels among the poor are improving even though the city's economy has been expanding rapidly. Most of the benefits of this growth have gone to the more affluent and little to the poor.

It is clear that the top three deciles in the population distribution have benefited from the economic expansion of the past three decades. It is also clear that the absolute and relative numbers of people living at an acceptable standard have increased – a fact reflected in the increased membership of social security schemes, the rising numbers of personal bank accounts, the expansion in professional and white-collar occupations, the rise in the number of middle-income homes and the proliferation of private cars. Many poor families also benefited from the city's economic growth especially during the sixties when industrial wages rose steadily (Urrutia, 1969: 237). The continued expansion of illegal settlement suggests that many poor families were managing to purchase lots on which to build homes, an increasing proportion of which were provided with basic infrastructure. The expansion of the

Table 4 *Structure of employment in Bogotá, Mexico City and Valencia*

BOGOTA DE

	1964[1]	1973[2]	% increase 1964–73
Manufacturing	25.3	24.5	+30.8
Commerce and finance	15.9 }54.6	25.8	+118.4
Services	38.7 }	33.3	+16.0
Construction	8.5	7.8	+22.6
Other specified activities	11.6	8.6	+0.7
Total specified employment	527,505	711,088	+34.8 } +43.5
Total unspecified employment	527,497	869,000	+51.6 }

MEXICO CITY

	1960[3]	1970[4]	% increase 1960–70
Manufacturing	30.7	31.0	+47.3
Commerce and finance	17.3	13.7	+15.7
Services	33.0	36.5	+61.5
Construction	6.8	5.9	+26.5
Other specified activities	10.46	7.0	−3.1
Total specified employment	1,812,815	2,646,917	+46.0
Total unspecified employment	1,843,296	2,764,488	+50.0

VALENCIA

	1965[5]	1971[6]	1979[7]	% increase 1961–71	% increase 1971–9
Manufacturing	NA (21.8)	27.5 (25.6)	33.1	(+87.2)	+120.2
Commerce and finance	NA (15.0)	18.4 (16.2)	22.9	(+72.5)	+128.3
Services	NA (26.3)	32.9 (31.1)	29.1	(+89.3)	+61.9
Construction	NA (5.6)	7.9 (7.1)	5.8	(+100.8)	+34.4
Other specified activities	NA (31.3)	13.3 (20.0)	11.1	(+1.9)	+25.0
Total specified employment	NA (96,164)	100,626 (153,571)	184,217	(+59.7)	+83.1
Total unspecified employment	NA (116,061)	120,315 (192,895)	192,013	(+66.2)	+59.6

Notes:
1. DANE (1967), XIII, *Censo Nacional de Población: Resumen General*, table 34.
2. DANE (1978), *La Población en Colombia*, p. 109.
3. Mexico (1960), *Censo Nacional de Población:* Federal District and municipalities of Naucalpan and Tlalnepantla, table 21.
4. Mexico (1970), *Censo Nacional de Población:* Federal District and municipalities of Atízapan de Zaragoza, Ecatepec, Naucalpan, Netzahualcóyotl, Tlalnepantla.
5. Data in brackets for 1961 and 1971 for the State of Carabobo, *X Censo de Población y Vivienda: Resumen general*, pp. 58-64. Vol. VIII, part C, p. 380.
6. Data for Metropolitan area of Valencia. *X Censo de Población.*
7. Venezuela, MINDUR (1981). Although the source is not cited its figures are compatible with those presented in BCV (1980: A-IV-10) which are for September 1979.

49

Table 5 *Economic, housing and servicing conditions in the three cities*

	Bogotá	Mexico City	Valencia
Basic economic and social indicators			
Population in 1981 (millions)	4.5 [1]	15.0 [2]	0.65 [3]
Intercensal annual growth rate (%)	6.0 [1]	4.5 [4]	4.8 [3]
Population per hectare	161 [5]	177 [6]	68 [7]
Population over 15 years employed	48.9 [8]	54.0 [9]	29.3 [10]
7–11 year-olds attending school (%)	64.5 [11]	84.3 [12]	63.8 [13]
Inhabitants per hospital bed	361 [14]	346 [15]	375 [16]
Infant mortality (per 1,000 live births)	46.7 [17]	74.7 [18]	38.2 [19]
Infant mortality (per 1,000 live births)			126.6 [20]
Population covered by social security (%)	19.2 [21]	65.0 [22]	72.3 [23]
Population covered by social security (%)	33.8 [24]		
GNP *per capita* in 1979 US dollars	1,010 [25]	1,640 [25]	3,120 [25]
Daily minimum wage *per capita* in 1979 US dollars	3.0	6.1	3.5
Comparative data for housing and land			
Irregular settlements (%)	46 [26]	42 [27]	47 [28]
Government housing (%)	11 [26]	11.5 [29]	14 [28]
Conventional private housing (%)	43 [26]	NA	39 [28]
Families renting accommodation (%)	51 [31]	58 [32]	29 [29]
Percentage of housing on invaded land	0.7 [33]	NA	45 [34]
Number of occupants per occupied dwelling	7.6 [35]	5.8 [36]	5.2 [3]
Number of occupants per home	5.1 [35]	NA	NA
Homes with one room (%)	31.1 [37]	29.7 [38]	NA
Number of occupants per room	1.6 [39]	2.0 [40]	1.3 [41]
Number of rooms per dwelling	4.8 [39]	2.8 [40]	4.5 [41]
Dwellings without water (%)	8.8 [42]	19.7 [43]	22.4 [44]

Dwellings without inside water connection (%)	23.7 [45]	39.6 [46]	27.9 [47]
Dwellings without drainage connection (%)	10.1 [42]	24.5 [48]	53.5 [49]
Dwellings without electricity (%)	5.3 [42]	8.8 [48]	NA

Notes:

1. Projected at the 6 per cent 1964–73 population growth rate.
2. Fox (1975: 19).
3. Provisional 1981 census results including Guacara. *XI Censo Nacional de Población y Vivienda.*
4. Fox (1975: 19), 1960–70 period.
5. Gilbert (1978: 91).
6. Mexico, CAVM (1978: table 3.1.2.1). Our calculations relate to built-up area in 1977 for the Federal District and municipalities of Atizapan de Zaragoza, Ecatepec, Coacalco, Naucalpan, Netzahualcóyotl, and Tlalnepantla.
7. Venezuela, MINDUR (1981); EITAV (1977: 42) estimated density at 60 persons per hectare for 1975.
8. Colombia, DANE (1977: 108).
9. Census 1970, adapted from table 22. Relates to work in 1969.
10. Feo Caballero (1979: 190).
11. Secretariat of Education. 1970 data, unpublished.
12. Census 1970, adapted from tables 4 and 17. The figure is somewhat lower in Netzahualcóyotl (74 per cent).
13. Feo Caballero (1979: 172). Data relate to 1975.
14. Bogotá, Secretariat of Health, *Plan de salud,* 1977.
15. Our calculations from Fajardo Ortiz (1978: 183) who notes that there were 26,009 hospital beds in the Federal District for approximately nine million people. The ratio of people to beds is likely to be higher for the urban area as a whole.
16. Venezuela, MINDUR (1981). 1981 data excluding the psychiatric beds.
17. Arias (1978: 164). Data refer to 1976.
18. Mexico, SPP (1979: 26). 1970 data for Federal District only.
19. Venezuela, MSAS, *Anuario de Epidemiología y Estadística Vital,* 1975.
20. Venezuela, MSAS, *Anuario de Epidemiología y Estadística Vital,* 1975. There were major problems in 1972 but the discrepancy between the two figures suggests an overestimation of the earlier figure and an underestimation in 1975.
21. Colombia, MSP (1969), 105. Data for 1965–6.
22. Mexico, DDF, *Plan Director,* chapter VII, p. 9.

51

Notes to Table 5 (*cont.*)

23. Venezuela, IVSS, *Anuario Estadístico*, 1979, recorded 434,900 beneficiaries in Valencia.
24. Bogotá DE, *Plan de salud*, 1971.
25. World Bank (1981), *World Development Report*.
26. Vernez (1973).
27. Ward (1976c). Proportion of the built-up area, 1970.
28. BANOP (1970). Data relate to 1969.
29. Venezuela, Banco Obrero (1970: 74). Data based on 3 per cent sample carried out in 1970.
30. Estimate based upon (Garza and Schteingart, 1978b) figures for public sector units built in the Metropolitan Area and assuming an average household size of five persons.
31. Colombia, DANE (1977: 54). *Arrendatarios and subarrendatarios* as a percentage of total homes (*hogares particulares*).
32. 1970 Census, table 32. Includes dwellings that are loaned or obtained through work (e.g. by caretakers).
33. Colombia, ICT (1976).
34. CEU (1977).
35. Colombia, DANE (1977: 52). Note some dwellings contain more than one home.
36. Mexico, CAVM (1978: table 3.1.2.5).
37. Colombia, DANE (1977: 53–4).
38. 1970 Census, table 33. Excludes kitchen, bathroom and passageways.
39. Colombia, DANE (1977: 52–3).
40. 1970 Census. Adapted from table 33.
41. Venezuela, *Dirección* (1978: 67). Our calculation.
42. Colombia, DANE (1977: 53). Dwellings (*viviendas*) without water connection.
43. 1970 Census, tables 32 and 35, our calculation.
44. Venezuela, *Dirección* (1978: 67). Dwellings (*viviendas*) without inside or outside connection. BANOP (1970: 74) estimates that 13.9 per cent of houses were without water.
45. Number of dwellings (Colombia, DANE, 1977: 52) minus the number of residential accounts by the Bogotá Water Authority for 1973. We assume that the latter registers connections to individual homes.
46. 1970 Census, tables 32 and 35. Census disaggregates dwellings (*viviendas*) with a supply inside and outside the home.
47. Venezuela, *Dirección* (1978: 67). Dwellings without inside connection.
48. 1970 Census, tables 32 and 35. Drainage system means a hygienic system for the removal of waste waters.
49. Venezuela, *Dirección* (1978: 70). Dwellings without toilet connected to drainage.

52

school system allowed a higher proportion of children to receive primary and even secondary school education.

Unfortunately, there is evidence of a less favourable side to the picture. First, although the distribution of income improved to some extent during the fifties and sixties (Urrutia and Berry, 1975: 130), during the seventies it almost certainly worsened. As the inflation rate leapt, so real industrial wages fell owing to the inability of manufacturing workers to achieve matching wage rises (Fedesarrollo, 1976: 42). In most societies, manufacturing workers are numbered among the more affluent manual workers and their failure to maintain their standard of living in Bogotá poses the question of what has happened to those people employed in the so-called 'informal' sector. For the poor employed in commerce, construction and services, information is scarce, but it would be surprising if these groups had done much better than maintain their real standards of living during the seventies. The trend is unfortunate to say the least in a city where in 1970 the top 5 per cent of income earners received the same 30 per cent share of income as did the bottom 70 per cent (Córdova, 1971).

Second, although there was a dramatic increase in the availability of services such as water, telephones and electricity, the relevant agencies were unable to cope with the pace of urban growth. Thus, although the relative numbers of houses with services increased markedly, the absolute numbers of houses without services such as drainage and water increased gradually. By 1973, some 700,000 people in the city may have been living in houses without water. Other services were much worse, with only 65 per cent of seven- to eleven-year-olds attending school and only one-fifth of the population covered fully by social security (table 5).

Third, the pace and form of urban expansion has lengthened the journey to work, has increased real land prices and has accentuated levels of pollution and traffic congestion. While all groups have suffered to some degree from these urban diseconomies, the poor have suffered more in the sense that they have had less access to compensatory benefits. Thus, they have suffered from worse traffic congestion and pollution without the compensation of possessing their own car. They have suffered from rising land prices without relief from income tax or easy access to credit facilities. There are also signs that, despite higher rates of home ownership among the higher income groups, the proportion of houses with renters has remained more or less constant during the past 30 years. Increasing prosperity, therefore, has not brought the advantages of home ownership, even in an illegal settlement, to around one-half of the population.

Mexico City

Mexico City is the largest of the three cities. Indeed in 1978, at an estimated 14 millions, it was the largest urban centre in the world.[6] As early as 1940, when 1.7 million people lived in the Federal District, representing 8 per cent of the total population, Mexico City's economic pre-eminence had been established. At that time it generated 32 per cent of the total industrial product and 30.6 per cent of the gross internal product. Little has changed; Mexico City continues to dominate the national economy. In 1970, its share of gross internal product stood at 37.4 per cent compared to its 18 per cent share of the national population. Since the *Porfiriato*, Mexico City has been the foremost centre of financial, commercial and political decision making. The nature of the political system and its reliance upon person-to-person contact and behind-the-scenes bargaining means that few decisions of any importance are made outside the city. The trend towards centralization throughout the twentieth century is proving exceptionally difficult to reverse. Despite recent attempts to build up specialized educational and health services in other areas of the national territory, Mexico City continues to dominate with 41 per cent of all places in higher education and 44 per cent of all specialist hospital institutions (Mexico, SPP, 1979: 237, 322). The city also received a disproportionately large share (57.5 per cent) of public sector low-cost housing constructed between 1963 and 1976 (Garza and Schteingart, 1978b).

The attractiveness of Mexico City to investors began to concern the government as early as 1955. It abolished the tax advantages available to new industry in the Federal District, although this initiative failed to slow industrial growth as new companies began to locate in the adjacent areas of the State of Mexico where the advantages still applied. Continued industrial expansion fuelled the demand for labour, which, combined with the declining opportunities and growing landlessness in rural areas, encouraged many migrants to move to the city. The growth of the city was dramatic: 3.1 millions in 1950; 5.2 millions in 1960; 8.7 millions in 1970 and 13.3 millions in 1978. During earlier phases of growth, direct migration was the most important component of city growth, accounting for 65 per cent of the 1940–50 decennial

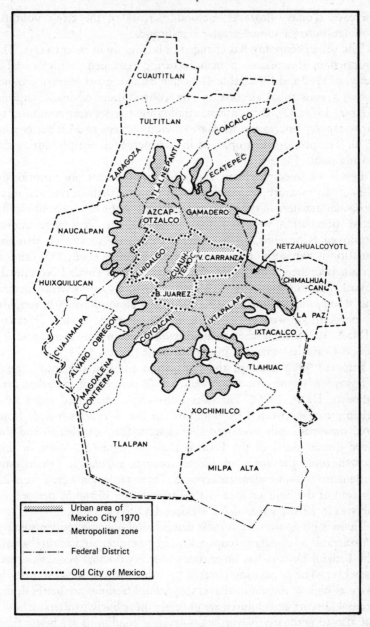

Fig. 3 Administrative and political boundaries of Mexico City, 1970 (after Unikel, 1972)

increase. Today, however, natural increase of the city's youthful population has assumed greater significance.

The urban economy has changed only slightly in recent years. The proportion of workers in manufacturing remained relatively stable between 1960 and 1970 (table 4) though data for gross internal product show a substantial decline in the contribution of manufacturing (Garza, 1978: 35). By contrast, employment in services continued to grow rapidly, increasing its share of employment to 36.5 per cent in 1970. The proportion employed in commerce fell sharply during the decade (table 4).

Levels of unemployment and underemployment are notoriously difficult to measure accurately, but it appears that, during the mid-1970s, somewhere in the order of 6 per cent of the city's economically active population were unemployed and 35 per cent were under-employed (Cornelius, 1975). There is evidence to suggest that the situation is worse among recent migrants (Muñoz *et al.*, 1973) and in certain poor neighbourhoods of the city such as Ciudad Netzahual-cóyotl. The minimum wage in Mexico City offers a subsistence income and stood at approximately 170 US dollars a month in 1979; roughly 70 per cent of workers earn the minimum wage or less (Mexico, BIMSA, 1974). Even when total household incomes are considered, 33 per cent earn less than the minimum wage (Evans, 1974: 50).

Prior to 1950 most of the population lived in the four central *delegaciones* of the city which made up 70 per cent of the urban area (Mexico, DDF, 1976). Thereafter, the city experienced rapid sub-urbanization between 1950 and 1960 in the *delegaciones* and, from 1960 onwards, spilt over into the adjacent State of Mexico and the more distant parts of the Federal District (figure 3). Much of this growth took the form of illegal *colonias populares*, low-income settlements without adequate services. These settlements grew from 23 per cent of the built-up area in 1952 to between 40 and 50 per cent of the area in 1976 (Ward, 1976; Mexico, COPEVI, 1977).

There is no doubt that in most respects low-income residents enjoy considerable advantages compared to their counterparts in rural areas. The Federal District has three times as many doctors *per capita* than elsewhere. The population covered by some form of social security is twice as high as the national average. School facilities are better in the Federal District and children are not only more likely to attend school, but also to graduate. Nevertheless, even if conditions are better than those in the rest of Mexico, rapid economic growth has failed substantially to improve living standards for the majority in Mexico City. Although most children go to school and a majority of the population is covered by social security (table 5), housing conditions are poor. In 1970, there was an average of two people per room, 39.6 per cent of dwellings had no internal water system, and 24.5 per cent were without any formal system of drainage (table 5).

Living in Mexico City also entails suffering many special difficulties. Pollution is a constant problem. Located in an upland basin, the city suffers from frequent temperature inversions which prevent the dispersal of pollutants. As a result, smog has reduced daily visibility from an average of 15 kilometres in 1967 to between 4 and 6 kilometres today. The population is also subject to the constant fumes emanating from the congested city streets. Indeed, transport is another major problem. Buses carry 44 per cent of daily passenger traffic in the Federal District and, while diesel fuel is subsidized and fares are low, the buses themselves are slow, overcrowded and uncomfortable. The Metro is modern, fast and cheap, but limited in its radius: in 1978 only 47 kilometres were in operation. This has since been lengthened to 85 kilometres and it is hoped that passengers will increase from 1.5 to 4.5 millions daily. Despite improvements and extensions to the road system, congestion continues to be an unresolved problem. On balance it seems that public transport costs people more in the way of time than money.[7]

Valencia

The population of metropolitan Valencia has grown extremely rapidly over the past few decades. From a town of 50,000 people in 1936 it grew 5.9 per cent annually to become a city of 653,000 in 1981 (Feo Caballero, 1979; Venezuela, *Dirección*, 1981). The rate of expansion has been especially rapid during the last three decades. Valencia has shared in the vast urban expansion that has been characteristic of Venezuela since the early 1950s. And, because of its location and the policies of its council, it has attracted more than its share of manufacturing companies during a period of rapid national industrialization. Manufacturing expansion has been very important to Valencia's growth; in 1980 one-third of its active population were employed in the sector. The city has benefited from its location 158 kilometres west of Caracas and 54 kilometres from the major port of Puerto Cabello (figure 1). Growing pressures on land in Caracas, together with other

urban diseconomies unrelieved by effective planning, led to a spontaneous process of industrial deconcentration along the so-called
Puerto Cabello–Tejerías corridor. The cities of La Victoria, Maracay
and Valencia, linked to Puerto Cabello and Caracas by motorway
since the early fifties, have all grown as a result. But Valencia was not a
passive recipient of growth, its council sought to attract manufacturing
companies to the city. In 1958, it began to make available 8 million
square metres of municipal land for industrial expansion, of which 5.7
million square metres were for sale (Venezuela, Banco Obrero, 1963).[8]
A special municipal agency, FUNVAL, was established in 1962 to
provide infrastructure and services needed for industrial expansion and
land was sold cheaply to a series of transnational corporations.[9] The
results were spectacular; during the fifties and sixties Valencia was the
fastest growing industrial centre of the country. The pace of its
expansion is shown by the fact that of the 651 industrial plants of the
city in 1971, 128 had been established between 1961 and 1966 and a
further 170 in the following five years (Lovera, 1978). In 1971,
Valencia contained 7.4 per cent of the country's manufacturing
workers (Feo, 1979: 186–9) and 9.1 per cent in 1979 (Venezuela,
MINDUR, 1981; BCV, 1980: A-IV-10). Clearly, manufacturing
activity has been a principal source of economic growth. Whereas the
total labour force increased by approximately 60 per cent between
1971 and 1979, employment in manufacturing had increased by twice
as much. By the later date manufacturing employed 33 per cent of the
labour force. Despite the strength of the manufacturing sector,
Valencia's occupational structure is dominated by tertiary activities:
51.3 per cent in 1971 and 59.1 per cent in 1980 (Venezuela, MINDUR,
1981). The most dynamic element within this sector is commerce and
finance; between 1971 and 1979 employment increased by 128 per cent.

   The high level of manufacturing employment, by Venezuelan
standards means that Valencia is not a poor city. Nevertheless, there
are large numbers of workers earning low wages. In 1980, it was
estimated that 53 per cent of the occupied labour force were earning
less than 350 US dollars per month compared to 63 per cent for
workers in Venezuela as a whole and 25 per cent in the central region
of the country (Venezuela, MINDUR, 1981). As in most Latin
American cities, incomes are highly concentrated, although the available statistics do not give a detailed picture. In 1975, however, 11 per
cent of families earned less than 120 US dollars, whereas 13.3 per cent
earned more than 700 US dollars (in 1975 prices).

The concentrated distribution of income combined with poor infrastructural and social-service provision makes the situation of poor people in the city particularly difficult. By a number of criteria, service provision in the City is unsatisfactory and actually worse than for Bogotá or Mexico City (table 5). While most of the city has access to electricity, supplies are frequently interrupted by black-outs. Some 20 per cent of households lack water and 30 per cent sewerage services (Venezuela, MINDUR, 1981). Until recently, the refuse disposal service worked very badly and few low-income settlements were included in the rounds. There was also an acute shortage of hospital beds for a relatively prosperous city: a ratio of 414 persons per bed (excluding the 805 psychiatric beds in Barbula). Of the 1,741 beds available in 1980, 23 per cent were for social-security patients, 20 per cent were in private clinics and 57 per cent belonged to the official public health service.

It is not entirely clear why service provision in the city is so unsatisfactory. Clearly, the city has not received sufficient investment from the national service agencies, either a consequence of the neglect of Carabobo or as a result of the failure of the service agencies to expand capacity throughout the country. Valencia's rapid rate of demographic growth has not helped the situation, but major responsibility must be placed on the failures of the service agencies, failures that are constantly documented in the media. Valencia certainly received less investment from central government after 1974, largely as the result of political circumstances.[10] Neither have the majority of Valencia's population been well served by the failure to control the pattern of urban growth. The logic of urban expansion has favoured real-estate interests and the construction industry, which have been prominently represented in municipal and state government. Municipal land-use planning has not functioned in the low-income areas of the city and has suffered from numerous evasions in the prosperous parts.[11] The result has been that urban land use has evolved rather chaotically from the point of view of the service agencies. In addition, these agencies have been less than effective in supplying the city. Competition between the private and the public electricity companies has prevented agreement over which parts of the city each should service; duplication of lines has been the result. The bus system has been a source of constant conflict as the private companies have attempted to persuade the municipal government to increase the subsidy and to modify the routes.[12]

It is unlikely that conditions for the majority of *Valencianos* have deteriorated. In 1961, for example, only 58 per cent of houses had access to water, and income levels have certainly increased given the huge rise in petroleum revenues and hence the gross national product. Nevertheless, the failure of any national government to redistribute income or to generate sufficient well-paid jobs and the weakness of government at the local level to control the patterns and processes of urban growth have meant that the city population has suffered worse conditions than it might have done with different policies.

Conclusion

This brief resumé of the national political and social systems and the basic structures of the three cities is merely the backcloth for the substantive chapters which follow. We have included this resumé to underline the point that housing, land and servicing are not issues that can be isolated from the wider societal context. The resolution of problems linked to these areas is not something that can be achieved simply through the introduction of technical initiatives. Such issues are part and parcel of the broader economy and society; as such any possible improvement in living standards depends upon the feasibility of governments introducing necessary reforms and changes in policy. Unless we understand the nature of the state, the prospects of the economy and the broad structure of interest groups, viable and relevant policies cannot be proposed. It is also essential to understand the limits to any policy initiative. Specific low-income housing policies, such as site-and-service schemes or regularization of illegal developments, may help the poor in certain circumstances or harm them in others. The particular outcome depends greatly upon trends in real wages for the poor, changes in the price of land and on the power of different interest groups to influence state policy. This chapter serves to underline a principal premise of this study that we are dealing with structures that link individual members of the poor into an urban, national and international economy. We are essentially interested in the nature of the linkages in those structures. Only in this way can we understand how land policies are formulated, how decisions are made about servicing the poor and the form in which the poor are encouraged to participate in the political system.

3

Access to land

As earlier chapters have demonstrated, one of the key issues which determines the opportunity for self-help consolidation in housing is the availability of land. Where land is accessible to the poor and tenure is guaranteed in law or in practice, home improvements will usually take place. In none of our three cities is land freely available. To obtain land, even poorly located land, is a struggle in each city. The purpose of this chapter is broadly to explain how the process of land acquisition takes place and to explain the differences and implications of allocation mechanisms in each city.

First, we examine how land is allocated to the poor as a group in society. What are the mechanisms by which the poor receive the 'worst' land and the more powerful and affluent classes receive the more desirable areas? Specifically, we consider the relationship between the coventional market for land, and its associated construction industry, and the low-income land market. In considering this relationship we must perforce examine the ways in which the state arbitrates and intervenes in the necessarily competitive process of land allocation.

Second, we examine in more detail the overt and covert intervention of the state in the process of land allocation. What is the purpose of residential zoning, building standards and urban perimeters, and how do they affect the market for land? In addition, and still more vital, how does the state handle the allocation of land to the poor given that most forms of access are illegal? Why, in short, does the state produce complicated regulations to control land development and then ignore those regulations in extensive swathes of the city? Why does it sometimes introduce convoluted procedures to subsequently regularize such illegally acquired land?

Third, we examine how those areas of land which have been allocated to the poor as a group are subdivided among individual

61

members of that class. How do individuals obtain land in each city and why do the forms of land allocation, invasion, subdivision, etc. differ so widely in the three cities and even within cities over time?

Finally, we consider the ways in which access to land has changed in each city. Has land become more difficult to acquire for particular groups of the poor? Is land invasion more or less common as a means of land acquisition? Where poor people purchase land how has the price of that land varied with respect to other prices and incomes? What effect has the increasing physical extent of the city had on land access? What effects and repercussions has the changing access to land had on tenure patterns? If land has become more scarce, do a greater number of people rent, share homes, occupy smaller lots, or live in multi-storey accommodation?

Land for the rich, land for the poor

It is clear that in any society the process of land allocation is highly competitive between groups. There has to be some mechanism by which particular groups gain priority over certain areas of land before others. In most capitalist societies it is the market which essentially allocates land. Those who can afford to pay more or, according to economic theory, are less indifferent to location acquire the more desirable areas. According to one's ideological perspective the process is efficient and equitable, or inefficient and inequitable, or somewhere in between. In all capitalist societies the process is one which creates residential segregation; the rich tend to live in one part of a city and the poor in another. Clearly, the greater the inequality of income and wealth, then the greater the degree of residential segregation and the greater the exclusion of poor people from access to the better land or, at times, any land at all. Thus, in societies with wide disparities in income and wealth, such as Colombia, Mexico and Venezuela, the degree of residential and land-use segregation is likely to be very great. This segregation is not only a reflection of the *inherent* characteristics of land, that is to say its height, soils, etc., but also of its *acquired* characteristics, its servicing, location relative to other activities, social character, etc.

In our three cities the poor occupy the worst land in terms of acquired characteristics: the areas with the worst pollution, the areas with least services and worst transportation. More often than not they also occupy the worst land in terms of inherent characteristics, the

areas most liable to flooding, areas subject to subsidence, the areas
with the poorest soils. Where rich areas develop on inherently poor
land, the difference is that negative elements are swiftly remedied,
indeed they may be turned to good advantage. In Bogotá, Valencia and
Mexico City the process of residential segregation is not only brought
about by differential powers to bid for well-located land but also by
the mechanisms which determine whether the land is serviced or not.

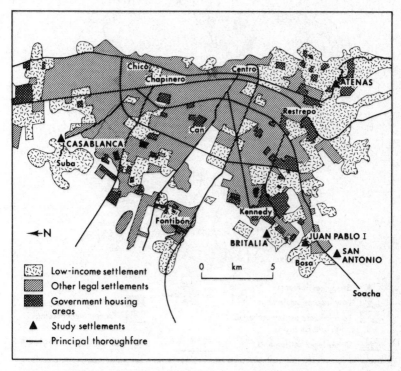

Fig. 4 Distribution of settlement by housing submarkets in Bogotá

As figure 4 shows, the poor in Bogotá tend to occupy broad swathes
of land to the southeast, south, southwest and northwest. By contrast,
the more affluent groups live in clearly demarcated zones in the north
of the city. Although the demarcation is by no means as marked as it
was in the Bogotá of the 1940s, homogeneous class areas are still found
across broad areas of the city. Needless to say, the affluent suburbs are
well planned, with green zones, good services, paved roads and street

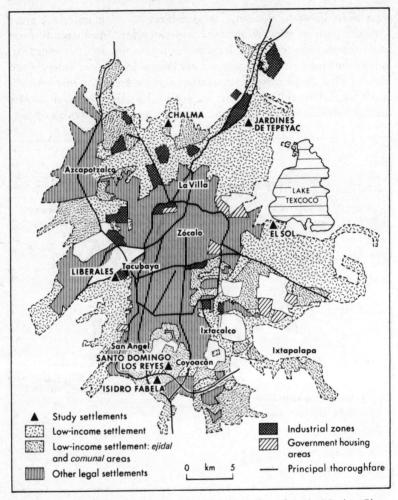

Fig. 5 Distribution of settlement by housing submarkets in Mexico City

lighting. The poor settlements are partially serviced and are located closest to the centres of pollution, flooding and heavy traffic. The middle-income groups are broadly distributed between the areas of high-income and low-income settlement. Broadly, these areas correlate closely with the inherent qualities of the land: the micro-climate of the north is superior to that of the south and the land most liable to flooding is occupied by the poor (Amato, 1969).

In Mexico, residential segregation is more difficult to describe because of the size and the complexity of the city. But, broadly, the poor live in the east, north and northeast, while the rich occupy land in the west and southwest (figure 5). Middle-income groups eschew the poorer zones and live as near to their would-be peers as possible, either in well-serviced subdivisions or in housing recently vacated by the rich. However, there are large pockets of low-income housing close to more affluent areas, mainly owing to the occupation of state or *ejidal* land. Where possible the rich have opted for hilly, wooded districts. Although the topography is often broken, the rich can afford to landscape their neighbourhoods and adapt house styles to the terrain to make the most of the views. The western hillsides suffer less pollution than elsewhere and enjoy easier road access to the rest of the city. With the major exception already noted, the poor occupy the two broad zones which are not highly desired by more affluent residential groups. The first is the area to the east and north of the Zócalo, where most rent accommodation, live in cramped conditions, suffer from deteriorating services and high levels of pollution. The second is the dessicated bed of Lake Texcoco where the soils are sterile, become waterlogged in winter, only to dry out in the summer to become subject to dust storms. The pattern of residential segregation has become more complex through time as the city has become larger and has absorbed more peripheral areas, as high-income groups have established new areas of preference and as infrastructural developments have transformed particular zones of the city.

In Valencia, the rich and middle-income groups live north of the city centre. The higher-income estates take advantage of certain physical features such as access to Lake Guataparo and the higher land but the main feature is their separation from lower-income areas and their good access to main roads. With one major exception, the area of Naguanagua to the northwest, the poor occupy the south of the city, the low-lying land liable to floods and closest to the industrial areas (figure 6). As in the other cities, the high-income areas are well laid out and serviced, the low-income areas are not. The pattern has changed little over the past thirty years except for the creation of the industrial parks in the southeast, the associated development of the Isabelica public-housing complex, and the general expansion of the city.

How can we best generalize about the similarities in the patterns of residential land use that have emerged in the three cities? Clearly, the processes determining land use are very complex. During the develop-

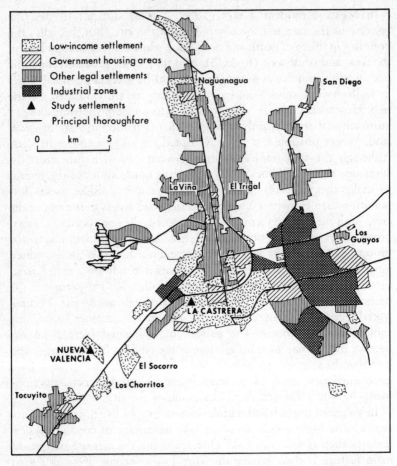

Fig. 6 Distribution of settlement by housing submarkets in Valencia

ment of urban areas, agricultural land is converted into residential, commercial, industrial, institutional or recreational land. Which it becomes depends upon the location of the land with respect to existing uses, upon the investment decisions of private and public institutions, and upon the planning decisions of the authorities. Over time, these initial land uses will change, low-income residential areas may be upgraded, high-income areas lose social standing, and residential land close to commercial and industrial areas may go through a process of urban renewal. All these changes influence the price of land. In developed societies most land is exchanged at commercial values in a legally binding process. In Latin America, however, a considerable proportion of land transactions are illegal in the sense that the land has been occupied against the wishes of the orginal owner, there are doubts about the legal documentation, or because the urban development, or the buildings themselves, do not meet the planning regulations. It is frequently suggested, or at least is implicit in most discussions of irregular and spontaneous housing, that land allocation in these illegally developed areas lies outside the market mechanism. Prices are irrelevant because the land is invaded by groups or individuals or because the prices are so much lower than the 'commercial value' as a result of the illegality of transactions. According to this argument there are effectively two land markets, the one legal and guided by the normal processes of supply and demand and subject to government intervention as planner, the other guided by non-market and usually political considerations. While there is some truth in this assertion, there are certain dangers implicit in it. In general, we would argue that the difference between the two sets of areas relates less to the method of valuation of the land, which is generally similar, than to the method of lot distribution. All areas, legal or illegal, have commercial values; the differences in price reflect differences in location, services, prestige, legality and transferability. If some illegal areas are initially allocated through non-market mechanisms such as invasion, their occupation gradually transforms the land into a marketable commodity. Thenceforth the value of individual lots is determined by the forces of supply and demand and influenced by servicing decisions and patterns of urban expansion.

Insofar as there are *initially* two land markets, the key question to be answered is why some land is subject to legal market transactions and other land is not? To some extent, of course, historical factors can explain this apparent separation. In Latin America, Spanish law established certain areas as reserves for indigenous peoples.[1] While many of these areas have been incorporated into the private land market in ways which we shall consider in a moment, there is no doubt that in some cities large areas are controlled by the public sector. In Valencia, for example, much of the land in the south of the city belongs to the municipality for this reason. In Mexico, most communal land was sold to private owners during the latter half of the nineteenth century but after the Revolution was reconstituted in the form of the *ejidos*.[2] There is no doubt that the presence of this land has an important influence upon the operation of the land market, notably upon the incidence of invasions.

Nevertheless, even in the case of *ejidal* and common land, we would submit that market mechanisms have intruded in a variety of ways to help determine the social distribution of land. First, the fact that it is often municipal land that has been invaded in cities such as Lima, Caracas, Valencia, and Barranquilla should be considered carefully. In general, invasions have occupied only those areas of public land that would fetch low prices on the market. For example, most land invasions in Lima have occurred on desert lands distant from the city centre (Collier, 1976), the invasions of Guayaquil have occupied swampland (Moser, 1982), those of Caracas the unstable hillsides (Marchand, 1966), and those of Barranquilla the land close to the river estuary (Foster, 1975). A few exceptions, such as the *favelas* in Copacabana or the Policarpa Salavarrieta invasion in Bogotá, have occupied central land and have been vigorously opposed and some-times eradicated. In these cases opposition has been generated by the fact that the land would have a high value if placed on the formal land market. Generally, valuable public land has not been invaded.

One reason is that the more valuable public land is sometimes held by the state for commercial or speculative reasons. The Beneficencia of Cundinamarca in Bogotá, for example, has held land since 1938 in a prime spot for urban development two miles from the city centre. Another reason is that the interests of private landowners may be threatened even by the invasion of public land. The occupation of land close to high-income residential areas, for example, would have a powerful negative effect on land prices in those areas. As such, private landowners are likely to persuade the state to oppose the invasion of land in those areas of the public domain which are contiguous to those of the private sector. In addition, it has been a common, and sometimes rather disreputable, practice in many Latin American cities for the private sector to alienate the more desirable public land. Collier (1976) notes how the more valuable public land around Lima has been used for agriculture by private interests. In Valencia, the council sold off up to 10 million square metres of land in the late 1950s and early 1960s for industrial use (CEU, 1977: 39). Ford alone bought 415,950 square metres for *bs.* 2 per square metre, a price far below its potential market value (CEU, 1977: 36).[3] If the market did not determine the sale price of this land, it is clear that the attractiveness of the land to the industrial purchasers was not unconnected with their view of the real market value of that land.

It can also be argued that much public land was acquired by the state for communal and public use because of its poor quality and low market value. Much of the *ejidal* land created in Mexico was of dubious agricultural value, its primary purpose. Similarly, the *ejidos* in Valencia occupy the low-lying land liable to floods in the south of the city, the least desirable land in colonial times. It was the absence of alternative uses that dictated the incorporation of land into the 'non-market' sector.

Finally, once public, or indeed private, land has been invaded, it rapidly becomes subject to market transactions. The fact that low-income areas begin illegally does not mean that they continue to be illegal. Indeed, in most cities such areas are gradually incorporated both functionally and legally into the urban fabric. This is true as we shall demonstrate both when the land has been sold illegally and when it has been the subject of invasion. As soon as the tenure of a settlement is assured, lots start to change hands. Invaders sell out to new occupants, as do speculators and the purchasers of lots who can no longer afford to build a house or whom other circumstances force to move. The price of these lots is determined by the commercial land market. The price, of course, is lower than in formal residential areas, but it is lower not because the land is outside the market, nor wholly because of the inherent characteristics of the land, but because of planning decisions. In short, the price is low because the land is outside the urban perimeter, or because it is not serviced, or because it is still technically illegal and therefore not serviceable or creditworthy. A favourable planning decision to service the land would automatically raise the price of the land.

We would submit, therefore, that there is some clear connection between the way in which public land is used and the potential price of that land on the commercial market. While some land is kept out of the 'formal' land market despite its commercial value, for example certain *ejidal* lands in Mexico, much of the public land in our cities is indirectly subject to market forces. If this is true of public land, it is still more true of illegal subdivisions and other kinds of private land. Indeed, we believe it is misleading to stress the distinctiveness of the two land markets. Clearly, the mechanisms by which purchase and servicing occur in legal and illegal settlements sometimes differ widely, but whether land is allocated to low-income or high-income groups is substantially determined by the market. High-income, commercial and institutional users bid for specific, well-located, areas of land. That which is left over becomes vulnerable to illegal land transactions, it is invaded, or is sold without servicing and planning permission. Indeed, there are relatively few differences between the present pattern of residential location in Latin American cities and what would have developed had all transactions been subject to legal sales on the 'formal' market. In every city, low-income residential uses are found on the low-value land. Government housing projects are relegated to distant, unserviced land because they cannot afford the higher value sites more accessible to service lines. In Bogotá, the annual reports of the National Housing Agency (ICT) since 1965 have consistently complained that the agency has been forced to purchase peripheral land which is expensive to service. In Valencia, the main public housing scheme, Isabelica, is located far from the higher-income areas. In Mexico City, too, housing developments by state agencies during the 1970s were, almost exclusively, located in the less accessible and initially unserviced periphery. We would argue that the market effectively determines land use whether the land is public or private, whether the use is public or private, whether the transaction is legal or illegal. In the process each bid affects the price of the land, further raising the price of high-value land and lowering that of low-value land. Of course, this does not go on for ever as some high-income areas become downgraded, some low-income areas, upgraded, but in general it maintains social segregation. In addition, and to anticipate a later argument, land-use planning in Latin American cities generally favours high-income uses. It often ignores low-income areas beyond making sure that low-income housing is systematically excluded from high-quality residential areas. These areas are not outside the market, nor in another part of the market, but an integral part of it. Planning decisions merely change the price of land. The desirable land is generally occupied by the more affluent, the least valuable land by the poor.

We must be careful, however, in our use of the terms desirable and valuable, for the value of, and the desire for, land does not depend only on its inherent qualities. In urban areas, the price of land depends upon externalities, neighbouring uses, government decisions about zoning and so on. Thus some land becomes expensive not because of its inherent qualities but because of decisions made with respect to it. Thus suburban development has often turned land of little inherent quality for, say, agriculture and with little suitability for other uses into high-value property. Where private or public investment has occurred it has raised land values, where it has not occurred it has reduced relative values, thereby increasing the probability of invasion.

The process of urban development and the decisions which influence it modify and redistribute land values.

This fact must be taken into consideration when discussing the ways in which individual members of the urban poor obtain land. The form in which land is acquired by the poor in our three cities varies considerably. But, despite this, the poor inevitably occupy the poorest land, both in terms of its inherent and acquired characteristics. This process of residential segregation has not occurred by chance. It has been the outcome of market forces, planning decisions and servicing policy. There is no space in which to develop this argument in detail, but it is clear from other authors' accounts of urban development in each of the three cities how land has been allocated to the poor.

The intervention of the state

We have already hinted at the heavy involvement of the state both in the conventional and the irregular urban areas. In fact, according to the particular state involved, public intervention takes a variety of forms. First, the state is frequently a landowner. In Valencia, the municipality owns large tracts of land, while in Bogotá and Mexico large areas are controlled by decentralized agencies and by ministries. Governments in all three cities are also landowners insofar as they own large institutional complexes and their housing agencies build for the city populations.

Second, the government affects the land market in that it stimulates and depresses the general price of urban land. Encouraging building activity, which has been done frequently by all three national governments, has an immediate effect on land prices. Plans such as the 'Four Strategies' of Colombia between 1971 and 1974 have stimulated a massive speculative wave in land and house prices (Ridler, 1979; Rosas *et al.*, 1972). In Venezuela, frequent changes in the incentives available to private builders, both to increase total activity and to increase the production of particular kinds of housing, have had a direct effect on land prices.[4] In Venezuela, the government accounts for 40–50 per cent of building investment, with an inevitable effect on land prices (BCV, 1978: A-283). Similarly, the intervention and non-intervention of government in the form of urban-land taxation has affected land prices and the distribution of benefits owing to increases in land prices.

Third, the state is also influential as an investor in buildings, infrastructure and services. A decision to build a road or a mass-transit railway through a a particular area has vital effects on the pricing of land. Similarly, by its refusal to service land in particular parts of the city, it reduces land values in those areas. In Mexico City, projects such as the *periférico*, *viaducto* and the *ejes viales* have, for the most part, raised the price of land belonging to middle-income and upper-income groups. In Bogotá, the construction of several major roads has had an important redistributional effect which has been only partially rectified by the incidence of valorization taxes.[5] In Valencia, Lovera (1978: 159) estimates, land prices in the far north of the city (Barbula) increased from *bs.* $0.4/m^2$ to $7.27/m^2$ as a result of motorway construction.

Fourth, the state exerts direct and indirect controls as land-use planner. Its planning decisions directly affect the price of land. Thus the planning authorities attempt to slow the physical expansion of the city by imposing a limit on the area within which the service agencies will provide infrastructure and the planning authorities will legalize *barrios*. Although the development of low-income housing in Bogotá has consistently gone beyond the perimeter, and has later been modified to take account of the new expansion (Losada and Gómez, 1976), its existence has limited the availability of serviceable land. It has thereby increased the price of land within the perimeter and lowered the price of land beyond. Similarly, zoning laws lay down the areas which can be dedicated to a particular kind of development – industrial, commercial, high-density residential, low-density residential, etc. – and indirectly affect land prices. In Mexico City, land-use zoning has been limited in scope; it has been employed mainly to legitimate government and to protect middle-income and upper-income land developments. In Bogotá, there is now a shortage of urbanizable land within the city limits and landowners and construction companies have exerted considerable pressure on the local authorities to shift allocations of land from the high-density (low-income) category to middle-density or low-density designations. The result of such a shift is to raise the value of the land. As a consequence, the amount of land available for the legal development of low-income settlements has been very limited, a fact which both increases the value of land in such settlements and encourages the emergence of pirate urbanizations.

Finally, the state indirectly controls low-income developments by its decisions on whether to permit land invasion, whether to prevent clandestine urban development, whether to service technically illegal urban areas, and by its decisions about extensions to the urban perimeter. These indirect influences are often more significant than the existence of zoning laws. Moreover, the state is a vital contributor to the form and level of land prices by its willingness to permit illegal land developments. We will deal below with the issue of why such illegality is permitted, but the degree to which it allows poor people to invade land, or prohibits such invasions, has a major effect on the supply of land and therefore helps to determine prices at least in the medium term.

In short, the state, through its overt and covert actions, and often through its failure to act in specific circumstances, is a critical element in the functioning of the land market. Directly and indirectly it has a major influence on the allocation of land in all three cities. It is essential, therefore, to gain some understanding of the motives behind state involvement, action and inaction.

The state, illegality and 'residual' land

We are certain that the general tolerance of illegality with respect to low-income housing in Latin American cities is not incidental to the survival of the Latin American state. Despite poor conditions, illegal settlements act as a safety valve to social tension. Through land invasion and illegal subdivision some of the poor receive land on which they can consolidate their homes. Low-income settlement provides them with a base from which they can seek work, raise their families and usually improve their absolute standards of living. Though the conditions in which they live are usually hostile and rarely conducive to a comfortable existence, comparison with rural conditions or with the lives of some low-income renters normally recommends their situation. As such, only where conditions deteriorate markedly is there any likelihood of their reacting politically *en masse*.

In addition, it is clear that more privileged groups in society gain certain benefits from the development of low-income housing. Elite residential groups are served in the sense that low-income settlement often indirectly maintains the sanctity of private property. If invasions can be confined to public land and illegal sub-divisions are kept to certain clearly demarcated areas, then high-income residential areas are not directly threatened. Indeed, by offering the poor some stake in the property system, low-income settlement upholds the property concept throughout the city and maintains the inequality of land holding. Elite construction companies and landowners are not averse to the system insofar as they may participate in the sale of land to the poor (Cornelius, 1975). Owners of land near to low-income areas may illegally subdivide their property as they will be unable to sell the land to the developers of middle-income settlements. Construction and building interests may make profits either through the sale of lots or through the eventual sale of building materials to the poor.

Industrial and commercial interests benefit to the extent that the labour force is housed cheaply and, therefore, is less likely to demand higher wages. Sales are helped by purchases made in these settlements and by the subcontracting that further reduces company production costs. Companies might gain still more from a better-housed population with a higher disposable income, but they are not threatened by the system and gain certain benefits from it.

Politicians are directly served by an increasing constituency and by greater opportunities for patronage (Collier, 1976; Nelson, 1979). It is only when the process gets out of hand because services cannot be provided or because land becomes too expensive that politicians are likely to lose the poor's support.

Only the state bureaucracy is directly threatened because it is required to respond to many of the problems created. Infrastructure, services and regularization need to be laid on at a price the poor can afford. If the state cannot satisfy the demand, it may come under pressure from a variety of sources. Nevertheless, even when its action is inadequate it may increase its power in a variety of ways. It may tap international lending sources to provide additional services, it may increase its fiscal base through increasing cadastral values in the low-income settlements, and it may take advantage of the whole range of opportunities for bureaucratic expansion and empire building created by the vigorously growing low-income settlements. At the very least, the proliferation of these settlements creates government jobs for professional architects and planners. Illegality also has its direct uses insofar as it allows the state to rid itself of particular settlements. Where land is needed for public or private work schemes, illegal occupants can be displaced (Gilbert and Gugler, 1982: chapter 5). Where opposition groups become established, the illegality of their land tenure may provide a means by which they can be moved. Compulsory purchase is not necessary where illegal settlement is concerned; the occupiers can simply be moved, as they have been throughout the Third World. Indeed, rather than being a disadvantage, the presence of illegality may be of positive assistance to the state.

We interpret the continued expansion of illegal low-income settlements, therefore, to the compatibility of these areas to the continuance of the urban system. Of course, as we shall constantly emphasize, that system does not remain stable; the economic structure changes, the political power balance shifts, urban development and the very process of low-income settlement modifies the macro-environment. As a result of these changes new responses are called for, most notably from the state. But Latin American societies have not changed sufficiently to eliminate the need for illegality. Illegality continues to be a useful way in which the state permits the poor to occupy the residual land of the city. The system needs to give them some land in order to reproduce the labour force; it also protects high-value legal land. The precise form of illegality varies from city to city. Indeed, the specific mechanism used to allocate land is that which best maintains political stability. In the following section we discuss why the forms of land allocation differ from city to city, and indeed within cities through time.

Methods of land acquisition

Low-income housing areas are generally outside the planning framework, are initially unserviced, are located in the least desirable parts of the city and contain homes designed and built largely by the occupants themselves. While these similarities have been documented in innumerable studies across the region there is one important difference in the way in which the low-income housing areas become established. This difference relates to the way in which the poor obtain land. There is in fact a multiplicity of ways in which poor people acquire land, within the broad generalization that they are generally illegal (Leeds, 1969). Within this range, however, two characteristic opportunities are open to the poor: the first is to invade land, and the second to purchase land beyond the limits of the conventional, legalized housing areas. At particular times, invasions have been the main form of land acquisition in Lima (Collier, 1976; Dietz, 1977; Turner, 1969), in most Venezuelan cities (Ray, 1969), in Rio de Janeiro during the fifties and early sixties (Leeds and Leeds, 1976) and in Chile between 1969 and 1973 (Lozano, 1975; Kusnetzoff, 1975; Collectif Chili, 1972; Cleaves, 1974). By contrast, land invasions have generally not been permitted in Bogotá (Vernez, 1973; Doebele, 1975), or in Rio de Janeiro after 1964 (Portes, 1979; Valladares, 1978), while in Mexico City their chances of success have varied under different administrations (Cornelius 1975; Ward, 1976a). The classic form of the invasion is well described in the above-mentioned works. But there are several variations on this form. Often invasion settlements have emerged through accretion, when individual families have occupied the area through time, with no apparent organization and in the absence of any real opposition from the state. In certain cases, the distinction between the land invasion and the illegal subdivision becomes blurred. Many cases exist where the subdivider has encouraged people to occupy the land even though he is not actually the owner of the land. The people believe that they are participating in a subdivision but they are in fact members of a *de facto* invasion. In other recorded cases, it has been the landowner who has organized the invasion of his own land in order to convince the urban authorities that they service the land, thereby increasing the value of his property, or that they include his land within the urban perimeter, thereby raising the market value because it can now be legally serviced (Leeds, 1969: 71; Nalven, 1978; Da Camargo, 1976).

Within this variety of forms our case studies contain examples of several interesting forms of low-income land acquisition. In Bogotá, the typical pattern is that the poor purchase lots from subdividers on land which lacks planning permission but which normally belongs to, or is in the process of being purchased by, the subdivider (Doebele, 1975). The tenure offered to the purchaser, while not supported by entirely valid papers, is secure. In Mexico City, there is a range of forms. Land invasions organized by politically linked groups have occurred, although they have become less common in recent years. Illegal subdivisions or *fraccionamientos clandestinos* have been a common form of land acquisition. Finally, the purchase of land on *ejidos* and the transfer of agricultural to urban land uses on *ejidal* lands is a further form of illegal land development in Mexico City. In Valencia, the land invasion is the typical pattern but such invasions occur on both public and on private land. Common to all three cities is the purchase of lots within illegal settlements once those settlements have become firmly established.

Figure 7 attempts to portray some of the main forms of land acquisition by the poor. In the following section we describe in detail these acquisition methods and attempt to describe why the forms of access vary so widely. As suggested earlier, the most satisfactory explanations require some detailed discussion of the reactions and policies of each national and local state.

Bogotá

Land invasions are uncommon in Bogotá. A major survey carried out in Colombia by the National Housing Institute in 1972 stated that only 0.7 per cent of Bogotá's housing was located in invasion areas (Colombia, ICT, 1976). This was something of an underestimate because it excluded from the invasion total settlements which had been formed through invasion but later legalized. Nevertheless, organized invasions on the Lima pattern are rare. A review of newspaper records, various documents of the planning department and the ICT inventory shows that only 21 settlements in the city have ever been referred to as invasions – a small number in comparison with Bogotá's 800 or so settlements.

Bogotá is neither typical of, nor peculiar among, Colombian cities for the incidence of invasions appears to be locally determined. In some cities invasions are the principal form of land occupation while in other invasions are almost totally absent. Thus ICT (1976) records the following percentages of homes founded in invasion settlements in different cities: on the one hand were cities such as Pasto 0.2 per cent, Manizales 0.4 per cent and Armenia 1.5 per cent; on the other Cúcuta 58 per cent, La Dorada 20 per cent, Valledupar 19 per cent. Ibagué 11 per cent and Barranquilla 9 per cent.

The difference in the frequency of invasions between cities has no legal basis; the same law applies in all urban areas. It prescribes that the police take action within 48 hours of a written complaint against a group of invaders. If the invaders cannot demonstrate a rental contract they will be removed immediately. The only real limit on this power is that removal must take place within 30 days of the act of invasion or within 30 days of the date when the complainant first knew of the invasion. If removal does not take place within 30 days, however defined, the invader can be removed only when the authorities are granted a possession order from a civil judge. Civil action can be supplemented, however, by the much stronger criminal law. Article 424 of the penal code declares invasion to be punishable by imprisonment of from 2 to 20 months. The law applies whether the land invaded belongs to a private individual or to the state, and has been

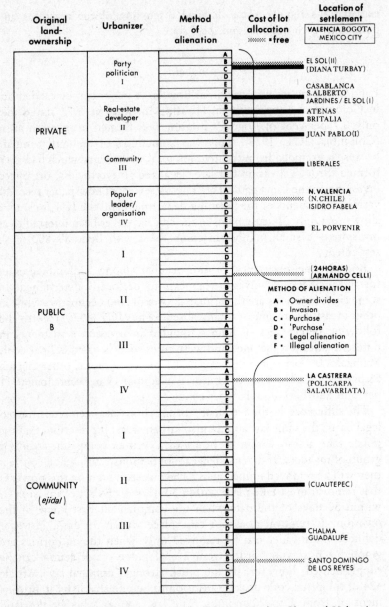

Fig. 7 Forms of illegal settlement in Bogotá, Mexico City and Valencia

invoked increasingly since the new security statute was introduced by the Turbay government in 1978. In Bogotá, at least, it is now especially difficult to invade land.

If the difference between cities is not explained by the letter of the law then it must be explained by how the law is applied. In cities such

Notes to Fig. 7

Original landownership

– Public land is that which belongs to a specific state institution or which is under the control of local government.
– Community or *ejidal* land is that which is controlled either by a group of people, as in the Mexican *ejido*, or by a cooperative.

Urbanizer

– The four categories listed below may overlap but generally the following are distinct:
– Party politician is a formally inscribed member of a major political party which may be the governing or a major opposition party.
– Real-estate developer includes any person who divides land with the principal aim of making a profit.
– The community may take the form of a group of *ejidatarios* or a cooperative group which purchases or invades land.
– A popular leader or organization includes those leaders who have no formal links with a major political party and members of minor opposition groups who have little in the way of influence with the government.

Method of alienation

– Owner divides includes all cases where the original owner divides the land. The owner may be a politician, a real-estate developer or even a popular leader.
– Invasion is reserved for those occasions where a group of people simultaneously occupy land against the owner's wishes.
– Purchase of land.
– 'Purchase' includes those cases where the intention is not finalized so that the vendor fails to receive the money owed to him/her. It also includes cases where sale is illegal, e.g. by *ejidatarios* in Mexico.
– Legal alienation includes those cases where the courts resolve that the urbanizer is permitted to occupy and subdivide the land. Such cases may be a result of political influence over the courts, or may stem from cases such as continuing possession or occupation which is sufficient to guarantee eventual title.
– Illegal alienation occurs where there is a *prima facie* legal right on which the possessor acts. On occasion, as in Juan Pablo I, the selling of lots by the illegal alienators of the land may appear to the owners to be an invasion; certainly the outcome may be very similar.

Cost of lot allocation

– Free includes all cases where no charge is levied (excluding perhaps contributions to legal costs).
– Charges include all cases where land is effectively sold.

as Cúcuta the police are not called to remove invaders, in Bogotá they are always called. In turn, this difference affects the propensity of poor people to invade land in different cities; the more probable ejection, the less likely people are to take the risks involved in invasion.

In the case of Bogotá, the absence of invasions is usually explained in terms of the following factors. First, it is claimed that the weather discourages invasion. This is a poor explanation because invasions have taken place despite the inclement conditions. It is true that in the Colombian cities where invasions are common conditions are much warmer than Bogotá, but this is coincidental. If people are prepared, as they most certainly are in Bogotá, to live in flimsy shacks on purchased land despite the weather, then they would invade land if they believed they could stay there. Second, Bogotá is located on the edge of a fertile and prosperous agricultural area. This means that most of the land on the edge of the city is cultivated and is valuable. In addition, most of the land has a legal owner, usually a private individual or company. The government does own land but on the whole it is not community (*ejidal*) land but belongs to particular government or semi-government agencies which act like private owners. Thus the water company owns most of the mountainside to the east of Bogotá and the Beneficencia de Cundinamarca owns a large wedge of land two miles to the west of the city centre. What Bogotá lacks is an area of land reserved under colonial Spanish law for public and specifically indigenous population use.[6] These areas have been prime targets for invasion in certain cities such as Cali and Ibagué. Their absence in Bogotá means that almost every plot of land has an owner with a legal title who is prepared to call in the police. Third, when the Bogotá police have been called in they have usually acted promptly and efficiently. This has been true even when invaders have eventually been allowed to stay. When the police have been ordered to move in, the invasion has usually been successfully repulsed. Fourth, it is said that there is no tradition to invade in Bogotá. Only one group has been actively involved in the invasion of land (a communist group known as the *Central de Provivienda*), but recently even that has been reluctant to organize or support invasions and has turned to the purchase of land to house its members.

There are three additional, and highly significant, factors which explain the infrequency of invasions in Bogotá. First, there is an alternative form of land acquisition for the poor in Bogotá: the illegal subdivision or, as it is known locally, the 'pirate' urbanization. For various reasons this mechanism seems to work fairly well in Bogotá in the sense that many of the poor seem to be generally satisfied with the process, and the cost of land, while rising fast, is still within the range of many poor families' budgets. Needless to say, this alternative would be gladly forsaken for free land if it were possible to invade. The presence of the 'pirate' urbanization market does not explain why the poor do not invade but it does serve as a safety valve permitting substantial numbers of people access to land and thereby reducing the need to invade. Second, those families which cannot afford to buy land are accommodated in a well-developed rental market (see below). Approximately half of the families in Bogotá rent homes in public, commercial and irregular housing areas. The high incidence of renting tends to increase occupancy levels and overcrowding (tables 5, 12 and 13) but, nevertheless, it provides poor families with a further alternative to invasion. Third, the political system in Bogotá has not used land as a source of patronage. In most cities where invasion has been the normal way for the poor to obtain land, politicians have been active in terms of organizing, or arbitrating, the process. Thus, in Lima, the government has been involved in the invasion process at least since the 1950s (Collier, 1976). In Chile, the wave of invasions which characterized the last years of the Frei administration was encouraged both by opposition and later by governmental groups (Cleaves, 1974). Recently, in Barranquilla, the fourth largest Colombian city, members of the council have been accused of encouraging the invasion of three hectares of land belonging to private owners. The National Council of State has ordered the removal of the 50,000 squatter families and the payment of compensation to the owner (*El Tiempo*, 19 June 1979). In Bogotá, by contrast, invasions have never become a significant weapon of the major parties. Invasions have been encouraged only by opposition groups which have had relatively little electoral support. In short, and as we shall develop in the next chapter, the political system has been better served by the use of employment and servicing patronage than by invasions. In this politicians have been helped by the 'pirate urbanization' process and recent accommodations by the planning authorities to ease that process.

Invasions, therefore, have been an occasional rather than a recurrent phenomenon and have tended to succeed only in exceptional circumstances – notably when there has been doubt about the ownership of land or where the owners have acted inefficiently and tardily in establishing their claim to it. Thus the Policarpa Salavarrieta settlement was founded in 1961 on land intended for the construction of a new hospital. Inefficiency on the part of several government organizations with responsibility for the land prevented the speedy removal of the initial invaders. A major police attack on the settlement in 1966 brought the deaths of a man and two children and the resulting outcry led to the gradual de-escalation of the conflict. Today, the settlement is well established even if it still possesses illegal services. In another Bogotá invasion Nuevo Chile, the owners also acted slowly and, although the invaders were initially removed, the authorities eventually ordered the police to return the imprisoned invaders to the settlement. This settlement is now serviced by the official agencies. In sum, therefore, invasions occur infrequently and only when there is indecision on the part of the owners and the authorities. Unlike the situation in many other cities, Bogotano politicians do not actively encourage the invasion process.

The phenomenon of pirate urbanization in Bogotá has been extensively discussed in the literature, though certain elements of the phenomenon merit further attention (Vernez, 1973; Doebele, 1975; Losada and Gómez, 1976; Losada and Pinilla, 1980). Illegal subdivisions are normally created on land fringing the city and the small lots are sold at low prices with, at best, limited services. Their illegality stems from the fact that the services provided, the areas of open land designated, the width of the roads and so on do not conform with local planning regulations. In addition, while the subdividers normally give contracts (*promesas de compraventa*) to the purchasers, there are usually legal deficiencies in the documentation.

In Bogotá, pirate urbanization is the principal means by which the poor acquire land. Arias calculates that 59 per cent of Bogotá's population lives in such areas (Bogotá, DAPD, 1973), and between 1972 and 1974 as much as 52 per cent of urban expansion was through this illegal process (Bogotá, DAPD, 1978). Clearly, it is a well-established process which is tolerated by the local authorities and which is accepted by the poor as their chief means of obtaining land.

The process works neither equitably nor efficiently (Gilbert, 1981b), but it does work well in the context of the way the city of Bogotá functions. At the same time, it cannot be assumed that it will always work well; it requires careful control by the state if it is to maintain the stability of the system. For this reason, the state has established a series of mechanisms to control pirate urbanization which have become both more insistent and more realistic through time. These changes have not occurred in a political vacuum but have been an outcome of pressure from the poor. The most important source of pressure came between 1966 and 1970 when ex-dictator Gustavo Rojas Pinilla and his party (ANAPO) offered a serious threat to the hegemony of the two major political parties. Attracting support mainly from the low-income population, he almost gained the presidency in 1970.[7] His political threat was neutralized after 1970 in part by a campaign to improve the conditions of the poor in the settlements of Bogotá. In 1971, a major initiative was launched by the country's president to provide water for the peripheral settlements. In 1972, a policy was introduced by the authorities in Bogotá to restrict the growth of new pirate urbanizations and to service existing areas. New decrees were approved which reduced the level of services required of an urbanizer; it was hoped that more urbanizers would establish legal rather than pirate urbanizations and that subsequent servicing would be easier and therefore less costly. The same decrees made legalization of illegal settlements achievable through three stages. First, the settlement had to be upgraded through the provision of basic services. Second, the settlement would be legalized, thereby permitting the issue of legal titles to the occupiers. Finally, the full range of infrastructure and community services would be provided which would regularize the settlements. This correction policy was complemented by the prevention of new illegal settlements through stiffer penalties and firmer application of the law. Essentially, the policy was to help the poor in existing settlements while holding back the growth of new pirate urbanizations.

The programme has not been unsuccessful. Many settlements have been legalized and services have been provided for large numbers of people. Together with a massive increase in the capacity of the water and electricity agencies, the policy has ensured that the proportion of unserviced homes in the city has not increased. It is also claimed that the rate of formation of pirate urbanizations has been slowed. In the five years to April 1979, 36 urbanizations were established under the minimum standards decrees. From December 1974 to February 1977, 24 per cent of the land in Bogotá was developed under the minimum standards decrees compared to 30 per cent through pirate urbanizations (Bogotá, DAPD, 1978). In 1979, *Acuerdo* 7 took the reduction of standards required of subdividers one stage further and eased the process of legalization (Bogotá, DAPD, 1981).

If the prevention element in the programme has been less successful than had been hoped, a major cause has been the cost of the land and the shortage of land suitable for minimum standards urbanizations

(Carroll, 1980: 92–5). Either because of inappropriate zoning regulations, bureaucratic delay, the concentration of land in the hands of large companies, or the shortage of land available for low-income settlement in Bogotá, there has been a constraint on the supply of land for this settlement form.[8] Such a policy, realistic though it clearly is, cannot work without more fundamental reforms to the land market and the planning system.

The other government initiative to control the pirate urbanization process operates through the Banking Superintendency (SIB). Responsibility was given to the SIB in 1968 to intervene in real estate companies which failed to comply with conventional accounting and business practice. The SIB is thus concerned with urban developments for all income groups. Its most important powers are to freeze the assets of responsible companies and to jail the urbanizers for up to six years. In fact, the law is inadequately applied and except for a short period in the later seventies has not constituted a satisfactory control over pirate urbanizers. It has been claimed that the office is both inefficient and corrupt; certainly the agency has taken some very strange decisions (Losada and Gómez, 1976). On the other hand, the SIB faces a genuine problem. As Paredes and Martínez (1977) put it, they have the power to stop the pirate urbanization process completely, but if this were done it would cause more problems than it solved. Too strict an interpretation of the law would severely restrict the poor's access to land. As a consequence, the SIB in its more energetic periods has acted merely to control the worst excesses of the pirate urbanization process. Where a settlement population has complained to the SIB about the urbanizer and where a major issue has been involved, the SIB has intervened. Some urbanizers have been put in prison and fines applied. The SIB has always suffered from a lack of flexibility and in some cases insufficient powers. This situation was improved towards the end of 1979 when the authorities resolved to take a still stronger stance on illegal subdivisions. Decree number 2610 increased the penalties that could be applied to illegal subdividers and increased the agency's flexibility. Together with modifications to the planning regulations in the city, the modification seems to have persuaded more subdividers to follow legal procedures.

But this reform has not solved another difficulty for the SIB: what to do with the pirate urbanizations once they have intervened. The normal procedure has been to appoint the National Housing Institute (ICT) as the agent to supply services to the settlement and to legalize its existence. Unfortunately, ICT's Special Agency in charge of intervened urbanizations has been unable to perform this role adequately. Indeed, it has been claimed that the agency is less able to service the settlements than the pirate urbanizer under pressure from the community and the SIB. In 1979, relations between the SIB and the agency deteriorated to such a point that the SIB began to appoint its own agents to intervened settlements in the hope that the pace of servicing and legalization would be accelerated. By 1981, relations between the SIB and ICT had been re-established and some improvement in the pace of legalization was apparent during 1982. Nevertheless, the Special Agency is starved of funds by its mother institution and there will continue to be major delays in legalization given these constraints.

Whatever the deficiencies of both the District of Bogotá's planning agency and of the Banking Superintendency, there is today much closer control of the pirate urbanization process than previously. This reflects the growing awareness among politicians and bureaucrats that the pirate urbanization mechanism has innumerable flaws and that its worst excesses must be controlled if the mechanism is to work at all. Most planners and some politicians want all low-income developments to occur through the minimum standards procedure. Indeed, Agreement 2610 and *Acuerdo* 7 have made this still more likely. Nevertheless, there are limits to such a development, mainly the fact that government in Bogotá does not always function on rational principles nor aim to provide the best possible solutions for the less privileged. Government policy is rather a response to the pressures exercised by several powerful interest groups. As such, the mayor, the daughter of the national president, and the Liberal presidential candidate all visited a newly established illegal subdivision during the build-up to the 1982 election. This instance reflects the fact that, with all their faults, pirate urbanizations serve the powerful groups in the city sufficiently well to impede any substantial attempt at reform (Bagley, 1979). Such illegality is certainly preferable to the nationalization of land or higher taxes on land. The poor undoubtedly suffer from the process but they accept the situation as the best available in an unfair world.

Mexico City

The case of Mexico City presents a rather more complex picture than either Bogotá or Valencia. This complexity results from its larger size, from the fact that there are three different modes of land development for low-income settlement, and from the fact that executive authority is split between the Federal District and the State of Mexico. Below we describe briefly each form of illegal occupation and attempt to explain the conditions under which each has appeared. This is followed by an account of state efforts to control and to regularize illegal settlement. Finally, we offer an interpretation of the changes in governmental response to the land market.

Illegal subdivisions – the 'fraccionamientos clandestinos'
Throughout Mexico the subdivision and sale of lots by landowners, usually without services, is a well-known if not widely documented phenomenon (for exceptions see Butterworth, 1973; Mexico, SAHOP, 1978a). Subdivision for sale represents the single most important form of land alienation in the city. Real-estate companies organize much larger settlements than those in Bogotá, or, indeed, elsewhere in Mexico. Located mostly upon the saline, dried-out marshlands of Lake Texcoco, they lie outside the Federal District. Originally national property, the land was sold off in the 1920s for agricultural improvement. Later the state tried unsuccessfully to regain ownership after it became apparent that no improvement had taken place nor was likely to (Guerrero *et al.*, 1974). During the 1940s, large areas were bought by a handful of private companies and gradually converted to urban use, specifically low-income housing. One single tract of land, later made into the municipality of Netzahualcóyotl, covered 62 square kilometres and was subdivided into 160,000 lots by 34 companies.

Like the pirate urbanizations of Bogotá, the subdivisions lacked most basic services and failed to comply with planning norms for service provision, open spaces and public utilities. Invariably they consisted of large blocks, divided into 200-square-metre plots, perhaps with the occasional standpipe and kerbstones to demarcate the incipient road network. Needless to say, roads were unpaved and during the rainy season became impassable (Fox, 1972). Often the titles sold to residents were not properly drawn up, and, particularly in the early stages of occupancy when it was anybody's guess exactly where one's lot began and finished, it was not unusual for titles to relate to different land parcels. Many contracts failed to include clauses promising service installation at a future date. Although many settlements were established during the 1940s and 1950s, few residents occupied their lots until the 1960s. Yet, by 1970, some 600,000 people lived in irregular settlements in Netzahualcóyotl alone. Today, the population exceeds one-and-a-half millions, though much of this increase has been accommodated in rental tenements and by sharing lots with kinsfolk who had acquired land in the settlement. Given that irregular settlement on this vast scale is both of major importance in Mexico City yet not widely replicated elsewhere in the country, we must try to account for its appearance in that city. In our view there are three principal reasons.

First, the rapid increase of population in the post-war period, fuelled by industrial expansion, demanded a housing form in which workers could be accommodated at low cost. Such motives had already led to a government-imposed freeze on rents which was concerned to reduce demands for wage increases (Connolly, 1982). Ironically, perhaps, this served only to reduce the incentive for the construction of cheap rental housing in and around the city centre and therefore contributed to rising demand for an alternative; an alternative met in large by the subdivisions. Although we do not believe that rent controls were deliberately manipulated by real-estate developers to force people to seek accommodation elsewhere, it is clear that self-build lots provided a lucrative opportunity for them. Unfortunately, we know little about the precise ways in which the ideology of self-build housing alternatives was propagated.

Second, and more importantly, the existence of a large area of land unsuited to any other obvious use made large-scale low-income subdivision an attractive proposition. Sub-soil conditions were not conducive to heavy industrial plant. Moreover, industrial zones had been designated for the northwest of the Federal District and indeed new taxes sought to discourage new industry from locating in the urban area altogether (see chapter 2). Neither did the former lake bed interest other real-estate developers at that time. During the 1950s, frenetic speculation for elite and middle-income housing was directed towards the west, south and southwest of the city (Unikel, 1972). Thus, almost by default, the Texcoco area was turned over to low-income residence. Although lots had to be cheap if the poor were to buy them, the profits made by the developers were still enormous. The very low prices at which companies had bought the land, together with their failure to invest in basic urban infrastructure, generated very large returns. One estimate, which documents land transactions in a settlement in the municipality of Ecatepec, describes how a one-million-dollar investment generated profits in the order of eleven million dollars over a ten-year period (Guerrero *et al.*, 1974; quoted in Connolly, 1982).

Third, the scale of operations of the real-estate companies involved in subdivisions in Mexico City is directly linked to the way in which government authority was exercised on both sides of the Federal District boundary. Within the Federal District strong controls were imposed by Mayor Uruchurtu after 1953 to restrict the expansion of low-income settlement. Many writers have argued that this action shifted the development of illegal subdivisions over the boundary into the State of Mexico where, of course, the ban did not apply (Cornelius, 1975). This interpretation fails, however, to account for the substantial development of low-income subdivisions in the east and northeast of the Federal District. Many of these areas appear to have been authorized for settlement prior to the ban, while others were invasions in which the landlords, unable to develop their land legally, chose to turn a blind eye in the hope of compensation at a later date (Mexico, INVI, 1958; López Díaz, 1978). Nevertheless, Mayor Uruchurtu's policy had a pronounced effect upon those areas within the Federal District over which he was able to exercise control, and the policy was sustained until he lost office in 1966. In contrast, there is evidence that the government of the State of Mexico actively supported the real-estate transactions. The 'improvement boards' established from 1952 onwards, ostensibly to coordinate the installation of services in the region, achieved little beyond the promotion of lot sales. Our interviews with leaders in one subdivision (Jardines) indicate that local municipal officers were in the pay of the company. Moreover, state authorities took no action against the common abuse whereby the same lot was sold several times over to different individuals. This practice was encouraged by the unwillingness of purchasers to occupy their lots until services were available and by contractual clauses which allowed the company to resell the plot if repayments were not paid on time. Nor did the authorities attempt to disguise their support for the companies, even when many settlers formed themselves into 'defence associations' to demand that promises of service installation be upheld. Despite comprehensive regulations governing the creation of low-income subdivisions (*Ley de Fraccionamientos*, 1958), neither the state nor the municipal executive pressed for sanctions against the developers. Rather, authorizations were made for further developments even where companies had failed to satisfy the conditions laid down for earlier settlements (Guerrero *et al.*, 1974).

Not until the 1970s was any serious attempt made to penalize the developers – a consequence of the extensive complicity between state authorities and the companies throughout most of this period (Guerrero *et al.*, 1974).

Transfer and sale of 'ejidal' land

Many Mexican cities have substantial areas of *ejidal* land contiguous to the urban area. Inevitably, therefore, city expansion encroaches upon *ejidos* and results in changing land uses either through their legal disestablishment or, more usually, through a variety of illegal practices. In Mexico City, *ejidal* and communal lands have provided widespread opportunities for low-income land acquisition. One study reports that 30 per cent of all low-income settlement has developed on such areas (Mexico, COPEVI, 1977: 62). As figure 5 indicates, settlement on *ejidal* land has occurred frequently in the south, southwest and west of the city and has often occupied marginal agricultural land which had been turned into *ejidal* property regardless of whether it afforded a livelihood to the 'beneficiaries'. The more marginal the land, then, the greater the incentive of the *ejidal* population to at last reap some reward from their holdings. However, even first-rate agricultural land cannot compete with the returns offered by urban or commercial land uses, and the *ejidos* located to the southeast of the city are increasingly under pressure of commercialization. So far, both *ejidatarios* and the government have resisted this pressure and it is likely that the authorities are unlikely to tolerate either the invasion or sale of these areas (Mexico, DDF, 1980). *Ejidal* lots can be handed down from father to son but never sold. The legal provisions governing *ejidos* are extremely complex and detailed. Moreover, their existence has firm ministerial backing under the Agrarian Reform Law, and further strong support is received from several farmworker unions integrated into a national confederation, itself one of the three pillars of the PRI. The law is quite clear. *Ejidal* land cannot be used to accommodate urban expansion (Articles 90 & 93 of the *Ley de Reforma Agraria*). The poorest area of land should be allocated for settlement by the *ejidatarios* and those families fulfilling community functions. The maximum size of lot in this 'urban zone' is laid down, and it is the only land over which the holder has alienable rights. *Ejidal* land use can only be changed through formal disestablishment through expropriation in the 'social interest' and an indemnity paid to *ejidatarios*, or by a swap of equivalent lands elsewhere (*permuta*) – also in the public interest.

Despite these extensive provisions, abuse has been widespread. Past presidents have, on occasion, authorized *permutas* of *ejidos* in the south and northwest of the city, substantial parts of which were later turned over to luxury housing in Jardines San Angel and to middle-income housing in Ciudad Satélite (Mexico, COPEVI, 1976: F-74).

More extensively, low-income settlement has resulted from the connivance between the *ejidal* community and officials in the Agrarian Reform Ministry. The most frequent procedure is for the former to apply for the creation of, or extension to, the urban *ejidal* zone, a process that involves some 138 separate legal steps. In the meantime, the local community sells lots providing purchasers with certificates of transfer which, in effect, constitute provisional title whilst the application is processed. However, the application collapses once it becomes apparent that the area is occupied by a large number of residents who are not legitimate members of the rural working community. The only option is for the state authorities to expropriate the land, regularize the land title, charging residents a second time, and finally, to indemnify the *ejidatarios*. There are many variations on this theme (Mexico, SAHOP, 1979), but the result is the same: irregular settlement, recourse to expropriation, compensation to the *ejidatarios* who thereby benefit twice over.

Housing has developed on *ejidal* land for four principal reasons. First, given the high level of demand for self-build lots in the 1950s and 1960s and the strict controls in force in the Federal District, there was pressure on the *ejidal* lands over which Mayor Uruchurtu's department held little authority. Formally, he could only block applications for service provision, a tactic used once to prevent a middle-income sale proposed by *ejidatarios* in the south of the city (Durand, 1978). Recently, the exercise of tighter controls against invasion and the clamp-down on company-sponsored subdivisions (see below) have left the *ejidos* as the only real source of cheap land.

Second, the existence of large areas of *ejidal* land in desirable locations was obviously critical. Indeed, luxury urban development in the southwest of the city resulted in substantial tracts of the Padierna *ejido* being sold illegally to upper-income households. Moreover, the fact that *ejidal* land often has little agricultural worth has provided incentive for *ejidatarios* to sell their holdings, albeit illegally and cheaply. Only where the land provided a regular source of employment and a reasonable livelihood for the *ejidatario* has development sometimes been resisted.

Third, regularization of *ejidal* land since 1973 has encouraged further irregular settlement. The requirement that *ejidatarios* receive compensation for the 'loss' of their land has quickened the pace of illegal land sales. It made sense for *ejidatarios* to sell their plots, particularly after the establishment of CoRett whose initial charter empowered the agency to acquire vacant *ejidal* land and to commercialize it for housing purposes. This threatened to deny the *ejidatarios* the opportunity to sell plots and, after pressure from them, the offending clause was revoked. Henceforth, CoRett was to be responsible for land regularization and compensation (*Diario Oficial*, 3 April 1979).

Fourth, illegal settlement on *ejidal* land has flourished because of the political patronage that *ejidatarios* enjoy. The powers of the Agrarian Reform Ministry and the Farmworkers' Federation rest upon their ability to control and manipulate the *campesinos*. The failure of past governments drastically to improve conditions of the small-scale peasants (Hansen, 1974) has been compensated, in part, by a knowledge that it can ill afford to alienate their support. It is our opinion that any concerted attempt to undercut the alienation processes outlined above would threaten that support. There are also other reasons. Illegal land sales are lucrative not only for *ejidatarios* but also for SRA officials. Engineers who draw up and authorize the certificates issued to low-income buyers take their cut, part of which is handed on to their bosses. Indeed, it is sometimes engineers who put the idea of selling land into the minds of *ejidatarios*.

Invasions

Invasions are of limited importance as a method of land alienation in Mexico City, though their size, conflictive beginnings and interaction with the state authorities have given them a certain notoriety. Invasions are likely to occur in two broad circumstances. The first is where prospective purchasers are prevented from buying lots in low-income subdivisions or from *ejidatarios*. Invasions occurred in two settlements where the owner threatened to renege on his agreement to sell land.[9] Similarly, the two most significant invasions during the early 1970s (Santo Domingo and Padierna) were, in part, a response to the refusal of *ejidatarios* to admit low-income households. Invasions also were the outcome of Mayor Uruchurtu's attempt to restrict the activity of subdividers within the Federal District. Second, invasions are occasionally the result of a politician or party using the settlement for political ends, for example, to strike at an enemy. No lesser figure than President Echeverría promoted an invasion of lands belonging to the national newspaper *Excelsior* in July 1976. The paper had been increasingly critical of his administration and this action was used to oust the editorial staff. Other political considerations may also serve to propagate invasions, for example, the desire by the leaders to create a personal clientele and basis of support within the invasion settlement, or agency aggrandizement where an agency initiates 'problems' that it can subsequently resolve. Invasion attempts appear to increase close to elections, and during the elections of 1979 were actively promoted by radical parties whose aim was to embarrass the PRI by forcing the government to eject squatters.

In Mexico City, squatter settlements have been established both by the gradual occupation of lots on land where the ownership is in doubt and uncontested, and by rapid invasion where the aim is to present the authorities or owners with a *fait accompli*. As in other Latin American cities, the latter are especially well organized: leaders have mapped out the street pattern in advance, applicant households have been vetted and are provided with identity cards, sympathetic propaganda is cultivated.

No land is immune to invasion though astute leaders normally avoid private land, knowing that the landlord will press the authorities to remove the fledgling settlement. Private land is only threatened where there are doubts about the ownership or where the owner is politically vulnerable (cf. pp. 81–2). We have already observed that public land is relatively scarce in Mexico City, but in any case we believe such land is usually well protected. Public agencies, for example, can eject squatters on the grounds that their presence prevents projects that are in the wider public interest. In general, it is *ejidal* and *comunal* land that has offered the best chances of success even though *ejidatarios* may resist such invasions and physical conflict may ensue.

Past governments have tended to respect private ownership and acted to remove invaders, but the sternness of their actions has varied with different administrations. Uruchurtu regularly took a hard line against invasions, seeking to discourage them through immediate removal, or, where impossible, by refusing to recognize and service them (Cornelius 1975: 194). The early phase of Echeverría's presidency created the impression that the moral claims of homeless groups who invaded unused lands would receive a sympathetic ear. Several massive invasions were highly successful at that time, including Santo Domingo and Padierna. But, given that these invasions involved such large numbers of people, it is difficult to imagine what other action the authorities could have taken. Thereafter, invasion settlements were usually swiftly removed, and in the Federal District invasions have once again virtually ceased. Discouragement has taken a variety of forms. The mayor has publicly announced his firm intention to uphold the rights of private owners and to prevent anarchic urban growth. Invasion settlements have been systematically eradicated despite tactics such as good organization, the selection of land with unclear ownership, and the use of legitimizing tactics such as calling the settlement after the president's wife. More careful vigilance of open spaces by the police and greater attention to fencing and boundary walls have also been an outcome of this stance. As a result, most poor people now prefer more secure methods of land acquisition. They prefer to purchase land, either from a subdivider or from *ejidatarios* so that they have some minimal documentation and have the moral claim that they bought in good faith.

The relative importance of these different methods of land acquisition by the poor is a product of the attitude that the state has adopted in previous decades. Below we demonstrate, briefly, the manner in which state intervention has altered over the years and focus attention upon the reasons for those changes.

Since 1941, the Federal District has had adequate statutory powers to ensure that any form of residential land development be properly authorized, registered and serviced prior to public sale (*Diario Oficial*, 31 December 1941). In addition, subdividers have been subject to taxes both on their land and their profits, although the taxes were not applied until Mayor Uruchurtu's ban on subdivisions was introduced in 1953.

As we have seen, the State of Mexico failed to control real-estate companies during the 1950s and 1960s. This attitude could not continue indefinitely, however, since by 1970 almost 900,000 people were living in Netzahualcóyotl and Ecatepec (Garza and Schteingart, 1978a: 69), most without basic services. Public utilities such as schools, markets and clinics were totally inadequate and levels of gastric disease and infant mortality were very high (Fox, 1972). Moreover, the late 1960s were marked by growing social unrest, and local community leaders, who had previously fought one another for the right to represent the informal constituencies, now formed themselves into a common movement. The MRC (*Movemiento Restaurador de Colonos*) called a strike on all further payments to the subdividers and both residents and companies turned to the federal government for help. The conflict posed an acute political dilemma for the incoming Echeverría administration, which was concerned to promote a closer link with disadvantaged groups and to take a more interventionalist stance on their behalf (Tello, 1978). The solution was highly political. It proposed to create a Trust (*Fideicomiso*) in which the companies were to receive the sums owing to them less 40 per cent, and the residents a discount of 15 per cent and legal title to their plots. Service installation would begin immediately, although charges would be levied on the residents. The agreement was accepted by all parties though it has been strongly criticized for favouring the companies; the latter were exonerated from responsibility for their illegal transactions, retained a large part of their profits and escaped the burden of paying for services (Guerrero *et al.*, 1974; Martín de la Rosa, 1974; Ferras, 1978). Nevertheless, the agreement marked the end of company-sponsored, low-income subdivisions. The companies recognized that the state would no longer tolerate their indiscretions and legislation was introduced to tax profits, which made only higher-income subdivisions and the development of condominia a profitable enterprise. It was not until 1977, however, that the State of Mexico determined not to compensate developers; perhaps the only direct attack upon the interests it had until then protected.

Elsewhere, however, the Echeverría administration was inconsistent in its attitude to the expansion of low-income settlement; new regulatory agencies and legislation on human settlements went hand-in-hand with the emergence of a large number of new settlements – mostly *ejidal* subdivisions and invasions. In part, permission for the new settlements was given in return for the political support that residents were expected to offer to the president (Cornelius, 1975; Ward, 1981a). Although some evictions occurred, they usually affected inner-city rental shantytowns where the land was required for redevelopment or where squatters had invaded lands belonging to someone influential.

Between 1977 and 1982, Mayor Hank González (formerly governor of the State of Mexico) acted vigorously to prevent the development of unauthorized low-income settlement in the Federal District. He evicted settlers in several large new invasions and issued local mayors (*delegados*) with precise instructions about the need for greater surveillance of vacant lands, about how to intervene quickly to prevent unauthorized settlement, and about the need for ready access to the police to secure evictions. In addition, the Urban Development Plan (Mexico, DDF, 1980) introduced policies to increase land-use densities and to control growth in the south of the city. One outcome of these policies has been to increase the demand for *ejidal* land; land, of course, which comes under the jurisdiction of other state agencies.

Servicing policies have not acted significantly to restrain or control the expansion of low-income settlements. Since 1965, all settlements in which *de facto* owners pay land taxes have been eligible for services. However, eligibility does not mean that services are received: agency criteria for installation vary with the service and the agency (see chapter 4). Nor have land regularization policies acted as a brake upon low-income settlement, though they reflect important shifts in government attitude. Regularization was a rare event under Uruchurtu but became commonplace after he left office in 1966 (Cornelius, 1975). The emergence of land tenure as a major issue of conflict from 1969 onwards led to the creation of several regulatory agencies between 1970 and 1973.[10] These agencies had relatively little success in terms of general programmes and most of their attention focused on the largest and most conflict-ridden settlements, particularly those in the Federal District. In the absence of strict land-use controls, the combined effect of a more enlightened state attitude towards low-income settlement, the regularization of large numbers of settlements, and the practice of compensating those responsible for illegal land sales was to stimulate settlement formation. Only since 1977 have the state and Federal District authorities adopted stricter controls.

In summary, while the authorities in Mexico City have displayed an increasingly enlightened attitude towards servicing low-income settlement and a greater willingness to intervene on the poor's behalf, it is almost always a belated response to circumstances. The authorities have not sought to anticipate settlement expansion and channel it into areas which would be easy to service.

It is clear that the existence of low-income settlements has not been dysfunctional to the interests of most groups in Mexico City. Over the years, the authorities have allowed developers in the State of Mexico to make vast profits (Connolly, 1982). The development and sale of *ejidal* land has been permitted due to the political strength of the economic interests involved and the electoral importance of the *ejidatarios* and the low-income settlers.

National interests have been served to the extent that labour for the booming Mexico City economy has been housed without substantial recourse to the exchequer; self-help has cut the need for expenditure on public housing. Moreover the land that has been allotted to low-income subdivision had few other competing uses and the inconvenience of its distance from employment centres has been partly overcome by heavy subsidies to public transport.

In addition, the state bureaucracy has benefited through graft, opportunities for empire building, patronage and manipulation – the *leitmotif* of the Mexican political system (Grindle, 1977; Smith, 1979). Politicians use settlement issues to exert influence over the electorate; local leaders also have used low-income areas as springboards for political careers. Finally, it must be recognized that the poor, too, have benefited even if they have suffered from prolonged insecurity of tenure, inadequate services, the loss of leisure time taken up in house building and neighbourhood improvements, and the high cost of paying for land, regularization, taxes and bribes.

If, therefore, the expansion of low-income settlement has benefited so many in Mexico City and functioned in the general interest, how may we account for the following anomalies? First, why were different approaches by the authorities followed in the Federal District and the State of Mexico during the 1950s and 1960s? Second, after the relaxing of controls upon low-income settlements in 1966 and the shift towards a more enlightened approach to servicing, how can we explain the imposition of restrictions in the State of Mexico from 1973 onwards, and in the Federal District from 1977?

In the fifties and sixties, Mayor Uruchurtu appears to have been concerned to prevent the Federal District from being overwhelmed by shantytown sprawl and, more specifically, by the enormous costs that the treasury would incur if any systematic attempt were made to service such areas. That he was able to pursue an anti-settlement policy may be explained by the absence of a powerful and coordinated group of low-income land developers within the Federal District; by the 'safety valve' that the expansion of settlement in the adjacent State of Mexico offered and, lastly, by the opportunities for settlement on *ejidos* or on those lands for which development permissions had already been authorized. Significantly, opposition mounted only after his refusal to install services, and, more importantly perhaps, once his policies began to threaten the more powerful groups involved in speculative land development in the south of the city. That his policies had become dysfunctional is indicated by the more circumspect and conciliatory approach of his successors.

Opposition towards invasions by Mayor Hank González in the Federal District may be explained by his personal position as a leading figure in real estate in both the Federal District and the State of Mexico. Not surprisingly, he is a vigorous advocate of private-property interests. Unlike his predecessors he has initiated a systematic programme of regularization and improvements to infrastructure, always endeavouring to ensure that the costs of the improvements are recovered from the beneficiaries (Ward, 1981a). Popular opposition to the mayor's policies has been defused by the opportunities for purchase in existing settlements and by the continuing provision of low-cost land outside the Federal District.

The sharp change in policy in the State of Mexico from one of implicit state support and complicity in company-sponsored subdivisions to one that has essentially frozen further expansion, and on recent occasions, has actually embargoed their land, can be explained both by Hank González' appointment as governor in 1970, by the scale of the settlements and their potential for political unrest. The numbers of people involved, the resources required to service them, and the intense social unrest that was moulded into a broad-based social movement in Netzahualcóyotl and Ecatepec, had turned the friendly Frankenstein, created by the companies and ignored by the authorities until the early 1970s, into a threat. Recent state intervention has demonstrated a determination that a similar situation should never again arise. At the same time, it is important to recognize that the provisions which terminated this era of company subdivisions were, on balance, favourable to those companies.

A growing technical awareness has also been a factor that has contributed towards the change of policy. An emergent interest in the planning of human settlements, the growth of policies aiming to legalize existing settlement and the early promotion of site-and-service type alternatives by agencies such as AURIS and INDECO were all, in part, a response to the emergence of self-help as an international conventional wisdom during the 1970s. López Portillo's administration took up many of these proposals. However, these ideas have been in existence for over a decade; their recent adoption in Mexico reflects state needs rather than a new-found technical appraisal of the problem.

Community participation significantly lowers servicing costs and allows the state to spread its limited resources more widely; legalizing land titles increases the amount of money that the poor can contribute to the city through land and valorization taxes, and payments for the installation of services.

Valencia

In contrast to Bogotá and Mexico City, invasions of land are the most common form of land acquisition in Valencia. Estimates vary, but approximately 45 per cent of the housing in the city is on land occupied initially through invasion (BANOP, 1970; CEU, 1977). In this respect, Valencia is not untypical of the rest of Venezuela which has experienced urban-land invasions in most cities under both military and democratic governments. While there have been periods of strong repression, as under Marcos Pérez Jiménez (1948–58), the land invasion has been the normal means by which the poor have obtained urban land in Venezuela.

The law in Venezuela certainly provides little explanation of this phenomenon. Indeed, the letter of the law is extremely favourable to the landowner *vis-à-vis* the invader. Pérez and Nikken (1982: 208) conclude that in the event of dispute over building on land belonging to someone else '. . . the landowner becomes the owner of the dwelling and does not have to compensate its builder'. However, as in the case of Bogotá, it is not how the law reads but how it is interpreted that is important. In Venezuela, 'official bodies take the side of the *barrio* inhabitants when they are in dispute with the presumed owners of the land on which they have built' (*ibid:* 224). In general, therefore, while the law does not permit the invasion of land, the authorities generally tolerate it. Certainly, in Valencia the whole of the south of the city has been occupied in one form or another by invasion (figure 6). This does not mean that there has been no repression; on numerous occasions during the past two decades squatter housing has been destroyed and people have even been killed. But, in most circumstances, large-scale invasions have been permitted and the authorities have later agreed to service the inhabitants. And, on those occasions when it has been necessary to remove established invasion settlements, the authorities have generally given compensation to the settlers for the destruction of their homes.[11]

An important factor encouraging this kind of interpretation of the law in Valencia has been the existence of a considerable area of community land; both the State of Carabobo and especially the municipality of Valencia own land. Both have suffered greatly from invasion: the State in the northwest of the city in the area of Naguanagua, the municipality in most of the south of the city. In addition, other land belonging to national agencies such as the National Sports Institute (IND) and the Electricity Authority (CADAFE) has been subject to invasion. Clearly, the reaction of the authorities in Valencia with respect to the occupation of government land is very different from that of the authorities in Bogotá or Mexico. But the difference in attitude does not apply only to public and community land. In 1968, it was estimated that between 40 and 45 per cent of invaded land belonged to private individuals and, in 1976, the 862.6 hectares of invaded private land probably represented a similar proportion (Lovera, 1978: 190). Most of the private land subject to invasion has been located close to that belonging to the municipality. Almost all private land invasions have occurred in the southwest of the city; while this land is not in any sense outside the commercial market, it is among the lowest value land in the city (Lovera, 1978). It repre- sents mainly fringe agricultural land located some five to ten kilometres away from the main city centre. Clearly, the authorities have not defended private land much more effectively than they have public or community land; there has been a tacit understanding with the invaders that a certain sector of the city is open to invasion.

In comparing Valencia with Bogotá and Mexico City another difference is apparent. We suggested that in the larger cities both renting and illegal subdivision reduced much of the pressure on the poor to invade land. Neither safety valve is present in Valencia. Whereas renting is common in the pirate urbanizations of Bogotá, it is prohibited in the *ranchos* of Valencia. Venezuelan law makes the renting of an unserviced dwelling illegal and the law is largely effective because of the shrewdness of its formulation; renters who denounce their landlords are entitled to take over the dwelling.[12] This means that renting is a risk for any landlord unless he has some expectation that the tenant will not denounce him. For this reason, the only renters we found in our household survey were either close friends of the landlord or illegal Colombian immigrants. The latter, of course, were unable to denounce the landlord without being deported. In this case, a *quid pro quo* existed between landlord and tenant; 'you denounce me for renting and I get you repatriated to Colombia'. Renting is common in the commercial and government housing sectors of Valencia, but overall renting levels are clearly lower than in Bogotá or in Mexico City (see table 13 p. 121). In addition, there is no direct equivalent to the illegal subdivisions of the other cities. Of course, this feature of Valencia may be either cause or effect; the presence of invasions may make illegal subdivision unnecessary or the lack of illegal subdivision may explain the proliferation of invasions. The former, however, would seem to be the most likely explanation if only because a form of illegal, commercial land market does exist in Valencia. This market develops once a land invasion has occurred and especially when it has been tacitly accepted by the authorities. Indeed, one of the recurrent complaints in council debates and from State governments about land invasions is that they have been organized for profit by professional invaders. To an extent, this view is correct for there is a rapid turnover of lots after an invasion. In the two settlements where we carried out our household survey, the people who had bought lots in the settlements once the invasion was a *fait accompli* far outnumbered the original invaders. Both settlements were founded by invasion around 1970, Nueva Valencia on private land and La Castrera on municipal land, and both contained large numbers of 'owners' who had purchased from the original invaders: 75 per cent and 57 per cent respectively. Not all of the invaders had left the settlement and many of the new occupants had been accommodated through the subdivision of invaded lots, but clearly many invaders had made some profit from the invasion. This profit was not large and we found few cases of the professional invader.[13] The main point at issue here is that the subdivision of invaded land meant that most occupants of invasion areas were not themselves invaders. They were more nearly the equivalents of those people in Bogotá who saved up and purchased a lot from a pirate urbanizer. To an extent, therefore, the groups involved in invading land in Valencia are performing the land-development role for low-income housing that the pirate urbanizer is performing in Bogotá.

One of the interesting features of the invasion areas in Valencia, therefore, is the relatively limited number of families who were involved in any kind of conflict with the authorities. The majority had either come into the settlement free, once the invasion had taken place, or had purchased their lot from an invader. The number of real invaders was limited and the leaders of invasions were often well known. As in Mexico and in certain Colombian cities where invasions have occurred, the occupation of land in Valencia required organization and most importantly a leader or group of leaders with experience. Ray (1969: 33–4) has argued that 'the outstanding credential of the leader (or leaders) is that he usually has the backing, either tacit or explicit, of one of the political parties that shares governing power in the city. He is not necessarily a member of such a party, but he must be closely affiliated with it. This link is essential because it protects the leader against official reprisal.' While correct, the point should not be overemphasized, for several invasions in Valencia have been successful even though they have lacked political contacts; around election time the authorities are generally reluctant to remove invaders whatever their political affiliation. Neither Nueva Valencia nor El Combate (another settlement in the south of the city) had political links or even strong leadership during their formation. While political links are clearly a major advantage to an invasion settlement, they are not indispensible. Settlements have been formed, have survived and eventually have been serviced without a political patron.

However, the link between partisan politics and invasions is undoubtedly present in Valencia. A major organizer of invasions in Valencia, Trino Medina, has had important political links throughout his career. In the invasions he organized near the bullring and which culminated in the occupation of land in La Castrera, he was said to have had a tacit agreement with the mayor. In the 1978–9 invasions, when he was an important cog in the COPEI party machine, his political links worked against him; the invasion of Brisas del Sur was several times repressed by the *Adeco* governor before it was eventually successful. It is also hardly coincidence that most invasions during the past fifteen years have occurred during the build-up to a national election. A strong wave of invasions was reported during the 1968 elections and again during the 1978–9 campaigns. During the 1973 campaign and between elections, invasions seem to have been very infrequent.[14]

To what extent the political parties actively stimulate land occupation is more difficult to assess. During the 1978–9 campaigns, there were several accusations against leading *Adeco* councillors. It was alleged that one council employee was dividing up municipal land near the bus terminal in the name of the mayoress and the opposition COPEI councillors demanded his resignation. The mayoress refused to dismiss the employee and 'offered him a new opportunity because he said that he acted in that way as he was dealing with people in great need' (*Gaceta Municipal*, 27 July 1979: 19). Few councillors would deny that both major parties, and previously the numerous minor parties active in Valencia, have deliberately encouraged land invasion. In addition, local politics have clearly affected the response of the council to invasion settlements. Where the invaded land is required for public works, the council normally offers the invaders land in another part of the city; one sector of the Monumental settlement was created in this way when invaders occupying the route of a proposed new major road were found alternative lots on *ejidal* land. Such invaders will also receive compensation for the destruction of their homes. Even where the council resolves to remove an invasion it may be unable to do so. Police action depends upon the decision of the state governor who may or may not find it congenial to remove invaders at the behest of the council; especially when the council is in the hands of another party. The control procedures of the council encounter further problems; the chairman of the Public Lands Commission declared that frequently he was unable to obtain a vehicle to visit lands under threat of invasion, an inference that the council did not control council workers affiliated to the opposition.

At times, of course, repression is applied against invaders – in the case of Brisas del Sur because the invasion was led by the opposition party and was countered by the party in power; in other cases because of the limited political leverage of the settlement. There are numerous cases of opposition to invasion in Valencia which have led to the destruction of *ranchos* and on occasion to the death of invaders. Fear of embarrassment can also motivate the council to adopt a firm attitude towards future land invasion. In 1971, fears that invaders would occupy the land where the 150th anniversary of the Battle of Carabobo was to be celebrated encouraged the council to pay the National Guard to patrol the grounds. But cases of severe repression and of careful control of municipal land are relatively rare; it is the exception rather than the rule.[15]

Perhaps the most consistent control on land invasion is the deliberate refusal of services to certain new invasion settlements. This policy has been applied to invasions on both public and private land, but has been much more firmly applied to the latter. Both the council and national government agencies have been stricter with settlements on private land. This is clearly demonstrated by the different experiences of our two case studies, Nueva Valencia, which was founded on private land, and La Castrera, founded on *ejidal* land. The former was refused water for nine years whereas the latter was supplied very soon after its foundation.

Clearly, however, this indirect control has not stopped the invasion of private land. In part, this is due to the expectation among the invaders that they will be serviced eventually. In Nueva Valencia, the provision of water came as a result of petitioning during the 1978 electoral campaign; the pipes were installed a few days before the national election. But, even though the authorities are much firmer with invasions on private land, it is interesting that these invasions are permitted at all. Certainly, in Latin America generally, such invasions are very much the exception; it is normally public or community land which is occupied. In Valencia, and in Venezuela as a whole, one answer may be that electoral politics are a more important consideration for the authorities than protecting the land belonging to important economic interests. But, it is also common for some arrangement to be reached between the principal landowners and the state. As Pérez and Nikken (1982: 214) have argued, despite the general policy of favouring the invader before the landowner '. . . favoured landowners regain their rights through expropriation in the public interest'. This may indeed be the reason why so few owners of land in southwest Valencia seem to have actively defended their land against invasion. Certainly, the late Luis Bigott mobilized the police and communicated with the governor and the minister for the interior when La Florida was invaded and brought in the police during the invasion of Nueva Valencia, but the land had not been extensively fenced off nor protected from invasion. Once the invasions had been established, the owner's efforts (and later that of his successors) were directed at the negotiation of a deal with the government in compensation. From the middle seventies, complicated deals began to be negotiated between the council and the Bigott company. One deal was to exchange council planning permission for the development of neighbouring land in return for the company's donating the invaded land to the municipality. At the national level, a way round this kind of difficulty was sought through a plan to purchase invaded private land from the owners and donate it to the country's municipal councils. In Valencia, in fact, no land was purchased although the preparations for such a purchase had been made. But, the possibility of such deals demonstrates that the relationship between the government and the individual landowner is critical in determining the terms of his compensation. At times, the landowner will suffer greatly through the loss of land; in certain circumstances he may receive more than the real value of the land (Lovera, 1978). Like so much in Venezuela, whether or not compensation is paid depends on the degree of political leverage. Without the right contacts at the right place and the right time compensation may not be granted; with the right contacts, suffering from land invasion may be good business.

In sum, therefore, Valencia's low-income population is housed on land belonging originally both to the government and to private owners. The limited repression is due in part to the low value of the land, in part to the electoral advantages to the party in power from permitting invasion, and in part to the compensation which the affluent Venezuelan state is able to give to invaders for their improvements (in the case of removal) or to the private landowner in the case of continued settlement. In any event, concerted action on the part of the state to remove invaders is unusual and few large-scale invasions in Valencia have been severely repressed for long periods. Private lands are better protected by the state than public land but the frequency of private-land invasions shows that this is a relatively ineffective deterrent. In general, it would appear that the balance of advantages to the politicians, to the local authorities and indeed often to private landowners in Valencia lies with invasion. The poor may not gain the best land, much of it may be relatively distant from work, but, unlike most of their Bogotá and Mexico City contemporaries, some poor people get free land. If only a minority of the poor actually invade land, the bulk of the urban poor benefit through relatively cheap land prices when they purchase lots in the newly invaded areas (see pp. 105–12).

Unlike Bogotá and Mexico City, the local authorities have not attempted to formally incorporate low-income housing land into the planning process. In Valencia, there has been discussion of ways to prevent invasion. The idea of reception areas was suggested in the early seventies and, more recently, Governor Gómez has written of plans to anticipate and prepare for low-income settlement (*El Carobobeño*, 1 September 1981), but no real action has materialized in either case. Petitions from settlements for servicing are referred to the Commission on Public Services but this does not represent anticipatory planning. Clearly, the pressure on the authorities to improve the allocation procedure has been insufficient; *ad hoc* reactions to invasion are clearly more congenial to the political and economic environment than a routine response. The fact that the opportunities to invade are not greater still is due to the limited capacity of even the Venezuelan authorities to compensate all landowners or to service all invasion settlements. If the rate of invasion were faster still, the sanctity of private property might be destroyed and servicing the settlements would prove to be an impossible task. In those circumstances one of the major principles of the Venezuelan state would be undermined; at the current rate of invasion, the process seems to function effectively. As a result there has been little pressure for change.

Comparative access to land

Our analysis so far has attempted to explain why different forms of land acquisition have evolved in each city. What we have not examined are the effects of these different land-acquisition systems on the housing situation of the poor. In terms of low-income housing it seems plausible to suggest that relatively easy access to land and/or low average costs of land acquisition relative to incomes would permit higher levels of ownership and faster rates of house consolidation. This section examines that proposition in our three cities. Specifically, we wish to test whether access to land is more difficult in certain cities than in others and whether land is becoming generally more difficult to acquire. We will explore also whether there is any broad relationship between tenure structures in each city and the price and availability of land.

Costs of land acquisition in each city

Using our own data as well as those of other studies we have examined whether the acquisition cost of land in each city varies in any consistent way. We have compared the prices of land in real terms and compared them to income. Table 6 contains estimates of the real cost of land in our survey *barrios* and the average for each city. The survey method has been described in appendix 1 but it is important to point out that, because of differences in forms of land acquisition in each city, the figures are not wholly comparable. Thus, land in invasion settlements, which may cost nothing, may offer the occupants little security of tenure and no possibility of servicing; more expensive lots in subdivisions may offer both security and servicing. The components of land costs also vary with the mode of acquisition. Obviously, the cost of land in illegal subdivisions is the market price of the land, but the cost of land acquisition in *ejidal* settlements in Mexico City is made

Table 6 Costs of land acquisition by city and settlement in 1978 US dollars

Settlement	Acquisition costs per sq m — Original owners (1) / (1a)	(1b)	Second owners (2)	Average monthly income of household head in survey (3)	Monthly minimum wage (4)	(4)÷(1) / (4)÷(1a)	(4)÷(1b)	(4)÷(2)	(3)÷(1) / (3)÷(1a)	(3)÷(1b)	(3)÷(2)
	(a)	(b)									
Bogotá	8.18		11.96	110.3	68.13	8.3		5.7	13.5		9.2
Atenas[1]	9.14		15.26	115.3	68.13	7.5		4.5	12.6		7.6
Britalia[2]	8.54		11.26	106.6	68.13	8.0		6.1	12.5		9.5
Casablanca[1]	6.30		13.96	117.3	68.13	10.8		4.9	18.6		8.4
Juan Pablo I[3]	6.76		*	86.9	68.13	10.1		*	12.9		*
San Antonio[1]	8.91		*	86.4	68.13	7.6		*	9.7		*
Mexico City											
Chalma[4]	4.98	2.91	6.9	216.0	145.4	29.2	50.0	20.9	43.4	74.2	31.0
El Sol[5]	*	*	6.09	229.2	145.4	*	*	23.9	*	*	37.6
Isidro	8.33	4.57	7.45	191.0	145.4	17.5	31.9	19.5	22.9	41.8	25.6
Fabela[6]	*	2.82	*	224.8	145.4	*	51.6	*	*	79.7	*
Jardines[7]	3.89	*	5.02	210.7	145.4	37.4	NA	29.0	54.2	*	42.0
Liberales[8]	NA	NA	NA	246.7	145.4	NA	NA	NA	NA	NA	NA
Santo Domingo[6]	*	2.62	*	212.9	145.4	*	55.5	*	*	81.3	*

(Note: columns under "Square metres bought by monthly wage" are (4)÷(1), (4)÷(2), (3)÷(1), (3)÷(2) for Bogotá, and (4)÷(1a), (4)÷(1b), (4)÷(2), (3)÷(1a), (3)÷(1b), (3)÷(2) for Mexico City.)

				(4)÷(1)	(4)÷(2)	(3)÷(1)	(3)÷(2)
Valencia	NA	3.50	420.9	139.5	NA	39.9	NA	120.3
La Castrera[9]	NA		444.0	139.5	NA	NA	NA	
Nueva Valencia[10]	NA		395.0	139.5	NA	NA	NA	

Source: settlement survey.

Notes on settlements:

1. Standard subdivisions with no special difficulties.
2. Subdivision intervened by Banking Superintendency and which faces difficulties over servicing.
3. Subdivision on land of doubtful ownership – no services provided as a consequence.
4. Subdivision and sale by *ejidatarios*.
5. Created by subdivision but most plots invaded or bought from original owner after 1973.
6. Invasion.
7. Subdivision in which plots were larger than usual, hence subsequent further subdivisions and sales.
8. Failed cooperative purchase where members invaded to retain their rights to buy the land.
9. Invasion of municipal land.
10. Invasion of private land.

Conversion to dollars: In November 1978 the average value of one US dollar was: 4.3 *bolívares*, 40.5 Colombian *pesos* or 22.8 Mexican *pesos*.

Notes on calculations:

1. In Bogotá original owners within subdivisions. In Mexico City:
   (a) bought from subdividers and payments include any further payments for regularization.
   (b) acquired through invasion and costs relate primarily to subsequent payments for regularization.
2. Purchases from original owner. In Mexico City may involve additional payment for regularization. In Mexico City the original owner may have purchased land from subdivider or may have invaded the land.
3. Regular income of household head excluding income of other family members and other incomes e.g. rent. Whole sample including renters' incomes of owner and renter household heads were in fact very similar.
4. Daily minimum wage in Bogotá January 1979 = 115 *pesos*
   Daily minimum wage in Mexico City January 1979 = 138 *pesos*
   Daily minimum wage in Valencia January 1979 = 25 *bolívares*

   *Less than five cases
   NA Not applicable

up of an initial payment to the *ejidatario* plus payments for regularization to the government. Notwithstanding these difficulties, table 6 gives a broad impression of the cost of land acquisition in each city. This is especially true of the data which report the prices paid by those people who bought from a third party (second owners), that is to say, those who bought-in after the establishment of the settlement.[16] The actual purchase prices were converted to 1978 prices using the respective consumer price index, and the average of the converted prices calculated in US dollars at the November 1978 exchange rate. This figure gives us an average of the prices paid through time in each settlement.[17] It clearly shows that the costs of land acquisition in Bogotá are relatively higher than those in Mexico or Valencia. For original owners in subdivisions, acquisition costs are almost twice as expensive as in Mexico City, and nearly three times more expensive when compared to the costs of acquisition in regularized invasion settlements. Land in Valencia for original owners is normally free. When comparing the costs of acquiring land in established settlements, the costs in Bogotá are again nearly double those in Mexico City, and three times those in Valencia.

We have also compared these acquisition costs with two measures of income. First, we have compared average acquisition costs with the incomes of household heads (owners), excluding income from rent and the contributions of other members of the household. This is justifiable in the sense that when most families purchase accommodation they do not have grown-up children contributing to the family budget. It is only when children have grown up that they contribute.[18] It is also justified in the sense that only a minority of families in three cities have more than one earner: in Bogotá 14.5 per cent, in Mexico City 23.7 per cent and in Valencia 12.9 per cent. Second, we compared these costs with the legal minimum city wage, a procedure most relevant in Bogotá and Mexico City, where large numbers of workers earn this minimum, and least relevant in Valencia where the minimum has not been increased in recent years and is exceeded greatly by most workers.[19] While this will exaggerate the difficulty of obtaining land in Valencia, it provides a measure of income independent of our survey data.

Table 6 shows that acquisition costs relative to income were many times higher in Bogotá than in Mexico City and higher still when compared to Valencia. Comparing acquisition costs to average incomes of household heads, more than three times as much land in subdivisions could be acquired per monthly income in Mexico City than in Bogotá. If the comparison is made between original owners in Bogotá and those households in Mexico acquiring land through invasion and later regularization, the difference is of the order of eight times. When the cost of land is compared to minimum wage levels, land in Bogotá appears still more expensive than previously when compared to Mexico City. Comparing costs to second owners in the three cities, it is again apparent that costs relative to income are much higher in Bogotá than in the other cities. For this group of inhabitants, three times as much land per monthly wage can be acquired in Mexico City as in Bogotá, and thirteen times more in Valencia than in Bogotá. When minimum wages are considered, the relative differences are nearly four times in Mexico City and seven times in Valencia.

In order to check these calculations we have used another way of estimating the percentage of the monthly household wage of our sample required to buy one square metre of land. This calculation takes lot prices as given and deflates current incomes to past values at the time of purchase. It assumes, therefore, that current incomes have changed little through time. This assumption is justifiable in Bogotá, for recent studies have shown that life-cycle income profiles are very flat, that is to say, workers earn more-or-less the same income irrespective of age (Mohan and Hartline, 1979). While there is also some sign that real wages for manufacturing workers declined in Bogotá from 1970 to 1977 and rose in 1978 and 1979, the fluctuation was never more than 16 per cent.[20] If the other cities are similar to Bogotá in these respects, and we lack data to demonstrate it, this procedure is not unreliable when combined with our other methods. The data support the earlier analysis very closely; land is more expensive in Bogotá than in Mexico or Valencia. Table 7 shows that, for all owners, land is much more expensive relative to monthly incomes in Bogotá than in Mexico, and more expensive in Mexico City than in Valencia. When the cost of acquisition in subdivisions is considered, the price is three times greater than in Mexico City. With respect to second owners, a pattern emerges almost identical with that for all owners. It is possible that our survey is biased in its selection of settlements so that we have an unrepresentative picture of average acquisition costs in low-income settlements. For this reason we have compared our data with those presented by other studies. These have also been converted to 1978 prices and then into dollars. The general picture conveyed by table 8 seems to support our own data except in

Table 7 *Land acquisition costs relative to incomes*

	Percentage of deflated monthly wages required to buy one square metre of land		Percentage of current monthly wages required to buy one square metre of land	
	Percentage	Sample	Percentage	Sample
All owners				
Bogotá	8.17	159	10.44	159
Mexico City	3.89	206	3.07	234
Valencia	1.04	77	0.94	79
Subdivisions – original owners				
Bogotá	7.92	148	10.04	148
Mexico City	5.92	40	3.44	53
Valencia	NA	NA	NA	NA
Invasions – original owners				
Bogotá	NA	NA	NA	NA
Mexico City	2.13	114	1.79	125
Valencia	0.00	55	0.00	55
Purchase from third party with or without shack*				
Bogotá	9.48	35	12.34	35
Mexico City	6.78	51	5.67	55
Valencia	1.14	70	1.03	72

Source: sample survey.
*In Valencia purchases from third parties are explicitly for the 'improvement' (*bienhechuría*) not for the land, although since such 'improvements' are normally rudimentary the implicit reason for purchase is to buy the land. In Bogotá and Valencia purchases are normally made either of vacant land or of an incomplete or complete house; the latter cases have been excluded from the calculations.

the case of subdivisions in Mexico where our data seem to have underestimated the cost of acquisition. This is because the two sampled subdivisions were somewhat atypical. El Sol contained cheap land because its isolation made lots difficult to sell; Jardines was sold in large lots ostensibly for agricultural use. It is also probable, however, that the costs of land calculated by the other studies are overestimated; most of these studies were attempting to show the high profits made by subdivisions and are likely to have selected from among the more

Table 8 *Costs of land by city according to other studies*
(1978 US dollars per square metre)

	Original owners		Sample	Range
Bogotá				
Our data	8.18		136	6.30–9.14
Carroll (Inside urban perimeter)[1]	9.46		11,540	NA
Losada and Gómez[2]	6.71		98	3.92–10.03
Peralta and Vergara[3]	19.02		99	15.43–22.37
	(a)	(b)		
	Subdivisions	Invasions		
Mexico City				
Our data	4.98	—	60	3.9–8.3
	—	2.91	145	2.6–4.6
FIDEURBE: Ajusco[4]	—	3.5	—	—
FIDEURBE: Padierna[5]	—	7.6	—	4.6–7.6
Sudra[6]	5.4	—	—	0–7.8
Sudra[7]	22.0	—	—	—
Guerrero *et al.*[8]	19.9	—	—	—
Martín de la Rosa[9]	23.2	—	—	15.5–31.0
Ward[10]	23.0	—	—	—
Schteingart[11]	13.2	—	—	11.0–17.6

Notes:

1. Carroll (1980) calculated average lot prices in 1976 prices for pirate *barrios* as 253 inside perimeter and 109 outside. We have raised these prices to 1978 values.
2. Losada and Gómez (1976: 104) calculated the average purchase price in five *barrios* at 152.73 *pesos* in 1975 prices.
3. Prices in the *barrio* of El Saucedal September 1976 to December 1979 from Peralta and Vergara (1981: table 15).
4. FIDEURBE (1976: 48–51). Amount is that charged for regularization. Most families (55%) acquired their plots free of charge or by small payment to leaders, López (1978: 22).
5. FIDEURBE (1976: 73). Cost of regularization but this would be reduced by 60% for low-income families (to 4.56 US dollars).
6. Sudra (1976: 196 and 352) for purchase into an *ejidal* subdivision. In addition the equivalent of a further 1.5 US dollar/m^2 was charged for regularization in 1971.
7. Sudra (1976: 352) notes that for low-cost subdivision 22 dollars/m^2 was the minimum for a partially serviced plot with legal tenure. For a plot in a 'remote location with very poor and difficult to improve environmental conditions' the cost would be 13.2 dollars.
9. Guerrero *et al.* (1974: 25). Company subdivision in Ecatepec (see also COPEVI, 1976: F90–F91).
9. Martín de la Rosa (1974: 8). Company subdivision in Netzahualcóyotl. Range notes different settlements.
10. Ward (1976a: 85). Field notes in 1973.
11. Schteingart (n.d. mimeo: 20). Data refers to Colonia Azul, a subdivision in Netzahualcóyotl.

expensive subdivisions. Few of these other studies were based on rigorous sampling designs.

The high costs in Bogotá reflect the greater security and legality of the process of land acquisition in that city. They also reflect the fact that commercial prices are charged for this land. In Mexico, the variety of modes of acquisition offer some families cheap land. Invasions are cheap, but at the cost of insecurity of tenure; more secure land sold in subdivisions appears to vary in price according to its physical quality and its location. Thus, land costs in Mexico appear to vary much more than in Bogotá; secure, well-located subdivisions appear to be more expensive but cheap land is available in poorly located subdivisions and in less secure invasions. In Valencia, few costs are involved in invading land but security depends upon the nature of the land invaded; private land is insecure and is not serviced quickly, public land is often secure and open to servicing. Clearly, the acquisition costs of land reflect these differences in availability and security. In addition, the costs of acquisition vary relative to average incomes. The high cost/income ratios in Bogotá reflect the lower income levels characteristic of that city and the low ratios in Valencia are also an outcome of the higher income levels in the Venezuelan city. The different costs are also reflected in resale prices. It is clear that original owners recoup their original outlays when selling their lot; resale prices in our settlements in Bogotá are much higher than in the other two cities.

In summary, land is cheap in Valencia and expensive in Bogotá. In Mexico City, prices vary dramatically according to the mode of acquisition and the characteristics of the subdivision. Invasions are clearly the cheapest form of land access but the price discount is due to the higher level of insecurity of tenure.

The changing price of land

In Bogotá, the poor gain access to land only through purchase in subdivisions. In Mexico, it has become increasingly difficult to invade land, and hence most households are required to purchase lots in subdivisions or on *ejidal* land. Even in Valencia, we have seen that the majority of low-income dwellers have purchased land after the invasion settlement has become established. For this reason, it seems critical to examine trends in acquisition costs through time. It would seem plausible that an increasing dependence upon the commercial market would lead to higher prices. Certainly, the literature on the

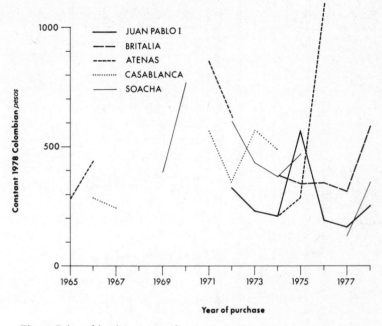

Fig. 8 Price of land in survey *barrios* in Bogotá by year of purchase
Note: years with less than one transaction are omitted

land market in other Third World cities has strongly suggested that such a trend is typical (Amis, 1981; Baross, 1983; Evers, 1977). Unfortunately, there is very little reliable information on this issue for our three cities. Our own data are inadequate to measure price trends because they record values in specific settlements that are not comparable in their locations. Our data are additionally susceptible to the problem of small sample size.[21] What they show in Bogotá is that in individual settlements lot prices tend to remain constant for the initial two or three years and then fall (figure 8). Although the fall may be due to sales of less desirable lots once the settlement has been established, the data do not support the idea of rapid price rises. It must be repeated, however, that these data are not totally reliable. As such, we have tried to supplement this information with more general city-wide data where this has been available.

By far the most reliable data are for Bogotá and come from the World Bank City Project (Villamizar, 1980; Carroll, 1980). Villamizar

Table 9 Evolution of real land prices by rings and radial sector in Bogotá

Ring	Centre					Perimeter
	1	2	3	4	5	6
Annual increase (1955–78)	−2.5	−1.1	0.3	2.0	6.6	9.5

Radial sector	Location and kind of housing	1955–77	1966/8–1969/71	1969/71–1972/4	1972/4–1975/7	1966/8–1975/7
		2	3	4	5	6
I	Centre	−2.5	3.2	−1.8	−7.3	−2.1
II	South – poor	4.5	6.7	2.2	0.7	3.2
III	Southwest – poor	6.8	−2.4	3.2	−0.7	0.8
IV	West – poor	0.8	−12.5	2.1	−0.3	−1.8
V	West – poor and middle income	1.1	0.7	1.3	5.9	2.6
VI	WNW – middle income	4.7	15.3	4.8	−0.6	6.3
VII	Northwest – poor, middle & high income	4.0	0.7	12.0	−1.5	3.6
VIII	North – poor, middle & high income	2.5	6.8	3.2	2.4	4.1
	North – high income	2.7	2.3	3.4	−0.2	2.1
	Unweighted average increase					
	Weighted increase	4.0				

Source: our calculations from Villamizar (1980: table 3).

analysed data provided by a Bogotá estate agent for the period 1955–78. The data show that in real terms land prices in the city increased by 4 per cent per annum between 1955 and 1978. Clearly, rates of increase varied greatly between areas of the city, with certain zones declining in real terms and others increasing. Table 9 shows the main pattern, whereby it is clear that the other rings of the city have experienced the fastest rates of change, and the inner city areas, including the city centre, have seen a decline. When the data are analysed by radial sector, however, it is not the high-income zone 8 that shows the fastest rates of expansion, but several of the areas which contain the majority of the poor, zones 2, 3, 4 and 7. In fact, this finding is substantially affected by the time period. For the period since 1965 our recalculations of his figures suggest that it is zone 8 and even more zone 6 (generally middle-income housing) that have experienced rapid price rises. It is clear, however, that the areas where most poor people live have experienced generally upward trends in land prices. Zones 2, 3 and 7, although not zone 4, have all experienced rapid price increases interspersed by periods of decline. However, the rates of increase for the 1966–77 period have generally been lower than those for the higher-income zones 6 and 8.

When we look at Villamizar's more detailed data for zones which include our sample *barrios*, then the evidence is more variable. The zone which includes Atenas has seen a consistent increase in land prices between 1968–70 and 1977–8 at an annual rate of 6.3 per cent; the zone which includes Casablanca the slightest decline in a price after a rapid rise to 1974–6 and a still more rapid decline; and in Britalia a small annual increase of 1.2 per cent. All this suggests, in combination with our own data, that the costs of land acquisition for the poor have been increasing in real terms but less rapidly than for higher-income areas.

A similar conclusion is drawn by CENAC (1980) which estimates that prices have increased in the whole city by 14.5 per cent per annum between 1971 and 1980. According to the disaggregated data, however, most of the very highest rates of increase came in the high-income zones. Nevertheless, in the west, southwest and southeast, popular zone land increased by 18 per cent annually between 1972 and 1980.

These data should not be interpreted to mean that poor people are necessarily paying more in low-income subdivisions. Both Villamizar and CENAC have used sources which record only formal-sector sales.

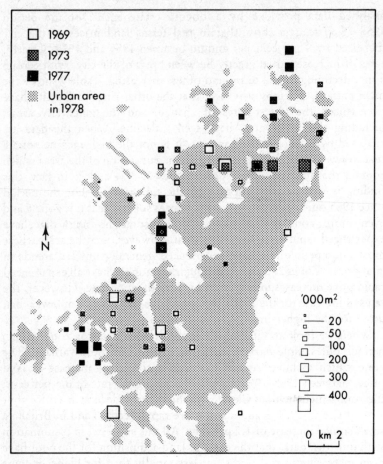

Fig. 9 Residential construction permits in Bogotá, 1969, 1973 and 1977

Their data is certainly compatible with the trends in housing construction in the city where the large construction companies have increasingly sought land in lower-status areas. Increasingly, middle-income housing has been built in what was formally low-income residential areas. This is demonstrated in figure 9 which shows how formal sector construction has gradually moved into what were previously considered to be undesirable areas for middle-income housing.[22]

However, another part of the World Bank study suggests that

land-price trends are indeed having a detrimental effect upon the poor. Unlike Villamizar's data, which come from a record of legal sales made by an estate agent, Carroll (1980) had access to data drawn from the records of pirate urbanizers.[23] Required to respond to a questionnaire circulated to urbanizers by the Banking Superintendency he has data on virtually all subdivision sales between 1967 and 1977. According to these data his figures show a doubling of real prices for illegal subdivisions in the four years from 1974 – an annual rate of 18.9 per cent, which is roughly comparable with Borrero's formal-sector sales data. However, the trend between 1960 and 1974 was much lower than that: real prices increased by just over one-third in the fifteen years (Carroll, 1980: 44). It is possible that the recent shortage of land zoned for low-income groups has pushed up prices artificially since 1974.

The general pattern in Bogotá, therefore, seems to be that land prices on the urban fringe are rising rapidly for all income groups. Land prices are rising much less rapidly in other parts of the city and in some places, including our settlements, land prices are actually falling. This is true both in the city centre and in certain low-income areas. It is also clear that particular areas have gone through dramatic fluctuations in land prices as they have passed through a speculative building cycle. For this reason, although the situation for all groups buying land in Bogotá appears difficult, we must interpret the situation with considerable care. Nevertheless, it is clear that the price of land for new purchasers of land in subdivisions is rising. And, although we have no systematic data to support it, we would be very surprised if trends during the seventies in Mexico City and Valencia were not very similar.

The effects of changing acquisition costs

This general pattern of findings is supported by our data on changing lot sizes through time. Our hypothesis is that in a high-price situation those low-income families that can still purchase land at all will tend to purchase smaller plots. We can check this hypothesis in two ways from our survey data. First, if we compare lot size in our survey settlements between cities then we should observe that where land is most expensive lot size will be smallest. Second, if we compare lot size in our settlements for each city through time we should observe a decline in the size of new lots.

Table 10 supports our first proposition. Average lot size does seem

Table 10 *Average size of lot for owners in Bogotá, Mexico City and*
Valencia

	Bogotá	Mexico City	Valencia
Average lot size (m^2)	137.2	233.5	451.7
–1969	156.7	310.7	531.4
1970–1974	128.5	241.8	431.8
1975–1979	131.3	180.5	456.9
Sample size	219	366	106
Lot density (m^2/person)			
mean	22.6	33.7	72.4
median	19.5	25.0	50.8

Source: sample survey

to be sensitive to price when compared across the three cities. The
higher prices of land in Bogotá have resulted in smaller lot sizes, the
very cheap land available in Valencia has produced very large lot sizes.
Mexico City, with its variable forms of acquisition, has medium-sized
lots but with considerable variation between certain settlements. The
limited data from other surveys generally support the finding (table
11). Lot sizes seem generally smaller in Bogotá than in Mexico City.

Table 10 also provides some support for the second hypothesis. Lot
sizes in Mexico City have fallen dramatically during the three sub-
periods depicted. In Bogotá, after an initial decline between the first
pair of sub-periods, lot size remained steady. In Valencia, lot size fell
during the first pair of sub-periods but then rose slightly between the
latter pair. The Carroll (1980) data presented in table 10 also support
this idea.

The corollary of these data on lot size is that lot densities are higher
in Bogotá than in Mexico City, and lowest in Valencia. When the
median figures are considered, lot densities in Valencia appear to be
half those of Mexico City, while Bogotá is one quarter greater than
Mexico City (table 10).

The effects of differential land access on tenure patterns

Our tentative conclusion is that during most of the sixties and seventies
land was most accessible in Valencia and least accessible in Bogotá,
where only those who could afford to purchase lots managed to

Table 11 *Lot size according to other studies (square metres)*

Bogotá	
Losada and Gómez (1976)	154.2[1]
Carroll (1980) in 1972	180.0[2]
Carroll (1980) in 1977	105.0[2]
Peralta and Vergara (1980)	72.0[3]
Mexico City	
Sudra (1976)	201.0[4]
López (1978)	500.0[5]
COPEVI (1976)	120.0[6]
Bazant *et al.* (1978)	220.0[7]

Notes:
1. Based on five *barrios* surveyed in 1975.
2. Based on a large sample for both years.
3. Based on the flooded *barrios* of Patio Bonito; some lots were as large as 131.4 m².
4. Mean lot size of owner households in five low-income settlements interviewed by Sudra in 1975. The range was from 100 to 300 m².
5. The usual lot size in the Ajusco settlement was 500 m², but almost half of the residents had further divided the lots so that the real average is much smaller.
6. The San Agustín *fraccionamiento*.
7. Two settlements, San Agustín and Colonia Auorora in Netzahualcóyotl.

acquire land. In Mexico, the variety of modes of land acquisition makes generalization more difficult: for some families successful invasion offered cheap land; for those purchasing in poorly located subdivisions land was also cheap; but for those purchasing in well-located subdivisions costs could be high. These differences between cities ought to have had some effect on the patterns of ownership, renting and sharing in the three cities. As a broad hypothesis we would expect that the highest ownership levels would be found in Valencia, where land is cheap, and the lowest levels in Bogotá where land is expensive. Of course, this is only one possible response. As we have just seen, smaller lot sizes may be acceptable to prospective buyers, so that the same proportions of people own homes but the land occupied by those homes is smaller. This is certainly the finding of Mohan and Villamizar (1980) who find that low-income populations in Bogotá are living at increasingly high densities. Clearly, too, other variables will enter into the land price/ownership relationship, the costs of building materials, governmental encouragement to home ownership, ideology and aspirations. But, in essentially similar kinds of society, it seems to

Table 12 *Tenure structure by city, 1978*
(percentages)

	Owners	Renters	Sharers	Others	Sample size
Bogotá	62.2	36.4	0.8	0.6	360
Mexico City	71.3	12.7	13.3	2.7	631
Valencia	94.9	4.5	0.0	0.6	178

Source: sample survey.

us a not unreasonable basic hypothesis that fewer households, and especially fewer low-income households, will be able to own property as land prices rise.

In general terms, it also seems to be supported by our *barrio* data. Table 12 shows that more people owned homes in Valencia than in Mexico, where more people owned homes than in Bogotá. Of course, the data are not to be generalized across all of the cities because the survey did not cover higher-income residential areas. Nevertheless, the patterns find some support at the city level in the limited amount of census and household-survey data available. In 1970, the only year for which direct comparisons are possible, the proportion of owned dwellings was the highest in Valencia where access to land was easiest. Marginally fewer dwellings were owned in Mexico City than in Bogotá, but it is interesting to consider the dramatic increase in home ownership which took place in the sixties. Relatively cheap access costs allowed large numbers of low-income people to buy the land becoming available in the municipalities outside the Federal District. In fact, there seems to be a general trend in all three cities during the sixties towards higher proportions of the population owning property. Our previous evidence on land prices, however, would suggest that the phase of expansion in home ownership is now past and that, despite smaller lot size, there will soon be an increase in rental and shared accommodation. This is especially likely in Mexico City where the late seventies saw the closing off of invasion and subdivision options. The subdivision of *ejidal* land or legal purchase by cooperatives now seems the only real possibility open to the poor in Mexico City, with a consequent upward effect on access costs. Similarly, in Bogotá Carroll's figures on the prices of land in illegal subdivisions suggest that renting levels in the city will increase, even though some families may buy cheap lots in municipalities beyond the Special District.

Table 13 *Percentage of dwellings owned and rented by city*

	Percentage owned			Percentage rented		
Date	Bogotá	Mexico City	Valencia	Bogotá	Mexico City	Valencia
1960		19.8				
1964	46.4			47.0		
1970	44.9	41.6	68.9	51.7		29.4
1971						18.8
1977				43.4		

Notes:
Bogotá: 1964 DANE Population Census, Bogotá volume, p. 124.
   1970 DANE *Encuesta de hogares*, p. 115.
   1977 DANE *Boletín Mensual de Estadística*, 328, November 1978.
Mexico City: 1960 Census includes Federal District and the municipalities of Naucalpan de Juárez and Tlalnepantla.
   1970 Census includes Federal District and the municipalities of Atízapan
   de Zaragoza, Ixtapaluca, Naucalpan de Juárez, Netzahualcóyotl, La Paz, and Tlalnepantla.
Valencia: 1970 Banco Obrero (1970) *Estudio sobre la situación del problema de la
   vivienda en las areas urbanas: segunda parte. Estudio por
   ciudades Tomo 11 Valencia.*
   1971 Dirección (1977) *X Censo de población y vivienda*, Vol. VIII, part F.,
   Tables 5 and 6.

Renters and sharers: survival strategy for the poorest?

It is clear from tables 13 and 14 that the rental population constitutes an important element in the low-income populations of the three cities and a significant proportion of the population in the *barrios* of Bogotá and Mexico City. In addition, sharers are an important component in the population of the Mexican settlements. Who are these renters and sharers? Two initial hypotheses may be ventured. The first is that the renters tend to be among the poorer and more disadvantaged members of the urban community. Such an outcome would result from a bidding process for accommodation whereby the better-off own their houses and the poor are unable to participate in self-help construction. This would occur insofar as 'each form of housing has a different range of prices set by the market, so that the alternatives available to individual households are determined by their level of income' (Edwards, 1982a: 131). This is a very common argument in the literature on tenure in developed countries which shows that incomes of rental

Table 14 *Economic and social variables by city and by tenure*

| | Bogotá | | | | Mexico City | | |
	Total	Owners	Renters	Total	Owners	Renters	Sharers
Head's monthly income[1]	45.3	46.4	42.9	49.2	49.4	46.8	50.5
Other sources of income[1]	13.7	13.8	11.8	17.9	19.6	13.5	11.9
Income of other earners[1]	44.7	47.7	35.3	55.3	57.7	45.5	45.6
Families with no other income (%)	83.3	76.3	95.1	86.8	85.5	87.1	93.8
One active worker in household (%)	58.0	54.4	64.8	65.8	63.3	78.2	64.2
Two active workers in household (%)	23.8	23.2	25.4	21.4	24.1	13.9	16.0
Age of household head	38.6	42.0	32.7	39.2	41.9	34.4	30.5
Persons in household	5.5	5.8	5.0	5.8	6.2	5.2	4.5
Head's employment – independent (%)	22.0	25.6	15.8	19.4	22.1	9.0	17.9
Head's employment – manual (%)	54.5	52.1	59.2	64.5	64.2	66.0	64.1

Source: sample survey.
Note:
1. In hundreds of local *pesos.*

122

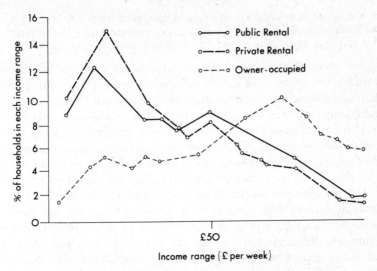

Fig. 10 Tenure distribution by income group, UK, 1976
(*Source:* Bourne (1980): Fig. 3.10)

households are generally lower than those for home owners (figure 10). It is also an increasingly common argument in the limited amount of work on renting in less-developed countries (Van der Linden *et al.*, 1982; Amis, 1981).

A second hypothesis is that rather than being forced to rent or share accommodation, many families effectively choose these options. They may choose to rent or share on grounds of preference, their lack of responsibilities, a wish to live in areas where ownership is difficult, the need to invest savings in a business, desire to spend money on goods other than housing, because of their family characteristics, and so on. Such a hypothesis is inherent in the Turner (1968) explanation of housing tenure whereby 'bridgeheaders' occupy rental accommodation and 'consolidators' occupy peripheral self-help accommodation. It is clearly spelt out by Hamer (1981: 68–9) for those he calls guests.[24]

Shared housing plays an important role in cities such as Bogotá, insofar as it gives access to housing for families whose age, income, size and degree of residential mobility suggest that, on average, they are in an early stage of their housing cycle, when flexibility counts most. This is due to a combination of undefined preferences with respect to future employment and residential location, of relative inexperience of the functioning of urban markets, and of limited resources that make it very difficult to acquire assets . . . 'As the guest family units get older, accumulate savings and increase in size, the attractions of acquiring a home increase and they tend to become owners. (p. 80)[25]

One method of testing between hypotheses one and two is to consider the incomes of owner occupiers compared to renting and sharing families. Under hypothesis one rental and sharing families should have lower incomes than owners. They would be forced to rent or share accommodation if free land was unavailable owing to a prohibition on squatting. If there was no significant difference between the families in terms of their family characteristics, constraint more than choice was the principal factor in their tenure selection.

According to the second hypothesis, however, the key difference between owners and sharers or renters is not income but family characteristics. According to this hypothesis there should be no significant difference between the incomes of owners and those of renters or sharers but there would be other significant differences in terms of other characteristics, for example, age, family structure or form of employment. Of course, there are other possible explanations but we will examine the available data with respect to these two hypotheses before moving on to somewhat more complex possibilities.

Our data for Bogotá and Mexico City suggest that *prima facie* there is little difference in the income levels of renters, sharers and owners (table 14). The incomes of heads of household are almost identical among owners, sharers and renters in both Bogotá and in Mexico City. When total household income is measured, however, there is considerable difference. This finding is substantiated by census data for the city of Bogotá as a whole, where renters' median incomes are lower than those of owners (figure 11), and by Hamer (1981) and Peralta and Vergara (1980). The principal reason for this difference is the additional sources of income received by owner families. There is some variation, for example, in other sources of income with owners receiving over one quarter more than renters or sharers in Mexico City, although in Bogotá the difference is negligible. A further source of difference between owners and the other families is that certain owners receive income from rent, although this should not be exaggerated for in Bogotá only 18 per cent of owning households had income from this source. The most important difference in terms of income is found in the monies coming from other members of the family. It is clear in both Bogotá and Mexico City that owners receive more from their families than do renters or sharers.

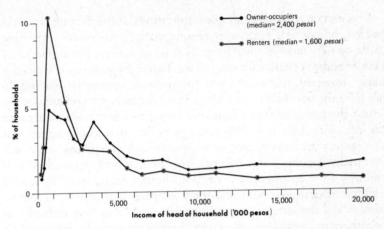

Fig. 11 Tenure distribution by income group, Bogotá, 1973
(*Source:* DANE (1977): *La vivienda en Colombia*, Bogotá)

The reason for this difference in income is that owners have more grown-up children than renters or sharers. In Mexico City, 78 per cent of renting families had only one earner compared to 63 per cent of owning families. In Bogotá, 54 per cent of owning families had only one earner compared to 65 per cent among renters. In fact, the principal difference between the three groups seems to depend upon family characteristics. Table 14 shows that rental and sharing households were younger and smaller than those of owners. On average the renters in Mexico City are 7.5 years younger than the owners, sharers 11.4 years younger; in Bogotá renters are 9.3 years younger than owners.[26] This age factor is linked to the smaller size of renting and sharing families: owning households in both cities had around 6 members, renting households 5 and, in Mexico, sharers 4.5.[27] The renting households also had more young children.

Age is also important for a number of other reasons. Renters are more likely to have arrived in the city later than owners, more renters are single, more owners are covered by social-security arrangements, and few renting families are living in extended or compound families. This difference in age structure between owners and renters was also found in the World Bank Study of Bogotá (Hamer, 1981) and by Edwards' (1982b) analysis of renters in Bucaramanga. The difference between owners and renters or sharers seems, therefore, to be primarily one of age.

Less certain, however, are the implications of this finding. It could be that the younger renters are renting through preference, expecting to be owners later in their lives. This is, of course, the argument of Hamer and of certain followers of the Turner hypothesis. It is equally likely, however, that renters and sharers would prefer to own but do not have the possibility of owning. There might be two reasons for the latter: the lower household income owing to fewer wage earners, or the increasing difficulty of obtaining plots. The first would suggest that the renters are saving money to purchase lots and that they will eventually become home owners. This process will be eased as their children grow up and contribute to the household budget. The second hypothesis is more pessimistic for it suggests that lots are becoming scarcer and that some or many of the tenants will have difficulty in becoming owners. The competing hypotheses could be examined by comparing the age at which household heads ceased to be renters or sharers and became owners. If today this tenure transition comes at an older age than previously then we could reliably conclude that tenure is determined more by constraint than choice. If the age difference is insignificant, or people are younger than previously, we might conclude that access is no more difficult and is perhaps becoming easier.[28]

A further possibility is that there are major differences between the roomers (households which rent one room) and more affluent tenants which masks the real differences among those forced to rent and those who choose to rent. For example, Edwards (1982a, 1982b) argues that there is an essential difference between households renting one room and those occupying apartments. Whereas the first can be clearly distinguished from owners, the latter have incomes equal to or often higher than those of owners. The important difference is not between owning families and renters but between owners and roomers. Of course, this division between roomers and apartment tenants is only one of a possible range of forms of heterogeneity. If affluent owners were separated from poor owners, for example, it could be that the income differences between owners and renters would be further diminished.

At first sight, however, there seems no reason to conclude that the renters are the down-and-out, the very poor and the most 'marginal'. Employment structures, income levels of households heads and general background appear to be very similar for both owners and renters. Renters and sharers do not have most of the old, sick and infirm. It is merely their youth and consequent differences in their position in the family and work cycle which explain the variations between owners and renters. This is not, however, sufficient reason to be optimistic as Hamer. For if, as we suspect, land prices are rising rapidly, young renters today face a much more difficult task in becoming owners than did their parents. The easy transition from renter to owner, from bridgeheader to consolidator, may well be a phenomenon of the past.

Conclusion

The poor acquire land principally through illegal processes but the form of this illegality varies considerably between settlements, and between cities. In Valencia, low-income settlements are developed primarily through invasions of public and private land, with many poor people buying into settlements at a later stage. In Bogotá, invasions are rare and the principal mechanism for obtaining land is the so-called pirate urbanization; these illegal subdivisions have provided the land on which half of the housing in Bogotá has developed. In Mexico City, the situation is more complex both because policy has changed over time and because the urban area includes two distinct administrative areas: the Federal District and the State of Mexico. Broadly, however, the most typical form of low-income settlement formation has been the illegal subdivision. Invasions were common for short periods within the Federal District but increasingly as the city has expanded the most common form of land acquisition has become the subdivision of *ejidal* lands. Despite the illegality of all these processes the state is integrally involved in monitoring and at times distributing this land. Such covert state action is essential to maintain political stability in a socio-economic environment where the poor are clearly limited beneficiaries of economic growth. Land allocation is an integral part of the political process; land invasions in Valencia occur more frequently close to election time, while the regularization of land in Bogotá and Mexico City becomes easier at moments of political stress. Illegal processes of land acquisition also have benefits for the process of economic growth, provided that the poor occupy only low-value land. Cheap, self-help housing reduces the pressure on the existing housing stock, limits social conflict and cuts the cost of labour to the 'formal sector'. Both invasions and illegal subdivisions are channelled in directions which do not directly threaten the residential areas of elite groups and which indirectly bring considerable benefits to the latter, notably in the form of cheap labour and services.

The process of land allocation is clearly part and parcel of the urban economy and the political system. Despite its illegality, land allocation constitutes an important element in the urban land market. In Bogotá and Mexico City, most lots are purchased and, as in the rest of the urban area, the price is determined by the market. There is considerable turnover of lots and houses in low-income settlements as people move into and out of consolidating settlements. Prices are determined by location, levels of consolidation and servicing and by the reputation of the settlement. The illegality of the settlement reduces the price of land but, as most settlers anticipate that regularization of tenure and servicing will eventually be achieved, most illegal settlements survive. In Valencia, despite the formation of settlements through invasion, land purchase is the norm for most settlers. The fact that most of these settlements continue to be irregular or illegal provides a lever which the state can use at difficult moments to ensure the compliance of specific settlements.

It is clear that the variations between the cities in the way that the poor gain access to land have substantial effects on the housing market. In general, it appears easier to obtain land in Valencia than in Bogotá or Mexico City. For our settlements the evidence is clear that the cost of land relative to income is very low in Valencia and high in Bogotá. In Mexico City access costs are highly variable, some poor people gain access to land relatively cheaply, others must pay a high price. It also seems as if access to land, at least in Bogotá and Mexico City, may be becoming more difficult. Although our own data do not provide a good basis for calculating price trends, certain other studies show that land prices are rising in real terms. In general, this trend affects the poor as well as the rich. The implication is that, as prices rise while real incomes remain stable or rise slowly, access to land for the poor becomes more difficult. Ideally, policy makers should attempt to address this issue.

The effects of differential and changing access costs seem to be as follows. First, lot sizes appear to be falling in the two largest cities. Given higher prices of land relative to income, poor families can acquire only smaller lots. This may be advantageous to planners in reducing the costs of transport and infrastructure; it is not a trend, however, that is welcome to most poor people. Second, it would seem that where access costs arise the proportion of households that can afford to purchase land must diminish. As a result, more households will share or rent accommodation. At the moment, there is no clear trend in our three cities in this direction. It seems that families are occupying smaller lots. But there is obviously a limit to falling lot sizes. If land prices, and indeed material costs, continue to rise the result will eventually be much higher proportions of renters and sharers.

In general, we would expect most poor people to disapprove of this trend. Self-help housing is a viable alternative in the sense that it is a difficult but possible route by which poor families can provide themselves with shelter. It is certainly not an ideal process but it is much superior to renting accommodation in the same environment. Our data analyses have not proceeded so far that we can prove the point, but we strongly suspect that more and more people are being excluded from the housing market. The average age difference between renters or sharers and owners in Bogotá and Mexico city owes little to choice and much more to the unavailability of money with which to purchase a lot. More families want the opportunity to build their own homes than can afford to do so. The irony of the Turner bridgeheader/consolidator model is that, as governments begin to accept its intrinsic worth, land and material costs relative to income are making consolidation more difficult. Renters and sharers are not the down-and-outs but they are an excluded majority, excluded from an alternative that few would regard as desirable in an ideal world. It is a sad situation to say that if poverty forces people to build their own houses, many households are too poor to do even that. We return to this issue in the final chapter.

4

Servicing low-income settlements

Once land has been acquired, communities petition the respective public utilities for services. In this chapter we are concerned with explaining how these services are supplied and distributed, the procedures of the agencies, the power they have, how they use that power, and how successfully they service the city populations.

In the first section, we consider certain theories that explain the growth of government intervention in the urban economy. How has the government come to be involved in these areas? Has it been stimulated by economic or by social considerations, has intervention been in the field of collective consumption or collective production? Has government commitment to urban infrastructure and services generally increased or decreased? Has government servicing of poor people been widespread, motivated by a genuine desire to improve living standards, or has it been limited, the outcome of campaigns to maintain legitimacy and social control? In the second section, we provide a resumé of the organization of servicing and government activity in each city. Which services are provided by government and which by the private sector? In the third section, we provide an institutional guide to the organization of servicing in each city, relating service activity to the structure of government in each country and city. In the fourth section, we consider how government agencies perform their role. What are the main characteristics of the agencies supplying services to the poor? Do they work primarily through technical procedures or through patron–client relationships? In what ways do politicians and technicians interact, to what extent is servicing a partisan and politicized process, to what extent is autonomy given to agencies to allocate resources according to need? Through what kinds of mechanism do poor communities express their demands for services and what kinds of response do they receive to those demands? And how has the response of the government bureaucracy with respect to servicing low-income settlements changed through time? Has it become more technical and subject to routines, has it become more politicized, has it become more responsive to community pressures? These general questions are considered in detail in the fifth section with respect to the provision of one service: water. Finally, we consider the different outcomes for the poor of these different servicing procedures. How do servicing levels vary between the low-income populations of the three cities? To what extent is variation a consequence of different state policies, different levels of government revenue, or of different styles of agency operation?

The growth of state intervention

Why does the state have responsibility for certain public services and not for others? This theme has been subject to much recent analysis which has considered the effect such intervention has on the politicization of the poor. Castells (1977, 1979), currently the most influential writer on these issues with reference to advanced capitalist societies, has argued that the growing intervention of the state is an inevitable outcome of the falling rate of profit in the capitalist economy. He has argued that the state is forced to intervene to maintain the rate of capital accumulation and does so by undertaking responsibility for what he calls 'collective consumption'. It intervenes in this area in part because these are generally areas of low profit to the private sector and in part because increasing organization by the working classes demands state intervention: 'the intervention of the state becomes necessary in order to take charge of the sectors and services which are less profitable (from the point of view of capital) but necessary for the functioning of economic activity and/or the appeasement of social conflicts' (Castells, 1979: 18). State intervention is both direct and indirect but is concentrated in urban areas and in the fields of infrastructure and servicing. He illustrates this point with reference to the changing areas of responsibility of government in France from 1872 to 1971, showing that the area of fastest-growing state intervention was in the fields of collective consumption.

In general, we find this argument unconvincing for our three case studies both because of the doubtful categorization of collective consumption and because the area of intervention in all three national economies has not been confined to the area of collective consumption. Previously, several criticisms have been made of the term 'collective consumption'. It has been argued that services are provided simultaneously for both social (consumption) reasons and to stimulate economic growth (production). It is therefore misleading to label those services as consumption rather than as production (Lojkine, 1976). The collective element in social services is dubious in the sense that most collective services, e.g., public housing, education and health, are consumed individually (Pahl, 1975; Saunders, 1979; Harloe, 1977). Second, while there has been a clear trend towards increasing responsibility by government for working-class groups, intervention has often grown fastest in areas linked directly to production.

In Colombia, Mexico and Venezuela, this second argument is crucial, for it has been the industrial, agricultural and commercial sectors which have been the principal recipients of state aid, involvement and policy. The basic aim of policy (and one constantly condemned by many critics in all three countries) has been to accelerate economic growth. Governments have become heavily involved in the provision of economic as opposed to social infrastructure, with the activation of economic growth rather than with the distribution of its benefits. In all three countries social policy has been largely an afterthought.

The same tendency is also clear in the three cities with respect to local expenditure. In Bogotá the four areas which have received greatest government intervention during the past two decades are electricity, water, roads and telephones. While all are provided to the population for social reasons, we would propose that they have been developed primarily not because of organized political pressure from residential groups but as a response to the organized statement of needs from powerful industrial and commercial interests. In general, it has been in those areas of critical interest to industry and commerce where services have expanded *not* in areas which have been primarily subject to growing working-class or even middle-class pressure. To use Lojkine's (1979) phrase, the intervention is better described as coming in the field of collective production, although this opens up further problems of definition. Public utilities have been required by the industrial and capitalist sector to sustain and stimulate productivity in manufacturing, commercial and indeed construction activities. In fact recent trends in Venezuela, as in Chile (Riesco, 1981) and the United Kingdom, reflect an increasing trend towards the privatization of community service provision. Rubbish collection in several Venezuelan cities has recently been handed over to the private sector.

That collective consumption has not been the principal area of intervention by the state is perhaps not surprising given that there is no shortage of ways through which each state has been able to sustain the rate of capital accumulation and maintain social control. All three states have used protection, incentives, exchange controls and a multitude of other economic policies to stimulate industrial, commercial and construction activities. In general there has been no crisis of economic growth in these countries during the past twenty years. Between 1960 and 1980 real gross domestic product in Colombia grew by 5.5 per cent per annum, in Mexico 6.3 per cent and in Venezuela 5.3 per cent (UNECLA, 1981). In addition, all three governments have sought to reduce wage demands by coopting trade unions and at times by using direct repression. One result has been that in Colombia real industrial wages declined between 1970 and 1977 (Sanin Angel, 1981). In addition, given the dependence on self-help housing among the poor in these countries, there has been little pressure to subsidize the costs of reproducing labour in the way that occurred in nineteenth- and twentieth-century Western Europe. In Britain, the state increasingly provided housing and services for lower-income groups. In Latin America, the very existence of self-help housing tends to maintain the rate of profitability of the industrial sector without such intervention (see chapter 3). With the help of government incentives and protection, growth sectors such as industry and construction have expanded rapidly in all three countries.

Given these facts, we believe that the state has become involved in those areas of urban activity where the private sector has been unable to supply itself owing to the nature of the collective good. Public utilities are the traditional area in which governments have first become involved, although as we have already seen state operation is not inevitable. In Britain, railway, gas, telegraph and telephone services were first developed by private companies. Although the state came to be involved increasingly during the nineteenth century, it was less as a producer than as a coordinator of these services; the private companies were not unprofitable but state intervention emerged because the form of competition was inefficient (Grove, 1962: 17). State efforts to collectivize the provision of utilities and public services came much earlier than attempts to take over such activities. For similar reasons, the state has become actively involved in service provision in Latin American cities. But two points should be emphasized. First, public intervention has often been in a form other than public ownership: the private sector has often been subsidized rather than nationalized. Thus bus services are run primarily by the private sector in all three cities although the service receives a large state subsidy.[1] Secondly, the state has normally become the sole provider of a service only when the size, complexity and inherently monopolistic nature of the product has created problems. Indeed, the trend has been for the services to be taken over by the state as demand has increased. Thus, the private electricity companies in Bogotá and Mexico City were gradually incorporated into the public sector as demand for power increased during the forties and fifties (Lozano, 1978). Similarly, the Bogotá municipal water authority was completely reorganized in 1945 as demand for its services increased and loans were required to increase capacity (Wiesner, 1978).

In areas of concern primarily to low-income groups and of little direct interest to the corporate sector – education, housing and public health – the amount of state intervention has been more limited. Where the affluent could satisfy their service needs through the private sector and the industrial sector through specially developed schemes such as social security, the poor have generally been neglected. In health and housing the state has failed to contribute substantially to the servicing of the poor. Growing state intervention has occurred in those areas necessary to the acceleration of economic growth not in those vital to the welfare of the poor; it has been in areas of collective production more than collective consumption that state intervention has been most marked. In making these distinctions we are in full agreement with Connolly (1981) who argues that governments intervene both for growth and legitimacy reasons. Every activity falls along a continuum which runs from directly productive (and therefore beneficial to capital) to unproductive; a related continuum runs from activities with high social content (that is to say they both contain and integrate the population) to those with little social content.

If government has intervened in the urban services field to an increasing degree, the form of that intervention (public ownership versus subsidies to the private sector, control or regulation, stimulus or restriction) has varied dramatically from country to country and indeed city to city. There has been a general need to improve urban infrastructure both for reasons of production but also to improve urban conditions for all social groups. At times there have been similarities in the form of its intervention. Health has been delivered to the industrial and organized labour force through social-security programmes, public housing has been provided for government workers, private bus companies have been heavily subsidized. But, the form of that involvement has often varied greatly according to the scale of the problem, the nature of the state in each country, the pressure upon it and so on. There can be no simple answer as to why the different patterns of state involvement have come about, even at the simplified level described in the matrices below. Sometimes, complex institutional responses have emerged as different groups' political demands have been gradually accepted; Malloy (1979) describes clearly this process in terms of social-security provision in Brazil. The form of involvement has been symptomatic of the political and economic environment in each country. Generalizations such as those of Castells are really rather unhelpful.

Responsibility for servicing

In order to simplify explanation of the mechanisms used to service the population in each city, we have produced matrices of responsibility for the various services (figures 12, 13 and 14). These matrices show the main responsibilities of the private and the public sectors with respect to low-income and higher-income populations; they show the national, local and regional responsibilities, they demonstrate the influence exerted by international agencies. Each matrix contains a series of row vectors which describe the responsibilities and influence of different kinds of public and private agency. The rows contain the major activities which affect low-income populations in their housing and settlement situations, that is land, building materials, housing, water, drainage, electricity and so on. The matrices are not comprehensive and include only a number of representative service functions. We have subdivided each row: the first sub-row contains information about the populations living in the 'conventional', legalized housing market; the second, those living in the 'irregular' low-income market. Clearly, this is a less-than-watertight distinction but it is not misleading at the level of generalization at which we are dealing. We wish only to depict the different roles of public and private sectors with respect to richer and poorer groups, the different ways in which poorer and richer groups in the city are housed and serviced. We are not suggesting that there are not vital links between the sectors, only sketching the

BOGOTA DE

		PUBLIC				PRIVATE	
		INTERNATIONAL	NATIONAL	REGIONAL	LOCAL	CORPORATE	COMMUNITY/INDIVIDUAL
Land	(U)		■[1] □[3]	■[4]	■[5] □[6]	■[7]	■[8]
	(B)		■[2] □[3]		■[5] □[6]	■[7]	■[8]
Building materials	(U)		■[1] □[2]			■[3]	
	(B)		■[1] □[2]			■[3]	■[4]
Housing	(U)		■[1] □[3]		■[5] □[7]	■[9]	■[10]
	(B)		■[2] □[4]		■[6] □[8]		■[11]
Water/ Drainage	(U)	□[1]		□[2]	■[4]	■[6]	
	(B)	□[1]		□[2,3]	■[4] □[5]	■[7]	■[8]
Electricity (domestic)	(U)	□[1]	■[9] □[2]		■[4]	■[6]	
	(B)	□[1]	■[9] □[2,3]		■[4] □[5]	■[7]	■[8]
Health	(U)	□[1]	■[2] □[4]		■[6] □[7]	■[8]	■[10]
	(B)	□[1]	■[2,3] □[4]	■[5]	■[6,7] □[7]	■[9]	■[10,11]
Public transport	(U)				□[1] ■[2] □[3]	■[4,5]	■[6,7]
	(B)				□[1] ■[2] □[3]	■[4,5]	■[7]
Rubbish	(U)				■[1]	■[2]	■[3]
	(B)				■[1]		■[3]

Fig. 12 Matrix of responsibility for housing and servicing – Bogotá DE

Bogota
U = urbanizations: i.e., 'conventional', legalized housing market.
B = *barrios:* i.e., 'irregular', low-income market.

Land
1. National government is owner of land, also the decentralized agencies such as ICT.
2. Site and service schemes.
3. National legislation and agency involvement, for example SIB, since 1968.
4. Regional government such as the land owned by the Beneficencia de Cundinamarca.
5. Local-authority land which is used to service community and is not open to land invasion. Also local authority's CVP runs site and service schemes.
6. Local land taxation, planning regulations, etc.
7. Large landowners.
8. Individual sales.

Building materials
1. Nationalized industries providing materials, for example Paz del Río steel plant.
2. Price controls, incentives, etc., to building-supply industry.
3. Private industry.
4. Small firms, recycling materials.

Housing
1. ICT and institutionally funded housing.
2. National government site and service programmes.
3. National policy for construction industry.
4. National policy on building materials, sites and servicing, etc.
5. CVP.
6. CVP site and service programmes.
7. Planning controls, building licences, zoning, etc.
8. As above plus regularization policies.
9. Building companies.
10. Small-scale building contractors.
11. Self-help and small-scale builders.

Water and drainage
1. World Bank loans and influence on pricing and operations.
2. National policy and controls on pricing.
3. ICT (Special agency).
4. EAAB.
5. Local planning and servicing committees.
6. Provision by urbanizer.
7. Provision by illegal subdivider.
8. Community action and illegal tapping.

Electricity
Matrix notes as for water except where noted.
4. The Bogotá Electricity Company (EEEB).
9. The National Grid.

Health
1. Pan-American Union, etc.
2. ICSS and sectional social-security funds.
3. Ministry of Health participation in local health services through the Servicio Seccional de Salud.
4. Ministry of Health policy.
5. Departmental hospitals.
6. Caja de Previsión Social fund for local-government workers.
7. Secretariat for Health.
8. Private clinics.
9. Charity hospitals.
10. Private doctors.
11. *Teguas, curanderos,* quacks, etc.

Public transport
1. Ministry of Transport subsidies to private bus companies.
2. Bogotá Transport company (EDTU).
3. Planning department (DAPD) route planning, bus stops, etc.
4. Bus companies and microbuses.
5. Fleets of taxis.
6. Private cars.
7. Small-scale bus, *buseta* and taxi drivers.

Rubbish
1. The Bogotá Institute for Sanitation (EDIS).
2. Private companies.
3. Small-scale informal activities.

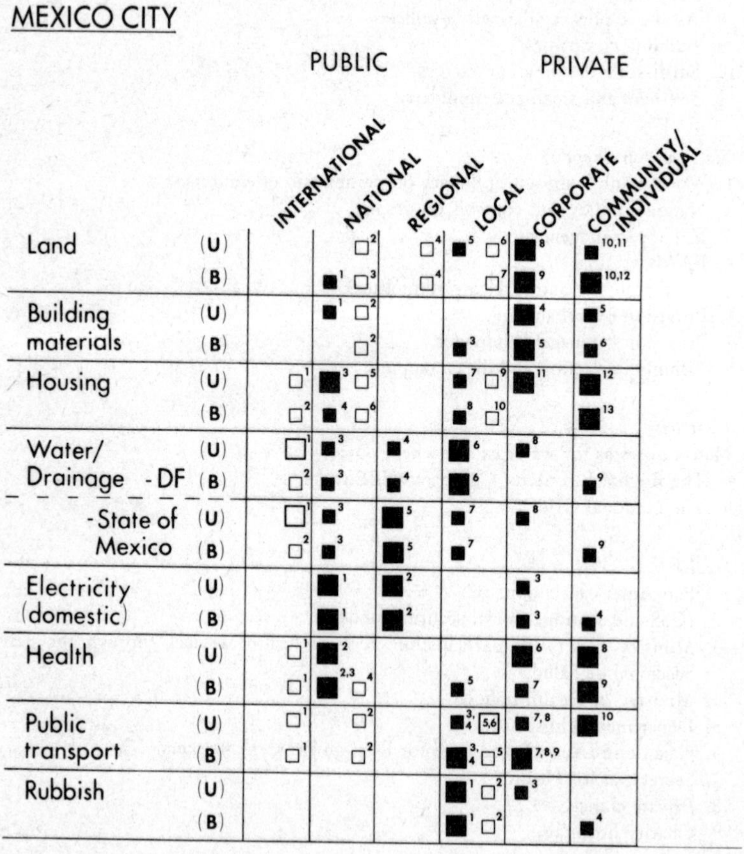

MEXICO CITY

		PUBLIC				PRIVATE	
		INTERNATIONAL	NATIONAL	REGIONAL	LOCAL	CORPORATE	COMMUNITY/INDIVIDUAL
Land	(U)		□2	□4	■5 □6	■8	■10,11
	(B)		■1 □3	□4	□7	■9	■10,12
Building materials	(U)		■1 □2			■4	■5
	(B)		□2		■3	■5	■6
Housing	(U)	□1	■3 □5		■7 □9	■11	■12
	(B)	□2	■4 □6		■8 □10		■13
Water/ Drainage – DF	(U)	□1	■3	■4	■6	■8	
	(B)	□2	■3	■4	■6		■
– State of Mexico	(U)	□1	■3	■5	■7	■8	
	(B)	□2	■3	■5	■7		■9
Electricity (domestic)	(U)		■1	■2		■3	
	(B)		■1	■2		■3	■4
Health	(U)	□1	■2			■6	■8
	(B)	□1	■2,3 □4		■5	■7	■9
Public transport	(U)	□1	□2		■3,4 [5,6]	■7,8	■10
	(B)	□1	□2		■3,4 □5	■7,8,9	
Rubbish	(U)				■1 □2	■3	
	(B)				■1 □2		■4

Fig. 13 Matrix of responsibility for housing and servicing – Mexico City

Mexico City

Land

1. Lands provided by the state for *barrio* overspill developments, site and service schemes, etc. Agencies involved: BANOBRAS 1960–70; INDECO 1976–81; INFONAVIT 1977–83.
2. National housing and economic policies, tax legislation on real estate, etc., all affect the supply of land.
3. National policy towards illegal land development affects willingness of developers to promote low-income settlement.
4. Conurbation Commission (1976–83) provides normative plans which affect future land uses and supply of land for residential purposes.
5. Agencies provide land for urbanizations (usually lower-middle-income housing) BANOBRAS 1960s–83; AURIS 1969–83; INDECO 1973–6; CODEUR 1977–83.
6. Local zoning policies or tax laws affect supply of land.
7. Local policy towards invasion and illegal land occupancy and willingness to regularize and service affect propensity to supply land.
8. Real-estate companies' speculatory developments (usually legal).
9. Real-estate companies' speculative developments, usually illegal, 1950s and 1960s.
10. *Ejidal* lands are alienated illegally by the *ejido*. Results mostly in low-income settlements but some notable middle-income residential developments have occurred.
11. Small-scale landowners also provide land for subdivisions.
12. Invasions and small-scale purchases of land by groups of residents.

Building materials

1. National enterprises produce steel and other goods used in the building industry.
2. Price controls and restrictive practices affect total output.
3. Cheap supply centres provide materials for self-help. Sponsored by INDECO, 1973–82; AURIS, 1970–5.
4. 'Industrialized', large company and monopolies sector.
5. Building materials produced by middle-sized enterprises.
6. Middle-sized enterprises, artisans, petty-commodity production, recycled throwaways, etc.

Housing

1. International assistance for 'social-interest' housing and international conventional wisdom affect national housing policies. Specifically, the Alliance for Progress provided 'seed' capital for PFV, 1963–4.
2. International agencies espousal of self-help affects national housing policy.
3. Social-interest housing projects provide housing. Specifically: BANOBRAS 1960s; INVI 1964–70; INDECO, 1973–6; INFONAVIT 1973–83.
4. Supply of site and service housing opportunities.
5. National housing policies, provision of credit, tax incentives, etc.
6. National housing policies towards self-help type solutions.
7. Housing projects produced by Habitación Popular, 1972–6; AURIS, 1970–5.
8. Development of self-help projects (Habitación Popular, 1972–6; AURIS, 1970–5; INDECO, 1977–82; FIDEURBE, 1973–6).
9. Local policies towards social-interest housing and urbanizations.

10. Local policies towards self-help and towards illegal settlements.
11. Corporate provision of private housing.
12. Individual provision via private architects' offices, etc.
13. Individual self-help.

Water and drainage
1. International finance for water procurement and regional drainage schemes.
2. International finance and pressure to provide service to low-income communities; pressure from WHO, etc. to reduce mortality and morbidity levels.
3. National procurement and supply to regional authorities. Prior to 1977 SARH, 1977–83 SAHOP.
4. CAVM supplies 20 per cent of DF's requirements. Sells to DF in bulk.
5. CAVM sells water to CEAS which supplies households in State of Mexico.
6. Procurement and supply within the DF. Water is obtained from wells and a proportion of the DF needs are brought from CAVM. Prior to 1977, responsibility of Dirección General de Operación Hidráulica and the Dirección General de Aguas y Saneamiento. Since that date merged into single Dirección General de Operación Hidráulica. The DCGOH today provides primary and secondary networks while domestic supply is the responsibility of the Delegación.
7. Secondary supplies of water procured and supplied by municipal authorities in State of Mexico.
8. Provision of network by urbanizer.
9. Self-help drainage, pit latrines, etc.

Electricity
1. CFE provides national grid.
2. Companía de Luz y Fuerza del Valle de México provides domestic supply.
3. Provision of domestic network by urbanizer.
4. Illegal wire taps supply households.

Health
1. Pressure from international health organizations to improve health standards and provision.
2. Social security affiliates. IMSS, ISSSTE, and those created for certain groups of workers in railways, military, petrochemicals.
3. State Sector (SSA).
4. National policy regarding treatment of low-income groups.
5. DDF Dirección General de Servicios Médicos provides some medical services, blood for transfusions, etc.
6. Private clinics and hospitals.
7. Charities, Red Cross, etc.
8. Private doctors.
9. Private doctors, chemists, *curanderos*, 'quacks', etc.

Public transport
1. 'Tied aid' from France for Metro.
2. National government policy towards fuel prices, subsidies and public transport.
3. Metro, trams and buses within the Federal District (since 1981).

4. Trolley buses (Servicio de Transporte Eléctrico).
5. DF policy towards servicing needs of private transport: car parks, freeways, etc.
6. DF policy towards transport in general (COVITUR).
7. Taxis.
8. Collective taxis.
9. Buses in the State of Mexico. The privately owned bus service that operated in the Federal District was nationalized in 1981.
10. Private cars.

Rubbish
1. Delegación cleansing department and outside the Federal District in hands of the municipalities.
2. Incentives for interest groups to invest in recycling materials.
3. Private services, industrial-waste-disposal services, etc.
4. Self-help tips and dumping.

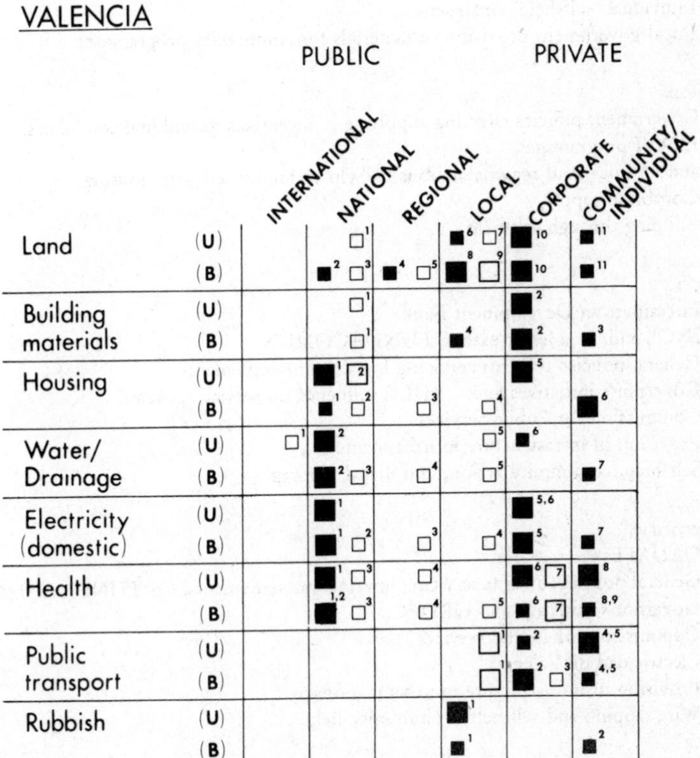

Fig. 14 Matrix of responsibility for housing and servicing – Valencia

Valencia

Land

1. National housing and economic-growth policies.
2. National institutes such as the Sports Authority supply invasion land.
3. National land and servicing policies.
4. Supplies land through invasions, e.g. Naguanagua.
5. Affects number of invasions through police control.
6. Owner of land of potential use to urbanizations.
7. Planning and zoning regulations.
8. Municipal ownership of *ejidos*.
9. Planning and zoning regulations. Land invasions.
10. Large landowners.
11. Small landowners especially lot speculators and *traspasos*.

Building materials

1. Price controls and industrial policies.
2. Corporate supply.
3. Individual, self-help construction.
4. Local-government provision of materials for community programmes.

Housing

1. Government policies affecting supply, e.g. incentives to building companies.
2. INAVI programmes.
3. and 4. Local and regional actions to help or hinder self-help housing.
5. Corporate supply.
6. Building through self help.

Water

1. Interamerican Development Bank.
2. INOS and, to a lesser extent, FUNDACOMUN.
3. General policies towards servicing low-income settlements.
4. Governor's initiatives and ORDEC influence on service agencies.
5. Commission for Public Services.
6. Provision of infrastructure in urbanizations.
7. Self-help, community action, and illegal tapping.

Electricity

1. CADAFE.
2. General policies towards servicing low-income settlements, e.g. FUNDACOMUN.
3. Governor's initiative and ORDEC.
4. Commission for Public Services.
5. Electricidad de Valencia.
6. Provision of infrastructure in urbanizations.
7. Wire tapping and self help, community help.

Health

1. Venezuelan Institute for Social Security (IVSS).

2. Ministry of Health (MSAS) supplied services and FUNDACOMUN provided the buildings.
3. MSAS health policy.
4. State pressure for hospital provision.
5. Council pressure for service improvements.
6. Private clinics.
7. Industries and firms affiliated to social security.
8. Private doctors.
9. *Curanderos*, etc.

Public transport
1. Municipal planning department, control on fares and routes.
2. Private bus and microbus companies.
3. Corporate works buses.
4. Taxis and *colectivos*.
5. Private cars.

Rubbish
1. Local council.
2. Individuals.

ways in which they are treated differently by the public and private service agencies.

For every function, each matrix depicts which of six public and private 'agencies' is responsible for provision. International responsibility, through the international lending institutions, aid agencies, private lending and commercial organizations, makes up the first column. There follow three public-sector columns which demonstrate the responsibilities of national-, regional- and local-government institutions. The final two columns deal with the private sector, one with the corporate and large-scale sector (that is to say manufacturing industry, commerce, large landowners, building companies, etc.), the other with the small-scale, individual and community sector (that is one-man businesses, individual home owners, community action, etc.).

For each area of responsibility the kind of influence of different institutions, individuals, etc., is depicted in terms of its direct or indirect responsibility for supply. Thus, where a group or set of individuals supplies a service, they are indicated as having direct responsibility (shaded squares), where they have partial responsibility (say through controlling prices, by prohibiting land invasions, through planning, etc.) they are represented as exercizing an indirect demand on supply (unshaded squares). Each agency's or group's level of responsibility and fulfilment of that responsibility is indicated: those with major responsibility are distinguished from those with minor responsibility. If one agency is solely responsible for a service but provides that service to only a minority of the population, it will be depicted as having lesser responsibility. The numbers accompanying each symbol relate to the notes of explanation.

It is important to underline the limitations of this method. It does not show the relationships between activities; for example, it does not show the influence of the water company on the supply of electricity. Each matrix is static and represents the situation in 1978–9: changes in responsibility through time are explained in the accompanying notes. The matrices do not demonstrate the nature of the relationship between different actors, for example between the government and the corporate private sector. They do not indicate the effects of other agencies and processes on servicing, for example the effects of employment policies on incomes and hence on servicing. Finally, they make no comment on the efficiency with which that responsibility is dispensed; while the public sector is depicted as being responsible for the poor, this does not signify that it performs this role well. The only qualification included is when an agency with major responsibility for servicing is depicted as having minor responsibility because its real action in supplying that service is minimal. Detailed discussion of these matters must await treatment in the following section. Here the matrices serve merely to help reduce a complicated universe of interrelating institutions, groups and individuals into a more comprehensible pattern. We are seeking to show in an easily assimilable way the similarities and differences between the areas of responsibility of the public sector in each city, the ways in which different or similar levels of government deal with similar services and functions, and the extent of international involvement.

We have already seen that, with respect to the supply of land, the state plays a different role in each city. The matrices help to draw out the direct influence of the private corporate sector in all three cities, and the different roles played by the public sector. While the corporate private sector is important everywhere in its role as an owner of land, in Mexico small communities also own usufruct land in the form of *ejidos*. Another difference lies in the levels of government which hold land in each city and in the ways in which each government distributes that land. In every case, the state is totally involved in determining the allocation of land through its planning and regulatory role.

In the case of building materials, the state has a highly restricted role because most building materials are produced by private companies; only a few materials are produced by the public sector, such as some steel items in all three countries. The state is otherwise involved in the supply of materials only in its role as regulator of the economy – mainly through its control of prices.

With respect to utilities, the situation is reversed; the state is the major supplier with the private sector playing a minor role. In Bogotá, electricity, water, telephones and rubbish collection are administered by the public sector. The same is true in Valencia except that Valencia is also served by a private electricity company, which both complements and competes with the public company.[2] In Mexico, the private sector is responsible for telephones but the other utilities are provided by the public sector.

Health and public transport are the responsibility of both sectors. In all three cities, much of the health care is provided by the social-security agencies which are financed by the state, private companies and individual workers. Those poor workers and their families who are not covered by social security are served mainly by the official, state health services, though extensive use is also made of the private sector in the form of pharmacists, mid-wives and local quacks. It is also important to recognize the major role played in the hospital service of Bogotá and Mexico by the charity sector. Higher-income groups have recourse to private health clinics and medical facilities. These three sectors overlap in terms of the populations they serve but, in broad terms, the poor are served by the social-security and official sectors and the better-off by the social-security and private sectors.

In the case of public transport, there are important variations between the cities. In Bogotá, buses and taxis are privately operated, although the services are monitored and controlled by the state and heavily subsidized. There is also a public company which runs a few bus and trolley routes, but which carries few passengers compared to the private bus lines. In Mexico, within the Federal District the Metro and the buses are publicly operated, but the bus service in the State of Mexico and taxi services throughout the city are run by private companies. The buses, like those of Bogotá, are heavily subsidized. In Valencia, bus services are provided by subsidized private companies and routes and fares are controlled by the local authority. In all three cities, the higher-income population provides its own transport in the form of private cars.

What cannot be shown easily in a matrix is the indirect influence of government and private sectors in each city. The critical point to make is that all three cities are very much part of a mixed economy, whereby the state is influential to one degree or another in every sector. Thus the building-materials industry is not controlled by the state but is critically dependent upon state intervention, patronage, investment and subsidies. We will return to this indirect influence in more detail below.

The local, regional and national states

The matrices show that, even when the state has become involved in the direct administration of services, it has not operated at the same organizational level in each city. One reason for the variation among our three cities is that Bogotá, Mexico City and Valencia occupy different positions in their respective national systems. Bogotá and Mexico City, for example, are national capitals whereas Valencia is merely an important provincial city. Because of their size and status both Bogotá and Mexico City have been given greater autonomy and responsibility than most other cities in their countries. Bogotá was made into a Special District in 1954 which gives it greater autonomy over its own affairs than that possessed by most other Colombian cities. Essentially, this status removes Bogotá from control by the intermediate level of departmental government; it means, for example, that the Mayor of the city is appointed directly by the president rather than by the departmental governor. In fact, dependent on its holder, the office of mayor is the equivalent to a middle-level cabinet post. The fact that Bogotá is a Special District means that he can appoint the heads of all agencies in the city; he has powers similar to those of a departmental governor and city mayor combined. He has a relatively large budget and, most importantly, the economic base from which to apply for outside loans with which to finance infrastructure programmes.

Similarly, the Federal District of Mexico occupies a unique position in the Mexican administrative structure. The mayor, or *regente*, is appointed by the president and occupies a top-ranking cabinet post. Thus, he is responsible to the president rather than to a state legislature. Although the president appoints the top six secretaries of the department and makes many lesser appointments, the *regente*, unlike state governors, does not have to submit any of his nominations to popular vote and, therefore, is largely responsible for the department's personnel. The city budget is very much larger than that of any state and, equally important, much of it is generated within the district; the mayor is not so dependent upon the federal government for his budget. The size of the budget also means that the *regente* has much greater opportunities for investing in urban infrastructure (Connolly, 1981). There are, of course, certain activities which are administered and financed directly by the federal government, such as public health and school and university teaching, but in this respect the Federal District is no different from any state. In the State of Mexico the situation is rather different. The governor is elected by popular vote; is always the candidate of the PRI and normally the nominee of the outgoing president. Although he manages a larger budget than his counterpart in any other state, his area of responsibility is quite limited. Major social and economic responsibility is in the hands of the ministries and decentralized agencies. His main source of power derives from his control over the state judiciary, the police force and public works. He also enjoys considerable scope for patronage through appointments to the state bureaucracy and nominations for elected municipal office. While the whole of Mexico City benefits from large budgets because it is in the president's backyard, the Department of the Federal District has far greater responsibility and autonomy over its administrative area than has the state government.

Valencia is a provincial city and falls under the jurisdiction both of the municipal council of Valencia and the Government of the State of Carabobo. The state governor is potentially much more powerful than the city mayor. He manages a much larger budget and is in charge of the police force.[3] The municipal authorities have control over a very limited range of services and few resources. In fact one characteristic of Venezuela is that neither state nor municipal authorities wield real power, for both form part of one of the world's most centralized bureaucracies. As Stewart (1977: 217) has put it, 'all national agencies have their headquarters in Caracas, and decisions of any consequence are normally made there. In fact, all decisions, whether important or not, are usually made in Caracas.'

Thus the three cities, and in the case of Mexico City different parts of the city, vary in terms of their autonomy from central-government control and in their ability to finance their own programmes. But, the cities also vary in the range of their responsibilities. The local authorities in Bogotá are charged with the provision of electricity, water, drainage, telephones and local roads. They have their own planning department, department of community action, housing corporation, education authority, bus company, rubbish-collection service, university, and social-security institute.[4] While important functions remain in the hands of the national government and there are numerous occasions when there is no coordination between the city and the national authorities, many urban functions are in the hands of the local authorities. If the city budget is inadequate it is superior in *per capita* terms to that of most other cities.

The same is true in Mexico City's Federal District where the department controls roads, water and drainage, the Metro, buses and trolley buses, land regularization, some housing, rubbish collection, street lighting, cultural activities, neighbourhood councils, primary- and secondary-school building and even runs a limited health service. As in Bogotá, *per capita* budget expenditure is far higher than elsewhere in the country. By contrast, the municipalities in the State of Mexico have only limited responsibilities. In fact, they are more akin to the decentralized units of local government in the Federal District, the delegations. The municipalities control the police, street cleaning, street lighting, and minor roadworks and repairs. Nominally they are also responsible for the household supply of water and drainage, but in practice this task is shared with the State Commission of Water and Sanitation (CEAS). They assess and collect taxes for the state and markets, and cultural events and tree planting also fall within their remit. Not only are responsibilities limited but the municipalities also suffer from limited resources. Inevitably, therefore, they tend to be very lightweight.

In Valencia, the city authorities control few of the key servicing functions. Water is in the hands of a national-government agency, road building largely the responsibility of the State of Carabobo and the national Ministry of Public Works, while electricity depends on two agencies, one belonging to the national government, the other a private company. Health is controlled nationally by the Ministry of Health and the Venezuelan Institute of Social Security, education is in the hands of a range of institutes belonging to the Ministry of Education. In fact, Valencia's municipal government has control over very few sectors of importance. The council is in charge of land-use planning, markets, sanitation, some schools, street maintenance and a few other activities. If they want anything done in the city, councillors must normally petition state or national agencies and are often forced to approach Caracas. As Cannon *et al.* (1973: 31) describe it, 'Valencia does not really have an urban government; rather a raft of single purpose hierarchies carry on their specialized activities with little or no cooperation or communication with local government or themselves.' While similar statements have also been made of Bogotá and Mexico City (Gilbert, 1978; Ward, 1981a), local government wields much greater influence in those cities.

These differences in the administrative structures of each city have important implications for the ways in which services are allocated in each – a point which we shall now develop.

Political and technical bureaucracies

We believe that the bureaucracies which distribute and allocate resources in our three cities vary considerably in the ways they operate. Indeed, not only do the ways of Mexican bureaucracy differ from those of Colombian or Venezuelan bureaucracy, but within each administrative system important differences can be observed. We believe that, although there has been a trend in all three countries towards growing 'modernization' and rationality of the bureaucracy, this trend has affected each country to different degrees and affected certain institutions before others. Broadly, our argument is that the first institutions which have been affected by this modernizing, rationalizing trend have been those which are directly linked to the public services deemed essential by the private sector to maintain and accelerate the pace of economic growth. Subject to the national political model, this trend has deeply or superficially modified the traditional form of government bureaucracy. Before discussing the local manifestations of these changes, however, it is necessary to make certain distinctions between the ways in which governmental agencies behave.

Definitions

Broadly we shall distinguish agencies according to their position on a continuum running from rational–technical to partisan–political. This distinction has important repercussions on the ways in which the agencies act, although we wish to underline that we are not saying that the urban poor inevitably benefit from one kind of bureaucratic style more than another. We are aware that many regimes in Latin America are highly efficient, but also highly repressive; others are less author-itarian while being highly partisan. An efficient bureaucracy can serve the most enlightened of regimes; the danger is that it can also serve the most despotic. For, as Weber (1962: 38) noted, 'A rationally ordered system of officials continues to function smoothly after the enemy has occupied the area; he merely needs to change the top officials.' It is also important to emphasize that technical bureaucracies serve political functions by the very rationality of their style (Batley, 1982; Dinkel-spiel, 1969). As Rivera Ortiz (1976: 152) notes, 'Notwithstanding how much technical and bureaucratic rationalities differ from political rationality . . . the fact remains that these actors, consciously or not, assume political positions . . . The super-technical or 'apolitical' attitudes of planners imply a passive acceptance of dominant political views.'

Despite this intermixture of political and technical goals and styles, there are still, we believe, major differences in the ways in which local and national bureaucracies act. Some act more rationally and tech-nically than others which often use patronage to win votes and influence people. Indeed, various authors have depicted particular Latin American institutions as constituting 'technical' agencies, most notably SUDENE, the Venezuelan Guayana Corporation and the Cauca Valley Corporation (Dinkelspiel, 1969; Robock, 1963; Posada, 1966). But, it is obviously vital that we define clearly the terms technical, rational, political, partisan and objective; this is the primary purpose of the following paragraphs.

We have reviewed some of the vast literature on bureaucracy and public administration in search of guidance through this minefield of value judgements. Much of that literature has been heavily influenced by the Weberian concept of bureaucracy. It will be obvious from previous chapters that we have major reservations about broad ele-ments of the Weberian approach. In particular, we are aware that Weberian definitions tend to be culturally and historically specific, tend to emphasize internal structure, reify objectivity and rationality, underplay environmental constraints on agency operation, and ignore the dynamics of change inherent in all bureaucracies. Nevertheless, with respect to our limited aims here, this approach has a clarity which is useful.

The literature has distinguished between 'functional rationality' and 'political rationality'. According to Friedmann (1965: 48), 'functional rationality consists of the exclusive consideration of technical criteria in making planning decisions. The key consideration is that of efficiency . . .' Or as Udy (1969: 343) defines it, social behaviour is rational 'insofar as it is purposefully directed toward explicit empirical objectives and planned in accordance with the best available scientific knowledge'. In contrast to technicians, who are guided by functional rationality, politicians are guided by political rationality. The latter implies the formulation of decisions on 'the basis of who benefits and who pays the costs of a particular decision' (Rivera Ortiz, 1976: 150). A critical interpretation of the latter is that:

In a political decision . . . action never is based on the merits of a proposal but always on who makes it and who opposes it . . . A course of action which corrects economic or social deficiencies but increases political difficulties must be rejected, while an action which contributes to political improvement is desirable even if it is not entirely sound from an economic and social standpoint (Diesing, 1962).

This quote implicitly puts the case for the efficient agency; the statement implies that political rationality is rarely concerned primarily with modifying economic or social deficiencies. As stated earlier, we are fully aware of the dangers of that argument. Nevertheless, the process of political rationality clearly operates in Latin American society, as elsewhere, and it is useful to our analysis.

The difficulty, however, comes in operationalizing the term in different political environments. After all, in Mexico there is essentially only one important political party, in Colombia two, linked until recently in a formal government coalition, and in Venezuela a competitive electoral situation with two and often three major competitors. Hence, when Stewart (1977: 215) defines 'political influence' as 'the straightforward use of party membership and connections to affect the implementation of national law', his definition takes on very different meanings in the different political situations. Thus, in Venezuela, political influence will favour one party's interests above those of a rival. It is also important to add that political influence in all three countries is not only used to favour *the* party but is used to support one faction of the party against another. Party and indeed bureaucratic factionalism are highly characteristic of Colombian, Mexican and Venezuelan politics, and 'political' decisions are often made by bureaucrats to help their party or bureaucratic faction. For this reason we would add to Stewart's definition the concept of intra-party and inter-group alliances and conflict.

Given these broad definitions of political and technical rationality, we can depict servicing agencies as falling along a continuum ranging from the wholly political to the wholly technical. Clearly, neither extreme is anything more than an 'ideal type', but such a distinction does allow the characterization of different behavioural types of bureaucracy. According to our previous definitions the 'ideal-type' rational, technical bureaucracy is one which is autonomous, stable, accountable and objective. We interpret these terms in the following way.

'Autonomy' means that once policy is established by political decision makers, whether on rational or partisan political grounds, the agency is then free to make day-to-day decisions without interference from extra-agency actors. Policy is determined at regular intervals and is not in a constant state of flux. Thus an autonomous agency is permitted to interpret and execute policy and to appoint its own bureaucrats to perform its functions. Manpower changes only after a crisis of accountability or after a change of government; the director and staff are not constantly under threat of dismissal. Its budget is either self-financing or protected from constant modification and is normally adequate to perform at least part of the overt function of the organization.

'Stability' means that the policy of the institution is modified only at regular intervals, for example after every presidential election. Manpower remains stable, budgets change no more than once *per annum* and the institution is largely guaranteed protection from major fluctuations in budgets.

'Accountability' means autonomy is granted on condition that specific measurable tasks are performed 'respectably'. Failure to perform these clearly defined tasks is punishable by loss of autonomy and resources and most severely by the creation of a rival agency to perform similar functions.

'Objectivity' means that the technical bureaucracy will discharge business primarily 'according to calculable rules and "without regard for persons"' (Weber, 1962: 35). Manpower is recruited on a technical, credentialist and career basis. Procedures are selected to maximize use of resources and/or minimize costs. Queues are established according to strict rules which makes queue jumping difficult or impossible.

Our definition of the 'politicized agency' is clearly the converse of the above. Such an agency will lack autonomy, will be unstable, constantly accountable and will not be objective (that is it will make politically rational as opposed to functionally rational decisions).

Which of these institutions, or which balance of these institutions, emerge in each city or country depends greatly upon the socio-political development of the country. According to our interpretation, the difference is quite clear in Bogotá, Valencia and Mexico City. Public administration in Valencia and Venezuela generally tends to be highly politicized and falls towards the political end of our continuum. By contrast, Bogotá contains a mixture of technical and political organizations. In Mexico, a similar mix is strongly affected by the philosophy of each national president. Given the extreme concentration of power he wields during his *sexenio*, he can cajole agencies to follow a much more political or a much more technical line. Such differences in presidential styles are characteristic of all three countries but seem much more marked in Mexico.

Modernization of the national bureaucracy

A major characteristic of development policy in Colombia, Mexico and Venezuela has been the attempt to modernize the economy in an effort to further stimulate economic growth. One element of this modernization has been the rationalization of the machinery of the state. Clearly, this latter process is of critical importance to our current analysis. All Spanish American nations inherited from the colonial period a government machine geared more to patronage than to the fulfilment of overt developmental tasks (Stein and Stein, 1970). In all three countries, while the state continues to be a source of patronage, national elites have attempted to modify the bureaucratic structure. This task was easier to achieve in Colombia because of the changes that took place in the political system in 1958. An important result of the National Front coalition and its implicit agreement to modernize the country, was to reduce 'the power of any specific political party in government decision making. In doing so, it favoured an increased reliance upon technocrats and on proliferating interest groups' (Hoskin, 1980: 108). This view has been echoed by Cepeda and Mitchell (1980: 253): 'Colombia's National Front coalition system removed many issues of development policy from direct exposure to political debate. With sixteen years of national power virtually guaranteed to a fairly homogeneous group of traditional party leaders, the probabilities increased that questions of economic strategy could be defined as "technical" and solved accordingly.' Although political rationality, personal loyalties, favouritism and many other traditional forms of political and bureaucratic action continue to dominate large areas of government in Colombia, there has been a major change in the way substantial parts of the bureaucracy operate. As we shall see, this trend has been particularly strong in Bogotá.

In Mexico, any assessment of bureaucratic changes must first take account of two peculiar but critical features of its political system. First, the enormous authority invested in the Executive means that during his six-year period, the president has an almost completely free hand to set his personal imprint upon the nation. Policy formulation is the exclusive prerogative of a small group and is characterized by limited information inputs, behind-the-scenes bargaining and low levels of public discussion and debate (Grindle, 1977; Smith, 1979). Once the overall guidelines of the administration are established, officials generate programmes with a view to impressing the president and winning his approval and support. The second overriding feature is the intensely personalistic and particularistic criteria that govern alliances within the political system. Ideology and party affiliation are relatively unimportant. Far more critical is loyalty to a group, or *camarilla*, organized around a particular leader (Smith, 1979). These two features account for the following characteristics of Mexican government: frenetic activity within six-year cycles; changes of policy and shifts of emphasis every six years accompanied by an almost complete change of personnel brought about not by a change of governing party but by movement of 'patrons'. Within this dominant and continuing pattern, it is not inappropriate to describe a recent 'rationalization' of the bureaucracy in Mexico. While the afore-mentioned ground-rules still apply, it is increasingly common for technocrats to fill important posts and there have been recent attempts to streamline the bureaucracy, reducing overlap and defining responsibilities (Law of Administrative Reform, 1977). Each ministry now has greater control over a number of decentralized agencies, public enterprises, commissions and development trusts, thereby limiting the rather 'maverick' status that many previously enjoyed. Within the Federal District there is now tighter organization of functions exemplified in the merging of three separate agencies responsible for regularization and low-income housing into a single organization (CODEUR). Local *delegados* also have been invested with greater responsibilities as part of this general trend towards rationalization of the city administration, in this case by encouraging decentralized control over certain local activities (Ward, 1981a). Another aspect of this 'modernizing' trend is increased emphasis upon financial accountability. Since 1977, cost recovery has been an important criterion for approval of servicing and regularization programmes. In general, the change in Mexico has tempered the political rationality of the bureaucratic system without altering it fundamentally. Nevertheless, it is important to note that the change has affected 'productive' agencies much more than those concerned with 'social' issues.

In Venezuela, a similar attempt to modernize the bureaucracy and to introduce more Weberian bureaucratic values has been underway. Some success has been achieved in those sectors where it has been agreed between the parties that efficient government is essential to the nation's development and where that efficiency could be implemented through some form of technical approach without directly affecting the day-to-day lives of large numbers of Venezuelans. Institutions such as the Ministry of Mines and Hydrocarbons, the Venezuelan Petrol Corporation and the Venezuelan Corporation for the Guayana clearly fall into this category. By Venezuelan standards, all are highly efficient in fulfilling their overt role of developing the country's resources. They employ technical criteria, indeed they deliberately exaggerate their use of those criteria, and are consequently protected from direct exposure to political debate (Dinkelspiel, 1969; Stewart, 1977: 223–4). But, despite this tendency, Venezuelan bureaucracy is still highly politicized. This derives from the fact that the Venezuelan political system since 1958 has been characterized by much inter-party and intra-party competition. Partisan political interests could clearly not be ignored in a situation where power could be lost every five years. Patronage has continued to be a vital ingredient in the operation of Venezuelan democracy. The patron–client system has been sustained to a greater degree than in Colombia, and jobs created in the government bureaucracy as a result. This has not been to the total exclusion of technical competence even in those institutions which could not be protected from direct political debate. As Stewart (1977: 222) has pointed out, 'a system has developed . . . which combines achievement and party status considerations. Under this system, employees are chosen on the basis of party membership and professional qualifications. Labourers, a large unskilled category, are generally chosen solely on the basis of party qualifications . . .' Affiliation to one or other of the major parties has been essential as the political system has become firmly established and as it has come to be dominated increasingly by the AD and COPEI parties.

To different degrees in all three countries, therefore, there has been an acceptance of the need to modernize the bureaucracy, in order both to maximize economic growth and to legitimize the social system through social welfare programmes, while maintaining political stability through the age-old method of giving jobs to supporters through the government bureaucracy (Nalven, 1978: 430). In Colombia, the coalition has, for some institutions at least, partially separated government from politics.[5] A number of agencies are relatively autonomous and concentrate primarily on their formal functions. Similarly in Mexico, despite a widely held notion that the PRI and the government are identical, they are actually quite distinct entities. The party political apparatus functions to ensure electoral legitimacy, to reduce the overall level of demands placed upon the system using its powers of cooptation and manipulation, and to provide a system of patronage (Hansen, 1974; Smith, 1979; Reyna, 1974). The role of the PRI in policy formulation and its ability to influence the day-to-day affairs of government is extremely limited. Neither does the party position appear to be a significant platform for stepping into the government. Party and government career tracks tend to remain separate (Smith, 1979). This contrasts markedly with Venezuela where separation of party political criteria from the allocation of government posts occurs only in a limited number of agencies.

Modernization of the local state

These trends towards modernization at the national level have clearly had their local and regional repercussions. Indeed, this same tendency towards improved efficiency, rationalization and agency autonomy has been apparent to differing degrees in our three cities.

Bogotá's administration, even more than the national government, has managed to establish several highly effective and efficient public utilities. The city authorities have set up a series of autonomous institutes which are partially shielded from day-to-day political influence. While such protection has never been afforded to institutes such as the garbage company or the bus company, it has been institutionalized in agencies such as electricity, water and telephones. Not every house is serviced but the companies are regarded as essentially technical agencies which are capable of providing services and gradually do so. Partisan political requests are made of these agencies but are contained. These agencies function according to a routine, established on technical grounds, and services are costed and priced accordingly. The same is true for Mexico City where certain agencies have consistently managed to maintain their autonomy from political interference. The electricity company and, to a lesser extent, the water and sanitation department are characterized by the stability of their personnel and the technical formulation of their programmes. To a considerable extent, their policies continue despite major changes in general government policy. Of course, their broadly technical nature does not guarantee efficiency nor the servicing of low-income settlements, points to which we shall return below. Nor are they totally immune from external, political pressure; something clearly demonstrated by the way President Echeverría intervened to favour specific settlements. However, this experience seems to have been exceptional and is not typical of the normal procedures of, nor the normal expectations about, these agencies. Valencia, by contrast, has no such technical agencies. The few functions which the municipal authority is expected to perform are carried out by direct dependencies of a highly politicized council.

Bogotá and Mexico City both have a certain number of these technical agencies, but all three cities have examples of the political agency. In Bogotá, the political agency is exemplified by the bus company which a past mayor has described as demonstrating 'all the ills to which a mistaken and improvized management can lead' (Bogotá, Alcaldía Mayor, 1976: 36). In 1979, the company had ten drivers for every bus and an accumulated debt of about 13 million pounds.[6] In Mexico City, the field of land regularization has proved most susceptible to political interference, particularly prior to 1977. During the 1960s, the Oficina de Colonias intervened in settlement issues as a means of garnering popular support for the CNOP wing of the PRI (see chapter 5). Later reconstituted as the Procuradaría de Colonias Populares, it continued to lend support to the CNOP but tended to function more as a troubleshooter in the low-income settlements. Under Mayor Sentiés, it furnished information about settlement conflicts, exercised largesse by distributing milk and free gifts, and provided a means of bypassing other agencies which had failed to resolve a crisis. The proliferation of agencies with overlapping responsibilities appears to have been a deliberate ploy aimed at enhancing the Executive's ability to manipulate factions and dissident resident groups as well as to provide opportunities for graft. No matter how much officials strove to operate rationally, they were beset by grossly inadequate funding, presidential insistence that they offer a sympathetic ear to all requests, and by frequent countermanding of their instructions by higher authority. The main purpose of these agencies for the Executive was to perform specific covert functions; their overt roles were almost incidental. In Valencia, the politics of agency operation are demonstrated by the fierce debates in the council over the appointment and dismissal of council employees whenever the party in power changes. The truth is that politicians do not expect these agencies to fulfil their overt, formal functions. Some potholes should be filled in and some rubbish should be collected but this is not their only or perhaps even their prime role. Their other functions are to provide jobs for political appointments and to offer favours. On the whole, they perform these roles quite effectively and it is certain that political stability and the form of electoral competition depends heavily on this kind of agency. Councillors in Valencia, and indeed in Bogotá, gain votes by getting political allies jobs in the bureaucracy; many poor settlement leaders rely upon this kind of patronage.[7] In Valencia, as in most Venezuelan cities, 'party politics pervades almost every aspect of local government' (Martínez, 1977: 314). To a limited extent Valencia tried to modernize its municipal machinery in 1978 when it set up more technocratic procedures and more 'responsible' recruitment procedures. But, this has been a much later development than in the other cities and, judged by the departure of certain key 'career' recruits, does not seem to have been markedly successful.

These differences in organization, responsibility and autonomy mean that power in each city is exercised in different ways. Economic, social and political stability is maintained and the growth of the city channelled through different mechanisms. In Bogotá, the authorities employ a complex mixture of accumulative and legitimizing tools. The technical service agencies maintain economic growth in the city by providing industry with water, light and telephones. But they also help to legitimize the social system by providing some services to the poor. Although they work on commercial criteria, the agencies supply the poor even if that process may be quite slow. Indeed, the poor actually benefit from cross-subsidization by the agencies; the more affluent housing areas pay much more for water than do low-income areas.[8] There is no legitimacy crisis in this sector in Bogotá, although there was a potential crisis in the late sixties. By contrast, there are serious criticisms made of the services provided by the more politicized, less technical agencies. These agencies' effectiveness is limited not only by their inefficiency but also by their budgets.[9] Because they are known to operate in the way they do, limited funds are made available to them. The consequence is that they perform little in the way of servicing and merely provide patronage to settlement leaders and political activists who might otherwise oppose the political and social system. In this way, they serve some poor people and indirectly maintain the stability of the system which favours the more affluent. Unlike electricity, water and telephones, the efficiency of service provision does not improve because industry and the rich do not depend directly on the service output. Education and health for the poor, for example, are provided inadequately by the politicized public agencies while the higher-income groups are covered by the private sector. There is consequently no sustained pressure from higher-income groups to improve education and health services. Budgets continue to be inadequate, and are deliberately held back both because the services are administered incompetently and because they are not needed by the influential. Given the choice between better services for the poor and higher taxes on land and incomes, the outcome is easy to predict.

In Bogotá, therefore, the lack of sustained political pressure from the poor and the degree to which the poor are genuinely serviced by the more efficient agencies maintains stability. In Mexico, stability is achieved through a combination of gradual service provision and by settlement cooptation and careful manipulation of political factions. In Valencia, stability is maintained much more through patron–client relationships. Because of Venezuela's affluence the government bureaucracy is relatively large and, despite inefficiency in the service agencies, budgets stretch to provide some utilities. It is clear in all three cities that the state operates most effectively and rapidly in areas critical to the interests of powerful economic and political groups. If industrial growth is threatened by the lack of electricity then the authorities are likely to improve its supply. If roads in the more affluent residential suburbs are not maintained, political pressure is exerted and action is taken. By contrast, state action in the poorer parts of the city or dedicated to improving the welfare of their populations is slow, inadequate and politicized. It is only when some major political threat is posed to the system that the poor receive greater attention in the process of resource allocation. In Bogotá, a major threat of this kind came when the National Front coalition was threatened by the ANAPO party in 1970; extensive improvements in water and sewerage provision soon followed. In Mexico, the emergence of a major protest movement (MRC) in the early seventies led to major improvements in drainage and water supply for the huge areas of low-income settlement in the east of the city. In Valencia, a political threat is posed every five years at election time; during the election period more invasions are permitted and more settlements are serviced.

Water and drainage provision

The differences in bureaucratic styles in each city, and in different agencies within each city, can be illustrated by comparing how the water and drainage companies have sought to supply low-income areas.

Bogotá

In Bogotá, the water agency is a good example of the technical kind of agency. Although it is accused, along with every other institution, of political partisanship in its relations with the *barrios*, it is our opinion that such political rationality is very limited. There are signs that some political influence affected decisions in the later sixties but since 1970 this has rarely occurred. It is not by chance that the water and drainage company (EAAB) acts primarily as a technical agency. Ever since it became a municipal responsibility in 1914, water provision has been deliberately protected from partisan political intervention. The main source of this protection has come through the board of directors, which has been appointed largely from financial institutions rather than by the political parties. This tendency was strengthened in 1946 when the forthcoming Panamerican Conference convinced the city authorities that they must expand public services. They took out large loans with several banks to improve the supply of water, and the lending institutions required that the financial viability of the water authority be guaranteed. As such, a board of directors consisting of three representatives of the lending institutions, the mayor, the head of the Central Bank, and two nominees of the municipal council was established. This board of functional representatives outnumbering party nominees was given autonomy to sign contracts and to take out loans. When the water company was merged with the drainage secretariat in 1955, the newly formed EAAB was given an identical board of directors and continued financial responsibility and autonomy.

One consequence of this autonomy has been that the directorship of the EAAB has never been under the same pressure from the political parties. Unlike the heads of most secretariats in Bogotá, and many of the decentralized agencies, the director of the water authority has remained in office for long periods. Between 1964 and 1975, there were only 3 directors. Since 1975, when the mayor took over responsibility for nominating the director from the board, the company has had 4 directors, an average occupancy period of about two years. But, this rate is still much lower than in the more politicized agencies. For example, DAAC had 17 directors between its formation in 1962 and 1979, IDU had 11 between its foundation in 1972 and 1982, an average of approximately one director *per annum* in both cases. This stability has an important effect on staffing within the agency; the officials are semi-permanent, technical appointees. The technical character of the EAAB was further reinforced in the middle sixties when a loan request was made to the World Bank to finance the giant Chingaza project. The World Bank sent down an evaluation team, was somewhat critical of the functioning of the agency, and from then on closely supervised the enterprise. The firm control exercised by the World Bank over the enterprise from 1967 to 1976 was on occasion denounced in the city council. When two members of the board of directors were elected to the municipal council in 1972, the Bank insisted on their resignations. Despite their annoyance at such demands, most politicians in the city accepted that this was a small price to pay for the flow of foreign loans and the development of a highly efficient enterprise. In general, the company has satisfied that desire. While there were long periods of water shortage during 1980 and 1981, this was primarily due to the failure of contractors to finish the giant Chingaza project. Once this project is completed, the city will again be well supplied.

The regular expansion in capacity of the water and drainage authority has reinforced its broadly technical procedures. Relations between the agency and the low-income settlements have normally been on a non-partisan basis. That relationship has also been influenced by the fact that the water company loses money in serving low-income settlements and has therefore been less than enthusiastic in its servicing of the more problematic parts of the city.[10] Indeed, the agency has sometimes been intransigent in its dealings, both with other

Bogotá agencies and with individual settlements, when it has felt that servicing a settlement would be expensive.[11] Its general line has been to persuade settlements to find some part of the cost of servicing. A range of schemes has appeared over the past few years, but a common characteristic has been that work would begin if the local community could raise 30 per cent of the cost of the project.[12] The agency has then been prepared to supply a low-income settlement even when it has lacked planning permission and legal status: an attitude that has caused some problems with the planning authority (Fuentes and Losada, 1978). The advantage of this self-financing strategy for the agency is twofold. First, it slows the rate of demands by settlements for services by placing a substantial, if not insuperable, hurdle across their path. The rule puts the onus on the community rather than on the enterprise. Where servicing is straightforward, and therefore cheap, the 30 per cent should not be too great a barrier to a reasonably well-organized *barrio*. Where servicing is difficult, however, the 30-per-cent deposit can be substantial. In this case, it protects the agency from having to service an expensive area. When, however, the settlement overcomes the barrier by finding the money (often as we shall see through partisan political processes), the agency will usually act. Second, the 30-per-cent self-finance rule means that the agency has some protection against partisan political pressure. If the 30 per cent is sometimes reduced to 25 per cent when the agency is sufficiently hard pressed by partisan influence, it still serves to protect the agency from continuous political pressure.

Since 1978, the growing capacity of the water company and the growing willingness of the World Bank to fund social projects has meant that there is a lot of money available for servicing low-income settlement in Bogotá.[13] This means that the initiative for servicing low-income settlements now rests much more with the agency and less with individual settlements. Partisan political pressures are likely to be weakened still further because of this situation.

These facts do not mean that the water authority has never indulged in partisan political behaviour nor that it has always been free of pressure from politicians. Indeed, our research revealed some interesting examples of political interference and involvement in the supply of water to low-income communities.

Before 1970, there are examples of political pressure being exerted successfully on the water authority. Atenas, one of our survey settlements, was serviced with the help of the pirate urbanizer's brother who happened to be on the city council; he persuaded the mayor to put pressure on the water authority. Without this assistance the location of the settlement would have made the installation of services problematic. Even here, however, the settlement was required to participate in the cost of installation. There are other examples of settlements which had clear political leverage and which were serviced surprisingly quickly. But of these cases several raised the money themselves, and of the rest all obtained water before World Bank influence was really established. Perhaps the clearest case relates to Casablanca where the settlement had been refused water consistently because it was too high to supply without pumping. It was not until an influential politician with an estate next to the *barrio* became mayor of the city that water was installed. Pressure from the new mayor soon brought a compromise: if the settlement found the pump and some of the pipes, the agency would provide technical help and water. The water supply was inaugurated in May 1970 with the mayor in attendance. Even in this clear example of political influence, however, the money was provided by agencies outside the water authority, one a charity and one an agency of the district government (Integración Popular).

But, if there are examples of successful political influence there are many other cases in recent years where such influence has been unproductive. In general, if there is a *prima facie* case of political influence before 1970 there is no real case after. Certainly, politicians have been active in the settlements promising to help obtain water, but we do not believe they have been very effective. More often than not, those politicians with knowledge of agency decisions have used their knowledge to seek political support in the *barrios*. For example, two appointees to the board of directors of the water company, who aspired to become city councillors, began visiting settlements in one area of the city, soliciting electoral support in return for the delivery of water. The fact that the board had already determined to supply the area was, of course, unknown to the communities and allowed the politicians to pretend that it was they who would obtain the water for the settlements. Rather than exercising partisan political influence on the technical agency to change its policy, they used its decisions to win electoral support – a vital but frequently ignored distinction. The only political decisions that have affected the policy of the water company have been those made at the top. For example, President Pastrana determined to increase the supply of water to low-income settlements in an effort to win back the support of the poor from ANAPO. He sought to implement such a policy by providing new sources of funds. This method, of course, did not distinguish between settlements according to their political affiliation. A large number of settlements were supplied, not individually favoured *barrios*. Water supply was made a specific political objective, made into agency policy and then introduced in a technical manner. Partisan political goals were, of course, instrumental in the decision-making process but the method of winning support was very different from what would probably have occurred in Valencia. The need for continuing technical expertise was accepted, hence no interference with the agency's procedures was apparent, and new funds were found to finance the operation. Indeed, in Bogotá, it seems that only by finding non-agency funds can politicians influence distribution policies.

Both features of this policy in Bogotá can be illustrated by recent decisions. In one settlement, Britalia, considerable pressure was being placed on the EAAB by the community, politicians and various government agencies. Yet, despite this pressure, the agency was able to delay supplying drainage time and again. Using technical arguments, sometimes we believe fallaciously, the agency managed to gain more time and to find a solution that was more convenient and cheaper to itself. It also protected itself from financial difficulties by relying on the 30-per-cent contribution by the community – collections were being made when a return visit was made to the community in 1982.

By contrast, high-level political pressure evokes a different response. In October 1979, floods hit thirty *barrios* including nine in the Patio Bonito area close to Britalia. Although most of the settlements were outside the sanitary perimeter, because they were below the level of the River Bogotá, a commission was immediately set up consisting of EAAB, EEEB and CAR representatives. This group agreed to fit a 'superpump' on the river, costing approximately 2 million US dollars, to divert water away from floodable areas (*El Espectador*, 8–9 November 1979). A crisis brought about an initiative by the Mayor which was transformed into a servicing policy for the *barrios*.

In sum, we would argue that the Bogotá water agency performs a political role on behalf of the governing party by acting principally according to technical rationale. When it is necessary to diverge from its broadly commercial policy, high-level politicians normally find additional monies to finance necessary works. At times, the agency comes under attack as part of the partisan political activity of the city, especially close to election times. But such debates are also conducted normally on technical grounds. The severe criticism that the agency suffered over the water shortages and its pricing policy during 1980 and 1981 focused on its technical competence and high-handed behaviour. It was difficult for parties to charge the agency with partisan political bias; criticism focused on real problems that temporarily faced the agency.

Mexico City

The supply of water to Mexico City is in the hands of agencies that act in a broadly technical fashion. The supply of water and drainage to individual households, however, is much more open to partisan political influence, even though it is administered by the same agencies.

There is no doubt that the image of the water agencies, the DGCOH in the Federal District and the CEAS in the State of Mexico, is broadly technical. Both have developed this image through their ability to provide a regular water supply to the city, through the manner in which they carry out their activities, and by the stability of their personnel. The Federal District Water Agency (DGCOH) and its predecessors, the DGOH and the DGAyS, have always been in charge of large budgets. Between 1971 and 1974, when the deep-drainage system was being built, from 30 to 40 per cent of the Federal District's total investment budget was in the DGOH agency's hands. The large budget has been an outcome of the demands of major commercial and industrial companies in Mexico City for a good water supply. It is our opinion that efficiency and stability have been demanded of the agency by the need to manage such a large budget. The evidence of this efficiency and stability are not difficult to demonstrate. First, the agency has managed to supply most of the business needs of the city despite the speed of urban growth. Second, agency personnel have not changed as regularly as in other government offices; the director general of the DGAyS, for example, remained in office from 1954 until his death in 1978 when he was replaced by his deputy.

In supplying domestic consumers the DGCOH and its predecessors have tried to develop technical routines for the distribution of water. In this area, however, the agency is more vulnerable to directives from politicians, notably the president or the mayor. Between them the latter decide the sort of service the agency is to provide and the priorities that are established. Occasionally, they even intervene directly to solve the problems of particular settlements, but such intervention is exceptional and the normal practice is for the agency to 'interpret' its guidelines in a technical fashion within the political and financial constraints imposed.

The priority which different administrations have given to the supply of water and drainage to low-income areas has varied markedly. Prior to 1977, the *barrios* were given low priority partly because the primary and secondary networks had not been completed. The agency could not take the initiative because there was no mechanism whereby they could recover the costs of installation directly from the consumers. Since investment had to come from the ordinary budget and be recovered by the treasury under a separate account, any commitment to servicing the poor required a major budget increase. Because additional appropriations were not provided by the DDF to supply low-income areas, servicing continued on a rather *ad hoc* basis.

In the 1960s, Mayor Uruchurtu responded to public pressure and relaxed the requirement that settlements be legalized before services could be provided: from then on anyone paying property tax was eligible. His successor continued and extended the practice, and service provision and land regularization soon came to be linked to the process of political patronage; those settlements that managed to create a link with a top government official were most likely to be serviced (Cornelius, 1975). These officials would sometimes exert pressure on the agency; when the directive came from the president or mayor the settlement was serviced. Yet officials from the agency argue that they tried to respond sympathetically to all settlement requests and tried to resist pressures that would result in queue jumping. Nevertheless, during Echeverría's presidency, when popular mobilization and petitioning was strongly encouraged and when a large proportion of the agency's expenditure was directed towards the deep drainage programme, few low-income areas were adequately supplied. Those settlements that were serviced gained from political intervention on their behalf. Most settlements were provided with hastily installed systems of public standpipes or supplied by water tankers. Both methods were inefficient and costly; standpipes led to a lot of water being lost, and because they are not metered the water was provided free of charge. Water tankers were still worse. In 1973, 1,000 litres of water delivered by tanker cost between 40 and 60 *pesos*; the cost of an equivalent piped supply was only 3 *pesos*. Politically, of course, the method had its uses. The mayor and president maintained their patronage systems and the total cost was less than that of providing a proper supply. The resident groups which shouted loudest, or had good links with high-level decision makers, were the most likely to receive some kind of service. Although the DGAyS disapproved, once the ground rules had been set by a combination of directive and financial constraints they were obliged to follow them. The agency could only act as efficiently as the circumstances permitted.

In 1977, new policies were introduced to improve the efficiency and coverage of the supply to low-income neighbourhoods. The agency's internal structure was reorganized and certain water and drainage functions were delegated to the *delegados*. The Federal District Water Plan identified the unserviced areas and planned to provide 1.2 million people with domestic water and 2 million with drainage by the end of 1982. Since 1977, decisions on the distribution of water to domestic users have rested with the *delegado*. Agency policy constrains their independence by obliging *delegados* to extend the network, recover costs, and encourage community works. However, the *delegado* has considerable power over the ordering of which settlements have highest priority. In effect, this means that politicians determine who gets water. Of course, the *delegado* receives technical advice and feasibility studies from his own engineers, but his final decision cannot be wholly technical. The *delegado*'s overriding concern is to maintain stability and control and to avoid upsurges of public protest. He is likely to accommodate political criteria alongside the technical advice that he gets from his subordinates. A settlement that is compliant to the *delegado*'s view, which presses hard for services and where the costs of installation are not prohibitive is likely to receive speedy attention. A weakly organized or non-compliant settlement may well be dropped from the programme, especially if servicing would be expensive. Therefore, although the operations of the water agency continue to be governed primarily by technical criteria, there is now greater opportunity for partisan rationality on matters concerned with domestic supply. The role of the DGCOH is now like that of the technical national agencies higher up the water procurement ladder; as with the CAVM, its function is one of providing the water and extending the primary network to get it to the distributors lower down the order.

One should not be misled by the apparently 'political' statements contained in the DGCOH budget proposals. In the normal manner of

Mexican bureaucracy, agency officials are not averse to using political arguments to justify their programme development. They are likely to argue that failure to provide an adequate supply of water or to prevent flooding will have serious repercussions on the government's image. The aim of the agency is not simply one of providing a service but also of preventing public discontent. In their words, 'water is used not simply to put out real fires but also to douse political fires' (Mexico, DDF, 1979: 36). Technical rationality is clearly not incompatible with political goals.

In the State of Mexico, water and drainage are the responsibility of a special commission created in 1973 (Comisión Estatal de Aguas y Saneamiento). Created with federal funds to help overcome the social unrest in Netzahualcóyotl and Ecatepec during the early 1970s, it installed services to most settlements by 1978. The costs of household supply are being recouped from residents over a ten-year period. It is staffed by trained officials who are responsible to the state governor. In theory, CEAS should sell water in bulk to the municipality, which is responsible for the supply and sale to residents. In effect, however, the municipality is too small a unit to have the necessary resources and personnel, so CEAS takes responsibility. In this respect, municipal intervention is less marked than that now given to their approximate counterparts, the *delegaciones*, within the Federal District.

Water and drainage provision in Mexico City, therefore, is predominantly 'technical' with respect to water procurement and to the supply of business, industrial and higher-income residential users. Water and drainage are essential if these sectors are to maintain their economic growth; consequently the water authorities receive high priority in government budgets. For those sectors that can afford to pay for their water there is no difficulty in being served; norms, charges and procedures are all clearly laid down by the agency and followed strictly. The poor, however, do not fall into this category. Whether they are serviced depends on the political priority given to satisfying their needs and the pressures that local groups exert on the government. The agency continues to act in a technically responsible way, but political rationality becomes more influential. Politicians influence the priorities list and press the agencies to favour certain settlements before others.

Valencia

Water in Valencia is provided under contract to the municipality by

INOS, a decentralized national institute dependent on the Ministry of the Environment (MARNR). The institute is divided into nine regional divisions, one of which has its headquarters in Valencia. There is no doubt that in most respects it is a much more politicized agency than the Bogotá water company.

With respect to personnel, the high-level posts in Caracas and in the regions are appointments based on political confidence; though most appointees have the technical competence to do their job, they resign when the national administration changes. Another indication of the intrusion of political rationality into the agency's operations is the way the budget fluctuates. The INOS investment budget for water and drainage in Carabobo during the seventies showed a cyclical pattern with high expenditures during election years. For example, more than half of the investment in water between 1969 and 1973 came in the 1973 election year, and the same was true in the 1974–8 period.[14] These increases have led to the supply of water to problem settlements close to election times (see pp. 102–3). A further indication of partisan influence on servicing is the fact that low-income settlements pay very little towards the cost of installation and nothing for water supply. In fact, INOS attempted to introduce supply charges in 1969 but was opposed by the municipality; since then the subject of charges for poorer groups has been regarded as a somewhat sensitive matter (Cannon *et al.*, 1973).[15] One outcome of this situation is that INOS, unlike the Bogotá water authority, is nowhere near to self-financing, one of the original aims of the organization. Between 1969 and 1975 the company's own sources of revenue accounted for 20.2 to 38.4 per cent of their total income (Venezuela, INOS, 1977).

At the regional level, the local office is highly dependent upon political influence in Caracas to determine its budget. Thus, only the intervention of the governor for Carabobo through the national president persuaded INOS to introduce a crash programme to construct a new pipeline in the early seventies. The new system served to overcome something of a crisis in the city's water situation and permitted the servicing of numerous low-income settlements. Partisan political influence is also a feature of certain decisions to service particular settlements. Thus, although the general policy of INOS had been to avoid servicing settlements which have been formed through the invasion of private land, during the build-up to the 1978 election a new governor and the INOS regional director agreed to provide water for as many of such settlements as possible. One of our survey *barrios* was a beneficiary of this programme, an official water supply being inaugurated very close to election day. Since that time, and despite national policy as adumbrated by CORDIPLAN, MINDUR and FUNDACOMUN, the service agencies have been supplying low-income settlements.[16] Local directors of INOS agreed that, while they had little control over their total budget, they did exercise full responsibility over which settlements would be serviced. In taking up cases they are strongly influenced by pressure from the council and the governor's office. This suggests that queue jumping is common practice, that particular settlements with access to key decision makers through party links are serviced before other less well-connected settlements. Certainly, communities such as Las Brisas and Renny Ottolina received water extraordinarily quickly compared to the normal pace of servicing *barrios* (see pp. 102–3). In the past, the municipal council was more inclined to intervene in the supply of water by splicing into the main water line and paying INOS the cost of the water, a process that was very open to political influence (Cannon *et al.*, 1973: 108).[17] In addition, INOS itself used to provide materials and supervision with which *barrios* could build their own water systems. Of course, it is by no means true that only settlements with political clout receive services; programmes were announced in 1971 and 1973 which embraced large numbers of settlements and which it was claimed would achieve 'a transformation of the conditions of daily life for marginal classes' (Governor Estopiñan quoted in *El Cara-bobeño* 13 March 1973). But, if political rationality is not the only criterion entering decision-making, it is an important influence in the way settlements obtain water in Valencia.

INOS differs from the water authority in Bogotá insofar as it is neither financially autonomous nor free to make major decisions about expansions in servicing. It must rely on alliances between regional and national politicians in order to obtain increased budgets. At particular conjunctures, the lack of such alliances has meant that the city has suffered from major shortages of water. Such shortages may well have had something to do with the fact that INOS supplies mainly commercial and residential users; the important industrial sector mainly supplies its own needs through wells. Given that a major pressure group has been largely unaffected by the recurrent shortages in the city, demands on the national agency for greater action may well have been more muted. There is also little pressure on the agency to employ a more technical rationale. The officials within INOS are clearly pressing towards this end but the fact that much of their budget comes from outside the agency means that they are forced to respond to political pressure. In addition, although INOS has applied for loans from the Interamerican Development Bank and although the Bank tried to modify agency procedures and tariff policy as a condition for its loans (Cannon *et al.*, 1973), it has never been under the same international pressure as the EAAB. The outcome of all these factors suggests that water provision is much more influenced by partisan political processes in Valencia. Such partisanship affects both the regional budget of the agency and the processes which determine the particular settlements selected for servicing. We would emphasize, however, that the provision of water through INOS in Valencia is not as open to local partisan influence as the allocation of other kinds of resources, notably land and municipal jobs. In large part, of course, this is because INOS is less open to local partisan political pressure than the municipality.

Conclusion

During the past thirty years the role of the state has expanded greatly in the three national economies. In the context of this study, it is most relevant to note that the state has become involved in those urban activities which the private sector is unable to supply itself owing to the nature of the collective good. Electricity, water, drainage and telephones are the most notable examples, together with some participation in health for the poor, social security, transportation and education. In general, the public sector has intervened most effectively and decisively in those areas essential to economic growth and in those sectors where more affluent residential groups could finance the service – notably water, drainage, electricity, roads and telephones. As a result, the quality of services by sector of the city is a function of socio-economic status. Wealthy residential areas have services installed before homes are occupied while low-income residential areas sometimes have to wait many years before servicing. The wealthy pay for the services when they purchase the land, the poor cannot afford to and consequently buy into illegal and unserviced communities. If state intervention has come in areas integrally linked to the process of economic growth, there has also been a concern for social legitimation and welfare. As a result, urban social conditions have tended to improve for most members of the poor even if a substantial minority continue to suffer from an unacceptably low standard of living.

We have distinguished between three different kinds of urban services: those which are of critical importance to powerful economic and residential interest groups but are too complex to be provided by the private sector alone; those which are of interest to all social groups but are provided by the private sector for those who can pay; and those 'social services' that are provided by the state for the poor. On the whole, we are concerned with the first and third of these services. It is our contention that the first is more likely to be provided efficiently by the state, the third is likely to be supplied with limited funds and effectiveness. Electricity and water receive large budgets while state health and education are provided cheaply and at low quality for the poor.

Indeed, we believe that within the same urban and national economy the manner in which state institutions conduct themselves varies according to the nature of the service. The first category of services is provided by relatively 'efficient' and 'technical' state companies, the last by relatively 'inefficient' and 'politicized' agencies. Indeed, in Bogotá the differences between the 'technically rational' water and electricity companies and the 'politically rational' rubbish-disposal and bus companies are most marked. It seems to us that the two sets of agencies play distinct roles in the urban society; the former is expected to provide a service efficiently at a price; the latter is expected to legitimate the state. The legitimation role may take the form of providing a service but it may also be linked to the 'politically rational' role of providing jobs for partisan political allies. Many of the state agencies in all three cities were competent only at providing jobs through the political patronage system; this, indeed, was their major role.

Clearly, this distinction between the 'technical' and the 'political' agency is city-specific. In Valencia, most agencies operated according to 'political rationality', in Bogotá some had been deliberately protected from partisan political activity. To some extent, these differences were reflected in servicing levels; water and electricity provision was more efficiently supplied in Mexico City than in Valencia.

Differences are also apparent in how the poor are actually supplied by these different kinds of agencies in the different cities. The technical agencies follow commercial criteria in the allocation of services. Those settlements which are located in difficult physical areas wait much longer than those close to existing water or electricity lines or those located at convenient altitudes for servicing. Older and more consolidated settlements are likely to be serviced more quickly. On the other hand, the more partisan agencies tend to follow more politically rational criteria in allocation. Political patronage is a critical variable in determining the rate of servicing in Valencia, but seems less important in Mexico and in Bogotá, at least with respect to lighting, water and sewerage. The extent to which politicians are directly involved in the servicing of settlements depends in part upon the political situation in each city and partly upon the nature of public utility organization. In Valencia, where the nature of Venezuelan democracy intrudes into most activities and where the capacity of the service companies is limited, political links are sometimes critical for a settlement's servicing. In Bogotá, where since the late sixties a deliberate effort has been made to increase energy and water supplies and to keep day-to-day partisan political activity out of their administration, political interference in favour of particular settlements is more limited. In Mexico, party political interference has had a limited effect upon whether or not services are granted to a *barrio*, though the influence and involvement of politicians appears to increase around election times.

There is an important difference in the policies of governments in the three cities with respect to the legalization and servicing of low-income settlements. In Bogotá and Mexico City, recent administrations have attempted to incorporate these settlements into the serviced area; in Valencia this attempt has not yet materialized. In part, this reflects the different capacities of the servicing agencies. In Bogotá and Mexico City, the agencies' capacity has generally kept up with demand and they are able to service the low-income settlements at a price. Social legitimation in these areas can be achieved through servicing rather than through political patronage. It also has the advantage of integrating the society into similar patterns of social and economic involvement. Home-owners occupying legalized lots with services are likely to feel more integrated and less hostile to the regime. There is political point to technical servicing and to the partial elimination of partisan processes of patronage.

5

Community organization: participation or social control?[1]

We now focus our attention at the *barrio* level and examine the structure of the community organizations that have emerged to defend and develop settlement interests. The need for brevity obliges us to concentrate our analysis around two key issues. First, how much impact does community mobilization have upon the upgrading process? What is the extent of resident participation and how far does participation significantly affect the likelihood of servicing? Second, what governs the response that the state makes to community-development issues? Here our concern is to identify the motives of the state and to account for the way in which it handles community issues. Is the state basically sympathetic, attempting to help the poor as much as it can with limited resources, or is it concerned with maximizing social control by containing demand making to acceptable (and probably low) levels? Our aim is to understand the forms and levels of community participation relating them to the structural characteristics of each city and society.

Few observers doubt the potential value of community participation in development although many question its practice in Latin America. Such a paradox has become increasingly obvious through time. A major gulf exists between reality and the way in which community action and participation should operate. Such a statement is true whatever the political stance of the observer. That right and left might agree about the state of community participation is at first sight surprising. But despite their differing perspectives both would agree that community participation should be encouraged, that community action is desirable. Many on the right support community action in poor capitalist societies in the sense of community self-help. Not only does self-help overcome resource deficiencies by producing community services and infrastructure, but it is also good in reducing dependence on the state. It promotes self-improvement and independence –

174

cherished right-wing values. For those on the left, community action may serve to improve physical standards but it is most necessary to raise consciousness. Herein lies the main difference from the right; the basic needs are to make poor communities aware of their class position and to encourage political action against those groups which monopolize wealth and resources. Between the political extremes, many see community participation as a means of improving both material standards and increasing the community's role in decision making. Good decision making depends upon planners and communities interchanging ideas and opinions. Community action not only helps supplement limited state budgets but is a way of modifying over-centralized state bureaucracies.[2] We portray the attitudes to community action within a poor capitalist economy in table 15. All three perspectives support active participation by the community; both material and community needs can be served in this way. The differences between the three viewpoints lies in the outcome of community action on the form of society and on the relationship between the state and the community. Those on the left trust that community participation will lead to a transformation of society; those on the right to the consolidation of traditional values and freedom (cf. Pearse and Stiefel, 1979).

If table 15 covers the range of ideals, the practice of community action in Latin America seldom reflects such hopes (Portes and Walton, 1976; Algara Cosío, 1981). The typical pattern in most low-income settlements is that there is little community participation, little collective activity, and few material improvements. Rather than community involvement leading to changes in the values or structures of society, the major influences originate from the state. In practice, it is apathy more than opposition or independence that is typical of most low-income communities. This situation is not the result of some 'culture of poverty', it is more a response to the attitude of the Latin American state. As Portes and Walton (1976: 108) note, 'relative absence of political radicalism is a consequence not of frustration but of the perceived impracticability of challenging the existing order'. Our argument is that a new objective of community action has been achieved in most Latin American cities. The main aim of community-action programmes is less to improve conditions for the poor or to modify forms of decision making than to legitimate the state. The main object of community action is how to help maintain existing power relations in society. The aim is not to change conditions for the poor as

Table 15 *Ideal–typical pictures of community participation and Latin American reality*

Perceived virtues of community participation	Priority or position adopted given the political perspective of observer			Outcome in practice in Latin America
	Left	Centre	Right	
Raising level of community activity and participation	High priority	High priority	High priority	Limited
Raising level of material improvements to community	High priority	High priority	High priority	Low
Relationship to the state	Opposition	Interdependence	Autonomy	Dependent
Effect on society	Social transformation	Reform of decision making and reduction of inequality	Raising of individual values	None

much as to make sure they cause no problems. Community action forms part of what Pearse and Stiefel (1979: 25) call the 'structures of anti-participation'. Most community-action programmes have been established by the state and are integrated into the state budget and bureaucracy. Rather than stimulating widespread community participation and endeavour, such 'bureaucratic institutionalization' (Dore and Mars, 1981: 13) tends to be diversionary and cooptive. Community participation in the sense of raising community awareness of social class and economic structure (*concientización*) has been limited to specific periods and governments (de Kadt, 1982).

The object of this chapter is to examine how community action and participation have developed in three Latin American cities. Our aim is to demonstrate how community action has been integrated into the wider patterns of state power and how social control has been achieved. We show how different political systems have developed similarly subtle but highly differentiated responses to low-income communities. State–community relations have developed according to the needs and abilities of the state. Because the state has adopted different patterns of response and control, the patterns of community participation vary.

A brief history of community participation in Latin America

Community participation in Latin America is hardly new. Twenty-five years have passed since the Alliance for Progress began to pour money into community participation and self-help projects in many Latin American cities. Whatever the precise aims of the Alliance, this approach was based on a particular view of community action. It was a view heavily influenced by the work of anthropologists and other social scientists who had worked in the settlements of Latin America in the fifties. Typical of this work was that of Mangin (1967) and Turner (1963) in Lima, Peru. Their observations of *barriada* formation on the outskirts of Lima helped to counteract the conventional wisdom of the day that the poor were subject to a 'culture of poverty'. Rather than apathy and exclusion, they demonstrated that settlement formation and community participation channelled the energies and aspirations of the poor in a positive direction. The picture that emerged from their accounts of swift overnight seizures of land was of highly efficient coordinated action by the poor; settlement formation both required and encouraged group organization. To gurantee the survival of a settlement, the community had to organize itself against any effort by the state to dislodge it. A clear image emerged: the autonomous community defending its rights and improving its position in society.

Later work suggests that community organization in Lima was much less autonomous than this picture conveyed and was born of exceptional circumstances. First, it seems that the state was in no sense divorced from the process of *barriada* formation. Collier (1976: chapter 4) shows how President Odría encouraged the development of settlements on state land as a means of consolidating support among the poor. His motive was to undermine the popularity of the recently deposed populist APRA party. He offered land to groups of the poor and kept the settlements sweet through the *ad hoc* provision of services and charity. Such an approach was necessary because APRA was one of the few mass-based parties to have developed in Latin America. Second, Odría used land to gather support among the poor because much of the land around Lima was owned by the State and because the land lacked alternative uses. 'Autonomous' communities could be encouraged in these circumstances because they posed little threat either to the state or to major vested-interest groups such as land-owners. Later administrations even modified Odría's policy by using invasions of peripheral state land to favour landowners by freeing valuable inner-city locations (Collier, 1976: 72–3). *Barriada* development and community participation in Lima, whatever their origins, helped create the image on which the community-action programmes of the Alliance for Progress were based.

The Alliance for Progress had a major impact upon national housing and community action policies throughout Latin America (Turner *et al.*, 1963). Created to foster reforms that would stem any widespread movement towards Cuba-style alternatives, the Alliance provided the funds for greater government intervention in the housing sector. In most countries, it provided capital for the creation of 'social-interest' housing banks which would offer loans to low-income home buyers (Connolly, 1982: 150; Murillo and Ungar, 1979). In many countries this period was unique in that government housing was made available to the poor. In Colombia, major loans under the Alliance allowed ICT, for the only time in its history, to build large housing estates for low-income groups (Stevenson, 1979).

As part of the developmental initiative of the Alliance, self-help and community participation became national priorities. Latin American governments made more formal commitments to 'community development' programmes than ever before. In Venezuela, for example, the Central Office for Coordination and Planning (CORDIPLAN) established a community development division which was particularly active during the early 1960s. Indeed, Turner *et al.* (1963: 372) wrote that 'Venezuela is the first Latin American Government to recognize the broad implications of community development as a vehicle for "democratizing" the country by strengthening local and regional responsibility and hence autonomy.' In Rio de Janeiro, most resident associations were formed with the support of the government of Guanabara State from 1960–2 and SERFHA (the Reclaiming Service for Favelas and Similar Housing) was particularly active at this time. In Colombia, the Community Action Department, created in 1958 as a part of the National Front agreement to provide a bipartisan political channel for demand making, received further support (Bagley and Edel, 1980: 282). The Alliance for Progress also fostered a more 'progressive' housing policy by ICT which introduced certain self-help initiatives through which residents could extend their core houses (Turner *et al.*, 1963: 385; Stevenson, 1979).

But, as the Cuban threat diminished in intensity and as US commitment to reform in Latin America declined, the flow of funds and initiatives slowed (Veliz, 1965). As direct foreign assistance declined so did the interest of many Latin American governments. In Rio de Janeiro the development of resident associations slowed, there was a major change of personnel in the housing agency, and new policies involving *favela* eradication and resettlement were introduced (Portes, 1979; Perlman, 1976). In Colombia, the reduced flow of external funds caused a major liquidity problem for the Housing Institute which shifted investment away from self-help programmes to accommodation that could be sold to higher-income groups (Stevenson, 1979). Community-action programmes in Colombia declined through lack of funding.

But, if Latin American governments failed to channel substantial resources to low-income communities, the latter were not ignored; governments continued to use neighbour associations as a means of enlisting support (Nelson, 1979: 270). Three basic mechanisms were employed. First, support was enlisted through the cooptation of leaders. 'Cooptation' describes the situation where 'an "informal", loosely structured group is led by its leader to formally affiliate with a supra-local institution' (Eckstein, 1977: 107). Cooptation may occur when the leader believes, often mistakenly, that formal affiliation will further the interests of those whom he represents by providing better access to the agencies distributing resources. Alternatively, the leader may seek affiliation for reasons of personal gain, for example to obtain a job or to advance his political career. Political parties and government departments may be eager to coopt leaders as a means of extending their influence over local constituencies. The important point to recognize is that the community may lose its autonomy and become subject to the orthodoxy of the coopting body. In some cases, for example the governing party in Mexico, cooptation may well reduce the chances of successful demand making (Eckstein, 1977); elsewhere it may provide an important foothold for successful negotiation where political support is exchanged for urban services (Leeds and Leeds, 1976).

A second mechanism of enlisting support is for the government or a political party systematically to institutionalize the channels of political mobilization, social control and neighbourhood improvement (Michl, 1973; Skinner, 1982). It seeks to develop formal channels to each community and therefore differs from cooptation which simply aims to influence selected leaders. Nelson cites the examples of the Committee for the Defence of the Revolution in Cuba, the National Organization for the Development of Pueblos Jóvenes (ONDEPJOV) in Velasco's Peru, and Promoción Popular in Frei's Chile as instances in which the state or party attempted to institutionalize local-community organization and affiliation into a single body (Nelson, 1979: 294–9). In these cases there were clearly twin aims: to foster allegiance and to stimulate community development. Some communities benefited from these programmes but there were dangers for both government and the communities involved. In Lima, for example, relations between SINAMOS and certain *barrio* organizations became very tense during the 1970s. The residents of Villa El Salvador, Lima's largest and most notorious low-income settlement, developed fairly radical demands which went far beyond issues of physical development and included proposals for a community bank, worker control over the industrial park, health and education. Ostensibly, these plans enjoyed the backing of the Velasco government and indeed offered a logical local outcome of the national strategy; in fact they received little concrete support from the state (Skinner, 1982). More importantly, once national priorities shifted towards the right, the government found that it could not 're-align' the community organization structure (Skinner, 1982).

The third form of support is based on clientelism. A patron–client relationship is an 'enduring dyadic bond based upon informally arranged personal exchanges of resources between actors of unequal status' (Grindle, 1977: 30). The relationship is typically informal and has no legal basis. In the case of the low-income communities, the leader, or 'broker', maintains a personal relationship with the politicians or administrators who control resources required by the community or members of that community. Patrons vary and in different contexts they may be politicians, landowners, agency heads, even the president himself (Collier, 1976; Ward, 1981a). President Odría used patron–client links to increase his influence over the residents of Lima's *barriadas*. In Mexico, such links prevailed throughout the 1960s and early 1970s; the fortunes of one settlement changed overnight when its long-standing 'patron' achieved high governmental office (Cornelius, 1975: 195).

Both military and civilian governments have used these, with the result that they have tended to undermine and suppress community autonomy and reduce active participation. Governments have also failed to channel resources to the poor especially in countries dominated by strong right-wing military regimes. Indeed, the tendency during the later sixties and seventies was for governments to rely much more strongly on repression as a means of social control. Certainly, recent experiences in Argentina, Brazil, Chile and Uruguay indicate little in the way of support for community action, let alone community autonomy. Even in Lima where Velasco's revolution promised to build a new Peru and where community participation was seen to be a major plank in national reconstruction, later regimes have held back on this commitment and have used more regressive methods (Skinner, 1981).

In the light of this experience, many observers on the left have sought to find ways by which low-income communities could break out of this stranglehold. They have shown how some communities have retained their ability to organize and fight for their rights in the city. Other writers, most notably Castells, have tried to show how the low-income settlement situation may even serve as a springboard for widespread political action and the arousal of class consciousness. Castells (1977; 1979) argues that the growing crisis experienced by the state in providing the means of collective consumption leads to potential sources of conflict around which class struggle can mobilize.[3] Urban groups respond to the crisis by organizing themselves into pressure groups demanding better conditions and, as consciousness increases, this leads to social change. Given an appropriate source of conflict around which definite 'stakes' can be identified, competent political leadership will establish an urban social movement. Castells is careful to distinguish between the urban social movement which creates a 'qualitatively new effect' in power relations, and 'consumer unionism' which focuses only on issues of consumption (*ibid:* 377). However, Saunders (1979: 118) argues that the major conflicts of interest among the poor (for example, between renters and owners or between established squatters and recent arrivals) makes mobilization unrealistic even given good political leadership. And, even if we assume that working-class solidarity is successfully forged, what should the next step be? 'How does a class in itself become a class for itself?' (Pickvance, 1977, quoted in Saunders, 1979: 119.) Despite these problems, examples of increased awareness and consequent political action have been examined by Handelman (1975), Montaño (1976), Castells (1977), Argüello (1982) and Janssen (1978). It has to be said however that, whatever the virtues of 'urban social movements', they seem to be thin on the ground.

Given the importance of leadership it is surprising that so few studies outside Mexico, have examined the issue of leadership in any detail (Ray, 1969; Roberts, 1973; Cornelius, 1973b, 1975; Ward, 1976a). Indeed, Nelson's otherwise comprehensive review of community politics contains only brief reference to the nature of leadership (Nelson, 1979: 261).

In the Mexican literature the nature of leaders and their links with outside institutions appear to range from those who represent the community and are 'elected' by them, to others who either impose themselves or are placed by groups from outside the *barrio* (Cornelius, 1973b). Some evidence also suggests that the type of leader may change as the physical status and demands of the settlement alter (Ward, 1976a: 301). The vital influence that a leader may have upon a settlement's physical development has been emphasized by Cornelius (1973b: 136).

Detailed descriptions for rural Mexico have identified many local leaders as *caciques*. A *cacique* is a 'strong and autocratic leader in local and/or regional politics whose characteristically informal, personalistic, and often arbitrary rule is buttressed by a core of relatives, 'fighters', and dependents, and is marked by the diagnostic threat and practice of violence' (Friedrich, 1968: 247). Cornelius argues that *caciques* have emerged also in urban areas and are primarily concerned with local-development issues (Cornelius, 1973b). The motivation is largely one of economic self-interest which they further through the misappropriation of donations and community savings and through backhanders from those members of the community who require favours. Their power stems from control over land allocation, often enforced by a gang of close supporters, and their ability to mobilize support from outside the settlement (Cornelius, 1973b: 143; Ray, 1969: 62). Abuses by the *cacique* are likely to be tolerated by residents so long as material benefits are obtained for the settlement. Herein lies a paradox. The *cacique* must avoid being too successful. If the settlement is quickly regularized and receives basic services it would undermine the need for his leadership; at the same time he must take care not to alienate his support from the community. The result may be deliberate 'foot dragging' whereby only slow progress is made towards the satisfaction of community demands (*ibid:* 143). This practice may be highly acceptable to the government insofar as it limits demands upon the bureaucracy (Cornelius, 1975: 200).

We must be careful not to generalize about the widespread existence of *caciquismo*, for even in Mexico its importance has been questioned. Montaño (1976: 69–72) challenges the concept on three counts. First, he criticizes Cornelius for confusing these utilitarian figures with other types of local leaders who are not *caciques*. Second, he suggests that it is highly unlikely that the PRI apparatus would readily allow the existence of a semi-autonomous power structure even though it believed that it could benefit by winning electoral support from *caciques*. Finally, Montaño complains that the concept directs too much attention to describing how the *caciques* exercise power rather than investigating the different mechanisms and functions of the state–community relationship. Montaño's own approach focuses more attention upon the relationship between settlements and the political and governmental systems. In his research, five categories emerge: collaborative and participative (*asistencialista*), clientelist, cooperative (with negotiation and exchange), oppositional, and confrontational. Unfortunately, he fails to identify the conditions which determine why different relationships emerge.

Community action programmes in Bogotá, Mexico City and Valencia

In Bogotá, Mexico City and Valencia the state has established formal frameworks for channelling demands for servicing, legalization and community upgrading. Needless to say, the forms of these structures differ in each city. In Bogotá the Department of Community Action has functioned, for many years, as the primary channel for *barrio*-bureaucracy relations. In Mexico City, until the neighbourhood councils (*juntas de vecinos*) were mobilized in 1977, there was no clearly defined structure. In Valencia, the improvement committees (*juntas pro-mejoras*) have changed form frequently in the twenty years since they were first established, but almost invariably have been controlled by whichever political party happened to be in power. In the following section we attempt to account for the different structures. Our aim is to describe briefly the political background shaping their creation and the way in which they work at a city-wide level. We examine the degree to which they involve party politics and ask the fundamental question: are they designed primarily to assist low-income populations or to control them?

Bogotá

As we argued in chapter 2, there is a long tradition for the state to constrain community organization and participation in demand making. The National Front and later administrations have continued to prescribe the terms on which they are prepared to negotiate with the poor. The channels they have developed to accommodate the petitions of the poor have been carefully modulated and controlled. They have offered much in terms of rhetoric but little in terms of real resources. This argument can be demonstrated clearly by the experience of the Community Action programme, the main institution developed by the National Front to handle community demands.

Community action was introduced into Colombia by law 19 of 1958 which empowered local authorities to establish *juntas de acción comunal* to improve community welfare. The national government would supervise the system through the Ministry of Government, and would provide technical assistance, subsidies and the training of personnel. In Bogotá, *Acuerdo* 4 of 1959 called for the establishment of *barrio juntas* which would be supervised by the Planning Department and assisted by social workers employed by that department.

Bagley and Edel (1980) point out that the structure of the community-action programme derived from the nature of the National Front political arrangement. The ruling class wanted to avoid political conflict between the parties, preserve its own power and status, but at the same time accommodate the demands from lower-income groups. As a result, while community-action programmes have sometimes been actively promoted, the political authorities have always taken care that community pressure is carefully channelled and circumscribed. Within these limits, community-action documents explain the *junta* as the embodiment of micro-planning, an organization designed to solve local problems in terms of local needs. The system is intended to increase the interchange of views between the communities and the planners, to foster community participation in the analysis and implementation of programmes and hence add to their efficiency and facilitate the contribution of human and economic resources.[4] In Bogotá, this continues to be the basic rationale despite various modifications in the organizational framework within which the local *juntas* operate. The most significant of these changes came in 1968 when the Department of Community Action (DAAC) was separated from the Planning Department (DAPD). We will confine most of our discussion to the period since this reorganization took place.

The *juntas de acción comunal* were originally intended to represent *barrios* with an average of approximately 4,000 inhabitants. This figure was modified nationally in 1969 to improve flexibility, and now *juntas* can be formed by as few as 15 neighbours. Until 1968, political parity was enshrined in the statutes of community action as it was in the National Front arrangement.[5] Since 1969, the eight members of the *junta* are elected democratically by the affiliated members of the community under the supervision of the Department of Community Action. In 1972, there were 560 *barrios* in Bogotá of which 340 had *juntas*; in August 1977, DAPD listed a total of 901 *barrios* with 587 *juntas*.

At first, community action received a lot of attention from National Front governments. Bagley and Edel (1980: 262) argue that 'From the second year of the Lleras administration through the administration of León Valencia, the National Front gave considerable support to Acción Comunal as a development program . . . The formal launching of the Alliance for Progress led to further initiatives related to Acción Comunal.' Even these critics suggest (p. 280) that 'By 1966, the Juntas de Acción Comunal were functioning effectively as channels of local participation in development projects. Indeed, with the creation of regional federations of *juntas*, the community program had even begun to assert a certain degree of independence from local, regional, and national political elites.' However, the reforms of Lleras Restrepo to the budgetary system limited the amount of patronage that individual congressmen had, forcing *juntas* to compete for that fixed amount. 'Under the new system, national allocations to community projects leveled off, ending the period of rapid growth in Acción Comunal' (Bagley and Edel, 1980: 268). And, in order to strengthen central-government control over these *juntas*, the Lleras administration limited and regulated available patronage, replaced the federations of *juntas* of community action with Integración Popular, and created a competitive *usuarios* organization paralleling the community-action *juntas*. 'These manoeuvres not only slowed the growth of community action but effectively curtailed virtually all popular pressures for basic societal reforms being channeled through *Acción Comunal*' (Bagley and Edel, 1980: 280).

Since these reforms a considerable gulf has separated theory and practice and no government has put much weight behind the programme. Community action has been publicly criticized on a variety of grounds including disorganization, lack of resources and a failure to communicate with or to help the communities. But the recurrent criticism has been that of *politiquería*, and we would place the DAAC within the category of the more partisan political kind of government institution described in chapter 4. Throughout the seventies, the press has reiterated a number of critical themes concerning the functions of the department and the community-action programme. It has been accused of inaction, excessive politicization, too much channelling of funds to political sympathizers, top-heavy paternalism, social control, poor accounting and auditing, and corruption among promoters. At the beginning of the seventies, the DAPD (1972: 282) accused the *juntas* of

having been highly politicized in practice even if formally they are not supposed to be . . . political parity has converted the *juntas* into the instruments of unscrupulous politicians, in search of votes in return for works. This has led to a lack of effective participation by the community in the *juntas*, with the limited power in the hands of cliques, which, in most cases, do not include the natural leader of the community.

Towards the end of the period the Liberal *El Espéctador* asked whether 'The twenty years of institutionalized community action represent a genuine and active entry into adulthood', and answered sadly that 'many of the ideals fell, not because of indolence, but due to the scourge of *politiquería* and greed' (*Editorial*, 31 March 1979).

It is useful to contrast this impression with the views of recent directors of the DAAC and with the evidence drawn from our communities. Many of the directors admitted the politicization and claimed that their main job was to remove it, others claimed that they were trying to make the department less legalistic, more open to the communities, better organized and more responsive to the needs of the low-income population. The ability of any of the directors to achieve these reforms has been limited severely, however, by their typically short periods of office. Between 1962 and 1979, the department had 17 directors, one of the clearest signs of a politically partisan agency. The high turnover is caused by the political controversy which the department attracts, because of its limited budget which discourages good directors from staying, and because many directors see the main virtue of the job as providing a good entry point into politics, especially the city council. The job certainly offers a platform from which a political career can be launched and generates the community contacts which can, though are not certain to, provide votes.

Despite these problems the department has been successful in stimulating community self-help around projects such as schools and community halls, encouraging communities to form *juntas*, channelling requests for help to the servicing agencies, and in mobilizing limited funds to help with community services. It is difficult to generalize because every director has his own priorities and methods and, since each has normally been appointed after some kind of crisis, he is anxious to distance himself from the policies of his predecessor. But, certain facts are clear. First, the department has a rather small budget (in 1980 the equivalent of around 1.7 million dollars) which is quite inadequate to provide much in the way of works. For this reason the department has sometimes promised money only to projects which have already had money from some other source, a sensible way of directing councillors' *auxilios* and other funds into useful projects. Although it provides communities with public services in this way, it nearly always insists on the communities contributing labour to the project.

Second, it does manage to organize *juntas* and the elections and to keep community organization working. The success of the agency can be seen in the expansion of the number of *juntas* from the 340 in 1972 to 587 in 1977. New *barrios* tend to approach the Department of Community Action or its local promoter about the possibility of setting up a *junta*. A visit is arranged for a Sunday when an official of the department will give a talk about the significance of forming a *junta*, the obligations and advantages of such a step, and the way in which the *junta* committee should be elected. *Barrio* leaders may then be encouraged to set aside a plot for the future construction of a community hall, to organize fund-raising events, and to purchase a loudspeaker system to aid community organization. The election is the method of legitimizing leadership and is subject to strict rules, although these are often waived in practice. Until 1968, the *junta* committees were required to have equal numbers of Liberal and Conservative members, in line with the nature of the National Front arrangement. Today, this requirement is no longer in force although DAAC's official policy remains strongly integrative in situations where conflicting tickets are in competition.[6] After the election the local DAAC promoter will maintain fairly frequent contact with the *junta* leaders, in the words of official rhetoric, helping the *barrio* to help itself.

Third, the DAAC also helps communities by providing contacts with the servicing agencies. The local promoter may advise *barrio* *juntas* as to which agency to approach and how best to prepare their request. The *barrios* cannot be supplied by the DAAC itself because of the agency's budget limitations. The role of the agency is much more as an intermediary between the authorities and the *barrios*, even though some of the larger service agencies have now developed their own departments of community action. This role sometimes places promoters in the difficult position of being both spokesmen for the *barrios* to officialdom and for officialdom to the *barrios*. They may have to explain to service agencies why the settlement spliced into the water mains, they may have to justify the failure of the service agency to provide a service. Given their association with an official agency, promoters are unlikely to support opposition groups or radical action, such as mass demonstrations. Indeed, at times they may be involved in countering the demonstrations of unofficial bodies; during the battles over the PIDUZOB programme the *juntas* were used to counter the work of the more radical Barrio Pro-Defensa committees (Revéiz *et al.*, 1977).

Increasingly during the seventies, this has been one of the main roles of community action. While the *juntas* retain an important role as a channel for petitions and settlement demands, they are also a channel by which the authorities seek to legitimize official action. Indeed, this is becoming more and more important as DAAC funds decline and as the major service agencies develop the capacity to supply settlements on their own initiative. These agencies have for some time had set procedures for servicing settlements; the *juntas'* role has been to mobilize the funds of their communities and to keep pressure on the authorities when the procedures do not allow *barrio* servicing. There has been a clear shift, however, towards more technical procedures and the *junta's* role has been transformed into a collector of funds for programmes determined by the agencies. While more services are provided, the decisions are made increasingly from above. There are few signs that community action is becoming an active participant in decisions about the allocation of resources.

Mexico City

Government–community relations in Mexico City were, until recently, less institutionalized than in Bogotá. Patron–client relationships, mediated by *barrio* leaders or 'brokers', have been the principal form of linkage between aspirant politicians or high-ranking government officials and the urban poor (Cornelius, 1975: 159). The leader or patron benefits insofar as he is able to demand the loyalty of those dependent upon him and to mobilize that loyalty on behalf of his superiors. Camp followers or 'clients' benefit insofar as they gain access to influential people who may intercede on their behalf and increase the chances of a successful outcome to their demand making. The informal and rather diffuse nature of patron–client networks acts to control the allocation of the limited resources available to the poor. Indeed, it is through this system that the government manages to curtail 'demands for expensive, generalized benefits that might "overload" the political system' (Cornelius, 1975: 160). Limited inter-party competition in Mexico means that partisan politics assumes a low profile in the *barrios* outside election periods. This does not mean that political parties do not seek to mobilize the vote in such areas; the PRI, in particular, is especially active around election time trying to secure a massive vote for official candidates. But at other times low-income settlements are largely ignored by the political parties.

Within this general pattern the manner in which the government has responded to community demands has changed significantly over time. These changes are best understood in the context of the different styles of successive administrations. Before 1970, there was little commitment to the creation of a structure to handle low-income community development issues. The rationale behind the few organizations that emerged had little to do with improving the welfare of the urban poor. The State of Mexico's Junta de Mejoramiento Cívico, Moral y Material, which was created in 1952, had negligible resources to help resolve the problems faced by the settlements in the east of the city. Its real purpose was to stimulate the proliferation of subdivisions and, through its close liaison with the CNOP wing of the PRI, to gain political and electoral control over the area (Cisneros, n.d.). Similarly, the Federal District's Oficina de Colonias played the roles of trouble-shooter, political patron and mobilizer of votes.

President Echeverría's administration significantly increased public intervention in low-income housing and land issues. This was a response to evidence of steadily deteriorating housing conditions, pressure to redevelop prime sites in the inner city occupied by rental shanties and, perhaps most important of all, the political crisis by resulting from the withholding of land payments in the eastern *fraccionamientos*. In addition, increasingly vociferous demonstrations outside government offices demanded greater attention from the state. Having resolved the Netzahualcóyotl crisis through a tripartite agreement between the government, residents and the company sub-dividers, the president established a variety of national and Federal District institutons to deal with servicing, land regularization and housing construction.

Two broad methods of handling community development emerged. First, the new Federal District constitution approved early in 1971 provided the first ever framework for community participation. *Barrio* residents were to elect block representatives and a community *junta*, the president of which would sit on the *delegación*'s *junta de vecinos*. Furthermore, each of the 16 *delegaciones* was to send an elected representative to sit on the Federal District's Consultative Council. The *juntas* were designed to report on the state of the settlement's services, to advise how they might be improved, to participate in civic occasions and to comment on housing, social services and administration within the *delegación* (*Diario Oficial*, 18 April 1979). The brief of the Consultative Council was somewhat wider, extending to the monitoring of public agencies, advising on plans for urban development and other public initiatives. Given the purely consultative functions of this structure it is hardly surprising that leaders did not rush to join the council. Six years were to elapse before the bodies were given 'teeth'; then leaders began to respond.

The second approach was much more flexible and relied on community problems being resolved through the traditional patron–client framework. Newly established agencies were encouraged to generate close contact with existing leaders and to attend to their demands (see chapter 4). The president meanwhile kept 'open house' to *barrio* residents and their petitions, responding personally to any crisis that threatened to cause major civic disruption. This free-ranging role gave him the power to modify agency programmes and to develop a wide patronage network. It gave him a platform to build up popular support and, when necessary, to take personal charge of any *barrio* unrest. Such a personal approach suited his somewhat populist style (Cosío Villegas, 1975).[7]

The potential advantages inherent in the second approach are critical in explaining the failure to use the *junta-de-vecino* structure as the main channel for community–state relationships. Any doubts in the administration's mind were resolved by the fact that the *junta* structure would have required a greater devolution of power and responsibility to *delegados*; a development which would have run counter to the personal control that Echeverría desired. In addition, an integrated structure would have drawn public attention to the limited resources available for community-development projects. The important point to recognize is that channels of community participation were *tailored to meet governmental needs* and were not intended to provide the best method of resolving community needs.

The result was that community mobilization was rife throughout the period 1970–6. The head of FIDEURBE complained that it was almost impossible to carry out regularization effectively owing to the constant stream of protesters and petitions passing through his office. Mobilization worked through patron–client links and residents expected to receive community benefits only in exchange for their support at political rallies. The power of a leader was assessed by the number of heads that could be mobilized on his own or on his patron's behalf. Our interviews with leaders about their activities, contacts and strategies throughout this period indicate that they understood the system and its rules quite clearly. Previously, most leaders had sought patrons within the party; now they aimed to ally themselves with the heads of government agencies.

The effect that these patron–client relationships had upon the pace of settlement improvements varied. One factor that clearly inhibited the chance of a successful outcome to demand making was the proliferation of factions within the community. Such factions emerged partly because of the range of interests that existed within many of the larger low-income settlements but also because the government was willing to receive the claims of all rival groups.[8] The sources of enrichment that settlements offered community leaders was an additional factor that encouraged factionalism. Since each rival leader tended to seek out different patrons, different government agencies found that they were backing rival factions. Multiple agency involvement invariably complicated matters. For example, in Santo Domingo, INDECO's early attempts to intervene in the settlement were thwarted when its social workers and engineers were run out of the area by rival factions backed by other patrons in the government. Meanwhile, the *delegado* (who supported the original *comunero* land holders) instructed the police to prevent the entry of construction materials, and even of personnel from FIDEURBE, the agency empowered to regularize the *barrio*.

Not all patron–client links proved ineffective, however, particularly where a single leader exercised effective control over an area. In return for real or apparent help, settlements were expected to supply participants for political rallies in support of the president, for the State of the Nation address and for visits of foreign dignitaries. Buses were organized by the CNOP to ferry people to rallies. Whether this was a successful method of gaining support is unclear, for our impression was that the majority stayed at home; it was the familiar faces seen among petitioning groups and at *barrio* open meetings who participated (Ward 1976a).

In retrospect, the high level of community participation that marked the Echeverría administration actually achieved little in terms of benefits to the *barrios*.[9] In the Federal District, there was no systematic programme to extend the water network to newly formed settlements. Water was provided by lorries (*pipas*) or from hastily installed public standpipes. The regularization of plots dealt with only a small proportion of the cases even though FIDEURBE's (unrealistic) brief had been to resolve the problem by the end of the *sexenio*. Other 'services' were blatantly palliative; the Procuradaría de Colonias Populares interpreted its deliberately vague terms of reference quite liberally and gave out land title, gifts, foodstuffs and free milk. According to one source it was 10 to 15 years behind the problem and tried to pacify the people by making it appear that something was being done (Montaño, 1976: 94–5). Even the electricity company, whose criteria and procedures for service provision appear to have been more clear-cut and efficient (chapter 4), was not immune from political directives and interference from above.

The important point to recognize in any assessment of the channels of community–state relations that existed during the Echeverría government is that a well-administered and adequately funded programme of service provision was never its principal aim. Rather, channels of community organization and methods of service allocation can only be understood in the way in which they contributed to the political objectives of the period. These were to keep the lid on social unrest, to provide a source of popular support for presidential policies and to limit the financial burden on the exchequer. Therefore a variety of channels for government–community linkages was encouraged. Multiple patron–client links between agencies and settlements offered better opportunities for social control. By involving so many agencies the executive appeared to be concerned and active; by encouraging competition between agencies it slowed the pace of problem resolution to acceptable levels. 'Popular' mobilization at rallies could be assured and any major crisis could be nipped in the bud by direct intervention of the president himself.

Few gained through this process. *Barrio* residents and organizations were deceived into believing that by participating in the political 'game' they would benefit from regularization and services. Agency heads were put under enormous pressure to handle community problems, yet they were given inadequate resources to cope and were vulnerable to external interference. Even the influence and penetration of the PRI appear to have been reduced. While the party was still expected to deliver the vote, leaders forged links with the government bureaucracy which had resources to dispense, and not with the party-political apparatus, which had few resources. Although few leaders alienated the PRI and most cooperated with party officials, it had become much more difficult for the latter to cultivate links with *barrios* than prior to 1970.

In chapter 4 we described how President López Portillo began his administration by streamlining and reorganizing the bureaucracy. It had become clear that some measure of decentralization of decision making was required to overcome some of the problems posed by the previous government's failure to improve servicing levels. An attempt was now made to come to grips with the servicing problem through self-financing programmes which required more efficient administration. There was also a need to increase the tax base both to finance major public works and to contribute towards the Federal District's massive external debt (Perlo, 1980).

As part of the general reorganization of the Federal District from 1977, many aspects of street paving, street lighting, water and drainage provision came under the purview of the *delegados*. The latter were given larger, though quite inadequate, budgets and they were left to draw up priorities for servicing the communities in their areas and to submit plans and cost estimates to the Federal District for special projects. In this way the mayor continued to control resources but had created a method for determining priorities which deflected criticism away from himself and the president towards the *delegados*. Community organizations were now encouraged to petition the *delegados*. The 'open door' of the previous administration was quietly closed and any settlement leader who mistakenly led his followers to the offices of the mayor or the service agencies would simply be told to go to his *delegado*. If this had already been done without satisfaction, then the mayor might telephone the *delegado* on the resident's behalf. The problem would usually be left to the *delegado* to resolve, though, of course, he would now have the mayor looking over his shoulder. Our interviews with leaders indicated that they had quickly adjusted to these new rules and would try to make contact with the top only when they had a deep-seated grievance that was not being resolved by their *delegado*.

The *juntas de vecinos* were now encouraged to be the principal channel for petitions. It was expected that leaders would be elected, and only formally elected *junta* presidents would be recognized by the authorities. Thus, elections became important. They were held every three years and became the subject of a major propaganda campaign to get out the vote. Lists of priority works were drawn up by the *delegado* in collaboration with the elected *delegación* committee of *junta* presidents. Finally, a *delegación* committee met the mayor and his advisers every month when complaints and special requests could be conveyed to them. At such meetings major projects or urgent demands which had not been included in the original *delegación* budget could be discussed. This combination of procedures to accommodate local demands through the *delegado* and a route through which exceptional demands could be made direct to the mayor had a major effect in raising the status and activity of the *juntas de vecinos*. These procedures are not applied consistently in all *delegaciones* nor are they equally effective for all settlements. Several *delegados* only half-heartedly adopted the *juntas de vecinos*, while others accord them an important role in deciding who gets what and when. In every *delegación*, however, the level of servicing is carefully constrained by the annual budget and the ordering of priorities strongly influenced by the statements of the mayor and the personal priorities of the *delegado*.

The adoption of an 'institutionalized' structure for community organization has several important implications for the degree of social control exercised by the state. The *junta* structure has increased the control that the *delegado* exerts over the local populace, which is arguably greater than that achieved by Echeverría's patron–client methods. The *delegado* is more autonomous and has greater authority to determine local improvement programmes than ever before. Moreover, decisions are taken in collaboration with the *junta* so that negotiation and competition between *barrios* effectively shifts responsibility away from the *delegado* and the central agencies and places the onus on the local neighbourhoods to sort out their problems. The central issue becomes one of how to divide the cake rather than how much cake is put on the table. As we have observed, the mayor also benefits. He is able to devolve many of the pressures associated with low-income demand making while retaining close control over resources and links to grass-roots leaders.

At an ideological level, it may be argued that the *juntas* consolidated the concept of low-income residents as 'good citizen' – an assessment often echoed by the public officials whom we interviewed. Community mobilization is identified much more with 'apolitical' civic issues and invokes less radical rhetoric about the rights of the poor and their class struggle. 'Good citizenship' further encourages the idea of citizen responsibility and reinforces the expectation that residents should pay for the services that the government provides.

Finally, the channelling of demand making through a uniform procedure dramatically reduced the opportunities for local factions, leaders and party-political groups to develop a significant power base built around civic issues. Only in very large settlements, where there are clearly demarcated areas of leader influence, do several representatives go forward to the *junta*. The effect has been to depoliticize demand making and to significantly reduce the myriad opportunities that the PRI and other parties previously held for popular 'mobilization'. The overall effect of the change is that the influence of the PRI is held in greater check than ever before. Most local leaders recognize the need not to antagonize PRI officials and support their candidates at election time. But, they recognize also that the PRI has little influence over the allocation of services and are therefore sceptical about the promises made to them by deputies and PRI militants at election times. Not surprisingly, this situation makes it difficult for the PRI to maintain the same sort of electoral legitimacy in the future as in the past against a stronger, more viable opposition. During the 1979 elections, several party members bemoaned the impotence of elected deputies who, they pointed out, were the only elected officials in the Federal District, One district organizer insisted that the *juntas de vecinos* had been nurtured by the PRI and that, somehow, the PRI must reinstate its influence over them. *Delegados* professed that they would resist such moves.

In the State of Mexico the arrangement for community participation is rather different, but confirms our general proposition that it is the outcome of governmental needs rather than the spontaneous expression of low-income organizations. The *consejo de colaboración* is broadly similar in nature to the *junta de vecinos*. However, for low-income settlements the *consejos* are hardly relevant as the resources available to the governor and to the municipal president are derisory compared with those of the Federal District. In Netzahualcóyotl no one had heard of them, but the new municipal president argued that they were about to be introduced. In Ecatepec they appear to have twin functions. On the one hand, the job of the *barrio* committee is to represent the interests of the residents and to liaise with the municipality over service provision and other matters. On the other hand, the so-called 'sub-delegates' represent the municipal president in the *barrio*, are charged with seeing that the peace is kept and have powers of arrest. Despite these very different roles, both sets of representatives are elected every three years on the same ticket. Like the improvement boards of the 1950s the arrangement appears to have brought few benefits for the *barrios*. They represent a chain of authority from the municipal president downwards rather than an effective upward channel for community participation in decision making.

Valencia

A formal programme of community action began in Venezuela, as in Colombia, as a reaction to the demise of a dictator. The *junta* that replaced Pérez Jiménez instituted an Emergency Plan that sought to remedy some of the problems facing the urban poor. An attempt was made to generate incomes for the population living in low-income settlements and to satisfy their most urgent physical needs. According to Ugalde (1972: 25), the only effect of this programme was to increase the already high rate of rural–urban migration; 48 per cent of the population surveyed in Caracas *barrios* in 1969 had arrived the previous year. An Emergency Works Plan replaced the Emergency Plan and sought to resolve some of the critical problems of housing, education, sanitation and paving through the establishment of *juntas pro-mejoras* and the construction of community centres in each *barrio*. Community action, local initiative and public participation were the keys to this plan. In fact, the political parties soon infiltrated the *juntas pro-mejoras*. In Valencia, most of the settlements were formed under the protection of the political parties and as a result leadership in the *barrios* was strongly influenced by those political parties (Ray, 1969). Even if control over the municipal council was divided, and relatively harmonious relations existed between the AD, URD and COPEI parties, the ruling national party, Democratic Action, had the best opportunities for influencing *barrio* leadership. Consequently, 'aggressive party leaders had managed to capture control of the federation of *juntas pro-mejoras* as early as 1958, and, although the individual *juntas* were not all in AD hands, the party's dominance was firmly enough established that it was never seriously threatened by the opposition' (Ray, 1969: 116).[10] The new plan was not generally successful and, despite the construction of numerous emergency works, was soon jettisoned.

By 1960, a new strategy was under way. Rather than introducing *ad hoc* improvements to individual communities, the new strategy sought to integrate community developments with the process of national modernization and growth. A hierarchy of organizations linking national, intermediate and local institutions had to be created. The National Programme for Community Development sought to change attitudes among low-income groups so as to increase productivity, integrate all social groups more fully into society, and reduce current levels of paternalism. Such an approach was also followed by private-sector groups established to encourage community action and religious belief (IVAC and Acción en Venezuela). Ugalde (1972: 28) claims that the Plan failed because it was 'an insignificant appendix' of the General Plan; while each ministry had its office of community development, ministerial priorities did not change. Community development was in reality an ideological tool to hide the disinterest of the government, as is reflected in resource allocation: between 1960 and 1969 only 21 production units were created under the National Plan for the Community at a total cost of 53,000 US dollars. Some investment in public works had occurred but nothing had changed which would tackle the underlying causes of poverty in the *barrios*. As a consequence it also became increasingly clear that local perceptions of need differed from those of the national planners.

The change of government in 1969 brought a new initiative and the development of two new government agencies: the Secretariat of Popular Promotion and, within the Worker's Bank, the Department of *Barrio* Urbanization and Servicing (DUEB). The former agency was intended to increase levels of popular participation, but once again the agency received too limited a budget. Resources were restricted because the Caldera government came to fear that popular participation would have effects similar to those in Chile; rather than integrating society it would encourage radical political protest. The DUEB had more success in part because it was one of President Caldera's first initiatives. It sought to encourage the community to establish its own priorities through Consultative Councils, made up of *barrio* representatives, which would then liaise with the Workers' Bank. Unfortunately, the results were often less than satisfactory: the funds were often misused by the *barrio* representatives; attempts to remove partisan political groups from the councils gave the impression that the governing party was trying to dominate the councils; differences between local promoters and the higher reaches of the Workers' Bank led to friction within the bureaucracy. The effect of these developments was to increase the Bank's interest in making physical improvements in the *barrios*, with a corresponding decline in its concern for local participation and education.

The administration of Carlos Andres Pérez introduced a wholly new kind of strategy. Its conception was very much a crude programme of physical improvements for the low-income settlements. Decree 332 of 1974 gave responsibility to FUNDACOMUN for carrying out a survey of all low-income urban communities, coordinating service promoters, and implementing the service programme. FUNDA-COMUN, which since its creation in 1962 had been primarily concerned with giving technical advice to municipal governments, received a vastly increased budget and responsibility for coordinating the actions of numerous main-line servicing agencies such as INOS and CADAFE.[11] As a further sign of presidential favour, the new director of the agency was Pérez' own daughter.

All *barrios* were grouped into units (UDOs) of up to 20,000 people.[12] In each state two committees were set up, presided by the governor, one for Physical Development, the other for Social Development. These committees would watch over the programmes for each UDO, and within each UDO a series of ministries and government institutes would carry out programmes and build services. The most important of these programmes was the construction of service modules which would contain health centres, schools, and subsidized stores. It was intended to build 225 such modules between 1975 and 1978 of which only three were planned for Valencia (Venezuela, FUNDACOMUN, 1978a, 1978b).

Little emphasis was given to community participation. FUNDACOMUN was to promote *barrio* organizations to consult with the Physical and Social Development Committees, but it was not until the very end of the Pérez administration that the functions and organization of neighbourhood associations (*asociaciones de vecinos*) were laid down. Decree 3130 of 1979 stipulated that these associations would solicit help for their communities and defend their general interests.

By contrast, the Herrera Campíns' administration listed as one of its major aims 'to increase the organization and participation of the population' (Venezuela, CORDIPLAN, 1981, Vol. 1, 18). It actively promoted the new neighbourhood associations which could be established within any community with more than 200 families. On presenting the signatures of 50 members, the association could be registered by the local planning office. While the introduction of party politics was prohibited, the formation of neighbourhood associations was subject to active encouragement by the COPEI party. In Valencia, as we will show below, sympathetic party members were encouraged to establish neighbourhood associations before opposition groups could do so. The formation of such associations proceeded apace: 72 were formed in 1979 and a further 33 during 1980.[13] Meanwhile, its *barrio* programme embraced the Decree 332 programme of the previous administration and it was concerned to complete the construction of service modules and the series of programmes coordinated by FUNDACOMUN aimed at improving the physical welfare of the 'stable' *barrio* populations.[14] Such programmes included loans to individual households for home improvement, establishment of community stores to sell cheap basic goods, the promotion of cooperatives to increase employment and incomes, and the initiation of productive enterprises which would each benefit several *barrios*. Despite this

continued emphasis on physical improvements, the new administration distanced itself from previous government policy by arguing for
greater government efficiency, less government paternalism and greater cooperation and participation from the low-income populations
(Venezuela, CORDIPLAN, 1981: Vol. 2). The previous government
was too paternalistic and had been too concerned with clientelism. It
had failed to adapt modules to local conditions – essentially owing to a
failure to relate activity to research effort (Batley, 1978) and to lack of
consultation with the community.[15] As basic planks of this strategy,
'integrated plans' and 'basic plans' were to be produced with the help
of the communities. These plans were to combine technical expertise
with the perceived needs of the communities; they would constitute
part of the process of consultation between the national government
and the people enshrined in Decree 478 on Regionalization and
Participation of the Community in Regional Development. In fact,
these plans only began to be produced during 1981 and none had been
prepared in Valencia by April 1982. In the meantime, it was left to
ORDEC, the state community-development office, to draw up an
inventory of *barrio* needs, consult with the respective service agencies
and then act. While ORDEC tries to decide the order of priorities on a
rational/technical basis, taking into account *barrio* needs, resources,
etc., this order is clearly disturbed by the political petitioning process
which often bypasses ORDEC altogether.

Settlement leaders tend to petition any institution in power which
they believe can help their cause. This petitioning can be directed to
the mayor, individual councillors, council commissions, to the governor, to ORDEC, to the servicing agencies, or wherever. This
suggests that the political nature of government in Valencia is very
diffuse in its organizational system. It is open to community organizations to petition directly any institution that can help, and specifically
those institutions and individuals which are members of the same
political party.

The general experience of community action and participation in
Venezuela, therefore, has not been encouraging. As we have seen, a
long series of efforts to encourage community participation has failed
to establish a reliable and trusted procedure by which *barrio* inhabitants can address the government. There are two major explanations of
this situation. The first is that community action has generally been
encouraged only so far as it has been in the interests of national and
local government to do so. As Ray (1969: 93) noted, 'most *juntas*

represent better the interests of the government than they do the interests of the communities which elect them'. When there has been any danger of community demands exceeding what the government was expecting to provide, government support has been withdrawn. Second, government support for community participation, like most other areas of public activity in Venezuela, is part and parcel of the process of party-political competition. What was true of the *juntas pro-mejoras* under Rómulo Betancourt is still true today: the party affiliation of *barrio* leadership is directly related to the national and local party-political situation. When the national, state and municipal governments change, so too does *barrio* leadership. The general result is that community needs are often sacrificed to party needs. Confidence in community associations has generally declined as a result.

Several important points emerge from this broad review of community-participation organizations in the three cities. First, it is apparent that organizations created to manage popular participation have a long and mixed history. In many cases formal channels have existed since the late 1950s. More important, perhaps, is the fact that their initiation and the form that they have taken has been carefully shaped from the top down. Demand making and organization has not emanated from the grass roots. Second, the real commitment of governments to community participation has been extremely limited. This is demonstrated by the low budgetary allocations to institutions made responsible for organizing popular participation. Furthermore, the ability of those agencies to provide direct access to funds for urban projects or, indeed, to act as intermediary between the community and servicing agencies or ministries has invariably been severely constrained. Often responsibility for community participation is invested in a multiplicity of agencies and departments, thereby weakening the visibility and effective influence of any single body. By and large, community participation has been used by government as a means of legitimizing the political system, either as a structure for garnering votes, or as a means of ensuring compliance with urban political decision making. Its value for governments has proved to be one of social control rather than an extension of power and decision making to local groups. Indeed, where community participation has led to greater demands of local control over resources and more active involvement in decision making, governments have usually backed off and have adopted measures to undermine such proposals. Third, formal channels of community participation have not led to major benefits for local communities. Any benefits that have been won are often superficial – such as the general-purpose meeting rooms favoured by Community Action in Bogotá. Elsewhere achievements are partial and unpredictable. However, it is important to recognize that, while affiliation to an institutionalized system of community participation is not a *sine qua non* for the receipt of urban services or other forms of governmental assistance, it is, nevertheless, often an important first step. If it were not, then few local communities would bother to involve themselves in the formal structure of community participation.

The community response

Besides the detailed records and interviews that we carried out in the survey *barrios* in each city, we talked also with leaders of many other communities. The following observations are based on both sources of information.

The existence of local community associations

Community associations evolve in a variety of ways. Their existence appears to relate both to characteristics of the settlement itself (history, security of tenure, class or ethnic composition, leadership, etc.) as well as to the attitude adopted by the authorities – such attitudes varying from one of 'supportive interest' to one of 'repressive hostility' (Nelson, 1979: 264). Clearly, the form of land acquisition is likely to be a key determinant of whether or not a community association is established. As we observed in an earlier chapter, the formation of a low-income settlement is rarely a spontaneous event. Land invasions, for example, require an organized group to arrange the capture of land; leaders sometimes screen potential residents, preferring young married couples and families with resources and excluding those who already own land (Mangin, 1967). Elsewhere, settlement formation is often sponsored by politicians or government officials hoping to make money or to develop a personal power base; sometimes opposition parties form settlements hoping to embarrass the government. Whatever the motive, an incipient organization is almost certain to exist from the outset of an invasion. Where land is sold a *barrio junta* may be created by the developer to promote land sales, to help further political ambitions or to coordinate the installation of services.

The form that *barrio* organizations may take varies considerably. At one extreme they may comprise a rather loose assembly of people whose functions are unclear beyond a general wish to improve the settlement. Leaders are often self-appointed and act for the community by allocating lots, settling minor boundary disputes, speaking to the press, negotiating for recognition and services, and so on. Residents attend regular general assemblies and elect, or are coerced to elect, a *junta* president, officials and committee (Butterworth and Chance, 1981: 162). Where the settlement is particularly large, block representatives may be appointed to coordinate opinion and to mobilize labour in community works. Sometimes an organization may draw up a formal constitution, levy regular quotas, draw up an approved agenda for community programmes, stipulate sanctions against those who fail to cooperate and, where appropriate, formally register with the authorities.

The initiative to create an association with a constitution, rules and elected representatives is generally stimulated from above. This has occurred in Bogotá, Valencia and Mexico City as well as in other Latin American cities. Sometimes, however, the community may want its *junta* to be formalized so as to exclude particular members of the settlement. In one of the Mexican *barrios*, residents insisted that only those who had contributed to community work schemes and were regularly contributing to the joint fund for land purchase should be allowed membership. Today, most settlements in Bogotá, Mexico and Valencia have a formal community organization, but the level of confidence in that *junta* varies greatly. *Junta* membership – and indeed the effectiveness of the *juntas* –will vary according to the leader, the extent of partisan political intervention, the age of the community, and the proximity of elections.

In Bogotá, most settlements have *juntas* recognized by the Department of Community Action. According to the results of our survey, participation in *junta* activities was much more common in Bogotá than in the other cities; with the exception of Atenas, around half of all the communities had been members at one time or another. (See table 16.) The low level of membership in Valencia must be understood in the context of the close links between political party and community action. Given the expectation that a change of government will bring a change of *barrio* leadership, formal affiliation with the *barrio junta* is likely to be lower than residents' actual participation in demand making. In Mexico City, only Isidro Fabela, Jardines and Liberales

Table 16 Levels of participation among owners by settlement

	Bogotá					Mexico City						Valencia	
	Juan Pablo I	Casa-blanca	Atenas	Britalia	San Antonio	Isidro Fabela	Santo Domingo	El Sol	Liberales	Chalma	Jardines	Nueva Valencia	La Castrera
Owner households in which a member participated (%):													
Land regularization	3	4	0	5	2	36	50	29	96	33	44	4	6
Installation of electricity	13	18	4	26	13	24	26	20	70	22	28	21	10
Installation of water	10	25	4	32	18	24	34	12	60	31	33	20	18
School facilities	6	4	6	3	2	12	19	15	29	7	19	3	1
Health centre	3	4	4	0	2	3	5	5	6	0	1	1	3
Number of replies	(31)	(44)	(49)	(62)	(45)	(90)	(97)	(84)	(47)	(54)	(75)	(91)	(78)
Principal participant (%):													
No one	67	68	83	54	48	47	36	53	4	53	35	68	65
Male head or husband	44	92	71	75	71	60	33	57	32	56	56	79	70
Female head or wife	55	8	15	11	21	18	38	22	20	16	4	21	30
Male and female jointly	0	0	14	14	8	22	29	21	48	28	40	0	0
Absolute number of participants	(9)	(13)	(7)	(28)	(24)	(45)	(58)	(37)	(44)	(25)	(48)	(29)	(27)
Participant in residents association (%):													
Never participated	32	55	83	60	47	66	78	77	4	82	68	80	81
Constantly involved	65	36	15	31	42	8	14	6	92	11	19	15	14
Involved mostly in the past	3	10	2	3	4	26	7	17	2	8	5	2	3
Involved mostly at present time	0	0	0	7	7	0	0	0	2	0	8	2	3
Absolute number of participants	(31)	(42)	(48)	(62)	(45)	(85)	(97)	(84)	(48)	(54)	(75)	(91)	(78)
Total number of households	(35)	(74)	(88)	(79)	(84)	(144)	(120)	(120)	(60)	(73)	(114)	(94)	(84)

Source: sample survey.

204

had ever created a formal *junta* structure, though elsewhere a few respondents declared that they had 'belonged' to an informal *barrio* grouping. We conclude, therefore, that community associations are not 'spontaneously' created by residents as an integral part of the mobilization process. Rather they emerge either in exceptional circumstances or where the city-wide rules of 'petitioning' demand it.

Resident participation in demand making

The household survey asked questions about the degree to which residents had participated in the securement of a wide variety of community services. When had members of the household been active in community petitioning, organization and politics, what had they done and had they been members of local organizations? The data are interesting in that they suggest that participation is often very limited; many households take no part in community affairs. This confirms Fisher's (1977) evidence collated from 19 neighbourhoods in Brazil, Chile, Mexico, Peru and Venezuela which showed that in all but three of those neighbourhoods as few as 20 to 40 per cent of respondents had taken part in some form of communal effort to influence the authorities (quoted in Nelson, 1979: 305).

Levels of participation in our cities were especially low in Bogotá and in Valencia. In Bogotá, non-participation increased because of the large numbers of renters living in the settlements. Only in Juan Pablo I, a settlement faced by crisis and with very high levels of 'ownership', were participation rates higher. In all three cities, there was a marked reluctance among renters and sharers to participate. This is not surprising given that they generally arrive once the community is well established and they have little stake in the securement of improvements. It is a finding that is supported by evidence for cities such as Bucaramanga (Edwards, 1982b). Nelson (1979: 253) also comments that 'neighbourhood associations are rare in older, more central, heavily rental low-income neighbourhoods'. The presence of renters means that many people within a community are not committed to its improvement. There may even be a conflict of interests between renters and owners insofar as the former recognize that legal title or the improvement of services may lead to rent increases that they cannot afford. In settlements with a significant number of non-owners there is likely to be less intensive petitioning for services and a reluctance to contribute to self-help programmes. High levels of renting may also weaken the potential for radical social movements focusing on community issues. However this is uncertain in the light of our finding that a large proportion of owners never become involved either.[16] Some 64 per cent of owners in Bogotá and 67 per cent in Valencia declared that neither they nor any member of their family had ever helped petition for services. In Mexico City, levels of participation appear to be consistently higher, even if 40 per cent had taken no part in servicing activities.[17]

Participation appears to vary not only by city and by tenure but also with the age of the settlement and the service sought. Table 16 suggests that in two Mexican settlements, Isidro Fabela and El Sol, participation was much higher in the past when servicing and regularization problems were greatest. Similarly, the fact that in the older settlements in Bogotá more people declared themselves to have been active only in the past than declared that they were active now suggests that the peak of mobilization in these settlements has passed. If community participation tends to decline through time, our evidence shows that this is not inevitable. San Antonio, where most of our interviewees had lived for some time, had high levels of continuing participation, as did Casablanca. Clearly, community mobilization can be maintained in certain circumstances, specifically when there is a strong community leader and the community lacks internal conflicts. Recently formed settlements or those with intractable servicing problems tend to have higher levels of participation.[18] Portes and Walton (1976: 94–5) are clearly right when they argue that community participation is not necessary all of the time: 'there is an upsurge of interest and collective spirit followed by periods of individualism and apathy . . . From the point of view of the poor, communal organizations are not artificial entities to be maintained for their own sake but instruments to be employed when necessary.'

It is interesting to note that there are important differences between the cities with respect to the issues which maximize community participation (table 16). In Mexico City, land regularization is of fundamental importance to the continued existence and future servicing of the settlement and therefore leads to active collaboration and petitioning. Concern over the securement of land title is both a product of the form of land alienation and the degree to which the government regards it as a major issue. Insecurity of tenure and government concern to regularize illegal land holdings in Mexico have made it inevitable that residents mobilize first and foremost around this issue. The variations observed between settlements in Mexico City are explained by local conditions: in El Sol illegality of land tenure was under resolution when most residents arrived, while many owners in Isidro Fabela arrived after legalization. By contrast, the security of land tenure in the pirate urbanizations of Bogotá explains why this is a non-issue there. In Bogotá, the service agencies are often prepared to provide services even when land has not been legalized (Fuentes and Losada, 1978) and once services have been provided one of the principal barriers to legality has been removed. Only in invasion settlements is security of tenure and regularization of the land situation likely to rank as a major issue.[19] Here, however, it may not give rise to mobilization because it is well known that the authorities are reluctant to regularize tenure. Very few invasions have been regularized in Bogotá and therefore there is little point to negotiations between invasion leaders and the authorities. Indeed, in one well-known case, the invasion leaders have deliberately sought to remain outside the regularized settlement system.[20] In Valencia, the lack of participation over the land issue, even though both of our settlements were founded through invasion, is at first sight surprising. Low levels of participation on this issue, however, are probably linked to the fact that relatively few of the households lived in the settlement at the height of the invasion and to the fact that besides purchase there is no mechanism for regularizing land tenure in Valencia until all services have been provided and twenty years' occupation has elapsed. In Nueva Valencia, where there was a clear need to legalize land tenure, the community only has the alternative of purchasing the land, an alternative that hardly appealed. Why mobilize when there is no clear objective?

Mobilization for services elicited much greater involvement in Bogotá and Valencia, although mobilization levels were still highest in the Mexican settlements. What is clear for all three cities is that the demand for certain services attracts higher levels of participation than others. The installation of electricity and water are important mobilizing elements in all three places. However, variations in intensity of servicing between settlements in each city reflect differences in local conditions; water was obtained with little difficulty in Atenas but both electricity and water have been the subject of major struggles in Britalia. Because of such differences it is difficult to establish from this kind of data whether there are universal patterns of settlement needs.

Previous studies have suggested that water, electricity and drainage elicit greater community interest than services like schools, health centres and paving (Daykin, 1978: 351, 356). Our results suggest that this is correct but that local variations are clearly also important; if electricity comes of right there is little need to mobilize; if it comes only as the result of petitioning it is likely to generate widespread community support.

Whatever the services involved, however, levels of mobilization were low in all three cities. Even when we add up such diverse settlement activities as attendance at community meetings, signing and delivering petitions to appropriate offices and pressing influential outsiders to act on the community's behalf, community activities rarely involved more than one-third of owners in any of the cities. And yet, mobilization would seem to be important. Petitioning draws attention to the settlement and may help to move it up the queue for servicing. But it does not appear to be a critical ingredient that determines presence or absence, nor does it always, or even usually, speed up the rate of installation. Only under abnormal circumstances, such as environmental crises, does petitioning gain major benefits for the communities. In Bogotá, the flooding of nine pirate urbanizations in 1979 created danger of a local crisis for the administration.[21] Its reaction was rapid and effective; the settlements were rapidly serviced, the populations received help and the tenants were offered sites in a specially developed government programme (Losada and Pinilla, 1980).

Community self-help

A continuing theme underlying community-action programmes has been the belief that settlements should mobilize to provide their own services. Numerous attempts have been made in Bogotá, Valencia and Mexico City to encourage this process either through the provision of materials, the offer of collaboration by the servicing agencies, or publicity given to the virtues of community self-help. Various directors of the Department of Community Action in Bogotá stated that one of their main aims was to mobilize settlement inhabitants to put their efforts into collective projects. In Bogotá, the water company has an office of community development which both negotiates with settlements about servicing and encourages settlements to contribute work to installation projects. Thus an interesting question is whether the settlements in each city actively worked as communities to improve their physical environment.

In Bogotá, the broad answer to this question is no. While a recent register of the Department of Community Action shows that most settlements had done something, few had done as much in the way of service provision as the communist settlements such as Nuevo Chile.[22] In Atenas, the community had contributed labour to some parts of the drainage and water systems and had built the community hall with the help of *auxilios* (small cash handouts from councillors). In Britalia, there has been a great deal of petitioning but very little work in terms of the construction of facilities. In Casablanca, collective action has been more highly developed. The community had worked together to provide water and had some parts of the drainage network.[23] At the time of the study they were about to build a new church. Where self-help community action was most highly developed was in Soacha. Community action had built much of the drainage system in San Antonio, had dug the holes for the electricity posts, had helped install the water, had contributed work on the neighbouring El Chicó school and was currently building a communal hall, office and theatre. The community had received numerous *auxilios* from the council and the United States government, which had helped considerably, but this was still an impressive record. This was due in part to the fact that Soacha is outside the area of the Special District and is therefore less eligible for help from the larger and better-financed Bogotá service agencies. The Bogotá service agencies supply Soacha under contract. These contracts sometimes specify that the communities must provide community labour.[24] The general outcome of this situation is that the settlements in Soacha feel there is no alternative but to contribute to the installation of the services.

In general, the state in Bogotá has increasingly sought to provide services through the technical agencies and to rely upon the communities to collect the money to pay for them. Hence, most *juntas* are concerned with the sometimes difficult task of collecting money from every household to pay for the cost of installing water or electricity. In this sense, community organization is a prerequisite for achieving services in Bogotá; water, electricity and drainage are usually not provided unless a minimum of 30 per cent of the total cost is paid to the respective agency.

In Mexico City, widespread resident involvement in physical improvements tends to occur only during the early phase of consolidation. The total absence of services encourages participation; difficulties over vehicular access prompt a community programme for street levelling; the lack of water leads to cooperation over the introduction of standpipes. Isidro Fabela during the late 1960s, Santo Domingo between 1971 and 1972, and Liberales between 1978 and 1979 were typical in this respect. Nevertheless, it is clear that continuing coordinated involvement in community improvement is exceptional. Once residents have achieved a minimum level of services and are reasonably certain that the settlement will not be demolished, mutual aid atrophies and people concentrate on upgrading their own houses (Nelson, 1979: 255). This does not mean that they are no longer interested in collaborative efforts to improve services, only that they recognize the marginal returns such action brings. They are aware that thenceforth better services are more dependent upon favourable government decisions than on community action. It will be interesting to observe whether recent government initiatives will generate greater community participation; some projects organized by the *delegaciones* require neighbourhood *juntas* to help dig drainage ditches and level streets. In the State of Mexico, further efforts have been made to encourage community action, notably Governor Jiménez Cantú's 'Army for Work'. Residents give a day's voluntary labour to this paramilitary force to collaborate upon public works – the construction of a school, installation of a water service, tree planting, slope stabilization, etc.

In Valencia, community action is notable for its absence – a point that Ray (1969: 74) makes about Venezuelan *barrios* in general: 'One of the prominent features of *barrio* politics is the extreme infrequency with which residents take the initiative to alleviate common problems through direct, cooperative action. When several of them do resolve to seek improvements, they invariably proceed by making a petition to a municipal or state government office.' The limited amount of work contributed by local communities is probably best explained in terms of the traditional expectation among the people in Venezuela that it is the job of government to provide services. While government often fails to perform this role, the expectation remains, and so long as people expect services to be provided from above they decline to work hard in installing them themselves. In general, therefore, community action is relatively limited and most participation in community affairs is directed to petitioning the service agencies. Certainly, there were few community works in either La Castrera or Nueva Valencia. Buia and Guerra (n.d.) found in a study of seven *barrios* that there was little belief that collective action had been practised. When asked which organizations had helped the settlement, in two *barrios* less than 10 per cent mentioned groups of neighbours, in four others it was less than 25 per cent, and in only one did virtually all people mention the *junta*. Indeed, the lack of community solidarity and unity was the main explanation given in all but one settlement.

Recent government statements have begun to recognize not only the limited community contribution to physical projects but also that they fail to contribute to decision making about works in their settlements. Thus, recent government activity has sought to stimulate greater community participation. For example, in 1980 the Governor of Carabobo State announced investment worth 40 million US dollars in the marginal areas but demanded that the communities help provide labour (*El Nacional*, 25 January 1980).

In addition, FUNDACOMUN has sought to stimulate participation in decision making through the preparation of integrated development plans. Whether this represents a new start to community participation can be determined only with hindsight. If the new start does not occur, then most *juntas* will continue to represent better the interests of the government than those of the communities which elect them.

Resident knowledge about community influentials

The fact that only a minority of residents, and even of owners, are constantly active in community-development affairs does not mean that residents are unaware of what is going on or who best represents their interests. The question 'Which person within the *barrio* has most helped the community?' elicited generally well-informed responses in every settlement, though the extent to which people were prepared to name particular individuals varied greatly. In some settlements in Bogotá, two-thirds or more of the households mentioned someone by name and among owners the proportion varied from a low of 71 per cent in one settlement to a high of 100 per cent. In Bogotá, therefore, even renters were aware of the personalities prominent in the community. In Mexico City and Valencia, the rates of recognition were much lower than in Bogotá, approximately one-half of the respondents failing to name a *barrio* leader (table 17). In Mexico, although recognition rates were higher among owners, the data show marked

Table 17 Recognition of leaders, by settlement

	Bogotá	Mexico City	Valencia	Atenas	Britalia	Casa-blanca	Juan Pablo I	San Antonio
Percentage of households naming no barrio leader by name or not answering	27.2	53.4	47.8	42.0	30.4	16.2	17.1	22.6
Percentage of owner households naming no barrio leader by name or not answering	17.7	44.5	46.7	28.6	24.2	0	16.1	15.6
Most mentioned individual leader as percentage of total mentions of leaders	60.0	45.1	57.0	45.7	70.9	61.8	51.2	64.6*
Total number of different individuals and institutions named	NA	NA	NA	11	9	10	8	15*
Total households interviewed	360	631	178	88	79	74	35	84*
Total owner households interviewed	231	449	169	49	62	44	31	45

	Chalma	Isidro Fabela	Jardines	Liberales	El Sol	Santo Domingo	La Castrera	Nueva Valencia
Percentage of households naming no barrio leader by name or not answering	76.7	59.7	44.7	13.3	64.2	47.5	46.4	48.9
Percentage of owner households naming no barrio leader by name or not answering	74.1	52.2	29.3	4.1	58.3	41.2	44.2	48.9
Most mentioned individual leader as percentage of total mentions of leaders	38.1	37.1	85.3	53.1	13.8	34.8	55.5	58.3
Total number of different individuals and institutions named	7	26	9	7	22	23	10	12
Total households interviewed	73	144	114	60	120	120	84	95
Total owner households interviewed	54	90	75	49	84	97	78	91

* San Antonio in fact consists of four small *barrios*. The individual *barrio* percentages, total number of different individuals and institutions mentioned, and total households replying were respectively (note, in three cases the same individual was mentioned in two of the sub-*barrios*):

San Antonio	82.0	4	41
El Chicó	33.3	8	19
San Alberto	54.5	4	12
El Triunfo	50.0	2	10

variations between settlements. In Liberales, only 4 per cent of owners failed to name a leader whereas in Chalma the figure was 74 per cent.

Why should the recognition of leaders be so variable between cities and between settlements? Certainly, higher recognition figures are associated with smaller settlements. In Bogotá, for example, the three smallest settlements all recorded high levels of recognition, especially for all households, but the difference was not marked when the replies of non-owners were excluded. In Mexico, the three largest settlements had low response levels; Liberales, the smallest, had very high rates, while Chalma – the second smallest settlement – had the lowest level of response. Small size clearly eases the problems of leadership but does not ensure recognition; in the large settlements fractionalism within the community is much more common.

This pattern is mirrored in the more detailed replies. In the generally smaller settlements in Bogotá and Valencia the majority of respondents named a single individual. Over 45 per cent of all personalities and organizations mentioned by households in Bogotá and Valencia referred to one specific individual. In some cases the figures were over 70 per cent. This suggests that the leadership in these settlements remained stable. In Bogotá, this reflected the fact that *barrio* leaders, while having clear political links, do not inevitably change after elections. Thus the leaders in settlements such as Casablanca, Atenas and San Antonio had been influential over a period of ten years. While some were recognized to be associated with a particular political party, the settlement either retained trust in them, as in Casablanca, or was of the same party anyway, as in San Antonio. In Atenas, however, while the leader was known to be an ardent Liberal, there were as many votes for the Conservatives in the 1978 elections. Similarly, in Britalia the fact that there was a Liberal leader did not preclude considerable numbers of people voting for the Conservatives.[25]

In Mexico City, the enormous range of different leaders named accurately reflects the size of the settlements and their internal conflicts; 23 different leaders were identified in Santo Domingo, and 22 in El Sol (see also Cornelius, 1975: 151). In Chalma, few leaders had attempted to establish a basis of community support and none had projected him or herself sufficiently to ensure recall from the residents whom we interviewed. Nevertheless, in some communities it was clear that a single leader had achieved dominance. In Jardines, nine different leaders were named yet Don Guillermo was named 68 times compared with only 2 mentions of his nearest rival. In Mexico, differences in settlement size, age, and leadership characteristics account for the variations observed.

In the Valencia settlements there were consistent mentions of a single leader. This was surprising given that the leadership normally changes after the national and local elections. Thus, although few people in Nueva Valencia or La Castrera wanted to be known as supporters of the losing Democratic Action Party, they were prepared to recognize that a leader of that party had helped the community. In Nueva Valencia, although more people voted *Copeyano*, the most mentioned community leader was an *Adeco*.

If there were major differences between the cities in terms of leadership style and levels of participation, the response to the issue of outside help was much more similar. In general, settlement residents named few outside individuals who had helped the community (table 18). In Bogotá, only Casablanca had a high level of recognition and even here the figure was artificially inflated in the sense that the individual named, a former mayor of the city, lived close to the community. In few of the other settlements did more than one-fifth of the households mention any outside influential. In Mexico City, outside influentials were mentioned in any number only in El Sol, and even here most of the wide variety of people mentioned had been involved in the attempt to resolve the regularization crisis of the whole area of Netzahualcóyotl. In Valencia, awareness of outside influentials was even lower.

In one respect these low recognition levels are hardly surprising. Links with outside organizations, agencies and individuals are usually maintained by the leaders directly. As Cornelius (1973b) has argued for Mexico, leaders possess an accurate knowledge about which patrons or departments are worth approaching for different development issues. Most residents are at least one-removed from the wide range of government and party personnel with whom leaders liaise. Hence, the people most often cited by householders are those who had contrived to make frequent 'appearances' in the *barrio*, or who had been repeatedly and favourably cited by the leadership as a staunch supporter of the *barrio*. In Bogotá, answers to this question were frequently accompanied by the comment that no one outside cared about the *barrio* or that the politicians only came when they needed votes, a few weeks before the elections. The few people mentioned were those who had taken some specific action to help the community. They had attended meetings with the authorities to help the commun-

Table 18 Recognition of extra-barrio personages and evaluation of settlement quality

	Bogotá	Mexico City	Valencia	Atenas	Britalia	Casa-blanca	Juan Pablo I	San Antonio
Percentage of owner households mentioning an extra-*barrio* individual or institution who/which had helped the settlement	73.2	73.7	89.3	89.8	75.8	53.7	93.5	60.0
Percentage of all households mentioning an extra-*barrio* individual or institution who/which had helped the settlement	75.3	NA	89.3	87.5	81.0	59.5	95.3	79.8
Percentage of households responding that the settlement was a good place to live	63.8	75.5	63.5	53.0	31.7	77.9	57.1	90.4
Percentage of households responding that the settlement was a bad place to live	23.5	11.0	30.7	33.3	46.0	5.9	32.1	8.2
Total households interviewed	360	631	178	88	79	74	35	84

	Chalma	Isidro Fabela	Jardines	Liberales	El Sol	Santo Domingo	La Castrera	Nueva Valencia
Percentage of owner households mentioning an extra-*barrio* individual or institution who/which had helped the settlement	81.5	76.7	82.7	77.6	61.9	68.0	85.9	92.3
Percentage of all households mentioning an extra-*barrio* individual or institution who/which had helped the settlement	NA	NA	NA	NA	NA	NA	85.7	92.6
Percentage of households responding that the settlement was a good place to live	67.6	92.1	67.6	85.7	55.0	77.4	86.8	40.6
Percentage of households responding that the settlement was a bad place to live	7.5	5.0	15.7	5.4	24.3	6.1	11.8	49.3
Total households interviewed	73	144	114	60	120	120	84	94

ity obtain services, or they had given money or land to the community for some community facility. But the general failure to name such personalities is wholly compatible with the apathy of the *barrio* electorate when it comes to elections: why vote for those who never help? The same was true of Mexico. The majority stated that no one had really helped the settlement or that they were not aware of anyone who had. Where names were mentioned they reflected the most recent specific patrons that individual *barrios* had acquired: the national president in Santo Domingo, a *delegado* in Isidro Fabela, the Catholic church in El Sol, CODEUR in Liberales. In Valencia, the pattern was the same but the number of mentions was very small. A former invasion leader, now living outside the *barrio*, and a former mayor of the city were the only individuals receiving more than two mentions in either *barrio* in Valencia. However, another survey of *barrios* in Valencia suggests that the level of help sought outside varies dramatically from settlement to settlement (Buia and Guerra, n.d.). In a survey of seven *barrios*, respondents were asked if help had been requested of outside organizations; the answers ranged from 100-percent affirmative in one settlement to lows in th e settlements of between 22 and 43 per cent.

These data confirm the existence of major qualitative differences in the nature of leadership, community mobilization and external linkages between the *barrios* of the three cities, differences that can be explained only in the context of the demand making and political structures in each city analysed in the previous section.

The importance of external political support

An issue of real importance in the process of community participation and petitioning is the degree to which community organizations are linked into the wider partisan-political system. The fact that community organizations are the only common level of social organization above that of the household means that inevitably they act as a magnet for supra-local political parties which seek to gain an advantage by working through them (Nelson, 1979: 292). However, the issue is whether communities are likely to enhance their chances of securing outside help or servicing if they use party-political linkages. Earlier in this chapter we observed that, with the exception of Venezuela, the party-political apparatus in each city did not appear to overlap significantly with the bureaucratic linkages between state and community. Below, we examine the degree to which partisan-political activity has been prevalent in our sample of *barrios*. In Bogotá, our impression is that while political contacts are useful they are not essential in the process of obtaining services. In Mexico, affiliation to the party-political apparatus, and to the PRI in particular, has never been a *sine qua non* for obtaining services (Cornelius, 1975: 182; Eckstein, 1977), although patron–client links to bureaucrats or to leading politicians have often been used successfully. In Valencia, political contacts through the political parties are indispensible in obtaining services, although they are no guarantee of full servicing. The invasion of private land, for example, may well preclude or substantially limit help from political allies, as in the case of Nueva Valencia.

In Bogotá, most communities direct their petitions to the appropriate service agency and several of the major agencies have developed community offices to deal with these demands. Politicians often act as intermediaries in this process and in some agencies are active within the bureaucracy to help their clients in the settlements. As we argued in the previous chapter however, water, electricity, and drainage are not generally allocated in this way. These agencies generally make an evaluation of the cost of a project and charge the settlement directly. They often provide loans to the community on condition that a 30-per-cent deposit is put down. This mechanism has been part of the deliberate process underway in Colombia to take partisan political activity out of certain key areas of decision making. Nevertheless, there is no doubt that partisan politics still intrudes, as it probably should, in the decision-making process. It is our clear impression, however, that this political influence has been much less marked since the capacity of the service agencies improved during the seventies. The levels of political involvement do vary considerably with proximity to the next election. Even though politicians recognize how few vote in the low-income settlements, they still strive for support in those areas. Our investigation was carried out in a non-election period, and we certainly observed less political involvement than is characteristic of pre-election periods. Gauhan (1975) noted the high levels of party-political activity in three Bogotá settlements, and in a return visit to the communities in 1982 a marked change was apparent. One leader was now a candidate for the Assembly and another a candidate for the Council of Soacha.

The political links that exist in Bogotá tend normally to be with personalities no higher than councillors. Few national politicians were mentioned in our settlements as having provided help. But, even where councillors or other politicians help the settlements, it is difficult to evaluate their effect. We noted the ambiguity posed by the activities of two aspirant politicians active on the Board of Directors of the Water Company: did they obtain water for communities close to Suba, or merely inform the settlements of a decision already made by the company? Only in the recent, notorious, case of *barrio* Diana Turbay was there a clear political link between the community and high-level politicians. Here a pirate urbanization obtained services and official help through the political links of the *ex-alcalde menor* who ran the housing cooperative. So successful was he that the national president and the mayor attended the inauguration of the settlement and the population turned out *en masse* to vote him onto the council.[26]

In Soacha, the situation is much clearer. Favours are allocated on a clear patron–client basis, and those settlements with good political links gain a clear advantage over those without. San Antonio provides a clear example of this situation. Once the *barrio* leader became an ally of the political boss of the municipality, he began to obtain more services for his settlement. He was elected to the council and then had access to the council grants, which can make a considerable difference to a community's existence: Soacha is a relatively affluent municipality because of its industrial development. Other community leaders admitted that they had got on to the council in order to help their settlement in this way. Those who had not reached the council did not receive grants.

In Mexico City, it is necessary to identify two forms of 'partisan-political activity': one which involves the party-political apparatus (including senators, deputies, district organizers, party militants, etc.), the other which involves senior government officials (president, mayor, governor, *delegados*, ministers, agency heads, municipal presidents, etc.), many of whom hold non-elective posts but who often make partisan decisions. We have already observed in chapter 4 that the degree to which government officials carry out their duties in partisan fashion varies according to the type of agency and between administrations. Cornelius (1975: 198) provides a good example of the improved fortunes of a *barrio* whose patron secured high office in 1966. He concludes that, while effective local leadership, substantial self-help efforts and careful recruitment of residents were all important factors, the critical determinant was the highly personalized relationship that the community sustained with key decision makers. In Isidro Fabela, conflict with the electricity company over how much the settlement should pay was solved overnight when its leader, Marta Andrade, secured an interview with President Echeverría to put the residents' point of view. The president's subsequent directive to the company resulted in the *barrio* jumping from 106th to 6th position on the waiting list and the service being charged at a below-cost price. In the past, therefore, patron–client links have been an important feature of the government–community relationship although they have not always benefited low-income settlements. Here, however, we are more concerned with the influence of party-political actors: those whose primary concern is oriented towards securing electoral support. What role have these actors played in securing resources for community organizations?

Prior to 1976 our data suggest that, while settlement penetration by political parties was widespread, party contacts were not usually viewed by leaders as an appropriate way to secure services. In part this was because of the attitude of the political parties. For the PRI in particular, low-income communities have fulfilled several important functions over and above that of providing electoral support. First, they have often provided a training ground on which *barrio* militants have cut their political teeth. We are aware of several individuals who used their election as *barrio* leaders as springboards into the party. Second, community organizations have helped the PRI control the low-income populations. The existence in some settlements of leaders who represent different factions within the PRI allows considerable scope for manipulation from party officials (Ugalde *et al.*, 1974). Elsewhere, a particularly able local leader who is putting pressure on the governmental system is likely to be coopted into the party, a process which normally leads to the reduction of that pressure and fewer benefits for the community (Eckstein, 1977). Finally, the widespread belief that cooperation with the PRI was essential if settlements were to receive help from the bureaucracy strengthened the CNOP wing of the PRI's hand in mobilizing support at rallies on behalf of Echeverría.

The extent to which election periods affect the outcome of community demand making is open to question. Montaño (1976) in his analysis of the 1973 Congressional elections found that the activity and interest of political parties in the *barrios* increased markedly near to the election. The need for electoral support provided local leaders with bargaining power with which to negotiate benefits for the local community. This occurred especially in those *barrios* which maintained a 'clientelist' relationship with the authorities (1976: 141). Montaño (1976: 84) also quotes a Federal District department head who says that the PRI channels most of its material help towards those *barrios* that might be hostile to it, and to those that have been exceptionally supportive of the party. These two arguments, that benefits accrue more rapidly around election time and that areas which present problems for the PRI are more likely to be singled out for preferential treatment, assume that the party-political apparatus is able systematically to influence decision making and resource allocation of government departments. We are unconvinced by either argument and we were fortunate that the later stages of our fieldwork coincided with the 1979 Congressional elections. During this period we monitored closely both the nature of *barrio*–party relations as well as the response of government officials whom we had observed throughout the year. Our aim was to identify the extent to which *barrio juntas* benefited by the proximity of elections.

Certainly all political parties increased their presence in the *barrios* during the three months before voting day. Some leaders allowed candidates to adopt the cause of their *barrio* and to accompany resident visits to government offices. Generally, however, PRI candidates were wary not to make promises that they patently could not fulfil; indeed, it became apparent that national-party speeches emphasised the promotional role that deputies might play on behalf of the *barrios*. PRI handouts in the form of services were rare and always insubstantial; a water lorry (hired by the PRI for the purpose) would be sent to *barrios* that had complained to their candidate; manilla folders with the district logo were provided to those actively soliciting land regularization. And, when *barrio* receptions were provided for candidates, the local residents (or leaders) paid. In short, we found little to suggest that the political parties used sizeable funds to 'buy' electoral support.

Leaders were not easily deceived by the party and their response varied from active support to extreme cynicism. Active support for the PRI was most likely from relatively inexperienced leaders or where the candidate was a big name whom leaders felt it would be unwise to alienate. Elsewhere leaders cooperated to provide PRI candidates with a platform to address *junta* meetings but did not go out of their way to garner support on their behalf. Weak rival factions within the settlements would commonly form linkages with opposition parties.

There was little evidence to suggest that government officials altered their programmes to help the PRI. Most received *barrio* delegations much as before, regardless of whether or not they were accompanied by candidates. As a general rule, opposition candidates were treated like those from the PRI so long as the group they accompanied were *bona fide barrio* residents. Decision makers acknowledged in interview that they came under extra pressure from candidate-backed *barrio* residents around election times, but also insisted that they did not respond any differently, nor did such considerations affect the resource-allocation programmes that were, in most cases, determined months earlier. Neither did we find evidence that *barrio*-servicing programmes had been affected significantly by the approach of elections. It seems that this is likely to occur only in exceptional circumstances where a particularly eminent or well-connected candidate gains the support of the *delegado* who hopes to provide a favour that may later be reciprocated.[27]

Valencia differs from the two previous case studies insofar as the processes of servicing, and public administration generally, are almost wholly partisan. It is assumed in many communities that only partisan *juntas* will be able to make the contacts necessary to obtain help from the authorities. Opposition leaders will not gain access to the mayor's office or to that of the governor. Consequently, they will not be recommended to the party-affiliated managers of the service agencies, nor will they gain favour with ORDEC, the state agency currently in charge of coordinating *barrio* petitioning. As a result most leaders belong to the ruling party, and leaders change after elections (see pp. 199, 203). In those few cases where a community *junta* contains members of different parties, the leading spokesman is likely to come from the political party in power. Thus, in La Castrera, a *Copeyano* was *junta* president during the Caldera administration and the secretary was an *Adeco*. The partisan nature of community–government relations is nicely demonstrated by the state community-development office, ORDEC. At the time of the field work, all 20 community promoters were affiliated to the same newly elected government party. While all lived in the low-income settlements of the city, few had previous experience in community organization or in the servicing agencies. In their promotional activities they seemed to deal only with the *juntas* belonging to their own party; when we used this link to meet people in the settlements we met only *Copeyanos*. Since it is the official function of ORDEC to draw up an inventory of *barrio* needs and try to indicate priority needs, the partisan nature of service demands is obvious. Clearly, community leaders can and do bypass ORDEC, going straight to the council or the governor, but they can do this only when they have influence with some other political figure.[28] Certain mayors have a good reputation among settlement leaders for helping their communities. Certain mayors were known to influence the servicing agencies in favour of settlements with which they had close links. The council also has funds to provide pipes, or gravel, or schools which leads to direct petitioning to allies in the council.

Thus, the Venezuelan political system encourages partisan petitioning. Hence settlements tend to elect leaders from the political party in power. Those leaders petition their patrons in the council, the state government and in the service agencies. Queue-jumping is frequent and technical rule-making by the service agencies much less common than in Bogotá.

Community leadership in the settlements

Two key issues in the nature of leadership were raised in our earlier literature review. The first relates to the sources of leaders' power within each community. Do they maintain power through force, through charisma and popularity in the community, because they are better educated, because they are known to have influential friends outside the community, because they are linked into a political-party apparatus, or because they are imposed from outside? Of course, these possibilities are not mutually exclusive; some imposed leaders are elected by the community, some *caciques* may even be respected and liked. Do the patterns of leadership vary with the circumstances of the settlement; do strong authoritarian leaders emerge at times of crisis such as the initiation of the settlement, or are less authoritarian leaders likely to emerge once major conflict over the land issue has been resolved and major services have been achieved? Over what time period do they lead the community? Do leaders remain in power only during the administration of one president or do they continue irrespective of changes in national and local administration?

Second, what is the nature of their links beyond the community and how far can they act on behalf of the community in the wider urban arena. Do they gain their legitimacy merely as settlement leaders or do they have some independent basis for action? What is the nature of their relationship to supra-local authorities? Are they imposed as leaders, as Ray (1969) has suggested is typical in Venezuela, or do they emerge autonomously from the community as is suggested by Cornelius (1975) for Mexico? Do they gain legitimacy within the community because of their personal characteristics?

Third, are there any systematic patterns which make it more likely that some individuals will be leaders? Are most leaders better educated, better off, older, etc. than the rest of the community?

To a considerable extent the nature of leadership varies in each city. For that reason we have chosen to discuss each city in turn and only to generalize about the kinds of leaders encountered in our survey settlements. We will return to this issue in the last section where we attempt to explain how leadership, community participation and settlement politics are determined in large part by the nature of land alienation, the form of service petitioning and the political organization of the settlements.

Bogotá

In Bogotá, the leaders showed a wide range of characteristics, bases of power, levels of political linkage and, indeed, degrees of success and popularity within the community. The few features which several had in common were: self-employment, and hence spare time during which they could conduct community affairs; extra-political links, though these had sometimes changed through time; election to the *junta de acción comunal* by popular vote; hope, but little expectation, of rising to political importance through their community role; a failure to use force, although several were strong personalities who were not averse to a certain amount of arm twisting; and some connection with the process of land subdivision (table 19).

The leaders had risen to power at different times. Some had lived in the settlement since its origin, others had taken over when the original leader had left, been voted out of office or had lost interest, some had played different roles in the community council. Few had an obvious source of power such as that conveyed by control over the allocation of land. Such influence over land allocation is clearly more likely in invasion settlements and therefore is largely absent in Bogotá. Nevertheless, frequent references were made in our survey settlements to the involvement between the community leader and the subdivider. In Atenas, the pirate urbanizer claimed that the community leader had chosen which families could participate in the subdivision, in Britalia

Table 19 *The characteristics of leaders in the survey barrios*

	Mexico City						Bogotá					Valencia	
	Isidro Fabela	Santo Domingo	El Sol	Liberales	Chalma	Jardines	Juan Pablo I	Casa-blanca	Atenas	Britalia	San Antonio	Nueva Valencia	La Castrera
Existence of factions?[1]													
Yes	x	x	x				x			x		x	x –
No				x	x	x		x	x		x		
Leader:													
employed	y	x	x				x		x		y		y
self-employed	xz	zy	y		xy			x			xz	x	
'unemployed'						x				x			x
male	xz	xz	x	x	xy	x	x	x	x		xyz	x	x
female	y	y	y	y						x			y
active in political party	xyz	xyz	y	xy	xy		x	x	x	x	x.	x	xy
unaffiliated						x					yz		

Source: interviews with settlement leaders.
Notes:
Different leaders within a settlement are depicted by different letters.
[1] Factions were identified when more than one organized group existed within the settlement with interests that were substantially different from the other(s).

224

there were strong accusations of dubious links between the pirate urbanizer and the original *junta*. In Juan Pablo I the subdividers were influential in the community organization and in San Antonio there is the suggestion that not everyone that wanted to buy into the community was permitted to do so. But, although these accusations were common and were also heard in other settlements we visited, the fact that subdividers are running a business and need to sell lots as quickly as possible is likely to weaken this tendency. Community leaders may receive free lots from the pirate urbanizer to keep relations sweet, and there is at times an alliance between the community leaders and the pirate urbanizer, but there is an inherent limit to the selection process. In three new 'pirate urbanizations' where aspirant councillors (or aspirant members of the Assembly) recently formed 'housing cooperatives', only one managed to achieve his objective.[29] It is difficult to guarantee that the settlers will vote for the leader or for the urbanizer when the population is buying the land. The only guaranteed basis for support is performance: Alfonso Guerrero in *Barrio* Diana Turbay obtained power because he gained powerful political support and obtained services for the community. Less successful leaders are unlikely to maintain support.

Nor, in general, do we believe that leaders are planted on the community. Most leaders have political links, but these have often changed and there is little evidence to support the idea of placement. Initially in Atenas and Britalia there was a common political alliance between the *barrio* leadership and the pirate urbanizer which worked to their mutual advantage, but we did not obtain clear evidence to support the idea of placement from above in the other settlements. In any case, this would be placement by the pirate urbanizer rather than by the political parties themselves.

More often, we believe, the credentials to run the community are accretitive. Leaders develop power as a result of talent, experience, growing contacts and simple force of personality. They achieve power through their position not the other way round. Initially, few had any obvious source of power. In Britalia, the leader lived outside the settlement, although she owned two plots of land in the settlement, and gained her position only after a sustained battle between the community and the urbanizer-linked *junta*. Although outside political actors were influential in her rise to power, these came from both the Communist and the Liberal parties, hardly the holiest of alliances. In Casablanca, the leader was the son of the original settlement leader and obtained power because of his higher level of education, knowledge and contacts. He had clearly worked hard on behalf of the community and it was this that constituted his prime source of continued support. Although he subdivided some land within the community and was, therefore, a small-scale pirate urbanizer, this occurred after he became leader. In San Antonio, the leader was one of the longest-established inhabitants of the settlement who ran a small business in it. While he also had political links before obtaining power, which may have helped, other leaders had been in charge before he took over. His subsequent election to the council of Soacha was gained through his role of community leader rather than the other way round. In the neighbouring Soacha settlements one leader had been elected after the original leader had moved, and another had been elected as being more amenable to the population; neither had obvious political links. In Juan Pablo I, the source of leadership is personal activity and energy; the informal leader was merely the most energetic of many people who work within the community to obtain some security of tenure.[30]

Certainly, most of the leaders were more affluent than the majority of families although they were not often markedly so. The leader in Atenas was a machine operative in a factory and was clearly typical of the working-class community that dominated the settlement.[31] The leader of Britalia came from outside and was married to a small restaurant owner in one of the factory districts of Bogotá. She was much better-off than the rest of the community, probably better educated, and much more self-confident. In Casablanca, the leader was a civil engineer, who owned a small construction business and who was much better-off than others in the settlement. He was clearly drawn from a different class and lived in a middle-class house on the very edge of the community. In Juan Pablo I, the leader was a manual worker like most members of the community. Of the four leaders in San Antonio, one owned a small café and ran two government stores, another worked as a printer and aspired to get into journalism, and a third was a taxi driver. In sum, while most were better off than their neighbours and had a measure of flexibility in their work timetables, it is difficult to generalize overmuch about their specific social and economic characteristics. Indeed, evidence collected from other Bogotá settlements revealed leaders from all kinds of background.

There was also little evidence of leaders using their positions to enrich themselves. The leader of Atenas may have gained some direct benefit from his ability to find jobs for some people in the settlement but this is uncertain. In San Antonio, the leader ran the two government stores but had done so before he took over as settlement leader. In Casablanca, the leader benefited insofar as he had developed a number of lots and, as settlement leader, he had obtained services for the community which increased the value of the land. But, even here, he could have made the money without having acted as community leader. In the other cases there was no suggestion that the leaders gained any pecuniary benefit from their involvement with the community.

Perhaps as a result there was little sign that Bogotá leaders maintain control through coercion. While Gauhan (1975) reports that one *junta* in an invasion *barrio* had indulged in force, including murder, we found no sign of physical violence being employed. Such coercion as took place was more subtle. The leader in San Antonio used his control over the government stores and the kerosene deposit to encourage community participation. Those who did not participate could not rely on obtaining supplies at times of shortage; we heard several complaints about this treatment within the settlement. He also insisted that all new owners join the community organization and clearly a mixture of threat and promise achieved the required result.[32] In the other settlements, the only pressure on the community was moral: failure to get involved and help to petition for services would rebound on all members of the settlement.

If coercion was not common, nor was clientelism. In few settlements did the leader have much in the way of resources to allocate; his basis of support, therefore, had to be performance, not favours. Only the leader in Atenas had used his ability to get jobs in the government as a means of mobilizing support within the community and here the principal aim seems to have been politics rather than money – not a terribly successful ploy, given the high community vote for Belisario Betancur in 1978.

The main basis by which leaders obtained and maintained their power within the community was their ability to mobilize the population and get services. Some of our leaders were very successful in performing this kind of role and received recognition for it. The leaders of Britalia, Casablanca and San Antonio had all been very successful in getting services for their communities, and in the past the leader in Atenas had probably been similarly successful. Since leaders are elected in Bogotá – though doubtful elections are not unknown – this seems to have led to leadership based on action. Surprisingly, it has not led to frequent change. Most of our settlements were characterized by continuity rather than change. Leaders do not change automatically after national or local elections; they continue in power. When they depart it is either because they wish to or because they have been elected out of office after scandal, internal community conflicts, or failure. This suggests that they are not planted by the political parties as is more common in Venezuela. The political parties seek to influence and coopt leaders but they do not often have the influence to do much to support their favoured candidates. Certainly, having obtained power it is relatively easy for leaders to retain it. By maintaining visibility, obtaining some services, organizing either community work or the process of petitioning, they are accepted as good leaders. They also obtain better contacts and power through their experience. As such the settlements are often prepared to accept them even if in Britalia and San Antonio the leaders are sometimes hard on the inhabitants.

At times, there has been evidence of competition between political parties within the settlement. Sometimes different party-backed slates of candidates are nominated, but until recently the Department of Community Action, rather than siding with one slate against another, has sought to merge them along the lines of the National Front. In general, while some leaders had enemies, both political and personal, there was limited evidence of settlement battles, feuds or tension.

The most plausible explanation of this situation is that there are limited rewards for leaders either politically or materially. We have already suggested that few leaders make a fortune, but it is also unlikely that they will win much fame. In the District of Bogotá, settlement leaders do not generally become councillors or rise to even medium-level political office. The community-relations jobs in the government agencies are for the educated professional not for the settlement leader. Councillors, except those in the Communist party, are drawn from higher social groups, although pirate urbanizers have become councillors. In general, the Conservative party draws its office holders from high social groups, the Liberals and ANAPO have gone down to the lower-middle class, but none have often gone much lower. As we noted earlier, although some of the leaders of the survey settlements had recently stood for political office, they had not been successful. The chances for political advancement are definitely limited. In Soacha, upward mobility is more likely. The leader of San Antonio was head of the Association of *juntas de acción comunal* and was a councillor of Soacha; so too were the leaders of two other settlements where we made visits. But, even here, it was claimed that the advantages of being a councillor were fewer for the individual concerned than for his community: his presence permitted a flow of *auxilios* to be channelled to his community.

In sum, community leadership in Bogotá is marked by its continuity, its lack of serious conflict, its limited opportunities for personal advancement and its reliance on popular election and hard work. The prizes and power available to settlement leaders are severely constrained.

Mexico City

In Mexico City the structure of leadership is complex and we concur with Montaño's (1976: 68) assertion that to regard low-income-settlement leaders primarily as *caciques* is a gross and inaccurate generalization. This view appears to be based largely upon evidence derived from several particularly conflictive invasion settlements which were established between 1965 and 1972.[33] As we shall observe below, there are many other types of leader who bear little relation to the characteristics of *caciques* outlined earlier.

Although the issue is complex, there appear to be two broad determinants of leadership structure in Mexican *barrios*. First, the nature of land alienation within the settlement is important, specifically the control that leaders are able to exercise over the allocation of plots. This control affects the power base of the leader, the potential for illegal earnings and, as a result, the propensity for conflict between competing-interest groups. The second determinant is the nature of the response of the authorities, specifically whether they encourage clientelism or the formation of single-community associations. In the case of Mexico it is difficult to generalize about leadership given that these two factors have changed over the past fifteen years. It is further complicated by the fact that as communities physically improve so the functions of leaders and their motivation alter. Unlike Bogotá, therefore, there is much sharper differentiation between leaders in Mexico and they come and go with greater frequency. Nevertheless, three broad features appear to emerge consistently in our analysis.

First, as in Bogotá, few leaders were employees (table 19). The only significant exception was in Isidro Fabela where the leader was an accountant. Usually leaders were self-employed. In Chalma, for example, the two leaders both worked from their homes, one as a baker, the other as a greengrocer. Elsewhere, leaders were 'unemployed', best understood as working full-time on community affairs. In the latter case, we assume that they drew a small salary and expenses from the community funds, though none openly acknowledged the fact. However, we did not get the impression that residents begrudged them the money so long as they felt the amounts were not excessive and the leaders were active on their behalf. Interestingly, in El Sol, it emerged that one leader received a small but regular retainer from the municipality, a fact she did not wish to advertise.

A second common feature was that leaders were not active members of any political party because they realized that there was little point. The PRI had little to offer in the way of services and traditionally appeared inclined to assist residents only during the run-up to elections. Moreover, overt affiliation with the PRI might be treated with scepticism by residents. However, as we observed earlier, it was not unknown for the PRI to attempt to recruit the most successful leaders into their ranks in an effort to coopt them. The leader in Liberales had turned down repeated offers. Other leaders did not: José Palacios had quickly abandoned *barrio* affairs in Isidro Fabela and risen to a high position within the CNOP. In Netzahualcóyotl, several leaders used their *barrio* networks as a springboard to election as deputies in the national legislature. However, party affiliation was the exception rather than the rule.

Third, leaders were usually better-off than most of their camp followers, at least insofar as levels of house consolidation were concerned. Interpretations about how this had been achieved vary. The cynical view of many government officials was that leaders exploited the local community. Alternatively, it could be argued that leaders emerge as a result of their particular abilities which are also put to good effect in earning their livelihood. Our evidence suggests that income derived from exploiting leadership functions is relatively unimportant. Even in those cases where it was likely that substantial misappropriations occurred (in Isidro Fabela and Santo Domingo), leaders' incomes did not appear to be dramatically out of line with those of the remainder of the settlement. While leaders usually figured in the upper quartile of each settlement's distribution of income, they were not especially ostentatious in their housing and lifestyles. It is difficult to generalize beyond these three common attributes. Leadership posts were not the exclusive prerogative of men; in all settlements women were active in improvement association committees though it was less usual for them to occupy the top position. Exceptions were Marta Andrade, who was elected to the key position in Isidro Fabela once the self-imposed leader José Rodríguez Cuellar had been removed; Josefa Torres in Santo Domingo, who also took over once the influence of the two strongest authoritarian leaders had waned after 1976; Doña Santos in El Sol; and Doña Lola of the husband-and-wife team in Liberales. *Prima facie*, it appears that women are less likely to exercise power during the early phase of community development, and that their legitimacy is based upon election rather than self-imposition. Authoritarian leaders on the other hand were almost always male and during the early 1970s dominated a number of large settlements where they could exercise authority over the allocation of plots. Their prospects for making money were brightest in such settlements.

Violence, conflict between factions and the intimidation of residents occurred in several settlements (Santo Domingo, Padierna, and on the slopes of Ajusco in the extreme south) where the extreme insecurity of tenure heightened the leverage that leaders could exert over residents. A further factor permitting conflict between residents within the settlements was the freedom from outside intervention by the authorities. Since 1976, the authorities have sought to reduce conflict by recognizing a single elected leader of the *junta de vecinos* and by stepping-up the campaign to regularize land tenure.

Leaders also had varying levels of previous experience. Several had been involved in earlier struggles for low-income settlement recognition or had cut their political teeth in union activities. Doña Lola had worked on behalf of residents evicted from the *barrio* in which she had lived previously. Juan Ramos had attempted an earlier invasion in the lands now occupied by Santo Domingo. Eleazar Flores in Isidro Fabela had worked in the bakers' union and now combined a relatively weak leadership role in the settlement with that of fringe preacher and leader of a defence organization covering the whole Federal District. Another leader who was actively trying to establish an invasion on the slopes of Ajusco during 1978 had worked previously as an organizer of the Independent Farmworkers' Confederation. He became disenchanted and set up his own Free Union, a principal activity of which was to organize land captures. Other leaders, especially women, claimed that this was their first (and last!) involvement. Previous experience was not a prerequisite for competent leadership. Motives varied for wishing to run the gauntlet of physical intimidation, verbal abuse, slander and the expenditure of enormous amounts of time. Many stated that it was a matter of chance; they had not sought the nomination. Don Guillermo from Jardines said that he was obliged to become leader because no one else was willing or competent enough. It is hardly surprising that none admitted that it was for their own personal advancement: pecuniary or political. However, there is little doubt that the primary motive of men like José Rodríguez Cuellar (Isidro Fabela), Manuel Romero and Juan Ramos in Santo Domingo, 'Pancho' and La Chabela in Padierna, and Doña Santos in El Sol was to exploit the settlement for their personal financial gain. Occasionally the motive was one of securing a job within the PRI or, more remote still, of entering politics.

In Mexico, community leadership is a precarious and often onerous affair. *Caciques* are less important than is commonly believed and opportunities for long-term domination and exploitation of residents have been eroded by more formalized arrangements of state–community relations and by programmes of land regularization. Effective leadership benefits residents insofar as they receive guidance and information, are 'protected' from unnecessary petitioning, and are not subject to arbitrary decisions and exploitation from their leaders. However, in our judgement, efficient leadership does not significantly advance *barrio* servicing and regularization.

Valencia

Ray (1969: 44–5) clearly sees community leadership in Venezuelan *barrios* as deriving from leadership of a land invasion. Since that leader is normally associated with a political party this means that, despite protestations that the *junta* will be non-partisan, it is closely linked into the party-political process from the beginning. He also suggests, however, that, as *junta* petitioning is seldom successful, popular support for the *junta* within the settlement atrophies and thenceforth there is no effective leadership for months, even years at a time. Only when there is some chance of obtaining services or, implicitly, when elections are near does the leadership gain a new lease of life, either the same group or another. Ray (*ibid:* 48) also notes a variation in this process in what he labels officially settled *barrios* – a process especially common, he claims, in Valencia. In such settlements the lots are allocated by a special office of the municipal council which appoints a *barrio* leader affiliated with the governing party to take responsibility for distribution lots within the selected area without charge to officially registered families. This process is most common in settle-ments which have been relocated from one part of the city to another. La Castrera, indeed, began as an unofficial outgrowth from just such an officially settled *barrio*. The formal link with government and the ruling party obviously determines the political connection and the nature of community organization. The leader's power over lot distribu-tion and official sanction of his role 'reinforces his power in the *barrio* and his control over its affairs' (Ray, 1969: 48).

Our information is of course based on a much later period. Nevertheless, there are certain elements of Ray's description that are still valid and which differ considerably, therefore, from the patterns of community leadership described for Mexico, and particularly for Bogotá. Clearly, *barrio* leadership in Valencia is defined as much by its party affiliation as by its identification with the community. As such the leadership changes with the national and local swings of fortune of the political parties. In both of our settlements, and indeed in most of the other settlements we visited, the victory of COPEI nationally in 1978 and locally in 1979 led to a change in *barrio* leadership. As one *barrio* leader said, 'For five years we sat with our arms crossed; now it is the turn of the *Adecos* to do the same.' However, it is important to point out that this was not true of every community in Valencia even in 1979 when COPEI won the local elections by a wide margin. Previously, Valencia regularly elected councils with a wide range of parties; it was only after 1974 that COPEI and AD came to dominate the council. This meant that *barrio* leaders affiliated to minority parties could still obtain support in the council. Since 1974, it has become more difficult for these leaders and it is probable that affiliation to AD or COPEI has become the norm, with the leader changing with the result of the election. These points can be illustrated by the experiences of La Castrera and Nueva Valencia.

The leader of La Castrera between 1971 and 1975 was a *Copeyano*. He obtained power in a junta election in which the original leader, with whom he had strong political disagreements, seems to have played no real role. The new leader led an active campaign to get services supported both by community petitioning and his party links. He also sent applicants for land to the council who allowed them to occupy the remaining lots in the settlement. For much of this time he was unemployed and claimed to live on his wife's income. He later became a security officer for a private company and there is no indication that he made money out of his position of responsibility.

His main source of legitimacy lay in the access conferred by his party and *barrio* position and his energy and resourcefulness in pushing hard for services. He lost power in 1975 when *Adeco* members of the Office for Community Development (under a new *Adeco* governor) sought to have him declare himself an *Adeco* or resign. He was replaced by a new leader who was nominated by the party. By 1979 the community organization had ossified and even *Adeco* supporters previously involved in community organization were critical of the lack of action since 1975. The change of government in 1979 brought a new leader, a *Copeyano* who was encouraged by ORDEC to found a new neighbourhood association. An employee of the University of Carabobo, the new leader had strong party links. By 1982, it seems as if the *barrio* was benefiting greatly from these links: a number of loans had been granted by FUNDACOMUN, CMA, INAVI and other government agencies.

The early leadership in Nueva Valencia was also linked to the process of land invasion. The leaders of the *Campesino* League led the community but were replaced by an *Adeco* leader in 1973 during the campaign of Carlos Andres Pérez. The new leader had recently arrived in the community and appears to have been elected to the leadership because of his past experience as an activist on behalf of rural groups and because of his ties with Democratic Action. Like so many community leaders he was self-employed, working as a gardener. As leader he faced a major problem insofar as the authorities were most reluctant to provide services to a settlement founded on private land. He was also hindered by the fact that the *Adeco* governor between 1974 and 1977 was unsympathetic to low-income settlement problems. With COPEI winning the 1979 election, he accepted that he could no longer lead the settlement. When we first visited Nueva Valencia, strenuous attempts were being made to get *Copeyanos* within the settlement to form a community *junta*. At the same time, a third group, linked to MAS, the main left-wing party, was trying to get itself recognized as the official *junta* for part of the settlement. The outcome was that two neighbour associations were established for the settlement, the first controlled by COPEI, the second by MAS. It seems, however, that neither has been successful in overcoming the basic difficulty facing the settlement: its location on private land. In three years the settlement seems to have made no progress in terms of servicing.

Leadership in Valencia changes more frequently than in Bogotá and

Mexico: a consequence of the close links that the parties develop with the *barrios* and the regular changes in the political complexion of national, state and municipal government. Some forceful and success-ful community leaders may retain respect during periods of inactivity and may be reinstated if the government changes again. It is very difficult, however, for such a leader to retain power when the opposition commands the major positions of political control. While the communities accept this reality, it suggests that local leaders are less representatives of the *barrios* than of the political parties them-selves.

Social movements

None of the settlements studied could be said to have participated in a social movement or even to have engaged in a major urban protest. In fact, such signs were very limited in all three cities, even if the terms are interpreted broadly. In Bogotá, the main urban protests have come in the form of occasional land invasions, in the burning of buses when fares have been increased and in the meetings and rallies occasioned by the plan to build a motorway along the side of the mountains in the east of the city (1971–4).

Certainly, the land invasions that occurred in Policarpa Salavarrieta, El Quindío, and Las Colinas were considerable breaches of the peace organized in the interest of those without homes. Central de Pro-vivienda, the major organizer, was seeking to discredit the National Front governments and to some considerable extent was successful in doing so. While the intention to increase class consciousness was succcessful within the settlements involved, the divisions in the Colombian left have consistently helped to undermine any popular support among the poor as a whole. The left obtains few votes in national or local elections except in hard-core communist areas.

If the outcome of the land invasions was little more than an urban protest, the same must be said of the *barrio* resistance that focused on the plan to build the motorway. Although Janssen (1978) has claimed that this opposition represented a social movement, the case is somewhat flimsy. Certainly, the *barrio* dwellers sustained their opposition to the plan but his claim that this was a wholly spontaneous movement of the inhabitants (p. 157), 'independent of politicians and parties', is belied by the major involvement of the *Anapista* councillor and leader Carlos Bula, and the considerable role played in discrediting the scheme by Liberal politicians and technical advisers (*Grupo de Estudios Urbanos*, 1978; Revéiz *et al.*, 1977). That it was temporarily a principal form of class struggle is beyond doubt. Some members of the squatter communities along the route were certainly well aware of the ideological potential of the conflict, but Janssen's own account suggests that tensions within the affected communities were equally responsible for the failure. The major threats to political stability in Bogotá have come from conventional working-class protest, such as the major strike in 1977 against low wages, or from recent guerrilla activity. Urban social movements have not been important in Bogotá.

In Mexico City, too, it is questionable whether any urban protest has been able to alter the power relations in society. The authorities have normally controlled demand making and community organization through a combination of patron–clientism, cooptation and repression. The nearest that community leaders have come to posing a major threat has been the Movimiento Restaurador de Colonos (MRC) and the Organizaciones Unidas de la Quinta Zona in Netzahualcóyotl and Ecatepec respectively. Both movements managed to unite settlements into an alliance against the company urbanizers. As we have already seen, however, repression and modified state policies managed to defuse the protest. After the FINEZA agreement had been negotiated, the CNOP began a systematic campaign to penetrate the MRC; some *junta* leaders were coopted and others were encouraged to use the power base that they had created as springboards for political careers (Cisneros, n.d.).[34] Likewise, in the case of the United Organization of the *Quinta Zona* the PRI had managed to subvert the movement by 1975. Guerrero *et al.* (1974) have argued that the government deliberately adopted a policy of differential servicing to *barrios* in this zone in order to generate divisions between settlements; but strong supporting evidence did not emerge in the course of our interviews with government officials and settlement leaders.[35]

In certain settlements, leaders have persuaded the residents to act beyond community issues of physical development and voice their protest about wider issues of social injustice. *Barrio* groups have taken up the cause of repressed minorities, political prisoners and workers' rights. Although the *barrios* that have achieved this are exceptional, they have been the focus of considerable attention.[36] The response of the government to individual radical settlements has varied. Campamento 2 de Octubre was subjected to a campaign of repression by the authorities: leaders were intimidated and the settlement was deliberately, but mysteriously, set alight (*Excelsior*, 26 January 1976; Montaño, 1976: 210). President Echeverría visited the Ruben Jaramillo settlement and authorized INDECO to intervene to regularize and install services. There is evidence that leaders here were also intimidated and murdered (Montaño, 1976: 193).

In Valencia, urban protests have been infrequent and have most often focused on issues related to land invasions, transportation and public housing. Deaths have occurred during the repression of land invasions, as indeed happened in Nueva Valencia, and major protests have been linked to the formation of settlements such as La Florida. A series of strikes by the bus companies created serious problems in 1980 and 1981. In August 1981, three people were shot by the police and 40 were detained when they protested about the poor state of the roads. This riot was occasioned by the refusal of the bus companies to use the roads any longer (*El Carabobeño*, 26 August 1981). There were also several attempts to invade public-housing areas which gave rise to police repression and civil disturbances. Attempts to occupy public housing in Ricardo Urriera and Isabelica were all repelled by the police using tear gas. In May 1980, a major riot involving school and university students and supported by the 'Popular Leagues' occurred in Isabelica and on one occasion spread to the centre of the city. Although some attempt was made to turn these protests into more general movements, these efforts were successfully controlled by the authorities.

In conclusion, we see little evidence in Bogotá, Mexico City or Valencia of any urban protest becoming sufficiently generalized to produce an urban social movement. Our observations suggest that the regimes in these cities have not lost control sufficiently to allow a social movement to develop. It is evident that government intervention has been successful in heading off urban protests, either by making concessions, coopting leaders, driving wedges between groups of residents or, as a last resort, by repression.

Conclusion

In Bogotá, Mexico City and Valencia, the state has established formal channels for settlement demand making. In Bogotá, the Community Action programme has been in existence since 1958, in Mexico City formal neighbourhood councils are more recent, beginning in 1977, and in Valencia, despite numerous changes, formal neighbourhood associations have been encouraged since 1958. The common link between the three cities is that these formal channels have served the interests of the state more than those of the communities. Partisan political links are apparent in most community organizations but it is only in Valencia that such links dominate the patterns of demand making and community affairs.

In the three cities, owners were the principal participants in *barrio* campaigns to secure services or the legalization of tenure. Yet even their involvement was limited; only 39 per cent of owner households declared that they had been active in some way or other. Petitioning helps secure servicing but is not the critical determinant. Participation was higher in Mexico than elsewhere, which reflects the greater need in that city to pressurize agencies for services and especially for recognition of land tenure. Participation obviously varies in the three cities according to the service required; the lack of water and electricity generates higher levels of community participation than the lack of utilities such as health centres and schools. Despite low levels of participation, the communities were well aware of the major personalities within the settlements. What varied was the number of leaders mentioned in each settlement; in general, fractionalism was most marked in Mexico City and least marked in Bogotá. There were low recognition rates for extra-community personalities in all three cities. In general, most people agreed that few major politicians or government officials had helped them. Party affiliated links were very different between the three cities. In Bogotá and Mexico City, partisan politics was not critical in the servicing process and therefore the communities did not demonstrate marked support for the major parties. By contrast, in Valencia where the petitioning process is highly partisan, petitioning was directed to friendly political links within the bureaucracy. In that city technical routines are secondary to political contacts. The characteristics of leaders, their levels of motivation, linkages with outside influentials and contribution to *barrio* improvements varied markedly, both temporally, as well as between cities. Valencia is characterized by close liaison between political party and the local leader; a change in the ruling party heralds a new leader at the *barrio* level. In contrast, few politicians in Bogotá appear to rely heavily upon a personal power base within the *barrios*. Affiliation to the majority party is not a *sine qua non* for favourable response from the government. While most *barrios* are affiliated to, and receive services from, the Department of Acción Comunal, a more important criterion is a leader's ability to demonstrate a settlement's need, promote a willingness on the part of residents to put up some of the costs, and to petition the relevant agencies. The same applies in Mexico, though here a personal patron–client relationship between government functionaries and leaders may be important, both in determining the local leader's power as well as the level of services and physical benefits that he or she wins for the community.

Leaders were generally better educated, self-employed, more prosperous and more highly motivated than most of their community. But the differences were not vast and leaders were normally members of the same class as the rest of the community.

Social movements were uncharacteristic of the three cities and indeed there have been relatively few 'urban protests' stimulated by issues related to 'collective consumption'. The regimes in each city have been successful in deflecting opposition by making concessions, by providing services, by coopting leaders or, in the last resort, through repression. This reflects the perpetual awareness on the part of local and national elites that they must respond to and channel community demands. Although the nature of that response has varied through time, the need for social control has been a consistent ingredient governing community–government relations. Our general conclusion is that the nature of *barrio* politics and its relative importance in determining service provision in each city is shaped by governmental constraints and needs rather than by local or settlement conditions. Better servicing might be achieved by higher levels of community mobilization but the authorities are well accustomed to handling such demands.

This conclusion is very discouraging, if not unexpected. It will satisfy few people who believe in community participation as a force to neighbourhood improvement and offer little hope to those who believe in participation as a form of raising class awareness. The truth seems to be that in Bogotá, Mexico City and Valencia the state has developed highly effective methods of channelling and controlling participation. There is certainly little sign of participation in the sense of growing control by poor people over the resources and institutions that determine their quality of life.

6

Conclusions

Most of our findings have been presented in the summaries at the end of each chapter and will not be repeated here. There are, however, a number of general statements which need to be made about our results. In particular, we would like to take this opportunity to emphasize those elements of our work which we believe to be original, affect planning practice or which warrant further development.

Our work has clearly underlined the point made in the recent social-science literature that issues such as housing, land use and servicing cannot sensibly be isolated from the wider social, economic and political environment. In the past, planners too often tried to separate these issues in order to better resolve urban problems; the practical mistakes that have been made often reflect that error. Work in the social sciences during the seventies has clearly shown that such a separation is unjustifiable. In this study we have tried to place the land, housing and servicing issues facing the poor in their broad socio-economic context. We have emphasized how home improvement depends upon income levels of the poor and upon the costs of land and materials. We have shown how tenure is less a matter of individual choice than an outcome of the broad working both of the capitalist land market and of the action of the state. We have demonstrated how methods of servicing low-income settlement vary with the nature of bureaucracy and political practice in each country. It is quite clear from this approach how the study of economy, politics and sociology merge with analysis of housing, land use and service provision. It can also be demonstrated that many elements in local housing conditions derive fundamentally not from local decisions but from those taken at an international level. Current work tends to emphasize the inter-linkages in the world system, both contemporaneously and historic-ally (Castells, 1979; Wallerstein, 1974). In this study we chose not to emphasize the international links nor to explore in detail the historical evolution of the societies involved. But there is no doubt that the roles of Bogotá, Mexico City and Valencia within their national economies and their past and present articulation with the world economy are critical. It is impossible to understand Mexico City without knowing of the Mexican Revolution and the impact of oil on the economy; Bogotá cannot be understood without some understanding of the background to the National Front and the role of Colombia within the world economy. Our already long study has taken much of this material as background; if we have not emphasized the historical and international context it is not because we do not realize their import-ance. Local housing problems can be understood only in the light of historical developments and in the context of international patterns of development.

We have studied three countries which occupy a broadly similar position within the world economy. Within this context we have found many interesting parallels. The processes that bring about residential segregation and the institutional structures developed to channel community demand making, for example, are not dissimilar in the three cities. This suggests that similar processes of development are at work and offers some hope that model-building about these processes is possible. Nevertheless, within each of these broad patterns of similarity there are fascinating variations which our comparative approach has forced us to consider. These variations are vital in two respects. They underline the point that dependency and structuralist analysis has recently discovered (cf. Roxborough, 1979; Palma, 1979; Cardoso, 1977), that deterministic models are of less help than models which explain variations within a broad conditioning pattern. The differences also challenge us as academics to explain their causes. Why, for example, are there such apparent differences in the land-allocation process in each city? We believe that our comparative approach has been rewarded by our having explained processes which previous writers have tended to ignore.

We believe that current social-science approaches are correct in emphasizing the critical importance of understanding the nature of the state. Public intervention in housing and servicing cannot be explained without a theoretical and empirical understanding of the role of the state in urban development; how, when, and with what motive does the state intervene? Our analysis of governmental responses to land, servicing and planning has been informed by three theories of the state. We have found none of these theories totally satisfactory as an explanation of how the local states in Bogotá, Mexico City and Valencia operate.

'Liberal' theories, and in particular the 'managerialist' strand of thought which argues that the major decisions lie in the hands of 'managers' who, given a large measure of autonomy from partisan political and popular pressures, allocate resources according to rules established by the bureaucracy, are lacking in several respects. Our data suggest that while 'managers' may indeed play an important role, they determine which individuals receive benefits rather than the still more critical issue of how many people will benefit. Thus, 'managers' determine how to allocate water standpipes rather than determining the number of pipes to be laid. While it is interesting and necessary to examine the goals and values of officials and the procedures they follow (cf. Shaffer and Lamb, 1981; Batley, 1978), the critical issue is how the constraints under which the agency operates are established. It is these constraints which largely determine the rules of operation of the bureaucracy; agencies with large budgets often act very differently from those with restricted funds.

Marxian 'instrumentalist' theories propose that the state intervenes directly or indirectly as the agent of the dominant capitalist class. The state acts in this way because there are close links between state functionaries and dominant private sector groups. Certainly, our city studies sometimes revealed a degree of overlap and occasions when intervention directly favoured the specific interests of those who governed. This was especially the case in Valencia (Gilbert, 1984). However, instrumentalism could not easily explain changes in policy nor the contrasts in policy in adjacent municipalities which we observed. The state also undertook too many programmes antagonistic to the interests of dominant groups for instrumentalism to be totally convincing.

'Structuralist' approaches argue that the state intervenes at an economic level to organize the labour process, at an ideological level to obscure class conflict, and at a political level to disorganize the dominated classes. Here the capitalist class and the state are separable, the latter enjoying 'relative autonomy' from the capitalist class and acting independently. Structuralist explanations are more consistent with our evidence. The weakness of structuralist theory, however, is that evidence of compatibility is insufficient proof of its validity as a theory. Structuralism is capable of explaining both the grinding down of the working class by authoritarian governments and the improvement of conditions for the poor. Since nothing is precluded, nothing is explained.

Our data suggest that individuals and institutions often enjoy a considerable degree of autonomy and their actions may have a very significant impact that cannot adequately be explained by either structuralist or instrumentalist theories. We conclude that no single theory is entirely satisfactory and that explanations about the role of the state must embrace different strands of analysis. Nevertheless, it is clear from our case studies that state intervention on behalf of the poor is only likely: (1) when the poor have raised a serious threat to social stability; (2) when the state has acted to foster capital accumulation (such as increasing the supply of electricity or water for industry), and the poor benefit indirectly from this action; (3) when assistance to the poor furthers the state's interest, an example being land-regularization schemes which also have the effect of integrating many *barrio* residents into the tax base thereby increasing revenue.

A general finding of our work is that processes of land allocation vary considerably. The specific process that is adopted in each city is determined by a combination of factors including the general price level of land, the pattern of landownership and the nature of the state involved. Whether land is invaded, community land is alienated, or land is subdivided illegally depends upon the local conjunction of these factors. What is invariable is that the poor tend to occupy the worst land in the city; theirs is usually the last claim on the available land.

It is important to emphasize that for many of the poor the process of obtaining land is similar in all three cities. Most of the poor actually purchase land from existing owners, whether those owners themselves bought the land, whether they invaded, or whether they alienated land in *ejidal* zones. Thus, the different processes of land distribution do not directly affect all poor people, they are relevant only to original owners. And, as we have seen in Valencia, a majority of settlement inhabitants often arrive after the formation and establishment of the settlement. This suggests that a process whereby land becomes a commodity with exchange value, in addition to use value, is soon underway (Conway, 1982; Burgess, 1978). Irregular housing areas are quickly incorporated into the land market.

Nevertheless, even if the land in each city soon becomes a potential commodity, the fact that there are different land-allocation processes is still significant. It is important to the welfare of the poor in the sense that it affects the cost of land to the poor. Access to land in Bogotá costs much more than in Valencia. The different methods also determine who among the poor will obtain land. In Bogotá, it is those who can afford to purchase a lot; in Valencia, it is those who are acquainted with or who hear about an invasion attempt. Political affiliation can be important in Valencia, but it is almost always money that counts in Bogotá.

In turn, the availability of land has a direct effect on housing tenure. We believe that the higher cost of land in Bogotá and Mexico City is an important explanation of the proportions of households that own, rent or share accommodation. It affects the age at which the poor obtain their first property and indeed affects the size of the lot and of the house. In this respect our findings are somewhat pessimistic. We detected a tendency for the cost of land access to increase. This trend is consistent with numerous reports from other Third World countries which argue that prices of land have risen because urban land markets are being commercialized by powerful economic and financial groups (Evers, 1977; Geisse, 1982; Negrón, 1982; Baross, 1983; Angel *et al.*, 1983). Growing government efforts to legalize land have added to this trend; previously illegal land is now attractive to higher-income groups (Brett, 1974). While our evidence does not wholly support this conclusion it does seem likely that real land prices will rise in the future and that self-help may become more difficult. Certainly in Bogotá and Mexico City, rising prices have led to smaller lot sizes for the poor. In the future it may well lead to smaller proportions of the poor owning property. The clear implication is that if lot sizes continue to fall, and household densities and the age of first ownership tend to rise, housing quality is in certain respects bound to decline.

In the three cities, most poor people aspire to ownership of a self-help home rather than living in rental or shared accommodation. Unfortunately, there are many barriers against owner occupation. But, the situation is by no means the same in the three cities and critical differences exist in the patterns of housing tenure. In general, home 'ownership' is much more common in Valencia than in Bogotá or Mexico City, renting is very common in Bogotá, and sharing lots with kin is frequently found in Mexico City. These differences are clearly linked to the nature of the land and housing markets in each city. The relatively low cost of land in Valencia, owing to invasion, allows even recent migrants without resources to own a lot. In addition, the legal prohibition on renting a shack acts to favour ownership or sharing a home. By contrast, the difficulties facing land invasion in Bogotá mean that all poor people are required to purchase land, which decreases the opportunities for home ownership. At the same time, there is no limit on renting, and rental accommodation is available throughout the city. Indeed, one of the advantages of home ownership to a poor Colombian is that he can eventually supplement his income by renting rooms to other families. The well-organized rental market and relatively high densities in the low-income settlements make sharing uncommon. Most recently arrived migrants and recently married couples rent a room rather than live with kin. In Mexico City, for those who do not invade, home ownership is expensive but lots in many parts of the city tend to be larger. Hence it is common for owners to allow kin and married children to establish themselves rent-free in part of the lot, though they usually share running costs. Rental accommodation is invariably developed as a speculative enterprise by absentee landlords, and is a process that is increasing throughout established low-income settlement.

If there is an undesirable (if expected) connection between the process of economic growth and rising land prices, there may also be a more positive association. Servicing levels do seem to be improving through time, at least with respect to water, drainage and electricity. Economic growth is dependent upon the successful expansion of those services. But the expansion of those services may well create excess capacity which may be made available to the poor. It is unlikely that the technical enterprises that provide this excess supply will provide the services free, but its very availability at a price represents a critical improvement for many poor people (World Bank, 1980b). The difference here between Bogotá and Valencia is pertinent.

It is clear that a major outcome of industrial growth and urban expansion is the need for greater organization of the urban fabric (Richardson, 1973). If such organization often goes by default (for example, controls on the traffic congestion), better administration is apparent in the two larger cities. This trend towards more sophisticated management of the urban fabric has numerous dimensions but it is clear in Bogotá and Mexico City that this trend is affecting methods of planning and indeed the general relationship between the state and the poor. The planning authorities in Bogotá and Mexico have sought to integrate poor housing areas into the urban area by introducing more realistic planning standards and by servicing as many low-income settlements as possible. They have also established formal frameworks for demand making and community participation. It is difficult to say whether this improved organization is necessarily to the benefit of the urban poor, a point we explore in more detail below.

What appears to be lacking is greater participation in decision making by the poor. If it is too crude to say that community mobilization is only encouraged by the state for reasons of social control, it is fair to suggest that the poor have little influence over the major matters that determine their housing and service conditions. They are permitted little say and few resources. Integral plans have been introduced in Venezuela, but in Mexico and Colombia both resources and participation are limited. Patron-client links still dominate, a form of relationship that is not conducive to increasing community participation. Low levels of participation are typical of the neighbourhood associations in the survey settlements. Such links are also reflected in the way the poor participated, making requests of the authorities either through political patrons or direct to the servicing agencies.

A further factor in the lack of community participation is the mixture of tenure types found in the settlements. The interests of owners, renters, and sharers often differ (Saunders, 1979; Edwards, 1982b). Non-owners are less likely to work hard for the legalization of tenure or the installation of services. Although most residents living in poorly serviced communities would wish for better conditions, improvement is not in everyone's interest. Improved services are likely to involve higher payments. The poorest section of the community, who may be owners or non-owners, may find difficulty in paying the new charges. Regularization and servicing may force some owners to sell or subdivide their lots. Low-income tenants may be forced out by higher rents or increased housing densities. In such circumstances, it is not surprising that many communities do not turn out *en masse* to fight for services. There is certainly reason to doubt whether class solidarity can develop around neighbourhood servicing issues. But the poor also participate relatively little in community projects presumably because of the lack of internal organization, lack of faith in leadership, and fractionalism in the communities. It must also be said that few groups would mobilize given similar living conditions. Most people are poor and are forced to work long hours; they simply have little time for community matters.

Issues that would repay further research

The price of land and trends in access costs

It is clear from our analysis how important the cost and availability of land is to the housing of the poor and to the wider process of urban development. Unfortunately, there seem to be few good studies of land prices and land policy in Third World cities. Bogotá now has a good data base for analysing land-price trends in the city (Villamizar, 1980; Mohan and Villamizar, 1980), but nothing is available for Mexico City or Valencia. Theoretically, too, our understanding of the land market seems to be weak. The literature is full of assertions about trends in land prices but there is often little notion of the complexities involved. Texts in urban economics on the other hand are long on theory but seem to get little beyond the subject of land-price gradients. While appropriate theories may be difficult to devise, the lack of good empirical studies of land prices is more difficult to understand. Of course, there are conceptual difficulties and the data base is often deficient; nevertheless it is an essential field for better understanding and better planning.

Land costs and housing tenure

We have begun to discover certain links between methods of land allocation, the price of land and the structure of housing tenure. We have argued that the size of the rental housing market lies in the alternatives available to the poor to obtain land. Where land is easily available, either through invasion, or because it is cheap, then more families are likely to construct self-help housing. Where land is difficult or expensive to obtain, then alternatives such as renting or sharing with kin are likely to be taken up and the proportion of home-owners will decline. But are these patterns general to Latin American cities, to African and Asian cities, to all capitalist cities, even to socialist cities? Is there, for example, a general trend in capitalist cities between cost of land access and levels of home ownership? *Prima facie*, such a correlation would seem true of the high rental levels in Indian and other Asian cities (Drakakis-Smith, 1981; Bhooshan and Misra, 1979). It would be very useful indeed to extend this kind of study to other cultural environments so as to test these ideas. Indeed, below, we make a general case in support of more comparative studies.

Renting and sharing

Although most poor people in Third World cities rent their homes, there is little in the literature on the nature of the rental population. Most housing studies have concentrated on owner-occupation in shantytowns: the most visible dimension of Third World housing.

Consequently, there are numerous unanswered questions about these rental populations and the subject would clearly repay greater attention (Gilbert, 1983; Edwards, 1982b). Are rental populations generally poorer than those who own or is there some alternative explanation of housing choice? Is rental accommodation occupied by the upwardly-mobile family or by those too poor to choose the form of their accommodation? How is the rental market organized? Is it a large-scale business or in the hands of owner-occupiers letting rooms in their own houses? Do renters move frequently, do they change tenure frequently or continue in one form of tenure, and what determines their mobility pattern? These questions are important because we simply know too little about the link between welfare levels and tenure. Irregular housing has correctly elicited a great deal of work; by contrast the rental market has been sadly neglected.

Methods of land allocation and tenure

We have begun to produce a typology of methods of land alienation and occupation. If we are correct in believing that forms of land allocation have an effect on individual access to land, it is important to examine which mechanisms are most appropriate to the needs of the poor. Squatting is often criticized in the literature for its inefficiency and for the anarchy that is associated with it, but for those who obtain land it is a blessing; in some cities it constitutes a highly redistributive policy. If there are additional costs for the servicing agencies and for transport systems these should be identified; ways should be found of providing cheap land in convenient places for the poor.

It is also important to examine whether legalizing land tenure is actually beneficial for the poor (Ward, 1982b; Burgess, 1978). We have suggested that there are circumstances when the poor actually suffer because of higher taxes, land prices, rising rents. But there is still too little empirical work which examines the effects of government initiatives in regularizing land tenure.

In addition, it would be useful to examine whether certain traditional forms of land might be encouraged in modern cities. In many Third World cities patterns of tenure such as community land, customary land, occupancy rights, common land and cooperative land are proven and widely understood by the poor. Rather than regularizing land according to individual ownership, a more sensitive and subtle approach might be to reactivate traditional forms of tenure. If land regularization sometimes constrains rather than assists self-help housing opportunities, we need to think more creatively about alternative forms of tenure (Angel *et al.*, 1983; Ward, 1982b).

Community action and participation

Few governments in the Third World doubt that some form of community action is desirable. Community self-help offers governments help in providing infrastructure and services; according to the government concerned, this contribution either complements or replaces state action. On the other hand, few governments are so keen on community involvement in public decision making; that process tends to increase demands upon the bureaucracy and already stretched budgets. The outcome of this dilemma is that governments tend to encourage a limited form of community action, one managed and controlled by the state for its own purposes. Selective patronage, often through patron–client networks, or favoured political parties, is often an effective form of social control. A frequent consequence of such community programmes is that the communities cease to participate actively in settlement projects. Most of the communities examined in this study fall into that category. Nevertheless, in some cities some communities do participate actively to help resolve their own problems. Such settlements even exist in cities such as Bogotá, Mexico City and Valencia where this is not the general pattern. In Bogotá, settlements linked to the *Provivienda* organization seem to be very active. Why do some communities engage in this sort of action and others not?

More comparative research

Detailed comparative studies of urban environments using the same methodology are not common in the literature. Our experience suggests that this approach offers considerable scope for increasing our understanding of urban phenomena. By its very nature, comparative work forces the observer to pose questions which might otherwise have been neglected. The fact that cities are different constantly raises the question why they are different. Having that question constantly posed is stimulating and in turn forces attention on why the similarities exist. Having previously carried out studies of a single city, we are convinced of the virtues of comparative urban research. It is important to underline that our recommendation is for *detailed* comparative work. The superficial glance at numerous cities is sometimes useful but there are far too many examples of this *genre* that have been highly misleading. A serious comparative approach requires detailed analysis of each city which in turn demands familiarity with the local environments. It also requires a combination of expertise; research teams should comprise both systematic specialists and researchers knowledgeable about the local environment.

Practical implications and responses

It cannot be assumed that more sophisticated and rigorous planning necessarily helps the poor. In the urban environments of most Latin American countries there are too many already powerful vested interests likely to benefit most from a better-organized urban fabric. Indeed, there is increasingly vocal support for the idea that the poor survive best in the interstices of the formal economy; they survive in those areas which are not subject to formal control by large-scale organizations whether of the private or the public sector. For example, there is increasing doubt about the benefits that legalization of land tenure may bring to the urban poor. The gradual tendency of the authorities in Bogotá and Mexico City to legalize illegal settlement, while fully in accordance with international planning wisdom, may pose major problems for the poor. It may involve the payment of taxes that were previously not levied. It may open up the land market to higher-income groups unprepared to occupy illegal or partially legal land. While resale of the land benefits certain poor individuals, it does not benefit most of the poor in an environment of rising land prices. This pattern appeared to be true in Bogotá, where minimum standard lots were being sold at a high price which put them beyond the pocket of the poor. Legality was being enhanced but at the cost of restricting the supply of lots in the pirate urbanization, the one source of land that the poor could afford. To examine the social effects of improved planning it is vital that the nature of the urban economy and the wider social and political system is understood. In theory, more rational planning ought to help all social groups; it should keep servicing costs down, allow poor people to buy land legally on which to build and improve their housing, allow a reasonable land-use pattern to develop. *But*, if land prices are constantly rising relative to incomes, if residential segregation is worsened by the planning process or by rising land prices, if services are well organized but are sold at too high a price, planning may not help the poor. The wish to regularize land titles may emanate from the authorities. It may be linked to new taxes, it may permit greater regulation of urban development, it may encourage an attitude of support for the government in power. Rather than enjoying full legality the poor may be content with the knowledge that they will not be turned off their land. Indeed, there are certain circumstances under which the poor may well be best left alone, protected by the very illegality which better planning seeks to remove. Some of the poor of Valencia undoubtedly benefit from the illegality of their tenure and the lack of rationality in the response of the authorities.

Clearly, the context is vital. In some circumstances improved planning processes will help the poor, but in others it will not. A widespread sites-and-services programme will help in most cities providing that land-price increases can be moderated. Easier servicing standards as in Bogotá may help but only if their introduction is not associated with higher taxes. Certain regulations and controls are clearly necessary, and generally we would support the trend towards the introduction of minimum standards and sites-and-services policies. But this is no panacea without greater control over the more inequitable forms of urban development. Monopoly control of land, acute residential segregation, and the lack of positive help for low-income groups need to be remedied at the same time.

Housing

Our investigation has found nothing to persuade us that the state is able to build sufficient cheap houses for the poor. The numbers of houses built by the state in Colombia, Mexico and Venezuela have been too few and too expensive for the poor. The capital invested would have been better spent on subsidizing service provision, or in establishing schemes to provide cheap building materials, credit, or architectural advice. It is clear, therefore, that the most effective housing policy is for the state to concentrate on the provision of urban infrastructure and for the poor to build their own housing. The role of the state must be to ease the task of the poor in building their own accommodation, not to do it for them. We are convinced that the current conventional wisdom, whatever the dangers about it expressed elsewhere in this conclusion, is essentially correct (World Bank, 1980a;

Habitat, 1982). Harrassing low-income settlements and attempting to rehouse them in other areas has proved to be counterproductive in too many areas.

Servicing

Many urban services can be organized on a relatively small scale. There are others, however, which can be provided efficiently and effectively only in quantity. These include water, drainage, electricity, roads, and telephones. Where such services are not organized on a large scale, provision is usually deficient and it is the poor who go without. We have seen how service provision in Valencia is less efficiently provided and that it is the groups in the low-income settlements who suffer most. Because efficiency may allow service agencies to supply the poor, we generally support the trend towards more technical and efficient public utilities. The development of water and electricity companies such as those of Bogotá and Mexico City would seem essential for every income group. We have no doubt that the efficiency of these agencies is due to the demands placed upon them by powerful economic interests, but the development of these services has been in every group's interest.

Nevertheless, certain factors need to be borne in mind. The costs of water and electricity provision should not be greater than the poor's capacity to pay; a measure of cross-subsidization seems to be acceptable in the way that has been practised in Bogotá. Service charges should rise with consumption, so as to discourage use, and therefore the rich, together with certain commercial and industrial users, should pay more than poorer consumers. But subsidies should be considered carefully because there is a danger that the poorest will not be supplied if the subsidy is too high (Linn, 1980). Poorly conceived subsidies may also benefit other non-poor groups such as landlords, who may charge tenants high prices for water while paying a low tariff themselves. In general, however, the pattern of charges should be progressive.

If we have reservations about the emergence of technical service agencies it is because they are so often run along purely commercial lines which bring few benefits to the poor. The practices of the São Paulo Metro, for example, is a model of efficiency to the neglect of the poor (Batley, 1982). Clearly, a balance is required between efficiency, to improve capacity, and equity, in the pricing and distribution policies employed. If the real cost of water is too high, then this vital service must be provided at a loss and the utility granted a subsidy. There are societies for which this might not be feasible but it is possible in the relatively rich cities of Latin America. Of course, the state may not be prepared to introduce such policies but, where it is, the conviction must be that technical agencies should be created. These should be broadly self-financing, and should provide a service at a price the poor can afford. The evolution of technical agencies following rational policies without recourse to partisan-political favours need not preclude greater community participation or political democracy. Partisan politics does not seem a good basis for running most public utilities especially those responsible for very large budgets.

Land

We have not examined the range of alternative policies to control the price of land. Nevertheless, the critical importance of the land market requires an improved response. Direct intervention by the state in the Third World (e.g. land banks in India) has not been terribly successful in controlling prices (Bose, 1973). Contrary to conventional wisdom, public land is often not used for low-income settlements; in Mexico City public land has often been used for speculative purposes, and in Bogotá a charity has held land for over forty years so as to benefit from rising land values. Elsewhere in the world, the public authorities may act as aggressive slum landlords, renting land for slum development and evicting residents to permit urban redevelopment (Boonyabancha, 1983). We should not expect too much from the public control of land (Angel *et al.*, 1983). The demands upon public agencies to balance their books may force them to use their land commercially; private-interest groups may persuade them to use the land for commercial rather than for social purposes.

What seems essential is to find some way of reducing the profitability of land speculation. Taxation of unbuilt land may be one answer to speed up the use of land. Taxation of excessive profits would seem another. Certainly, high land-and-building taxes on residential uses would seem to be desirable. We have not examined the full range of possibilities, but something needs to be done. Rising land prices benefit few people. At present governments neither know how to control prices nor understand fully the need to act. This has been one cause of the failure of urban reforms in Colombia and Venezuela.

The paradox of planning

Ultimately, the positive and negative features of planning depend upon the nature of the state and the political views of the observer. On the basis of this study we see limited evidence that the Colombian, Mexican or Venezuelan states, despite current rhetoric, are very concerned about the poor. Where the state bureaucracy comes into contact with the poor, its actions are too often legalistic, corrupt, arbitrary and unfair. In these circumstances, we must have severe reservations about increasing the scope of state action. As a result, we would like to see the regulative side of the state reduced to a minimum and communities having greater responsibility over purely local matters (Turner, 1976). Disputes between neighbours, the treatment of undesirable neighbourhood activities, and greater participation in health and education programmes all seem appropriate matters for community associations. The state should devolve low-level functions of this kind to the communities. At the same time, support for the process of self-help housing needs to be increased. Improved servicing, cheaper supplies of building materials, architectural and credit services are among the responsibilities of the state. There is no shortage of appropriate actions to be taken by the progressive state. Unfortunately, the progressive state is not often found in Latin America. Attempts to improve planning and to provide assistance to Third World governments should consider this point carefully. If the state is corrupt and preferential, it is often best to reduce its power rather than increase it. If unmitigated capitalism has a mainly unacceptable face, a corrupt state acting on behalf of the rich is still worse. In such circumstances, little is to be gained by even trying to improve the system.

Appendix 1: The methodology in detail

As we noted in chapter 1, there are few truly comparative studies of Third World urban development and we regard this as an important feature of our work. However, as we quickly discovered, comparative analysis of several cities undertaken by a group of researchers is not easy, and generates a whole host of methodological problems that the lone researcher working in a single context does not have to face. Therefore, we feel justified in including here a detailed account of our methodology in the hope that the staff of future projects might learn from our experience and from our mistakes.

Levels of field-work analysis

The team was formed in April 1978 and worked together until September 1980, when funding of the project formally ended. The first four months were spent in London making revisions to our methodology, refining our research questions and propositions, and in agreeing an outline questionnaire. In August, Ward and Raymond went to Mexico City where they stayed for one year, while Gilbert and Murray left for Bogotá where they spent seven months before moving to Valencia for their final five months. Midway during the period of field work a two-week meeting was arranged in Mexico City to allow the teams to discuss progress and to make whatever revisions and adjustments were necessary and practical at that stage of the programme. As we argue below, the split-team arrangement had numerous drawbacks, even though we had attempted to structure very carefully a common research strategy. The latter comprised several levels of analysis of which broad 'contextual' analysis occupied the initial phase of data collection in each city. Inevitably, however, eventually the different elements of the investigation overlapped. The phases described below, therefore, do not represent a chronology of the field work.

Evolution of housing and land-use patterns in each city

A picture of each city's recent evolution was required to place housing development in context. In particular, we were concerned to know the extent to which commercial decisions had been primarily responsible for land-use evolution and to understand how planners had sought to influence this process. What plans had been produced for each city and what impact had they had upon its evolution? Who were the key decision makers and what were the principal decisions determining the shape and structure of each city? Information was obtained from a wide variety of sources. As a first step past studies, planning legislation, official documents, and interviews with local analysts of each city's development proved fruitful. A review of past newspapers, while time consuming and sometimes providing material of dubious accuracy, allowed us to identify crises in urban management and conflicts between the urban poor and the authorities.[1]

Second, housing policies in each city were examined in an attempt to outline the change of attitudes to housing development over the previous twenty years at both the national and the local level. Information was sought from national housing agencies, local planning departments, politicians, commercial developers, etc. on the following issues: the importance of public housing projects; changes in policy towards irregular low-income housing; attitudes to invasions and the legalization of land holdings; incorporation of the poor into the city tax base; the nature of zoning laws and building regulations.

Third, data were gathered on the emergence of irregular settlement since 1950. The aim was to gain a dynamic picture of how each city had developed: the types of settlement process in evidence; original forms of tenure of lands affected; changing patterns and levels of servicing and a chronology of city-wide servicing provision; the form that legalization had taken; the total population accommodated and the current and past socio-economic status of settlements. Census data proved invaluable here, and were complemented by planning lists on *barrio* locations and dates of origin. Air photographs, where available, were consulted for different dates. Also a growing body of case studies, many the basis of undergraduate and postgraduate theses, provided detailed insight into specific settlements.

Fourth, the key agencies in past and present administrations were identified. Here the aim was to document the changing nature of that section of the bureaucracy with responsibilities in servicing, housing and health. We reconstructed the functions and responsibilities of agencies at different times and levels of political jurisdiction. Data about the status of each institution, its responsibilities, relationship to other entities, and crude budgets, principal activities and programmes were usually available in the form of annual reports and institutional prospectuses. Inevitably, coverage was partial and further information was gathered during interviews with agency personnel.

Interviews with major decision makers

We attempted to talk with past and present directors of agencies concerned with the supply and planning of public services. Since there were too many services and agencies to cover comprehensively, we chose the following as representing the main types of servicing functions: water and drainage, electricity, health, planning, community participation and land regularization. In addition, mayors, councillors and other local and political representatives were approached. Inevitably, the large number of institutions involved and the fact that many no longer existed meant that coverage was incomplete. Despite this, a total of 38, 43, and 22 interviews with high-ranking personnel were conducted in Bogotá, Mexico and Valencia respectively. The aim of the interviews was to identify the way in which decisions affecting low-income settlements and their populations were reached. What were the key criteria in the creation of an agency programme and in determining the order in which settlements benefited? How did directors account for the apparent anomalies that arose in our survey of *barrios*? To what extent had the agency received adequate financial and political support to sustain its activities? What were its principal successes and failings? Why did policy changes occur? Clearly, the answers to many of these questions were not easily come by. Our 'elite' interviews varied in length, locale, degree of respondent openness and overall success. Most fruitful were those interviews obtained by referral from a close colleague of equal status. On the few occasions when, despite all our efforts to secure an hour-long conversation, it became obvious that we would be received only for a brief 'courtesy' visit, we confined questions to a single issue and requested that we be referred to lower-level personnel who could provide additional information.

An unstructured interview format was used whereby the respondent was encouraged to talk freely on selected topics. Empty rhetoric was questioned by the interviewer who would introduce hard facts about agency performance or about particular events that had occurred in settlements known to us and to the interviewee. Interviews were not recorded, although one pirate urbanizer in Bogotá insisted on taping our conversation in the presence of his lawyer! It was felt that recorded interviews would inhibit the sort of 'off the record' conversation that we desired. Instead, brief notes of names, data cited and key words to facilitate recall were taken and a full transcript of the interview was written up the same day. The time and care spent in setting up these meetings proved extremely rewarding. While much of the information cannot be presented in this book, it was critical to our understanding of the overt and covert nature of agency functions, the relationship of each to the wider political system, the key factors influencing decisions, and the vitality of each institution. In short, only by combining the information gathered at interview with internal and published documents were we able to test many of our original hypotheses.

Invaluable too were the interviews we had with lower-level officials. Here we probed more deeply into the way in which specific decisions were carried out. Once policy was formulated, how was it implemented in both low-income and middle-income districts? How did officials view local leaders and how had they responded to them on a day-to-day basis? How did they interpret specific settlement crises to which we alluded?

Interviews with barrio representatives

Different kinds of leadership develop at different stages of a settlement's formation. This fact, together with the contrasts of tenure in the three cities, meant that several types of leader were encountered. Our concern was to describe the attributes of leaders, their motives, early experience, and skills, and to evaluate their contribution to *barrio* improvements. Those involved in *barrio* formation were asked about the initial phases of organization: which officials were approached, and how did they go about securing acceptance and credibility both for the *barrio* and themselves as leaders? What form did *barrio* organization take? Those involved in particular struggles for services or crises were asked about the tactics employed and about the whole process of *barrio* negotiation with supra-local authorities. Many leaders had been involved in *barrio* affairs over a long period of time and we were interested in their views about how the process of *barrio*–government relations had changed. Who were the key personnel in the bureaucracy and under what circumstances were they approached? Faced with an impasse over *barrio* servicing, what had they done to resolve it? A further feature of leadership, particularly in the larger settlements of Mexico, was the existence of different factions, often with alternative patrons and routes into the bureaucracy. In these cases, we explored the impact of intra-settlement struggles upon successful settlement development and its significance for *barrio*–government relations.

Most leaders were willing to meet us and to be interviewed. Indeed, their support and approval was carefully sought before we embarked upon detailed field work in the settlements. The need to convince leaders that we were not government spies, that our findings would not prejudice the interests of residents and that our work had some value was vital. Once good relations were established we sometimes became closely involved in *barrio* affairs and, so far as we were able, sought to offer any assistance that leaders requested of us. Discussions were unstructured and, rather like our interviews with agency heads, we attempted to encourage a free and open format. Similarly, only brief and occasional notes were taken and the interview was written up immediately afterwards. Some Mexican leaders who in the past had been involved in sharp or fraudulent practice were reluctant to talk to us so that coverage was incomplete. Most leaders, however, once they got to know us, were open, friendly, and extraordinarily helpful. Insights that we gained from them about the settlement–bureaucracy relationship proved a critically important ingredient in the analysis.

The household interview survey

The aim of the household survey was to obtain information about the origins, socio-economic characteristics, political attitudes and housing responses of low-income populations in each city. More specifically, the questionnaire sought information on the following issues: (1) The main factors influencing the household's choice of the settlement: work, friends, kin, location, price of land, etc. (2) The changing housing locations and situations of the interviewees: where did they live previously, were they renters or owners, what were the principal barriers to their improving their housing conditions? (3) The degree of involvement in the community and political activity of the settlement:

what role did families play in the formation of the settlement, what were their relations with and perceptions of the community leaders, how involved were they in the community organizations? (4) The principal problems facing the settlement and how they might be overcome: who was responsible for overcoming the problems? (5) The extent to which there were consistent linkages between forms of employment, levels of education, size of family and migration background and the housing and residential history.

The choice of settlement

We intended to carry out structured questionnaire surveys in selected settlements representative of the low-income housing universe in each city. Given the size of the settlements, we knew that we would be carrying out a minimum of 70 interviews in each settlement, and in combination with the time and personnel constraints this determined the number of settlements which we included in each city. More settlements were to be studied in the larger cities because of the greater complexity of the urban structure and its development; it was eventually determined to carry out interviews in six settlements in Mexico, four in Bogotá and two in Valencia.[2]

Like most cities in the world, Latin American cities contain clearly demarcated residential areas. In Spanish American cities these are known as *urbanizaciones*, *barrios*, *colonias*, according to class, country and city. Normally, the different parts of a settlement have a common history: the settlement was founded by a single urban developer, or through a particular invasion, or constituted a single government housing project. Typically, though not inevitably, community services are organized on a settlement basis. In many cities, *barrios* have their own committee for community action. Of course, there are settlements which lack a clear identity, where certain groups feel they are really part of some sub-community. This is often true in those settlements which developed incrementally without clear-cut origins and in those which are very large. But, on the whole the people in each settlement associate with that settlement. They perceive that they are part of that community, whether they are pleased with that situation or not. The problem facing the research was not that it was difficult to identify particular low-income areas within the urban sprawl but rather which settlements to choose? In Bogotá there are some 900 *barrios*, in Valencia some 177 *urbanizaciones* and *barrios* and in

Mexico some 1,300 *colonias*. Clearly, we did not intend to select higher-income housing areas or government housing projects but this still left a vast array of low-income housing from which to select our specific study areas.

To some extent our research focus dictated the criteria by which we eventually chose the settlements. Since we were concentrating on the period since 1965, we could not choose settlements that were too old if we were to use the information in testing how such *barrios* were formed and serviced. Nor did we want settlements that were very young which had few services and which, therefore, had a limited history of negotiations with the servicing authorities, politicians and planners. Our final compromise was to choose settlements which were founded between 5 years and 15 years before the start of our field work. In the two larger cities, however, we would include one young *barrio* which would demonstrate differences in the settlement process in the more recent period. This young settlement should have been founded in the previous years and would be relatively unconsolidated. Initially, we measured the age of the settlement by talking to the population and from contextual information. In some settlements there was considerable doubt about the real date of foundation, especially where the settlement had evolved gradually. Of course, once we had conducted the household survey we had a much more accurate idea of the date of original settlement, and we have chosen to use the latter data as the basis of our estimates in the tables. We have used the mean date when households moved in, whether they purchased directly from an illegal subdivider or bought from *ejidatarios*. The aim was to make the average age of *barrio* foundation similar in each city and we were to aim at producing an average age of between 7.0 and 8.5 years.[3]

In order to maintain comparability between the settlements it was important to ensure that the different settlements were of broadly comparable income and servicing level. We did not want to include either totally serviced or wholly unserviced settlements nor to choose qualitatively different settlement types in the three cities. We therefore drew up a list of service variables on which we would rank each candidate for *barrio* selection. Our major problem here was that there were genuine differences between cities in terms of their servicing levels and of the consolidation of settlements which contained very similar social groups. In general, Mexican settlements, especially in the State of Mexico, were vast and consequently had a wider range of infrastructural, commercial and service characteristics.[4] For example, such settlements typically had a church and a market whereas the smaller settlements in Bogotá lacked such amenities, though they were normally located in a neighbouring community. Our final points system attempted to include a mixture of variables which were dependent both upon size and age. The maximum points total was 20 and we were to choose settlements which fell within the range 6 to 15, excepting the case of the young settlement which should have a total of less than 6. Appendix tables 1 and 2 show how the chosen settlements in the different cities ranked on our points system.

A further criterion in our choice was that within the above-mentioned constraints we wished to include as wide a range of tenure types as possible. In Mexico, the three main forms of settlement formation should be included, that is to say the invasion, the illegal subdivision and the sale of *ejidal* land; in Bogotá, the illegal subdivision and the invasion; in Valencia, invasions of both private land and on public land.

Another constraint was the size of settlement. We did not want settlements that were very small and resolved on a minimum settlement size of 500 families, subsequently reduced to 400. This minimum was a compromise between the dictates of sampling fractions and the size of settlements in each city. To obtain a representative sample of a small settlement requires almost as many interviews as does a sample of a large settlement; interviewing economies of scale accrue in larger settlements. In addition, the large settlements of Mexico contrasted markedly with the numerous small settlements in Bototá and some kind of compromise minimum figure had to be reached.

The final constraint was our desire to select settlements as far as possible from different parts of the city. We wished to avoid making generalizations about the urban poor that would be based upon residents from a particular sector of the city, particularly if that sector was somehow favourably or unfavourably located *vis-à-vis* industrial employment opportunities, upper-income residential districts, etc. By choosing a range of settlements from different parts of the city we hoped to ascertain if proximity to such districts affected public response to low-income settlement. As figure 2 (page 26) shows, we surveyed a wide spatial distribution of settlements in both Bogotá and Mexico City. In Valencia, practically all low-income *barrios* are located in the south so our choice was confined to that zone. Where the built-up area spread across a formal political boundary we also endeavoured to survey at least one settlement that fell outside the city

Appendix table 1 *Services and public utilities used to derive points systems for settlement selections*

Service	State of supply to settlement	Points
Electricity	Settlement lacks mains connection	0
	Mains connection but some houses have illegal hookups (75%)	1
	Virtually all have legal supply	2
Water	No access to mains	0
	Partial: (spiggots in the streets)	1
	<75% have private taps	2
	>75% have private taps	3
Drainage	No mains drainage	0
	Part of settlement lacks sewer	1
	>50% settlement has connection to sewer	2
	>75% settlement has connection to sewer	3
Roads	No paved roads to or from settlement	0
	Paved access roads	1
	Paved access roads and some paving of residential streets	2
	Extensive paving of residential streets (26–75%)	3
	Extensive paving: 75% of streets	4
Public telephone	No telephone	0
	Only public *or* private phones	1
	Both public and private phones	2
Public transport	Buses/taxis do not enter nor run along outer limit	0
	Buses/taxis/trains enter or run along outer limit	1
Church	No church building	0
	Catholic church or non-Catholic church	1
	Catholic church with resident priest	2
Market	No market	0
	Periodic market (<5 days per week)	1
	Daily market (>5 days per week)	2
Police patrols	No foot or daily car patrols	0
	Daily foot or car patrols	1
	Total range	0–20
	Our range	6–15

Appendix table 2 *Service and public utility scores for selected 'barrios'*

	Maximum score	Mexico City						Bogotá					Valencia	
		Isidro Fabela	Santo Domingo	El Sol	Liberales	Chalma	Jardines	Juan Pablo I	Casablanca	Atenas	Britalia	S. Antonio	Nueva Valencia	La Castrera
Electricity	2	2	2	2	2	2	2	0	2	2	2	2	0	2
Water	3	3	2	3	1	2	3	0	3	3	1	3	3	3
Drainage	3	0	0	3	0	0	3	0	3	3	0	3	0	3
Roads	4	2	1	0	0	1	1	0	1	3	0	0	1	3
Telephones	2	2	1	0	0	1	0	0	2	2	1	1	0	1
Transport	1	1	1	1	1	1	1	0	0	1	1	1	1	1
Church	2	2	2	2	1	2	2	0	1	1	1	0	1	0
Market	2	2	1	2	0	1	2	0	0	0	0	0	0	0
Police	1	1	1	1	1	1	1	0	0	0	0	1	0	0
	20	15	11	14	6	11	15	0	12	15	6	11	6	13

or district limits. This allowed us to study the approaches of different authorities to low-income settlement.

Needless to say, selection was not without its problems and it was necessary to modify our initial criteria at times. We several times modified our service-points system. We were unable to study an invasion settlement in Bogotá because there are so few, because the older invasions had already been studied, and because the newer settlements were members of the communist-led *Central Provivienda*, which, while it was very helpful to our study, was less than keen that interviews be carried out in its settlements. Eventually, we chose our survey settlements, descriptions of which are given in appendix 2.

Survey design and interviewing

In Bogotá and Mexico City we carried out a household listing, either of the whole settlement, or in the larger settlements of at least 300 households in randomly distributed blocks. This meant that we had a minimum ratio of four households to every one that we interviewed. In Valencia we did not conduct a household listing because few homes had renters and because, as renting a *rancho* or a room in a *rancho* is illegal, few would answer accurately if asked about their tenure in a household listing. The nature of the listing varied in Bogotá and Mexico. In Bogotá, we listed the name and address of every family and the form of its residential tenure. In Mexico, where illegal land tenure made ownership a more sensitive issue and where renting might involve both tenant and owner in legal and fiscal wrangles, the collection of detailed information would have been indelicate at this stage. Our aim was to generate an accurate listing of all households so that we could identify specific households in multi-occupancy lots. This was achieved by asking the Christian names of heads of households, or by an indication of the location of the dwelling on the plot. In this way, we avoided the bias towards owners which would have resulted from random visits to individual plots. In Valencia we merely listed the number of occupied houses.

In the three cities we then drew representative samples by means of random number tables from our household or house counts. In Bogotá we could check that this sample matched the settlement-wide distribution of renters, sharers and owners. In Mexico this was impossible, but our method of household listing should have avoided any bias. In Valencia, since our final interviews showed little evidence of renting or sharing, the lack of a household count is unlikely to have led to any distortion.

Interviews were carried out when the occupants were at home and free to talk. No systematic call-back system was employed in Bogotá. If a family was absent for two call-backs it was thenceforth ignored. In a few settlements where many families were out, additional names were added at random from the household listing. In Mexico, our sampling method required numerous call-backs to be made. If, after three separate visits on different days an interview was still not possible, additional households were selected from a reserve list taking special care to include the same proportion of households occupying shared lots. In Valencia, visits were made to every eighth house on randomly selected blocks. If a family was out then the interviewer proceeded to the next house on the list.

The study team carried out many of the interviews themselves but also employed university students. The latter were given a comprehensive explanation about the questionnaire and strict instructions about interviewing only those families appearing on the household listing. They were paid on the basis of successfully completed questionnaires.

Interviewing took place mainly on Sundays when there was a good chance of finding the head of household at home. Each interviewer carried letters which contained the name and identity number of the interviewer and the address of the local project director. The letters explained the aims of the survey, the random choice of households, the fact that it had nothing to do with taxes or government information, and that answers would remain confidential. The letter was normally left with the family and was successful in allaying most fears. While there was a refusal rate of a few per cent, the interviewers were received generously, by British standards extraordinarily so.

The completed questionnaires were checked on the spot by the project staff. Unsatisfactory interviews were rejected or the interviewer asked to return to the house to repeat certain questions. When doubt remained about reliability of the questionnaire, it was rejected at the coding stage. The checking procedure was vital and could *never* be relaxed. While most of the students were conscientious they were often careless; at the very least this procedure made them more careful. There is no doubt, however, that we lost some information because of interviewer carelessness. Unfortunately, too, the system was not totally proof against more serious difficulties. One interviewer in Bogotá visited 25 households, recorded the name of the family, and made up most of the rest of the interview. His tactic was not discovered until one of the project staff himself checked one of the households where the questionnaire had been badly filled in.

Questionnaire design, testing and preparation of the coding guide

A draft of the questionnaire was prepared in Mexico and sent to Bogotá where it was amended. The questionnaire was then tested on a small number of households and, after discussions between the two teams, shortened and revised. A coding guide was produced which pointed to further deficiencies in the questionnaire and which required further modifications. The still imperfect questionnaire was then launched on an unsuspecting public.

The questionnaire was long but could normally be completed in 30 minutes. Some households with large families and grown-up, working children, who had migrated from the countryside and who had lived in numerous homes within the city, took much longer. Slight differences were apparent in the final questionnaires applied in the three cities because of local variations in terminology and land tenure. But, because of the long period of testing and checking the questionnaire, it was not necessary to change questions during the survey period.[5]

Coding was done by the project team and not, as had originally been intended, by the interviewers. This tedious exercise proved to be a vital check on consistency and the accuracy of the survey. Like many other experienced academics we now know what not to do and are in a position to advise others. The questionnaire data were recorded onto coding forms which were sent back to London for punching onto cards.

Computation and analysis of the results

The household-survey data were analysed using an SPSS Package (version 700) on the 7600 ICL Computer at the University of London Computer Centre. Missing data were excluded in most cases from the tables which explains why column totals vary from table to table and often differ from the total number of interviews carried out. The data file was fully documented thereby allowing the creation of properly labelled tables and statistics. Unfortunately, the SPSS package facilities in London do not allow direct on-line analysis of the data nor do they provide suitable mapping programmes. Consequently, survey data for a range of variables were transferred to the Department of Geography's PRIMOS 300 system with its user-interactive facility. Base maps of each city were digitized and a special programme written to allow us to plot locational data. Place of work, previous residence, location of medical treatment, and similar data were mapped, controlled by variables such as *barrio*, migrant status, year of arrival in the city, and household tenure.[6] The analysis of our field-work data and the writing of the report were completed in several stages. After coding we compiled a document which identified all of the potential flaws and problems related to our data. Incomplete information, ambiguous responses, incompatibility between cities, the significance of missing data were carefully documented in order to minimize the number of spurious conclusions. Next, we generated frequency distributions for each variable for each city and *barrio* and this was written up as a 'base document'. Gradually, as we began to test specific hypotheses, the computations became more complex, and necessitated controlling for other variables, amalgamating data, recomputing indices and so on.

Three other base documents were prepared for each city dealing with different themes: the land market, the urban bureaucracy and servicing, community organization and public participation. Preparation of these base documents occupied the best part of a year – rather longer than we had anticipated. An agreed structure was formulated and our research materials were assembled, catalogued and referenced in the summary analysis of the base document. The aim was to produce a manageable resumé of the vast amount of data and our findings for each city, so avoiding our constantly having to return to our specific data files and interview notes. Regular meetings attempted, with partial success, to ensure compatibility between documents for structure and depth. This essential stage occupied a great deal of time, and with hindsight we would have programmed more time to allow for this interim work. We would also have sought tighter control over the format, ordering and depth of analysis.

Writing up was undertaken jointly by the project leaders. The usual procedure was to prepare a chapter outline, when one or other would write a preliminary draft incorporating information for the city or cities with which he was most familiar. The draft was then handed over for supplementation and revision. Inevitably, the need to generalize across three countries required that we omit large amounts of fascinating detail. We hope that the information and argument contained in the preceding chapters constitute a satisfactory blend of detail and generalization.

Methodological problems in retrospect

Neither of the principal researchers had previously directed a major study of this kind. Both had engaged in personal study without assistance in the form of research associates. For this reason we learnt as we went along and, inevitably, made several mistakes. However, we feel that our experience was a very positive one and we are grateful for having been given this opportunity. We hope that others might similarly benefit in future and therefore conclude this chapter with a brief retrospect on our research methodology.

On the negative side the following problems arose. First, while one can only speculate about what would have happened had the whole team worked for about five months in each city, we believe that the split-team format was not the most efficient. Despite careful preparation, a common programme, clearly understood tasks, several problems arose. Delays in communication between the two teams, due to the post, led to frustration and unnecessary duplication in drawing up the final questionnaire. The inevitable need to adopt contingency plans to overcome local difficulties led to some divergence in data collection between the two teams. Similarly, our different levels of interest in the various facets of the study produced an imbalance in the depth of material collected on several topics. Likewise, the specifics of each city affected the sort of material collected so that directly comparable data were not always obtained. Flexibility to modify the agreed strategy became almost impossible as it required an exchange of several letters which took some months. We suspect, too, that mutual pressure derived from a group of four or five persons would have achieved a more intensive and efficient work rate than two pairs of two.

Second, as we have already indicated, our interviewers sometimes left much to be desired. While those who worked with us over several weeks performed very satisfactorily, many others fell quickly by the wayside and proved to be a hindrance. Much time was spent training and preparing them for work in the *barrios*, yet one young lady still turned up in high heels and with painted nails. Other interviewers were unreliable, failing to appear or arriving late. In a city the size of Mexico where travel to the *barrios* usually took an hour by car, ferrying a group of interviewers to and from the settlement to work between 10.00 a.m. and 3.00 p.m. became a major task.

Third, despite reducing the scale of the study on the advice of academic referees, it remained overambitious. The selection of smaller cities would have made our task simpler, even if the findings might not have had the same interest for many readers. We might also usefully have reduced the number of services to be studied, although this would have weakened our ability to make meaningful comparison of different levels of performance and behaviour of public utilities in the three cities.

On the positive side, there were certain very important benefits arising from our approach. First, we were correct in our belief that the authorities would receive us and talk openly and responsibly about their work. Although access to the very highest-level decision makers (e.g. mayors, cabinet ministers, agency heads) is more difficult in the larger cities, our perseverance was usually rewarded. We also experienced few difficulties in our discussions and interviews with people in the low-income communities. Leaders were, for the most part, friendly and cooperative; very few settlements refused to cooperate, usually those which had a difficult relationship with the authorities, and in only one settlement where we wished to work was this impossible. Similarly, most households were open, helpful and patient. Very few questions caused any concern (enquiries about voting in Valencia and presence of renters in owner households in Mexico were the main exceptions) and if we suffered problems it was due to our design of questions or to our wish to be more precise about dates and figures than most Latin American, or even British, households are wont to be. In general, we could not believe how well we were received.

Second, our strategy of comparing different cities in different countries was particularly profitable. It required that we focus upon common themes and not be channelled along set routes of enquiry by the specific characteristics of each city. It concentrated our search upon the identification of general processes of urbanization and state intervention. Obviously, the differences between cities themselves provoked our interest: why did such differences exist and what were their implications for the theories and hypotheses that we were trying to test? What was critical about the comparison was that it forced us to account for the differences and similarities between cities. By itself the comparative component demanded that we avoid mere description. It also cautioned us not to make generalizations on the basis of limited evidence, for it brought us into contact with a great variety of housing responses, forms of land tenure, leaders, community organizations and bureaucratic structures.

A third positive element of the study derived from working as a team. The multidisciplinary nature of the team – three geographers, a sociologist, a political scientist and an economist/lawyer – gave added depth to the investigation because it introduced different perspectives on any given problem. In addition, certain economies of scale accrue in that different individuals have different skills. Team work allows a mutually supportive division of labour; some people are better at questionnaire design, others at computer calculations, others at writing.

In sum, our methodology had faults but we believe that the basic strategy was correct. We also believe that it is replicable in other cities and would encourage the testing of some of our findings in other political and economic environments.

Appendix 2: Description of the survey settlements

The details of the settlements are summarized in table 1 on page 24 and the locations are depicted in figure 2 on page 26.

Bogotá – Atenas

Atenas is located on the mountain slopes along the road which leaves Bogotá for Villavicencio. Most of the settlement is on sloping terrain although there are several relatively flat sections. It is largely surrounded by low-income pirate urbanizations although there is still a limited amount of open land to the northwest. The settlement was developed in two parts beginning in the middle sixties, the first of which is now largely occupied and serviced, the second of which is less consolidated, lacks services and contains open ground.

The pirate urbanizer divided land which had been inherited by his father in the late twenties. He began to sell this land in the early sixties and provided certain services in an attempt to comply with the then ruling planning code: standpipes, road layout with paving stones and rough street surfacing. He later became a member of the Bogotá council and was identified with a campaign to service not only Atenas but several surrounding settlements. He used his contacts in the Liberal party to obtain services for these communities. He lost his position on the council in 1970 and indeed lost political influence generally. This has to some extent affected the recent servicing of the settlement. Nevertheless, Atenas is the best serviced of the five Bogotá communities partly because of its age and partly because of its early political links. Many of its roads are paved, there is a nearby health centre, the houses have water and drainage, there are public telephones, a large new church near completion and a regular bus service along the road to Villavicencio. The major problem is that certain parts of the settlement are located on unstable land; eight houses had

271

recently collapsed and numerous others were suffering from severe cracks. Parts of the drainage system are totally inadequate, and sewage escapes across the lower parts of the settlement after heavy rainstorms. The second sector lacks many of the services available to the rest of the community. As a result of these problems the community has many complaints and the settlement gives the impression of no longer continuing its consolidation.

The majority of lots are occupied and there are over 600 houses in the settlement accommodating approximately 1,050 families. There are almost as many families renting accommodation as there are owners; large numbers of owners are letting rooms.

Bogotá – Britalia

Britalia is located in the southwest of Bogotá between the suburb of Bosa and the new wholesale market. It is on low-lying land which is liable to flooding in winter. It is flanked to the west by open land belonging to a large estate and to the east by other pirate urbanizations. Sales began in 1973 but possession was not granted until 1974 when most lots were in fact sold. The pirate urbanizer bought, or at least promised to buy, the land from the two owners. By 1976 he had paid off the smaller debt but still owed the bulk of the purchase price. The urbanizer hoped that the settlement would be legalized under the 1972 minimum-standards decree, but this was not permitted because one-fifth of the planned area lay outside the urban perimeter and because the water company felt it would be difficult to drain the lower parts of the settlement. The request was formally refused in January 1975. In May of that year the community-action *junta* denounced the urbanizer to the authorities. The latter did not intervene, ostensibly because they lacked confidence in the state authority (ICT) to service the community, and signed an agreement with the urbanizer to legalize the community providing he brought the *barrio* up to minimum-standards servicing levels. He complied with part of the request, paid for the installation of electricity, paid off part of his debt to the original owners, and made considerable efforts to install some water and drainage services. But his efforts were insufficient and in June 1976 the authorities intervened strongly, urged on by the community. The settlement was then run by ICT but little further servicing took place. The community was exerting great pressure on the authorities to improve the services but without great success with respect to water. The community was successful, however, in mobilizing certain government agencies and more particularly private groups to help it. The second school was inaugurated in 1978, a bus route was initiated in 1978, the city's first UNICEF health centre was located there in 1979, and in the same year SENA established a corrugated room for classes in practical work.

The settlement had approximately 1,650 families in 1979 who occupied 1,450 lots out of the 2,846 total available. The mean purchase date of the original households was towards the end of 1974 and the mean moving-in date the beginning of 1976. The settlement was less consolidated than several of the other settlements in part because of its youth and in part because of the servicing difficulties. As a consequence, there was a much higher proportion of owners than of renters.

Bogotá – Casablanca

Casablanca is located in the northwest of the city on a hillside with a spectacular view over the more affluent northern area of Bogotá. It is surrounded not by low-income settlements but by higher-income estates, a military school and open land. It forms part of the low-income settlement which developed round the outlying village of Suba during the sixties and seventies.

Originally, the land belonged to the Pantaño family and at the time of the subdivision belonged to various siblings. Different members of the family subdivided their parts of the land beginning in the late sixties. Somewhat later the son of the original leader of the community bought land and subdivided it.[1] The settlement therefore developed more incrementally than Britalia and did not have such a well-developed street plan – partly a consequence of the steep slopes over which most of the settlement has occupied. Most of the occupants have legal tenure, but many have only *promesas de compraventa*. The settlement is reasonably well serviced, having light, water, some drainage, public telephones and a school. The major deficiencies are road paving and transport; no bus route serves the settlement and a walk of ten minutes is required to reach the main road. The settlement was regularized in the early seventies after strong pressure from the community council. The community has benefited considerably from the help of important people who live in the vicinity. The settlement has not suffered from any special problems and the community seems remarkably harmonious and content with the settlement. There is a large number of renters, the majority of whom live in a room in the same house as the owners. Approximately 600 families live in the settlement, occupying almost 400 houses.

Bogotá – Juan Pablo I

Juan Pablo I is located just beyond the perimeter of the District of Bogotá in the neighbouring municipality of Soacha. It is on the fringe of a huge area of consolidated pirate settlement which has developed in Bosa, one of the main industrial areas of the city. In the case of Juan Pablo, however, there is little sign of consolidation because there are major doubts over the land-tenure situation. Many charge that Juan Pablo is an invasion and the land-tenure situation is certainly complex and shrouded in controversy. Originally the land is supposed to have been purchased by Father Carvajal's Asociación Provivienda de Trabajadores, a non-profit-making organization selling housing to the poor. He was president of the association until 1956 when he left Bogotá for Venezuela. Certain famillies were invited to live on the land and look after it, but in 1971 three of these families started to subdivide the land to sell lots to low-income groups. The 'invasion' was not opposed by the Asociación, seemingly because its new head was not in Bogotá at the time; it has been suggested that he was following his own rather than the Asociación's interest. In the following years a legal suit was initiated and with the help of political influentials linked to the Asociación the police were persuaded to harass the settlement. In July 1977, for example, many houses were destroyed in the *barrio*. Police harassment has been inconsistent, however, because the governor of Cundinamarca, who controls the police, has often been at odds with the political authorities in Soacha. It is clear that the three individuals who sold, and continue to try to sell, lots are acting as pirate urbanizers, but they are regarded by most of the inhabitants as fellow strugglers in the fight against the Asociación.

The land itself is low-lying and is often partially under water. There are no community services beyond what mutual help has provided, that is illegally tapped electricity, an underground water hose and a provisional drainage system. The settlement has received little help of any kind from outside the community, no financial assistance from the council and no legal help. At the time of our study there were signs of improvement insofar as local politicians were beginning to conduct political campaigns in the settlement and *personería jurídica* had been granted to the community so that its *junta de acción comunal* could be officially recognized.

The effects of uncertain tenure and police harassment are obvious. The level of house consolidation is low, the people have stopped paying for the instalments on their lots. There are 130 houses and the vast majority of the inhabitants are 'owners'; the level of consolidation precludes the widespread renting of rooms although a few houses are rented. We interviewed 35 households in this settlement because it provided a marked contrast with the normal pattern of pirate urbanization in Bogotá and because it provided clear evidence of the problems facing a community which lacks secure land tenure.[2]

Bogotá – San Antonio

San Antonio is located on the edge of the industrial suburb of Soacha, a municipality administratively separate from the rest of Bogotá. The settlement has developed as a series of separate subdivisions during the past 18 years. It is located on flat and rather sandy land in an unpicturesque part of the town. San Antonio is really four separate settlements which have been linked closely in their development. Until quite recently they were all represented by the same community *junta* though they now have separate representation. They share numerous services, notably the school which was built by collective effort and the IDEMA shop and kerosene deposit. The fact that the average size of settlement in Soacha is much smaller than that in Bogotá together with the common elements in the history of the settlements persuaded us to interview households in all four communities. The largest and oldest settlement is San Antonio which began in 1961 with the sale of land without services by a small landowner; El Chico was a separate subdivision where sales began in 1965; San Alberto was founded in 1973 and El Triunfo about the same time. Through its own efforts the community has built a school, installed a drainage system, put up posts for electricity and is now building a health centre, a theatre and a community centre. But, it has also received considerable help from outside. The US Embassy helped fund the school, one pirate urbanizer paid for the cost of the servicing in San Alberto and, most important, the head of the San Antonio community council (and the most influential community politician) has obtained funds from the local council, supply from the Bogotá electricity and water company and a store from IDEMA, the National Marketing agency. In fact, the settlements are a fascinating mix of inspired self-help and political brokerage and are well consolidated, with health care, paved roads and public transport being the most notable deficiencies.

There are just over 400 families in the settlements of which 55 per cent own their property and 38 per cent are tenants. According to our survey, the average purchase date for the four communities was the middle of 1968 and the average moving-in date towards the end of the following year.

Mexico City – Liberales

Despite being the newest *barrio* in which we worked, Liberales was the most centrally located. Situated in a disused sand pit one kilometre west of the Observatorio Metro station, the *barrio* enjoys excellent access to public-transport facilities and to the downtown area. Its formation and history are quite unlike any of the other settlements studied. The original owner acquired the land in 1951 but never registered the title. Nevertheless, in 1974 negotiations were opened between the owner and a group of would-be residents who wished to buy the land in order to create a cooperatively organized low-income subdivision. The leaders were known personally to the director of one of the Federal District's housing agencies (the Procuradaría de Colonias Populares) who acted as intermediary and arranged a provisional agreement for the lands to be acquired at the relatively expensive cost of 120 *pesos* per square metre plus sundry taxes (in effect a total of 14,400 *pesos* a plot). However, the proposal broke down for several reasons. First, the bureaucratic procedure involved in getting planning permission proved time consuming and threatened to be very expensive insofar as the authorities refused to recognize the subdivision as 'working-class', a classification which would have entitled it to significant tax concessions. Second, the change of government in 1976 meant that the *barrio* lost its patron in the Procuradaría. Third, devaluation of the *peso*, also in 1976, led to the landowner's complaint that he would now be paid in *tostones* (50-cent pieces) rather than *pesos*: in short he wanted to renegotiate. Fourth, the residents were becoming increasingly impatient and a small disaffected breakaway group threatened to invade the land, which forced the leaders' hands. Thus, what began as an attempt legitimately to purchase land became, in effect, an invasion. The creation of a new agency, CODEUR, heralded a new phase in the settlement's tenure history. Faced with constant harassment from the local mayor, the residents appealed to CODEUR to carry through regularization. In September 1979, agreement had been reached whereby members of the *barrio* association would buy the land at a somewhat higher price than that agreed previously.

By Mexican standards, the settlement is relatively small, comprising approximately 640 plots which accommodated 750 households at the time of survey. The large majority are owner-occupiers and the small plot size (120 m^2), combined with its location and growing pressure within the city to share plots with kin, accounts for the already high population density (see table 1, page 24). The *barrio* scores very low on our servicing index (6 points). Electricity was in the process of being installed while water was provided by a few standpipes. The low level of services is due to its youth and also because of opposition from the local mayor who is primarily responsible for service installation. Despite this opposition, community participation and morale were high. Many attended the weekly *juntas*, most volunteered for the Sunday-morning work parties, a brick-making workshop had been created to supply the community, and a kindergarten and an adult education centre organized. Most households have improved their homes and substituted their shacks with two-roomed or three-roomed brick-built dwellings.

Mexico City – Jardines de Tepeyac

Located 16 kilometres northeast of the city centre in the municipality of Ecatepec, Jardines is just one example of a company-sponsored low-cost subdivision in the area. Created in 1962 by the 'Texcoco Company', the *barrio* originally contained 1,366 plots each with an area of 500m^2 offered at ten *pesos* a square metre. The company sold the land as *granjas* (a sort of market garden) which enabled it to sidestep certain servicing clauses, and the contracts issued explicitly renounced responsibility for the installation of services. The relative isolation of the area, together with the inhospitable environment and complete lack of urban services, meant that only 360 dwellings existed in 1970. Governmental commitment to service the region from 1970 onwards, combined with the installation of a school in the *barrio* in 1971, stimulated the occupation of plots from that date. In addition, approximately eighty unoccupied plots were invaded. The large plot size provided ample opportunity for further subdivision so that today most plots are about 250 square metres in size, still quite large by Mexico City standards. As a result, population density per unit area is much lower than for other settlements of comparable age. Our pre-survey enquiries gave a total of 1,324 house plots, many of which had been further subdivided to provide rental rooms or dwellings for kin; on average there are 2.43 households per plot. The land is flat, saline, and largely lacking in vegetation and forms part of the dried-out bed of Lake Texcoco. Legalization of land tenure has yet to take place, though responsibility was taken out of the hands of the company in 1977 when the state took over.

Although the settlement has had a domestic electricity supply since 1972 and water and drainage since 1977, it does not lack problems with its services. During the field work residents had begun to receive abnormally high bills for the installation of water and drainage. In addition, there was no street lighting, no health centre, no public telephone and, with the exception of the main access road, the streets were unmade and became impassable during the rainy season. There seems little doubt that the community would have been much worse off had it not been for the influence of Don Guillermo, the principal leader throughout the 1970s. His success as leader, notable though it had been, was, he argued, constrained by the fact that the low population density raised the costs of service installation and also meant that the total population was considerably less than that of neighbouring settlements. Therefore their claims drew less weight. Nevertheless his political judgement was shrewd. When really pressed he knew exactly whom to approach, the arguments that needed rehearsing and the manner in which they should be put across. His influence as a local leader was widely respected and went beyond the confines of Jardines.

Mexico City – Chalma Guadalupe

Located in the extreme north of the Federal District on the flanks of Guadalupe Sierra, the settlement contains 124 blocks arranged along eleven streets which run parallel along the hillside. So steep are the interlinking streets that many residents jokingly said that a cable car was the most needed service. In 1979, there were approximately 2,300 plots in the *barrio*, mostly about 200 square metres in size and a total of around 4,100 families.

The land formed part of the San Miguel Chalma *ejido* which had been created in 1928 on rough pasture with little agricultural value. In 1969, the *ejidal* committee applied to the Agrarian Department for permission to create an urban *ejidal* zone, a ploy to allow them to sell off plots and to give out certificates of land cession. The settlement has been gradually colonized since 1970. Most of those who arrived at the outset paid 2,500 *pesos* for a plot on the gentle lower slopes though cheaper plots were available higher up the hillside. By 1979, only a few plots remained vacant and purchase in the steep, least accessible sections cost around 9,000 *pesos*. The 'sale' by *ejidatarios* was illegal and the land was expropriated in 1974 and handed over to CoRett (the regularization agency responsible for *ejidos*) in 1976 for the transfer of title to residents.

Although several services have been installed, not all of the settlement benefits equally. Water standpipes were installed in the lower section in 1974 and recently households in the first three or four streets were provided with a domestic supply; those higher up still have to carry water from public hydrants. All have a domestic supply of electricity though the uppermost streets lack street lighting. The school, church and market are all located in the lower sections.

The relative security of land tenure, the internal differentiation with respect to service provision, and a history of changing and uninspired leadership have contributed to a lack of integrated mutual-help efforts among residents. However, while residents were mostly apathetic, a few had joined to protest to the authorities about the high taxes on land and construction that had begun to be imposed upon them as an outcome of land regularization.

Mexico City – Isidro Fabela

Isidro Fabela is one of several large invasion settlements located in the south of the city on broken terrain that forms part of a relatively recent lava flow from the Xitle volcano. Original ownership of the land is unclear. There is evidence to suggest that it was unregistered and belonged to a foreigner, two factors which made it especially susceptible to invasion. Plots were allocated to residents by the principal leader during the 1960s, but the pace of invasion quickened during 1967 and 1968 as public works for the Olympic Games brought services to adjacent areas. The land was expropriated in 1968 and most of the 1,300 200m^2 lots regularized by the 'Colonias Office'. After 1968, conditions in the settlement improved dramatically. Electricity was installed, standpipes were placed in each street, the main access road was paved and one side of the settlement ran alongside the newly constructed ringway. Legalization, the arrival of services and the proximity to the motorway have made this settlement particularly attractive to higher-paid households, many of whom bought out original invaders and built substantial homes. Their arrival has had a pronounced upward effect on land prices in the settlement.

The *barrio* was 'adopted' by President Echeverría (1970–6), who wanted it to become a 'model' self-help settlement, and it received favoured treatment with respect to servicing. During 1977–8, water was installed in each plot and all roads were being paved; by that date a purpose-built community centre/clinic had been provided by the *delegación* and in two streets cosmetic remodelling of house frontages had been undertaken by the authorities.

The settlement has an early history of conflictive leadership, but by 1973 the need for an active committee had declined and today leaders are mostly party-political activists. Our survey data suggest that lot densities are increasing markedly as families get larger, as elder children get married and share plots with their parents, and as entrepreneurs buy plots and develop rental tenements housing from six to ten families. In 1979, there were approximately 3,500 households living in the *barrio*.

Mexico City – Santo Domingo los Reyes

Santo Domingo is located several kilometres north of Isidro Fabela on the same volcanic terrain. It also began by invasion but its origins are both complex and confused. Different sources suggested that a government minister, the Jesuits, agency heads, unscrupulous leaders, or the *comunero* land holders were the principal promoters of the invasion. Certainly all were intimately involved very soon after Santo Domingo had been established but it is unclear which group was primarily responsible. The invasion took place in September 1971, the day of the President Echeverría's first State of the Nation Address. Within a few days an estimated 4,000 families were in occupation of the 261 hectares of land which belonged to the *comuneros* of nearby los Reyes. The invasion involved mostly young households who were sharing or renting in nearby *barrios*. In 1977, there were over 7,500 plots (Mexico, FIDEURBE, 1976: 57) and around 12,000 households. Most plots are 200m², though in northern sections where many of the *comuneros* lived they are much larger. The land was expropriated in 1971 and there have been major arguments since about how compensation should be paid to the 1,048 *comuneros* and about how much residents should pay for regularization.

From the outset the community has been riven with violence and factional strife between three principal leaders. Partly because of their failure to agree, but also because of divisions within the bureaucracy, the record of public intervention has been mixed. The several agencies that have been involved with the settlement at one time or another achieved little. In the first three years electricity was stolen from neighbouring settlements and, despite the attempts of the company to supply individual houses after 1973, local conflict meant that completion was delayed until 1977. Water was provided by tanker lorries and a few hydrants until 1977 when a domestic supply was installed through a combination of mutual help and Federal District assistance. Unfortunately, although the network is complete the water comes only as a trickle in the early hours of the morning. As in Isidro Fabela, the basalt is free draining and home-made latrine pits provide an adequate system of drainage. By 1979, most of the tension had disappeared as the authoritarian leadership lost control over community affairs.

Mexico City – El Sol

El Sol forms the northernmost part of the swathe of illegal subdivisions to the east of the city on land reclaimed from the lake bed. Located in the municipality of Netzahualcóyotl on the fringe of the lake, it is relatively isolated and though it was one of the first *colonias* to be created it was one of the last to be populated. It was established in 1950 when the subdividers began to sell off the 6,740 plots. Although approximately 1,200 families lived in El Sol in 1953, there were only 25 still there by 1961; a result of harassment by the Water Resources Ministry which claimed ownership to the land. A Supreme Court action favoured these 25 families but, nevertheless, the settlement failed to grow rapidly and only 600 families lived there in 1970. At the time, servicing was almost non-existent: no drainage, eight water hydrants, and only a provisional electricity system. Most contemporary residents arrived after 1973. In response to a payments strike by the 700,000 or so inhabitants of the *colonias* of Netzahualcóyotl in 1970 and major protests to the government about the lack of services and the failure of the company subdividers to fulfil their obligations, a Trust was established (Fideicomiso Netzahualcóyotl). So powerful were local community factions that the Trust was obliged to give local 'committees' the right to allocate remaining parcels. In El Sol the plots were distributed by four committees and most residents acquired plots by paying a set contribution of 2,000–3,000 *pesos* to the leaders. A few others simply invaded. As a result of this process, patterns of land tenure are complicated. A few in our sample had owned property since the 1960s, most had acquired a plot through the committees, the rest had invaded. In many cases, those who had bought in the 1960s arrived in the settlement in the early seventies to claim their plots only to find them already occupied. The government agency responsible for regularizing the land tenancy had an unenviable task; where multiple claimants existed they usually sought agreement whereby the occupier compensated the original (but previously absent) owner. Elsewhere, they divided the plot between occupant and claimant or simply omitted to pass judgement. By 1978 the settlement contained around 11,000 families and scored high on our *barrio* consolidation rating. Part of the Trust agreement of 1973 established a programme of regular monthly payments by residents to pay for a water-and-drainage service, which had been fully installed by 1976. Other services include permanent markets, schools, churches and regular police patrols. The settlement's major need is for paved roads although two primary access routes were being paved during 1979.

Valencia – La Castrera

La Castrera is located in the south of Valencia and forms part of the largest continuous area of low-income settlement in the city. It was first settled in 1970 after municipal land, in what was known as La Castrera but is now called José Gregorio Hernández, was distributed among fifty or so families who had been relocated from a settlement destroyed by the police. Despite doubts about the suitability of the land – 'only animals can live there', it was said – the Council distributed lots because they were under considerable criticism and pressure. La Castrera itself was invaded by some of the relocated families. The principal leader of the invasion distributed land to families on a first-come, first-served basis charging only a small sum except for corner lots, which were reserved at a price for commercial or more affluent residents. By 1971, however, potential residents were being sent to the municipal council to request lots. This explains why different people in the settlement said that they invaded land, others that they received it from the invasion leader and others received land from the council. In our survey, in fact, only 38 per cent were original invaders or settlers compared to 57 per cent who had bought lots from previous owners or from people who had subdivided their lots. The settlement has suffered no repression from the authorities and received services quite quickly. At the time of our survey it had light, water, some drainage, paving, public transport, public telephones and a school. Like most low-income settlements in Valencia there are few renters (5 per cent), and the level of house consolidation is high. In 1979 there were around 850 families.

Valencia – Nueva Valencia

Nueva Valencia is located in the far southwest of the city close to the neighbouring municipality of Tocuyito and near the motorway to Barquisimeto. It was formed in haphazard fashion after the Campesino League organized a small invasion of the land belonging to an important local landowner. The latter had subdivided the land in an attempt to urbanize it for middle-class families. The original invasion was soon overwhelmed by the arrival of a much larger group of invaders. The lots were first allocated by the League but soon the new group organized a community *junta* and took over the distribution. The *barrio* suffered severe repression from the police over a three-year period and several deaths are reported to have occurred at one point. Since 1973, there has been little active repression and the settlement has undergone rapid consolidation. Attempts have been made to regularize the land situation, specifically a plan for the nation to purchase the land and donate it to the municipality, but nothing has materialized. However, it has long been clear that the settlement will survive. Its main problems relate to services since it has long been council and national agency policy not to service settlements formed through the invasion of private land.[3] Thus, although the settlement is the same age as La Castrera, it lacks paved roads, a sewerage system and an official electricity supply. It received water only on the eve of the 1978 national election, eight years after its foundation. The situation now appears to be changing; there are plans to start a sewerage system and the beginnings of some improvement in the roads was underway in 1979. It is a large settlement with approximately 1,200 families of whom over 95 per cent are 'owners'. Few of these families are original invaders and three-quarters of our interviewees had bought lots from the previous occupants.

Notes

1 Introduction: the research issues and strategy

1 Gilbert had made numerous visits to Bogotá, carrying out doctoral and post-doctoral research in Colombia and acting as consultant to the Bogotá Urban Development Study in 1972 and 1973. He had visited Venezuela several times and had advised the government on new-town policy in 1975. Ward had carried out doctoral and post-doctoral research in Mexico City and, while working on the project in Mexico, was adviser on low-income housing to the Ministry of Human Settlements (SAHOP). He had also made two research visits to Venezuela in 1974 and 1975.

2 *Ejidal* land was established after the Mexican Revolution and comprises agricultural land held by the community but worked individually by named peasants. A detailed description may be found in chapter 3.

2 Bogotá, Mexico City and Valencia

1 Much of the following section is informed by an internal project working paper written by Bill Bell. This paper has appeared as Bell, 1982.

2 It also led to the examination of non-military regimes, such as those of Mexico and Colombia, in search of parallel political practices and forms of authoritarianism.

3 Articles 121 and 122 of the Constitution.

4 Levels of abstention in recent presidential elections in Colombia were 46 per cent in 1974 (Losada, 1980: 90, 95) and 68 per cent in 1978 (*Latin American Political Report*, XII (22)). In Mexico, abstentions reached 31 per cent in 1976 (Smith, 1979: 55) despite strong efforts by the PRI to increase voting. In Venezuela, where voting is compulsory, the abstention rate was only 3.5 per cent in the 1973 presidential election but rose to 12.5 per cent in 1978 (Silva Michelena and Sonntag, 1979: 155). In the municipal elections of 1979, abstentions rose to 30 per cent (Lascano, 1979).

5 This interpretation appears to differ from that of Smith (1979: 214), who argues that the elite, while highly fragmented, fall into one of two distinct and competitive camps: the business elite and the political elite. In his view relations between these two elites are characterized by minimum career overlap and by an ongoing struggle for control over the country's development process and resources. This interpretation, at least in part,

appears to have been influenced by events that arose during the Echeverría presidency, though Smith's analysis of career patterns goes back much further.

6 The boundaries of Mexico City require explanation. Throughout this study Mexico City refers to the contiguous built-up area. It includes most of the Federal District, with the exception of three sub-districts (*delegaciones*) in the south which are still largely rural (figure 3). Since the 1950s, substantial portions of the urban area have spilled over into surrounding municipalities of the neighbouring State of Mexico. Depending upon the date in question, several of these districts may also be included in our discussion of Mexico City.

7 Interestingly, while many of the poor spend two or more hours travelling to and from work, our survey data indicate that the average time *barrio* residents spent in daily travel was similar in Bogotá and Mexico (around 80 minutes: Gilbert and Ward, 1982a). Given the difference in city size and similar inefficiencies of public transport in the two cities, this finding suggests that there has been greater decentralization of employment and consumer services in Mexico than in Bogotá. Once isolated villages such as San Angel, Tlalpan, Mixcoac, Tacubaya, Tacuba have been incorporated into Mexico City and each offers a major source of employment and services reducing traditional dependency upon the downtown market area (La Merced).

8 Up to May 1961 1.3 million square metres of this land had been sold.

9 Ford, for example, was charged only two *bolívares* per sq m in 1959 for 415,950 m² (CEU, 1977: 39).

10 From 1974 to 1979 Valencia was controlled politically by a group of the Democratic Action Party that was out of sympathy with Carlos Andrés Pérez. From 1979 to 1982, although the local party was controlled by sympathizers of Luis Herrera Campíns, the national party was controlled by supporters of Rafael Caldera. Both situations have led to the neglect of the city compared to, say, Barquisimeto, the next major city to the west.

11 Council minutes are full of denunciations of notorious planning developments.

12 A series of major bus strikes in 1981 brought the city to a standstill on several occasions.

3 Access to land

1 The Spanish crown reserved certain areas of land for the use of the indigenous Indian population. These are often known as *resguardos indígenas*.

2 The *ejidos* in Mexico were established after the Revolution, usually through the break-up of extensive *haciendas*, and the lands made over in usufruct to be held by the community.

3 The Council did this in a campaign to attract industry to the city. Between 1959 and 1968, 43 per cent of Valencia's municipal land was sold to private industrialists (Lovera, 1978: 150).

4 The Venezuelan state gives major incentives to the construction industry both to reduce problems during building slumps and to encourage the

private sector to build housing for lower-middle income groups. Indeed, the Venezuelan state is frequently criticized for making the incentives too attractive (Cilento, 1980; Bolívar and Lovera, 1978).

5 Valorization taxes are charged on the increased property value owing to public works. One of the principal problems in Bogotá is that it is only in high-income and commercial areas that roads are built under this system. The limited ability of low-income groups in other parts of the city makes this system difficult to use.

6 Cali had extensive areas of such land but Bogotá very little.

7 In Bogotá, Rojas Pinilla won 44.6 per cent of the total vote in 1970 compared to the 40.8 per cent won by the elected president Pastrana Borrero. Among the lower-middle, lower and *tugurio* groups of the population Rojas won respectively 50, 62.7 and 84 per cent of the vote (Colombia, DANE, 1972: 297). Some kind of policy response in favour of the urban poor was clearly indicated.

8 *Acuerdo* 7 also increased the amount of land available for low-income housing.

9 This occurred in one of our settlements, Liberales. A similar case (Ajusco) is described by López Díaz (1978).

10 Specifically, AURIS in 1970, INDECO in 1972, and FIDEURBE, CoRett and FINEZA in 1973.

11 *Ley de Bienhechurías*, Article 557 of the *Código Civil*.

12 Article 20 of the *Ley de regulación de alquileres*.

13 The individual most nearly approaching such a description, Trino Medina, who had been involved in four out of the nine settlements for which we have detailed information, certainly supplemented his income in this fashion but equally clearly allocated many lots free to those without land. His motives were at least as political as they were speculative.

14 This judgement is based both on a review of the press for the 1968–79 period and on the evidence of our interviews with a number of *barrio* leaders.

15 Repression is much more common during 'invasions' of public housing – a very common occurrence in Venezuela due in part to the long waiting lists for government housing.

16 Note that we have eliminated the improvements made to the lots from the costs paid, but the prices still include any betterment brought about by improvements in servicing and general *barrio* consolidation.

17 It obviously does not show the changes in price through time because of the averaging process.

18 A point clearly demonstrated by the age differences between heads of owner households and heads of renting and sharing households (table 14).

19 The minimum of 30 *bolívares* in 1982 was well below the average industrial wage in the state of Carabobo which during a newspaper interview with a Ministry of Labour official was estimated to be between 45 and 65 *bolívares* (*El Carabobeño, Suplemento Industrial*, March 1982).

20 Sanin Angel *et al.* (1981) show that incomes were broadly stable 1970–2, fell to a low (with respect to 1970) of 92.8 in 1975 in a period of general decline (1973–7), and rose 1978–80 (116.2 in 1978).

21 Many of our interviews did not generate reliable information and were

eliminated. In addition, disaggregating the data by year soon reduces a *barrio* total of 40 or so owners to negligible yearly sub-totals. The data cannot be aggregated because the settlements are in different locations and at different points on the land-price gradient.

22 The data were obtained from the Bogotá Planning Department and record official approvals for the urbanization of land. The data included are typical of the 1968–77 period for which data were collected.

23 Carroll (1980) obtained his data from the SIB which had circulated all pirate urbanizers and compelled them to comply with the law in disclosing details about prices charged and cost of land acquisition, urbanization and administration. The evidence is generally considered to be reliable despite the obvious problems involved.

24 Meaning paying guests, a euphemism for renters. His terminology is rather confusing, however, when he refers to housing being shared by owners and renters. Sharing in this sense is not equivalent to our use of the word.

25 Translated from the Spanish.

26 In Bogotá, Hamer's (1981: 73–5) analysis of two sets of data show that: (i) among heads of household, 35.6 per cent of renters were under 30 compared to 18.7 per cent among all sample families; (ii) 37.9 per cent were under 30 compared to 23.7 per cent among all sample families.

27 Peralta and Vergara (1980) found little difference in the family sizes of renters and non-renters in the Patio Bonito *barrios*, but Hamer's evidence for Bogotá is very similar to our own.

28 Gilbert (1983) found that in Bogotá the average age at which the move from renting or sharing to ownership occurred was 35.8 years, a mature age at which to obtain a self-help lot which suggests that the transition to ownership is very difficult. Current renters had an average age only 2.7 years lower. The evidence also suggested that many tenants have been in rental accommodation for many years; it is not a stage of short duration before they obtain an independent home. Indeed, among the 114 tenants in Bogotá for whom there was information, the average number of years living independently of family is 8.4. Among this group were many who had lived for a long period in rental accommodation: 21 had lived for 10–14 years, 14 for 15–19 years and 9 for over 20 years. Only 27 had lived in rental accommodation for less than 3 years.

4 Servicing low-income settlements

1 Bus transport in the Federal District of Mexico was nationalized by the government in 1981. Private operators continue to run the service in the surrounding State of Mexico.

2 Rubbish collection recently changed hands.

3 1978 State budget = 339.5 million *bs*. City budget income = 142.2 million *bs*.

4 Bogotá differs in its control over public services from other cities in Colombia in that it has the equivalent of departmental control over education and social welfare and much greater control over police and transport.

5 'Generally speaking, there exist two isolated, distinct compartments in the

system: the government proper and the political parties. Each is staffed by different people . . . access to government posts through the party channel tends to be quite restricted' (Latorre, 1974: 268–9).

6 For detailed discussion of how parties allocated jobs, at least in Cali, see Nalven, 1978.

7 See Daykin (1978: 385) for a similar point with reference to Ciudad Guayana. He suggests that the poor do not greatly use, or trust, politicians beyond the search for jobs.

8 The Bogotá water company in 1973 charged the lowest-tariff group 0.7 *pesos*/m^3 of water compared to 4.72 *pesos*/m^3 to the highest tariff group. This meant that the lowest-tariff group, constituting 17 per cent of all accounts, consumed 12 per cent of the water and paid 4.5 per cent of the total tariffs, compared to the highest-tariff group which made up 0.4 per cent of all accounts, consumed 4.0 per cent of the water and paid 10.0 per cent of the total tariffs. Linn (1980) calculates for water, sewerage, electricity, garbage and telephones that in 1974 the top two deciles of the income distribution subsidize the rest, but of the rest most subsidy is received by those who have access to those services, namely the fourth to seventh deciles.

9 In 1979 the budgets of the main Bogotá agencies were as follows: electricity 10,007 million *pesos*, water and drainage 3,329 millions and telephones 4,456 millions. By contrast, rubbish received 479 millions, buses 160 millions, community action 73 millions, health 191 millions, education 560 millions, public works 367 millions and planning 40 millions.

10 See note 8.

11 For example, Britalia was not supplied with drainage because the proposed scheme did not commend itself to the company.

12 For example the Fondo de Redes Locales, 1967–9 and a similar scheme introduced in 1974.

13 *Barrios Periféricos* plan in 1974, IBRD 1979–82 loan to service low-income *barrios*, and the PHIZSU plan.

14 Total expenditure 1969–73 was 191 million *bolívares*, of which 85 millions were spent in 1973. Between 1974 and 1978 total expenditure was 658 millions of which 367 millions were spent in 1978 (INOS, 1977).

15 The municipality has the right to approve or reject proposed tariffs. An illustration of its attitude to the issue is given by the statement made by the mayor on 30 September 1975 (Council minutes p. 20): 'the Council could hardly raise tariffs for people in the north of the city, when INOS is such an incompetent and poor provider of services . . . he believed that tariffs could only be reduced for the marginal classes'.

16 Interview sources confirmed this. In addition, invasion settlements occupying private land have been included in the INOS/State of Carabobo coordinated budget. For example, Nueva Valencia was programmed for drainage according to the 1979 budget although nothing had actually been built by April 1982.

17 Debates in the council make frequent reference to the gift of materials to settlements before 1970 but no reference afterwards, and it appears that the council agreed to desist from this practice in 1970.

5 Community organization: participation or social control?

1 A shortened version of this chapter appeared in *World Development*, 12, 1984.

2 These three positions hold good in all Latin American countries except Cuba and possibly Nicaragua. In those countries the position of the observers with respect to the perceived virtues will largely be reversed.

3 'Collective consumption' is essentially social infrastructure such as housing, schools and hospitals. Unfortunately, there are numerous ambiguities in the term (see Saunders, 1980: 121–7).

4 Bogotá, DAAC (1968).

5 Until 1968, under the National Front policy of parity, *juntas* were officially required to display identical numbers of Liberal and Conservative representatives (Bogotá, DAPD, 1968). Although the parity requirement is no longer in force, DAAC's official policy remains strongly integrative in situations where conflicting slates of candidates (aligned on party political lines and/or focused on leading individuals) compete in *junta* elections.

6 In Santa Marta Sur, for example, one slate easily overcame the other, though the latter's leader had a significant portion of the vote for *junta* president. Over the initial objections of the losing group that it would refuse to work with the other, the Community Action promoter forcefully pushed an integration, based on a complicated manipulation of voting tallies, that gave the losing slate's leader the vice-presidency of the new *junta* and other members lesser posts. In this situation of mildly divisive conflict, with no strong personalities from the *barrio* involved, the promoter was well placed to impose an integrationalist policy. In *barrios* with strong, entrenched leaders, as in Atenas, Casablanca, and Britalia, such integrative behaviour on the part of the promoter is unlikely. He is also likely to permit illegal procedures, for example, an individual occupying the presidency for more than three years or a president who does not live in the *barrio*.

7 His style was not populist in the sense of involving true social mobilization with him identified as the figurehead.

8 An example of different interests that existed in low-income settlements during this period is observed in Padierna where there were *ejidatarios*, approved *avecindados*, and squatters, each with conflicting claims and wishes regarding the costs of regularization.

9 The record is somewhat better if we include low-income settlement in the State of Mexico.

10 At least up to 1968 when Ray wrote his book.

11 FUNDACOMUN is the Foundation for Community and Municipal Development.

12 A UDO is a unit for planning and administration.

13 By the end of June 1981 there were 115 in Valencia (OMPU files), a city with approximately 177 *barrios* and *urbanizaciones* in 1976 (Feo Caballero, 1979: 139–50).

14 The distinction between 'stable' and 'unstable' *barrios* was made on a mixture of criteria including the nature of the terrain and the previous

ownership of the land. Invasions of private land were automatically classified as 'unstable' *barrios* – i.e. there was no mention of such *barrios* in the lists of 'stable' *barrios* in Valencia drawn up by FUNDACOMUN and OMPU in 1979. Similarly, FUNDACOMUN's (1982) points schedule for servicing makes it impossible for a *barrio* on private land to qualify for servicing.

15 Interview with Alba Illaramendi, the president of FUNDACOMUN.

16 This finding was valid even when we controlled for later arrivals to the settlements.

17 Fagen and Tuohy (1972: 88–9) note that, with the possible exception of Cuba, Mexico more than any other Latin American country encourages structured, controlled political contact by citizens.

18 But this was in part biased by the fact that we were talking to current owners in these settlements and not to past owners who had left the settlement as in the case of the older *barrios*.

19 The fact that it did not involve the population in Juan Pablo I is due to the way the question was posed.

20 Policarpa Salavarrieta has had a long struggle with the authorities and has established an effective contraband electricity system in the *barrio*. While the electricity agency wishes to legalize the situation, the *barrio* prefers to obtain free light.

21 The Patio Bonito area was flooded at the end of October 1979. The *barrios* had little in the way of services at the time of the flood (Peralta and Vergara, 1980).

22 In inaugurating the water and drainage network in the *barrio*, the head of the EAAB praised the 'high level of organization and effective group coordination' which he wished was typical of most communities in Bogotá (*El Espectador*, 22 April 1979: 17-A).

23 This has in fact backfired on the water company, which has been involved in various disputes with the communities on technical matters. For example, the community has laid pipes to a different specification to that recommended by the agency and the latter has refused to service.

24 In the communist-led Nuevo Chile settlement there was a persuasive method of community mobilization. Help given to the community and financial contributions to the service improvements were listed on the wall of the community organization (*Provivienda*) office. Since the list contained the names of all families in the settlement, any lack of participation was obvious and presumably subject to strong moral pressure.

25 In 1981 the community had in fact elected a new leader with Conservative affiliation.

26 The case was publicized when voter-registration figures showed that a new unknown *barrio* had the highest number of eligible voters of any *puesto* in the city. Besides the election of the urbanizer to the council, the political battles revolving round the *barrio*'s formation led to the resignation of the city's planning director.

27 Montaño (1976: 142) describes a similar case in which a powerful candidate wanted to mobilize the electorate to provide him with a strong mandate in order to add weight to his political aspirations once elected. All stops were

pulled out to ensure that everyone was registered to vote and, when he was called upon to act on the *barrio*'s behalf by securing regularization, his (apparent) intervention was successful within three days. However, it seems hardly credible that 20,000 titles were drawn up in three days as Montaño describes. It is more likely that a handover of title was already imminent or had been withheld. The candidate's intervention had the effect of 'unblocking' the hold-up.

28 Thus one infamous invasion leader claimed to go straight to the governor in order to obtain services; now he is *persona grata* with the COPEI party.

29 Américo Moreno (Movimiento Reginista) who was selling land near Suba was unsuccessful, as was Hildebrands Olarte (Movimiento Cívico Popular) who had developed a pirate urbanization in Bosa (*El Tiempo*, 1 and 18 February 1982).

30 This had changed by 1982, however, when a Conservative had taken over, almost certainly in alliance with one of the invaders/pirate urbanizers.

31 He has since been replaced by a poor, self-employed worker.

32 In 1981 he was assassinated. People in the *barrio* suggested that he had made too many enemies, but the exact reasons for the killing are unknown.

33 For example, Colonia 'Nueva' (Cornelius, 1975), Padierna, Santo Domingo los Reyes, etc.

34 Several PRI deputies elected in 1979 were ex-MRC leaders.

35 Though our discussions with leaders did suggest that, while regularization of land was jointly fought for, resolution was achieved at different times. No single trust was established – as had been the case in Netzahualcóyotl.

36 See Montaño (1976) for accounts of Campamento 2 de Octubre, Ruben Jaramillo and others.

Appendix 1 The methodology in detail

1 *El Tiempo* in Bogotá (1968–78), *El Carabobeño* in Venezuela (1970–9) and *Excelsior* and *El Día* in Mexico were consulted.

2 In fact, we included a fifth settlement in Bogotá where we carried out only 35 interviews. This was Juan Pablo I, an unconsolidated settlement which faced major problems over consolidation because of uncertain land tenure and which was faced with a difficult dispute with a company which claimed ownership.

3 The desired average age differed slightly in Bogotá because we required one young *barrio* (0–5 years) and three older *barrios*. This worked out at $(3 \times 10$ years $+ 1 \times 2.5)/4$ years $= 8.125$ whereas in Mexico with two young settlements it worked out at $(4 \times 10 + 2 \times 2.5)/6 = 7.5$ years. In Valencia the formula did not work and we simply aimed to find two settlements which would be approximately 7 to 8 years old.

4 We attribute the differences in settlement size to the nature of land alienation. Large settlements occur in land sales, sponsored either by real-estate companies of large landowners, or in invasions where success is likely to be enhanced by force of greater numbers. Both situations are typical of Mexico City. Land sales sponsored by small-scale developers tend to lead to much smaller settlements – as in Bogotá.

5 Clearly, no matter how hard one tries no questionnaire will ever be perfect. However, we did not have to change or delete questions because of glaring ethnocentrism or to avoid annoyance by constantly tapping only the respondent's ignorance – problems to which Eckstein (1979) alludes.

6 We are grateful to Mr John Barradale who assisted in the preparation of this programme, and to the Department of Geography for a grant towards the expense incurred.

Appendix 2 Description of the survey settlements

1 He claims that this was to prevent its being invaded. The number of lots was in fact relatively limited and for this reason he has not been classified as a pirate urbanizer.

2 A return visit to the community in April 1982 revealed a much more consolidated settlement. Although it had suffered from further police harassment during 1980 and the subdividers had been jailed briefly, more people had occupied lots and there were definite signs of consolidation. It seems no longer to be under real threat.

3 This policy seems to have changed during 1979 but it is still much harder to obtain services as an invasion on private land.

Bibliography

Abrams, C. 1964. *Man's struggle for shelter in an urbanizing world*, MIT Press.

Abu Lughod, J., and Hay, R., eds. 1977. *Third World urbanization*, Maaroufa Press.

Algara Cosío, I. 1981. Community development in Mexico, in Dore, R., and Mars, Z., eds. *Community development*, Croom Helm and UNESCO, 337–432.

Amato, P. W. 1969. Environmental quality and locational behaviour in a Latin American city, *Urban Affairs Quarterly*, 83–101.

1970. Elitism and settlement patterns in the Latin American city, *Journal of the American Institute of Planners*, 36, 96–105.

Amis, P. 1981. Capital and shelter: the commercialization of 'squatter' housing in Nairobi, 1960–1980. Mimeo. Urban and Regional Studies Unit, University of Kent at Canterbury.

Angel, S. 1983. Upgrading slum infrastructure: divergent objectives in search of a consensus, *Third World Planning Review*, 5, 5–22.

Angel, S., Archer, R., Tanphiphat, S., and Wegelin, E., eds. 1983. *Land for housing the poor*, Select Books, Singapore.

ANIF (Asociación Nacional de Instituciones Financieras). 1976. Empleo y desarrollo, Bogotá.

Argüello, M. 1982. Los movimientos urbanos en las regiones paupérrimas de Costa Rica. Paper presented in the symposium, Housing, poverty and urban development, 44th International Congress of Americanists, Manchester.

Arias, J. 1974. Estudio de estratificación socioeconómica de los barrios de Bogotá, DE, DAPD.

1978. Bogotá, in Paine, L. H. W., ed. *Health care in big cities*, Croom Helm, 161–78.

Avramovic, D., ed. 1972. *Economic growth of Colombia: problems and prospects*, Johns Hopkins Press.

Bagley, B. M. 1979. Political power, public policy and the state in Colombia: case studies of the urban and agrarian reforms during the National Front, 1958–1974, unpublished doctoral dissertation, University of California, Los Angeles.

Bagley, B., and Edel, M. 1980. Popular mobilization programs of the National Front: cooptation and radicalization, in Berry, R. A., *et al.*, eds. *Politics*

293

of compromise: coalition government in Colombia, Transaction Books, 257–84.

BANOP (Banco Nacional de Ahorro y Préstamo). 1970. Estudio del mercado real de vivienda en Venezuela. Primera serie de resultados parciales, Valencia.

Baross, P. 1983. The articulation of land supply for popular settlements in Third World cities, in Angel, S., *et al. Land for housing the poor*, Select Books, 180–210.

Bataillon, C., and D'Arc, H. R. 1973. *La Ciudad de México*, Sepsetentas, Mexico DF.

Batley, R. 1978. Urban services and public contracts – access and distribution in Lima and Caracas, International Labour Office, Programa Regional del Empleo para América Latina y el Caribe Working Paper 165.

1982. Urban renewal and expulsion in São Paulo, in Gilbert, A. G., *et al.*, eds. *Urbanization in contemporary Latin America*, John Wiley, 231–62.

Bazant, J., Espinosa, E., Dávila, R., and Cortés, J. 1978. *Tipología de vivienda urbana*, Editorial Diana, Mexico.

BCV (Banco Central de Venezuela). 1977. Series Estadísticas 1977, Caracas.

1978. La economía venezolana en los últimos treinta y cinco años, Caracas.

1980. Series Estadísticas 1980, Caracas.

Bell, W. S. 1982. Tilting at windmills: considerations on the nature of the state, University College London, Department of Geography, Occasional Paper No. 40.

Berry, R. A. 1980. The National Front and Colombia's economic development, in Berry, R. A., *et al.*, eds. *Politics of compromise: coalition government in Colombia*, Transaction Books, 287–326.

Berry, R. A., Hellman, R. G., and Solaún, M., eds. 1980. *Politics of compromise: coalition government in Colombia*, Transaction Books.

Berry, R. A., and Soligo, R. 1980a. The distribution of income in Colombia: an overview, in Berry, R. A., and Soligo, R., eds. *Economic policy and income distribution in Colombia*, Westview Replica Edition, 1–45.

eds. 1980b. *Economic policy and income distribution in Colombia*, Westview Replica Edition.

1980c. Urban building and income distribution in Colombia: some relevant aspects, *Studies in Comparative International Development*, 15, 39–60.

Berry, R. A., and Urrutia, M. 1975. *Income distribution in Colombia*, Yale University Press.

Bhooshan, B. S., and Misra, R. P. 1979. *Habitat Asia: Issues and responses, Vol. 1, India*, Concept Publishing Company.

Bigler, G. E. 1977. The armed forces and patterns of civil–military relations, in Martz, J., and Myers, D., eds. *Venezuela: the democratic experience*, 113–33.

Bogotá DE 1979a. Presupuesto 1979.

1979b. Proyectos de presupuesto de las entidades descentralizadas y los fondos rotatorios de Bogotá DE 1979.

Bogotá, Alcaldía Mayor. 1976. Informe del Alcalde de Bogotá al Honorable Consejo, Bogotá.

Bogotá, DAAC (Departamento Administrativo de Acción Comunal). 1968. Manual de instrucciones para promotores de Acción Comunal, Bogotá.

Bogotá, DAPD (Departamento Administrativo de Planeación Distrital). 1972. Políticas de desarrollo urbano 1972, Bogotá.

    1973. Mercado de tierras en barrios clandestinos en Bogotá. Mimeo.

    1978. Normas mínimas de urbanización y de servicios. Consideraciones a su aplicación. Mimeo.

    1981. Ordenamiento y administración del espacio urbano en Bogotá.

Bogotá, Servicio Seccional de Salud. 1977. Plan de Salud 1977.

Bolívar, T., and Lovera, A. 1978. Notas sobre la industria de la construcción en Venezuela, Centro de Estudios Urbanos. Mimeo.

Boonyabancha, S. 1983. The causes and effects of slum eviction in Bangkok, in Angel, S., *et al. Land for housing the poor*, Select Books, 254–80.

Borrero, O. 1981. Crecimiento en los costos de la vivienda en la década del 70–80 en Bogotá, CENAC.

Bose, A. 1973. *Studies in India's urbanization 1901–1971*, Tata McGraw-Hill.

Bourne, L. 1980. *The Geography of Housing*, Edward Arnold.

Brett, S. 1974. Low income settlements in Latin America: the Turner model, in De Kadt, E., and Williams, G., eds. *Sociology and development*, Tavistock Publications Ltd, 171–96.

Bromley, R., ed. 1978. The urban informal sector: critical perspectives, *World Development*, 9/10, 1031–198.

Bromley, R. J., and Gerry, C., eds. 1979. *Casual work and poverty in Third World cities*, John Wiley.

BUDS. 1974. Bogotá Urban Development Study Phase II. Vol. 1, The structure plan for Bogotá.

Buia, C. E. de, and de Guerra, A. R. no date. Factores sociales y económicos de las barriadas marginales en Valencia, Universidad de Carabobo, Centro de Planificación y Desarrollo Económico.

Burgess, R. 1978. Petty commodity housing or dweller control? A critique of John Turner's view on housing policy, *World Development*, 6, 1105–34.

Butterworth, D. 1973. Squatters or suburbanites? The growth of shantytowns in Oaxaca, Mexico, in Scott, R. E., ed. *Latin American modernization problems*, University of Illinois Press.

Butterworth, D., and Chance, J. 1981. *Latin American urbanization*, Cambridge University Press.

Camacho, O. 1982. The role of the oligarchy in the spatial concentration of the Venezuelan economy, 1777–1870, University College London, unpublished doctoral dissertation.

Cannon, M. W., Fosler, R. S., and Witherspoon, R. 1973. *Urban government for Valencia, Venezuela*, Praeger.

Cardona, R. 1969. *Las invasiones de terrenos urbanos*, Tercer Mundo.

Cardoso, F. H. 1977. Current theses on Latin American development and dependency: a critique, *Boletín de Estudios Latinoamericanos y del Caribe*, 22, 53–64.

    1978. Capitalist development and the state: bases and alternatives, *Ibero-Americana*, 7 and 8, 7–19.

    1979. On the characterization of authoritarian regimes in Latin America, in

Collier, D., ed. *The new authoritarianism in Latin America*, Princeton University Press, 19–32.

Carroll, A. 1980. Pirate subdivisions and the market for residential lots in Bogotá, City Study Project No. 7, The World Bank.

Castells, M. 1977. *The urban question: a marxist approach*, Edward Arnold. Original French edition 1972.

1977a. Marginalité urbaine et mouvements sociaux au Mexique: le mouvement des 'posesionarios' dans la ville de Monterrey, *International Journal of Urban and Regional Research*, 1, 145–50.

1979. *City, class and power*, Macmillan.

1981. Squatters and politics in Latin America: a comparative analysis of urban social movements in Chile, Peru and Mexico, in Safa, H. I., ed. *Towards a political economy of urbanization in Third World countries*, Oxford University Press.

CENAC (Centro Estadístico Nacional de la Construcción). 1975. Inversiones y Construcciones del Instituto de Crédito Territorial 1942–1975, Bogotá.

1980. El valor del suelo urbano y sus implicaciones en el desarrollo de la ciudad: análisis del caso de Bogotá, Bogotá.

Cepeda, F., and Mitchell, B. 1980. The trend towards technocracy: the World Bank and the International Labor Organization in Colombian politics, in Berry, R. A., *et al.*, eds. *Politics of compromise: coalition government in Colombia*, Transaction Books, 237–56.

CEU (Centro de Estudios Urbanos). 1977. La intervención del estado y el problema de la vivienda: Valencia, CEU, Caracas.

Cilento, A. 1980. La mercancía vivienda en Venezuela: su producción, circulación, y consumo, Instituto de Desarrollo Experimental de la Construcción, Facultad de Arquitectura y Urbanismo, Universidad Central de Venezuela.

Cisneros, A. no date. La colonia El Sol. Mimeo, Mexico City.

Clarke, S., and Ginsberg, N. 1975. The political economy of housing, in Political Economy Housing Workshop, Political economy and the housing question, Conference of Socialist Economists, London.

Cleaves, P. S. 1974. *Bureaucratic politics and administration in Chile*, California University Press.

Collectif Chili. 1972. Revendication urbaine, stratégie politique et mouvement social des 'pobladores' au Chili, *Espaces et Sociétés*, 6–7, 37–57.

Collier, D. 1976. *Squatters and oligarchs: authoritarian rule and policy change in Peru*, Johns Hopkins Press.

ed. 1979. *The new authoritarianism in Latin America*, Princeton University Press.

Colombia, DANE (Departamento Administrativo Nacional de Estadística). 1972. Colombia política: estadísticas 1935–1970, Bogotá.

1977. La vivienda en Colombia, 1973. Bogotá.

1978. La población en Colombia, Bogotá.

1980. XIV Censo Nacional de Población y III de Vivienda. Octubre 24 de 1973. Bogotá DE.

1981a. Anuario Estadístico de Bogotá DE 1976–9, Bogotá.

1981b. Colombia Estadística 1981, Bogotá.

Colombia, ICT (Instituto de Crédito Territorial). 1976. Inventario de zonas subnormales y proyectos de desarrollo progresivo, Bogotá.

Colombia, MSP (Ministerio de Salud Pública). 1969. Estudio de recursos humanos para la salud y la educación médica en Colombia: Métodos y resultados, Bogotá.

Connolly, P. 1981. Towards an analysis of Mexico City's local state. Mimeo, Mexico City.

1982. Uncontrolled settlement and self-build: what kind of solution? The Mexico City case, in Ward, P., ed. *Self-help housing: a critique*, Mansell Publishing Co., 141–74.

Conway, D. 1982. Self-help housing, the commodity nature of housing and amelioration of the housing deficit: continuing the Turner–Burgess debate, *Antipode*, 14, 40–6.

Córdova, P., et al. 1971. La distribución de ingresos en Colombia, *Boletín Mensual de Estadística*, 237, 55–95.

Cornelius, W. A. 1973a. The impact of governmental performance on political attitudes and behaviour: the case of the urban poor in Mexico, in Rabinovitz, F., and Trueblood, F., eds. 1973. *Latin American Urban Research*, 3, 217–55.

1973b. Contemporary Mexico: a structural analysis of urban caciquismo, in Kern, R., ed. *The caciques: oligarchical politics and the system of caciquismo*, University of New Mexico Press.

1975. *Politics and the migrant poor in Mexico City*, Stanford University Press.

Cornelius, W. A., and Kemper, R. V., eds. 1978. *Latin American Urban Research*, Vol. 6, Metropolitan Latin America: the challenge and the response, Sage.

Cornelius, W. A., and Trueblood, F. M., eds. 1975. *Latin American Urban Research*, Vol. 5, Urbanization and inequality, Sage.

Cosío Villegas, D. 1972. *El sistema político méxicano*, Cuadernos de Joaquín Moritz, Mexico.

1975. *El estilo personal de gobernar*, Joaquín Moritz, Mexico.

Cox, P. 1970. Venezuela's agrarian reform at mid-1977, Land Tenure Center Research Paper No. 71, University of Wisconsin.

Da Camargo, C. P., et al. 1976. *São Paulo: crescimento e pobreza*, Ediçoes Loyola, São Paulo.

Daykin, D. S. 1978. Urban planning and quality of life in Ciudad Guayana, Venezuela, unpublished doctoral dissertation, Valderbilt University.

De Kadt, E. 1982. Community participation for health: the case of Latin America, *World Development*, 10, 573–84.

De Kadt, E., and Williams, E., eds. 1974. *Sociology and development*, Tavistock Publications Ltd.

Dinkelspiel, J. R. 1969. Administrative style, in Rodwin, L., ed. *Planning urban growth and regional development*, MIT Press, 301–14.

Diesing, P. 1962. *Reason in society*, University of Illinois Press.

Dietz, H. 1977. Land invasion and consolidation: a study of working poor/governmental relations in Lima, Peru, *Urban Anthropology*, 6, 371–85.

Dix, R. H. 1967. *Colombia: the political dimensions of change*, Yale University Press.

1980. Political oppositions under the National Front, in Berry, R. A., *et al.*, eds. *Politics of compromise: coalition government in Colombia*, Transaction Books, 131–80.

Doebele, W. 1975. The private market and low-income urbanization in developing countries: the 'pirate' subdivisions of Bogotá, Harvard University, Department of City and Regional Planning, Discussion Paper D75–11.

Dore, R., and Mars, Z., eds. 1981. *Community development*, Croom Helm and UNESCO.

Dowse, R. E., and Hughes, J. A. 1972. *Political sociology*, John Wiley.

Drakakis-Smith, D. W. 1981. *Urbanization, housing and the development process*, Croom Helm.

Dunleavy, P. 1980. *Urban political analysis: the politics of collective consumption*, Macmillan.

Duque Escobar, I., and Samper Rodríguez, G. 1980. Urbanizaciones intervenidas, Instituto de Crédito Territorial.

Durand, J. 1978. La ciudad invade el ejido. Mimeo, Mexico City.

Durrand Lasserve, A. 1983. The land conversion process in Bangkok and the predominance of the private sector over the public sector, in Angel, S., *et al.*, *Land for housing the poor*, Select Books, 284–309.

Dwyer, D. J. 1975. *People and housing in Third World cities*, Longman.

Eckstein, S. E. 1977. *The poverty of revolution: the state and the urban poor in Mexico*, Princeton University Press.

1979. On questioning the questionnaire: research experiences, *Latin American Research Review*, 14, 141–9.

Edwards, M. A. 1982a. Cities of tenants: renting among the urban poor in Latin America, in Gilbert, A. G., *et al.*, eds. *Urbanization in contemporary Latin America*, John Wiley, 129–58.

1982b. Cities of tenants: renting as a housing alternative among the Colombian urban poor, unpublished doctoral dissertation, Department of Geography, University College London.

EITAV (Estudio Integral de Transporte del Area de Valencia). 1977. Características actuales socioeconómicas y de transporte, 1975.

Evans, H. 1974. Towards a policy for housing low-income families in Mexico, unpublished thesis for Diploma in Architecture, University of Cambridge.

Evers, H. D. 1977. Urban expansion and land ownership in underdeveloped societies, in Walton, J., and Masotti, L. H., eds. *The city in comparative perspective*, Halsted Press, 67–79.

Fagen, R., and Tuohy, W. 1972. *Politics and privilege in a Mexican city*, Stanford University Press.

Fajardo Ortiz, G. 1978. Mexico City, in Paine, L. H. W., eds. *Health care in big cities*, Croom Helm, 179–93.

Fanon, F. 1967. *The wretched of the earth*, Penguin. First published in French 1961.

FEDESARROLLO. 1976. *Coyuntura Económica*, 8.

Feo Caballero, O. 1979. *Estadísticas consultativas del Estado Carabobo*, Gobernación de Carabobo.

Ferras, R. 1978. Ciudad Netzahualcóyotl: un barrio en via de absorción por la Ciudad de México, Centro de Estudios Sociológicos, El Colegio de México.

Fisher, J. 1977. Political learning in the Latin American barriadas: The role of the Junta de Vecinos, unpublished doctoral thesis, Johns Hopkins University.

Foster, D. W. 1975. Survival strategies of low-income households in a Colombian city, doctoral dissertation, University of Illinois, Urbana-Champaign.

Fox, D. J. 1972. Patterns of morbidity and mortality in Mexico City, *Geographical Review*, 62, 151–86.

Fox, R. 1975. Urban population growth trends in Latin America, Washington, Inter-American Development Bank.

Frieden, B. 1965/6. The search for a housing policy in Mexico City, *Town Planning Review*, 36, 75–90.

Friedmann, J. 1965. *Venezuela: from doctrine to dialogue*, Syracuse University Press.

1966. *Regional development policy: a case study in Venezuela*, MIT Press.

Friedmann, J., and Wulff, R. 1976. *The urban transition: comparative studies of newly industrializing societies*, Edward Arnold.

Friedrich, P. 1968. The legitimacy of the cacique, in Swartz, M., ed. *Local-level politics: social and cultural perspectives*, Aldine, 243–269.

Fuentes, A. L., and Losada, R. 1978. Implicaciones socioeconómicas de la ilegalidad en la tenencia de la tierra urbana de Colombia, *Coyuntura Económica*, 8, 1–28.

Garza, G. 1978. *Ciudad de México: dinámica económica y factores locacionales*, Temas de la Ciudad, No. 5, DDF.

Garza, G., and Schteingart, M. 1978a. Mexico City: the emerging metropolis, in Cornelius, W., and Kemper, R., eds. *Latin American Urban Research*, 6, Sage, 51–85.

1978b. *La acción habitacional del estado mexicano*, El Colegio de México.

Gauhan, T. O. 1975. Political attitudinal orientations in three low-income barrios of Bogotá, Colombia, unpublished doctoral dissertation, Rice University.

Geisse, G. 1982. Studies in urban land policy in Latin America: issues and methodology, in Cullen, M., and Woolery, S., eds. *World congress on land policy*, D. C. Heath and Co., Lexington.

Gilbert, A. G. 1975. Urban and regional development programmes in Colombia since 1951, in Cornelius, W. A. and Trueblood, F. M., eds. *Latin American Urban Research*, 5, Sage, 241–76.

1978. Bogotá: politics, planning and the crisis of lost opportunities, in Cornelius, W. A., and Kemper, R. V., eds. *Latin American Urban Research*, 6, Sage, 87–126.

1981a. Pirates and invaders: land acquisition in urban Colombia and Venezuela, *World Development*, 9, 657–78.

1981b. Bogotá: an analysis of power in an urban setting, in Pacione, M., ed. *Urban problems and planning in the Modern World*, Croom Helm.

1983. The tenants of self-help housing: choice and constraint in the housing market, *Development and Change*, 14, 449–77.

1984. Planning, invasions and land speculation: the role of the state in Venezuela, *Third World Planning Review*, **6**, 225–38.

Gilbert, A. G., and Gugler, J. 1982. *Cities, poverty and development: urbanization in the Third World*, Oxford University Press.

Gilbert, A. G., and Ward, P. M. 1978. Housing in Latin America, in Johnston, R. J., and Herbert, D. T., eds. *Geography and the urban environment*, John Wiley, 286–318.

1981. Public intervention, housing and land use in Latin American cities, *Bulletin of Latin American Research*, 1, 97–104.

1982a. Residential movement among the poor: the constraints on Latin American urban mobility, *Transactions of the Institute of British Geographers*, 7, 129–49.

1982b. The state and low-income housing, in Gilbert, A. G., Hardoy, J. E., and Ramírez, R., eds. 1982. *Urbanization in contemporary Latin America*, John Wiley, 79–128.

Gilhodes, P. 1973. *Luchas agrarias en Colombia*, Editorial La Carreta.

Gil Yepes, J. A. 1981. *The challenge of Venezuelan democracy*, Transaction Books.

Goldrich, D., Pratt, R., and Schuller, C. 1967. The political integration of lower-class urban settlements in Chile and Peru, *Studies in Comparative International Developments*, 3, No. 1.

Grimes, O. F. 1976. *Housing for low income urban families*, Johns Hopkins University Press.

Grindle, M. S. 1977. *Bureaucrats, politicians and peasants in Mexico: a case study in public policy*, University of California Press.

Grove, J. W. 1962. *Government and industry in Britain*, Longmans.

Grupo de Estudios 'José Raimundo Russi'. 1978. *Luchas de clases por el derecho a la ciudad*, Editorial Ocho de Junio.

Guerrero, Ma. T., *et al.* 1974. La tierra, especulación y fraude en el fraccionamiento Nuevo Paseo de San Agustín. Mimeo, Mexico.

Guzman, G., Fals Borda, O., and Umaña Luna, E. 1963. *La violencia en Colombia*, Ediciones Tercer Mundo, 2 vols., Second edition.

HABITAT (United Nations Centre for Human Settlements). 1982. *Survey of slum and squatter settlements*, Tycooly International, Dublin.

Hamer, A. M. 1981. Las subdivisiones no reglamentadas de Bogotá: los mitos y realidades de la construcción de vivienda suplementaria, Corporación Centro Regional de Población, La Ciudad Documento No. 24.

Handelman, H. 1975. The political mobilization of urban squatter settlements: Santiago's recent experience and its implications for urban research, *Latin American Research Review*, 10, 35–72.

Hansen, R. D. 1974. *The politics of Mexican development*, Johns Hopkins University Press.

Harloe, M. 1977. *Captive cities*, John Wiley.

Hart, K. 1973. Informal income opportunities and urban employment in Ghana, *Journal of Modern African Studies*, 11, 61–89.

Healey, P. 1974. Planning and Change, *Progress in Planning*, 2, 143–237.

Holloway, J., and Picciotto, S., eds. 1978. *State and capital: a marxist debate*, Edward Arnold.

Hoskin, G. 1980. The impact of the National Front on Congressional behaviour: the attempted restoration of El País Político, in Berry, R. A., *et al.*, eds. *Politics of compromise: coalition government in Colombia*, Transaction Books, 105–30.

Inkeles, A. 1969. Participant citizenship in six developing countries, *American Political Science Review*, 63.

International Labour Office. 1972. *Employment, incomes and equity: a strategy for increasing productive employment in Kenya*, ILO, Geneva.

Janssen, R. 1978. Class practices of dwellers in *barrios populares*: the struggle for the right to the city, *International Journal of Urban and Regional Research*, 2, 147–59.

Johnson, J. J. 1958. *Political change in Latin America: the emergence of the middle sectors*, Stanford University Press.

Johnson, K. F. 1971. *Mexican democracy, a critical view*, Allyn and Bacon, Boston.

Kalmanovitz, S. 1978. Desarrollo capitalista en el campo, in Arrubla, M., *et al. Colombia Hoy*, Siglo XXI, 271–330.

Kline, H. F. 1980. The National Front: historical perspective and overview, in Berry, R. A., *et al. Politics of compromise: coalition government in Colombia*, Transaction Books, 59–83.

Kowarick, L. 1975. *Capitalismo e marginalidade na America Latina*, Paz e Terra, Rio de Janeiro.

Kusnetzoff, F. 1975. Housing policies or housing politics: an evaluation of the Chilean experience, *Journal of Interamerican Studies and World Affairs*, 17, 281–310.

Lascano, J. A. 1979. Los resultados electorales, *SIC* 417, 298–9.

Latorre, M. 1974. *Elecciones y partidos políticos en Colombia*, Universidad de los Andes, Bogotá.

Laun, J. I. 1976. El estado y la vivienda en Colombia: análisis de urbanizaciones del Instituto de Crédito Territorial en Bogotá, in Castillo, C., ed. *Vida urbana y urbanismo*, Instituto Colombiano de Cultura, 295–334.

Leeds, A. 1969. The significant variables determining the character of squatter settlements, *América Latina*, 12, 44–86.

1971. The concept of the 'culture of poverty': conceptual, logical, and empirical problems, with perspectives from Brazil and Peru, in Leacock, E. B., ed. *The culture of poverty: a critique*, Simon & Schuster.

Leeds, A., and Leeds, E. 1976. Accounting for behavioural differences: three political systems and the responses of squatters in Brazil, Peru and Chile, in Walton, J., and Masotti, L. H., eds. *The city in comparative perspective*, Halsted Press, 193–248.

Lewis, O. 1966. *La Vida: a Puerto Rican family in the culture of poverty – San Juan and New York*, Random House.

Linn, J. F. 1980. Distributive effects of local government finances, in Berry, R. A., and Soligo, R., eds. *Economic policy and income distribution in Colombia*, Westview Replica Edition.

Linz, J. J. 1964. An authoritarian regime: Spain, in Allardt, E. and Littunen, Y. eds. Cleavages, ideologies and party systems: contributions to comparative political sociology, *Transactions of the Westmark Society X*, 291–342.

Linz, J. J., and Stepan, A., eds. 1978. *The breakdown of democratic regimes: part one*, Johns Hopkins Press.

Lipset, S. M. 1959. Some social requisites of democracy: economic development and political legitimacy, *American Political Science Review*, 53, 69–105.

Litterer, J. A., ed. 1969. *Organizations: structure and behaviour*, John Wiley, Second edition. First published 1963.

Lloyd, P. 1979. *Slums of hope? Shanty towns of the Third World*, Penguin.

Lojkine, J. 1976. Contribution to a Marxist theory of capitalist urbanization, in Pickvance, C., ed. *Urban sociology: critical essays*, Tavistock, 119–46.

López, J. E. 1963. La expansión demográfica de Venezuela, *Cuadernos Geográficos*, 2, Universidad de los Andes, Mérida.

López Diaz, C. 1978. La intervención del estado en la formación de un asentamiento proletario: el caso de la colonia Ajusco, tésis de licenciatura, Departamento de Antropología, Universidad Iberoamericana, DF.

Losada, R. 1980. Electoral participation, in Berry, R. A., *et al.*, eds. *Politics of compromise: coalition government in Colombia*, Transaction Books, 87–104.

Losada, R., and Gómez, H. 1976. *La tierra en el mercado pirata de Bogotá*, Fedesarrollo, Bogotá.

Losada, R., and Pinilla, L. 1980. *Los barrios ilegales de Bogotá: su desarrollo histórico y su impacto sobre la ciudad y la Sabana de Bogotá*, Pedro Gómez y Cía.

Lovera, A. 1978. Desarrollo urbano y renta del suelo en Valencia, Universidad Católica Andrés Bello, Facultad de Ciencias Económicas y Sociales, Caracas.

Lozano, A. A. 1978. Empresa de Energía Eléctrica de Bogotá, in Cámara de Comercio, *Bogotá: Estructura y principales servicios públicos*, Bogotá, 264–73.

Lozano, E. 1975. Housing the urban poor in Chile: contrasting experiences under 'Christian Democracy' and 'Unidad Popular', in Cornelius, W. A., and Trueblood, F. M., eds. *Latin America Urban Research*, 5, 177–96.

Lubell, H., and McCallum, D. 1978. *Bogotá, urban development and employment*, International Labour Office.

Lukes, S. 1978. Power and authority, in Bottomore, T. B., and Nisbet, R. A., eds. *A history of sociological analysis*, Heineman, 633–76.

McGreevey, W. P. 1980. Population policy under the National Front, in Berry, R. A., *et al.*, eds. *Politics of compromise: coalition government in Colombia*, Transaction Books, 413–32.

Malloy, J. M. 1979. *The politics of social security in Brazil*, Pitt, Latin American Series, University of Pittsburgh Press.

Mangin, W. 1967. Latin American squatter settlements: a problem and a solution, *Latin American Research Review*, 2, 65–98.

Marchand, B. 1966. Les ranchos de Caracas, contribution a l'étude des bidonvilles, *Cahiers d'Outre-Mer*, 19, 104–43.

Martín de la Rosa, 1974. *Netzahualcóyotl: un fenómeno*, Testimonios del Fondo, Mexico DF.

Martínez, I. J. 1977. The performance of local government in democratic Venezuela, in Martz, J., and Myers, D., eds. *Venezuela: the democratic experience*, Praeger, 309–22.

Martz, J. 1977. The party system: towards institutionalization, in Martz, J.,

and Myers, D., eds. *Venezuela: the democratic experience*, Praeger, 93–112.
1980. The evolution of democratic politics in Venezuela, in Penniman, H. R., ed. *Venezuela at the Polls: the national elections of 1978*, American Enterprise Institute for Public Policy Research, 1–29.
Martz, J., and Myers, D., eds. 1977. *Venezuela: the democratic experience*, Praeger.
Marx, K. 1967. *Capital*. 3 vols. International Publishers Edition.
Mexico, BIMSA (Bureau de Investigación de Mercados S.A.). 1974. Mapa mercadológico del área metropolitana de la Ciudad de México. Mimeo.
Mexico, BNHUOPSA. 1966. Obras para México, Número especial, Mexico DF.
Mexico, CAVM. 1978. Diagnóstico del consumo de agua en el Valle de México. Mimeo.
Mexico, Census 1970. Secretaría de Programación y Presupuesto, *IX Censo Nacional de Población y Vivienda*.
Mexico, CODEUR (Comisión de Desarrollo Urbano). 1979. Programa de acciones y presupuesto 1979–1982. Mimeo.
Mexico, CONAPO. 1978. México demográfico, Handbook.
Mexico, COPEVI. 1976. Análisis del comportamiento del mercado de bienes raíces en la zona metropolitana de la Ciudad de México, Capítulo F. Mimeo.
1977. *La producción de vivenda en la zona metroplitana de la Ciudad de México*, Mexico DF.
Mexico, DDF, (Departamento del Distrito Federal). 1976. Estudio de economía urbana del plan director para el desarrollo urbano del distrito federal, Capítulo 3, Estructura del uso del suelo. Mimeo.
1979. Plan hidráulico del Distrito Federal. Report by the Dirección General de Construcción y Operación Hidráulica.
1980. Plan de desarrollo urbano: Plan general del plan director, versión abreviada, DF.
Mexico, FIDEURBE. 1976. Fideurbe 1973–76, Informe.
Mexico, INVI (Instituto Nacional de Vivienda). 1958. Colonias proletarias: problemas y soluciones, Mexico DF.
Mexico, SAHOP. 1978a. Caracterización de la vivienda precaria en Ciudad Juárez, Chihuanua, Internal document, DGCP.
1978b. Plan Nacional de desarrollo urbano, versión abreviada.
1979. La incorporación de los procesos que generan los asentamientos irregulares a la planeación de centros de población, Internal document, DGCP.
Mexico, SPP. 1979. *La población de México, su ocupación y sus niveles de bienestar*, 2.
Michl. S. 1973. Urban squatter organization as a national government tool: the case of Lima, Peru, in Rabinovitz, F., and Trueblood, F., eds. *Latin American Urban Research*, 3, 155–78.
Miliband, R. 1969. *The state in capitalist society*, Weidenfeld and Nicolson.
1977. *Marxism and politics*, Oxford University Press.
Millikan, M. F., and Blackmer, D. L. M. 1961. *The emerging nations*, Little, Brown and Co. Boston.

Mingione, E. 1977. Theoretical elements for a Marxist analysis of Urban Development in Harloe, M. ed. *Captive cities*, John Wiley, 89–110.

Mohan, R., and Hartline, N. 1979. The poor of Bogotá: who they are, what they do and where they live. Mimeo, The World Bank.

Mohan, R. and Villamizar, R. 1980. La evolución de los precios de la tierra en el contexto de un rápido crecimiento urbano, en estudio de caso de Bogotá y Cali, Colombia, Corporación Centro Regional de Población, Series La Ciudad No. 22.

Montaño, J. 1976. *Los pobres de la ciudad de México en los asentamientos espontáneos*, Siglo XXI, Mexico.

Morón, G. 1954. *Los orígenes históricos de Venezuela*, Madrid.

Moser, C. O. N. 1978. Informal sector or petty commodity production: dualism or dependence in urban development?, *World Development*, 6, 1041–64.

1982. A home of one's own: squatter housing strategies in Guayaquil, Ecuador, in Gilbert, A. G., *et al.*, eds. *Urbanization in Contemporary Latin America*, John Wiley, 159–90.

Muñoz, H., De Oliveira, O., and Stern, C. 1972. Migración y marginalidad ocupacional en la ciudad de México, in UNAM, *El Perfil de México en 1980*, Vol. 3, Siglo XXI, 325–58.

Murillo, G., and Ungar, E. 1979. *Política, vivienda popular y el proceso de toma de decisiones en Colombia*, Universidad de los Andes, Bogotá.

Myers, D. 1980. The elections and the evolution of Venezuela's party system, in Penniman, H. R., ed. *Venezuela at the Polls: the national elections of 1978*, American Enterprise Institute for Public Policy Research, 218–52.

Nalven, J. 1978. The politics of urban growth: a case study of community formation in Cali, Colombia, doctoral dissertation, University of California San Diego.

Navarette, I. 1972. La distribución de ingresos en México: tendencias y perspectivas, in UNAM, *El perfil de México*, Vol. 1. Siglo XXI.

Negrón, M. 1982. Crecimiento económico y deterioro de la calidad de la vida de los sectores populares urbanos en Venezuela: necesidad de un nuevo enfoque y posibilidades de una acción transformadora, Paper presented to the symposium 'Housing, poverty and urban development', 44th Congress of Americanists, Manchester.

Nelson, J. M. 1969. Migrants, urban poverty, and instability in developing countries, Occasional Paper 22, Centre for International Affairs, Harvard University.

1979. *Access to power: politics and the urban poor in developing nations*, Princeton University Press.

Nun, J. 1969. Sobrepoblación relativa, ejército industrial de reserva y masa marginal, *Revista Latinoamericana de Sociología*, 4, 178–237.

O'Connor, R. E. 1980. The electorate, in Penniman, H. R., ed. *Venezuela at the polls: the national elections of 1978*, American Enterprise Institute for Public Policy Research, 56–90.

O'Donnell, G. A. 1973. *Modernization and bureaucratic-authoritarianism: studies in South American politics*, University of California Press.

1977. Corporatism and the question of the state, in Malloy, J. M., ed.

Authoritarianism and corporatism in Latin America, University of Pittsburgh Press.

1978. Reflections on the patterns of change in the bureaucratic-authoritarian state, *Latin American Research Review*, 13, 3–38.

Oliveira, F. de. 1972. A economia brasileira: crítica á razão dualista, *Estudos CEBRAP*, 2, 5–82.

Padgett, V. L. 1966. *The Mexican political system*, Houghton Mifflin, Boston.

Páez Celis, J. 1974. Ensayo sobre demografía económica de Venezuela, Dirección General de Estadística y Censos Nacionales, Caracas.

Pahl, R. E. 1975. *Whose city?*, Penguin.

Palma, G. 1979. Dependency: a formal theory of underdevelopment or a methodology for the analysis of concrete situations of underdevelopment?, *World Development*, 6, 881–924.

Paredes, L. R. 1980. Colombia's urban legal framework, Bogotá City Study of the World Bank.

Paredes, L. R., and Martínez, L. G. 1977. Alternativa para la solución del problema de la vivienda para grupos de bajos ingresos: el sector privado y las normas mínimas, Paper presented to INTERHABITAT Medellín.

Payne, G. 1977. *Urban housing in the Third World*, Leonard Hill.

1982. Self-help housing: a critique of the Gecekondus of Ankara, in Ward, P., ed. *Self-help housing: a critique*, Mansell Publishing Ltd, 117–139.

Pearse, A., and Steifel, M. 1979. Inquiry into participation – a research approach. United Nations Research Institute for Social Development, Geneva.

Peattie, L. 1974. The concept of 'marginality' as applied to squatter settlements, in Cornelius, W., and Trueblood, F., eds. *Latin American Urban Research*, 4, 101–9.

1979. Housing policy in developing countries: two puzzles, *World Development*, 7, 1017–22.

Peil, M. 1976. African squatter settlements: a comparative study, *Urban Studies*, 13, 155–66.

Penniman, H. R., ed. 1980. *Venezuela at the Polls: the national elections of 1978*, American Enterprise Institute for Public Policy Research.

Peralta, G., and Vergara, A. J. 1980. *Informe sobre la zona de Patio Bonito*, Pedro Gómez y Cia.

Pérez Perdomo, R., and Nikken, P. 1982. The law and home ownership in the *barrios* of Caracas, in Gilbert, A. G., *et al.*, eds. *Urbanization in Contemporary Latin America*, John Wiley, 205–30.

Perlman, J. 1976. *The myth of marginality: urban poverty and politics in Rio de Janeiro*, University of California Press.

Perló, M. 1980. Algunas consideraciones sobre los problemas financieros de la Ciudad de México, *El Día*, 4 December 1980.

Pickvance, C., ed. 1976. *Urban sociology: critical essays*, Tavistock, London.

1977. From social base to social force: some analytical issues in the study of urban protest, in Harloe, M., ed. *Captive cities*, John Wiley, 175–86.

Portes, A. 1979. Housing policy, urban poverty, and the state: the *favelas* of Rio de Janeiro, 1972–76, *Latin American Research Review*, 14, 3–24.

Portes, A., and Walton, J. 1976. *Urban Latin America: the political condition from above and below*, University of Texas Press.

Posada, A. J. 1966. *The C.V.C.: challenge to underdevelopment and traditionalism*, Tercer Mundo.

Poulantzas, N. 1973. *Political power and social classes*, New Left Books.

Pradilla, E. 1976. Notas acerca del 'problema de la vivienda', *Ideología y Sociedad*, 16, 70–107.

Quijano, A. 1974. The marginal pole of the economy and the marginalized labour force, *Economy and Society*, 3, 393–428.

Purcell, S., and Purcell, J. 1980. State and society in Mexico, *World Politics*, 194–227.

Ray, T. 1969. *The politics of the barrios of Venezuela*, University of California Press.

Revéiz, E. *et al.* 1977. *Poder e información*, Universidad de los Andes, Centro de Estudios Sobre Desarrollo Económico (Colombia).

Reyna, J. 1974. Control político, estabilidad y desarrollo en México, Centro de estudios sociológicos, 3, El Colegio de México.

Richardson, H. 1973. *The economics of urban size*, Saxon House and Lexington Books.

Ridler, N. 1979. Development through urbanization: a partial evaluation of the Colombian experiment, *International Journal of Urban and Regional Research*, 3, 49–59.

Riesco, J. 1981. Community participation and the housing and municipal decentralization policies under the Chilean military government: some implications for the urban poor, MA dissertation, Institute of Latin American Studies, London.

Rivera Ortiz, A. I. 1976. The politics of development planning in Colombia, unpublished doctoral dissertation, State University of New York at Buffalo.

Roberts, B. 1973. *Organizing strangers*, University of Texas Press.

1978. *Cities of peasants: the political economy of urbanization in the Third World*, Edward Arnold/Sage.

Robock, S. H. 1963. *Brazil's developing northeast: a study of regional planning and foreign aid*, The Brookings Institution.

Rodwin, L. L., and Associates, eds. 1969. *Planning urban growth and regional development*, MIT Press.

Rosas, L. E., *et al.* 1972. Controversía sobre el plan de desarrollo, Corporación para el Fomento de Investigaciones Económicas.

Roxborough, I. 1979. *Theories of underdevelopment*, Macmillan.

Sanin Angel, H. *et al.* 1981. El salario real en la industria manufacturera colombiana 1970–1980, *Boletín Mensual de Estadística*, 360, 35–73.

Saunders, P. 1979. *Urban politics: a sociological interpretation*, Weidenfeld and Nicolson. Penguin edition 1980.

Schteingart, M. no date. El proceso de formación y consolidación de un asentamiento popular en México: el caso de Netzahualcóyotl, Mimeo, Mexico City.

Sethuraman, S. V. 1976. The urban informal sector: concepts, measurement and policy, *International Labour Review*, 114.

Shaffer, B. and Lamb, G. (eds.) 1981. *Can equity be organized: equity, development analysis and planning*, Gower and UNESCO.

Silva Michelena, J. A., and Sonntag, H. R. 1979. *El proceso electoral de 1978: su perspectiva histórica estructural*, Ateneo de Caracas.

Simmons, A. B., and Cardona, R. 1973. *Family planning in Colombia, changes in attitude and acceptance, 1964–69*, International Development Research Centre.

Skinner, R. 1981. Community organization, collective development and politics in self-help housing: Villa El Salvador, Lima 1971–1976, unpublished doctoral dissertation, University of Cambridge.

1982. Self help, community organization and politics: Villa El Salvador, Lima, in Ward, P. M., ed. *Self-help housing: a critique*, Mansell Publishing Co., 209–29.

Smith, P. 1979. *Labyrinths of power: political recruitment in twentieth century Mexico*, Princeton University Press.

Solaún, M. 1980. Colombian politics: historical characteristics and problems, in Berry, R. A., *et al.*, eds. *Politics of compromise: coalition government in Colombia*, Transaction Books, 1–58.

Solaún, M. F., Cepeda, F., and Bagley, B. 1973. Urban reform in Colombia: the impact of the 'politics of games' on public policy, in Rabinovitz, F., and Trueblood, F., eds. *Latin American Urban Research*, 3, 97–132.

Stein, S., and Stein, B. H. 1970. *The colonial heritage of Latin America: essays on economic dependence in perspective*, Oxford University Press.

Stevenson, R. 1979. Housing programs and policies in Bogotá: an historical/descriptive analysis. World Bank City Study Research Project RPO 671–47.

Stewart, W. S. 1977. Public administration, in Martz, J., and Myers, D., eds., *Venezuela: the democratic experience*, Praeger, 215–34.

Sudra, T. L. 1976. Low-income housing system in Mexico City, unpublished doctoral dissertation, Massachusetts Institute of Technology.

Svenson, G. 1977. *El desarrollo económico departamental 1960–1975*, Inandes, Bogotá.

Tello, C. 1978. *La política económica en México, 1970–1976*, Siglo XXI. Mexico.

Travieso, F. 1972. *Ciudad, región y subdesarrollo*, Fondo Editorial Común.

Turner, J. F. C. 1967. Barriers and channels for housing development in modernizing countries, *Journal of the American Institute of Planners*, 33, 167–81.

1968. Housing priorities, settlement patterns and urban development in modernizing countries, *Journal of the American Institute of Planners*, 34, 354–63.

1969. Uncontrolled urban settlements: problems and policies, in Breese, G., ed. *The city in newly developing countries*, Prentice Hall, 507–31.

1972. Housing as a verb, in Turner, J. F. C., and Fichter, R., eds. *Freedom to Build*, Collier Macmillan, 148–75.

1976. *Housing by people*, Marion Boyars.

Turner, J. F. C., *et al.* 1963. Dwelling resources in South America, *Architectural Design*, 33, 360–93.

Turner, J. F. C., and Fichter, R., eds. 1972. *Freedom to Build*, Collier Macmillan.

Udy, S. H., Jnr. 1969. Administrative rationality, social setting, and organizational development, in Litterer, J. A., ed. *Organizations: structure and behaviour*, John Wiley, 343–51.

Ugalde, A., *et al*. 1974. *The urbanization process of a poor Mexican neighbourhood: the case of San Felipe del Real Adicional, Ciudad Juárez*, special publication of the Institute of Latin American Studies, Austin.

Ugalde, L. 1972. El 'locus' político del desarrollo de la comunidad en Venezuela, *Cuadernos de la Sociedad Venezolana de Planificación*, 106–7, 21–34.

UNECLA. 1981. *Statistical Summary of Latin America 1960–1980*, Santiago, Chile.

UNESCAP. 1982. *Policies towards urban slums and squatter settlements in the ESCAP region*, ESCAP, Bangkok.

Unikel, L. 1972. *La dinámica del crecimiento de la Ciudad de México*, Fundación para estudios de población, Mexico DF.

   1976. *El desarrollo urbano de México: diagnóstico e implicaciones futuras*, El Colegio de México.

Urrutia, M. 1969. *The development of the Colombian trade union movement*, Yale University Press.

Urrutia, M., and Berry, R. A. 1975. *La distribución del ingreso en Colombia*, La Carreta.

Valladares, L. do Prado 1978. Working the system: squatter response to resettlement in Rio de Janeiro, *International Journal of Urban and Regional Research*, 2, 12–25.

Van der Linden, J., *et al*. 1982. Situation and processes of informal housing in Karachi, Free University, Amsterdam, Department of Sociology and Geography of Developing Countries. Mimeo.

Veliz, C., ed. 1965. *Obstacles to change in Latin America*, Oxford University Press.

Venezuela, Banco Obrero. 1963. Informe General de Valencia, Caracas.

   1970. Estudio sobre la situación del problema de la vivienda en las areas urbanas: segunda parte. Estudio por ciudades. Vol. 11: Valencia, Caracas.

Venezuela, CORDIPLAN (Oficina Central de Coordinación y Planificación de la Presidencia de la República). 1976. *V plan de la Nación, 1976–80*, Caracas.

   1981. *VI Plan de la Nación 1981–5*, 3 vols., Caracas.

Venezuela, Dirección, 1978. Ministerio de Fomento, Dirección General de Estadistica y Censos Nacionales, *X Censo de Población y Vivienda*.

Venezuela, FUNDACOMUN (Fundación Nacional para el Desarrollo). 1978a. La acción del estado y el ordenamiento de las áreas marginales en el país. Paper given to Seminario Nacional sobre Políticas de Bienestar Social y de Población, Caracas 15–19 May, 1978.

   1978b. Boletín Estadística 1969–78, Caracas.

   1979. Manual del vecino. Caracas.

   1982a. Participación popular y desarrollo de la comunidad, Caracas.

1982b. Primer seminario sobre participación integral en el desarrollo de las areas marginales – material de apoyo, Caracas.

Venezuela, INAVI (Instituto Nacional de la Vivienda). 1979. INAVI: Programa de Vivienda, Caracas.

Venezuela, INOS (Instituto Nacional de Obras Sanitarios). 1977. Información estadística del comportamiento del presupuesto para el período 1969–1975, Caracas.

Venezuela, IVSS (Instituto Venezolano de Seguros Sociales). 1979. Anuario Estadístico 1979, Caracas.

Venezuela, MINDUR (Ministerio del Desarrollo Urbano). 1981. Distrito Valencia – Area Urbana: Estudio Eco-ambiental y socio-económico. Plan de Desarrollo Primer Informe, Valencia.

Vernez, G. 1973. Bogotá's pirate settlements: an opportunity for metropolitan development. Unpublished doctoral dissertation, University of California, Berkeley.

Villamizar, R. 1980. Land prices in Bogotá between 1955 and 1978: a descriptive analysis, World Bank City Project Paper No. 10.

Wallerstein, I. 1974. *The modern world system: capitalist agriculture and the origins of the European world economy in the sixteenth century*, Academic Press.

1980. *The modern world system II: mercantilism and the consolidation of the European world-economy, 1600–1759*, Academic Press.

Ward, P. M. 1976a. In search of a home: social and economic characteristics of squatter settlements and the role of self-help housing in Mexico City, Unpublished PhD dissertation, University of Liverpool.

1976b. Intra-city migration to squatter settlements in Mexico City, *Geoforum*, 7, 369–83.

1976c. The squatter settlement as slum or housing solution: the evidence from Mexico City, *Land Economics*, 52, 330–46.

1981a. Political pressure for urban services: the response of two Mexico city administrations, *Development and Change*, 12, 379–407.

1981b. Urban problems and planning in Mexico City, in Pacione, M., ed. *Urban problems and planning in the modern world*, Croom Helm, 28–64.

1981c. Financing land acquisition for self-build housing schemes, *Third World Planning Review*, 3, 7–20.

ed. 1982a. *Self-help housing: a critique*, Alexandrine Press, Mansell Publishing Co., London.

1982b. Informal housing: conventional wisdoms reappraised, *Built Environment*, 8, 85–94.

Webb, R. 1975. Public policy and regional incomes in Peru, in Cornelius, W. A., and Trueblood, F. M., eds. *Latin American Urban Research*, 5, 223–38.

Weber, M. 1962. *Basic concepts in sociology*, Citadel Press.

1969. Bureaucracy, in Litterer, J. A., ed. *Organizations: structure and behaviour*, John Wiley, 29–39.

Whitehead, L. 1979. The economic policies of the Echeverría sexenio. What went wrong and why? Paper delivered at the Latin American Studies Association, Pittsburgh.

1980. Mexico from boom to bust: a political evaluation of the 1976–9 stabilization program, *World Development*, 8, 843–63.

1981. On 'governability' in Mexico, *Bulletin of Latin American Research*, 1, 27–47.

Wiesner, F. 1978. Aguas para Bogotá, in Cámara de Comercio, *Bogotá: estructura y principales servicios públicos*, Bogotá, 239–52.

Wionczek, M. A. 1971. *Inversión y technología extranjera en América Latina*, Editorial Joaquín Mortiz.

World Bank. 1978. Urban policy issues and opportunities, Vol. 1., World Bank Staff Working Paper No. 283.

1980a. *Shelter*, Washington DC.

1980b. *Water supply and waste disposal*, Poverty and basic needs series, Washington DC.

Zorro Sánchez, C. 1979. Normas jurídicas y realidad social: la evolución reciente de las disposiciones en materia de urbanismo en Bogotá. Document for ODA-financed project on 'Public intervention, housing and land use in Latin American cities'.

Zorro Sánchez, C., and Gilbert, A. G. 1982. Tolerancia o rechazo de los asentamientos urbanos irregulares. El caso de Bogotá, *Revista Interamericana de Planificación*, 16, 138–70.

Author index

311

Subject index

CAMBRIDGE LATIN AMERICAN STUDIES